363

ALSO BY RICHARD SCHICKEL

Clint: A Retrospective

Film on Paper

The Essential Chaplin (ed.)

Elia Kazan: A Biography

Woody Allen: A Life in Film

Good Morning, Mr. Zip Zip Zip: Movies, Memory and World War II

Matinee Idylls: Reflections on the Movies

Double Indemnity

Clint Eastwood: A Biography

Brando: A Life in Our Times

Striking Poses

Schickel on Film

D. W. Griffith: An American Life

Intimate Strangers: The Culture of Celebrity

James Cagney: A Celebration

Cary Grant: A Celebration

Another I, Another You

Harold Lloyd: The Shape of Laughter

Second Sight: Notes on Some Movies, 1965–1970

His Picture in the Papers

The Men Who Made the Movies

The Disney Version

The Stars

Conversations with **Scorsese**

Conversations with **Scorsese**

UPDATED AND EXPANDED

RICHARD SCHICKEL

ALFRED A. KNOPF · NEW YORK · 2013

THIS IS A BORZOI BOOK PUBLISHED BY ALFRED A. KNOPF

Copyright © 2011, 2013 by Richard Schickel

All rights reserved. Published in the United States by Alfred A. Knopf,
a division of Random House, Inc., New York, and in Canada
by Random House of Canada Limited, Toronto.
www.aaknopf.com
Knopf, Borzoi, and the colophon are registered trademarks
of Random House, Inc.

Photograph of Martin Scorsese and Thelma Schoonmaker in the editing room
of *Goodfellas* used with permission of David Leonard.

Library of Congress Cataloging-in-Publication Data
Scorsese, Martin.
  Conversations with Scorsese / Richard Schickel [interviewer]. — 1st ed.
    p. cm.
  Includes bibliographical references and index.
  Includes filmography.
  ISBN 978-0-307-38879-7 (pbk)
  1. Scorsese, Martin—Interviews.   2. Motion picture producers and directors—United States—
Interviews.   I. Schickel, Richard.   II. Title.
  PN1998.3.S39A3   2011
  791.4302'33092—dc22   2010034250

Front-of-jacket image © Bureau L.A. Collection / Corbis
Jacket design by Chip Kidd

Manufactured in the United States of America
Published March 10, 2011
First Paperback Edition, January 13, 2013

CONTENTS

We are an odd couple, Marty and I. I grew up in a placid suburb of Milwaukee, Wisconsin, cosseted by my middle-class family—loving, indulgent, always avoiding openly expressed emotions. I'm certain that I gravitated to the movies because I was looking for melodramatic excitement, a relief from the "niceness" that was the highest value of that time and place. Marty's young years were, of course, the opposite, spent mainly in Little Italy on New York's Lower East Side—working class, but also criminal class, with the Mafia providing much of the neighborhood's half-hidden social organization and control. There was an element of danger on— well, yes, all right—the Mean Streets of his boyhood. And there was an element of anxiety in his home, which was rife with discussions of complex family issues tensely, if lovingly, argued out. He was escaping a vastly different sort of reality when he went to the movies—melodrama and fantasy, to be sure, but of a kind that was actually less threatening than the harsh realities this asthmatic little boy encountered in his daily life.

We've more than once laughed about this: he envies the peace of my picket-fence childhood; I would have loved the stir and occasional menace of Little Italy. But it speaks to the appeal of the medium in the 1940s and even the 1950s, when the movies were thought to be dying, that members of our youthful demographic almost universally went to them—their sheen and shimmer were that irresistible. The difference between Marty and me and the rest of our friends is that they drifted away from the movies, except as a form of casual entertainment, while we almost helplessly professionalized our passion. That process, as Marty experienced it, is what much of this book is about. In talking with him I've often felt we are like immigrants from two different countries meeting on neutral ground and discovering that we can communicate in a third language: the language of film.

It helps, of course, that in addition to being a filmmaker Marty is a passionate film scholar, a man who devotes almost as much time to studying and preserving the movie past as he does to making new films. This is a matter that naturally concerns me as a critic and film historian. It may also help that I eventually, much more modestly, became a filmmaker myself, a documentarian specializing in movie history. Technically, as well as historically and aesthetically, we communicate easily, instinctively, in the shorthand of shared experiences.

That was not always the case. We met for the first time in 1973, when I was working on the first television programs I wrote and directed, a series of interviews with American movie directors of the classic age. I was running their pictures of an evening at my apartment and I casually asked Jay Cocks, at the time my reviewing colleague at *Time* magazine, if he'd like to take a look at Howard Hawks's *His Girl Friday* some night. This was well before the home video revolution, when you had to haul out a cumbersome 16mm projector to see movies in your living room— a bigger, rarer deal than it is now in the digital age. Anyway, Jay was, and is, one of Marty's oldest friends, dating back to their days at the New York University film school, as well as his occasional screenwriting collaborator, and he asked if he could bring Marty along, which he did. I can't recall anything memorable being said. We all just had a merry time rewatching one of the greatest of all romantic comedies.

No friendship arose out of that encounter—largely, I think, because I was, at the time, not particularly fond of a lot of Marty's films. I did not, for example, greatly care for *Mean Streets*. It was Marty's breakthrough film, and though I have since come to respect it, I still don't quite love it. I enjoyed the lightsome *Alice Doesn't Live Here Anymore*, but had to wrestle hard with *Taxi Driver*, before giving it the good review it deserved. I remember Henry Grunwald, *Time*'s great managing editor, scribbling this note on the proof of my piece: "You don't like this movie as much as you say you do." He was right at that moment, though he would be wrong now.

A little later, Marty and I shared one of the most awkward moments of my career. This was in 1977 when the producer of Marty's *New York, New York*, Irwin Winkler, set up an early screening of the film for me. It was, you may recall, a drama with music about the troubled relationship between a bandleader (Robert De Niro) and his vocalist (Liza Minnelli)—in part, a tribute to the kind of musical comedies MGM had made in the 1940s and '50s, in part a dark and painful romance. These two ideas never really meshed, and the production had also been attended by all sorts of troubles, personal and professional, that rather obviously afflicted the finished product. Irwin invited Marty and me to dinner after the screening—at which I found I couldn't say a word about the film that would not have hurt Marty's feelings. So we awkwardly talked around the only subject that was of interest to either of us. I didn't know at the time that Marty, Irwin, and almost every one else connected with the film had the gravest doubts about it, and were perhaps hoping against hope that an objective observer might see something more promising in it than they did. Nor did I know that Marty was on the verge of a life-threatening illness, the result of exhaustion and the interaction of a wide variety of drugs—prescription and, shall we say, nonprescription—he had been taking to keep himself going through a brutal schedule.

Somehow, Marty survived—many of his friends insist that it was quite a near thing—and when he was recuperating in the hospital De Niro visited him to insist that he at last focus his attention on a project on which the actor had invested a profound passion: *Raging Bull.* Marty had always been dubious about the film, if only because he had never had the slightest interest in boxing (or any other kind of sports). De Niro, however, thought boxing was just a pretext for the film and judged that Marty, having now touched bottom in his own life, might forge an emotional connection with this story about the boxer Jake LaMotta reaching a similar condition. De Niro was obviously, spectacularly, right, and *Raging Bull* became in my opinion—and I was scarcely alone—Marty's first fully realized masterpiece.

When the movie was released, most of the critical and audience response focused on the unprecedented brutality of its boxing sequences, though when you re-encounter it now you tend to see it rather differently. Its more profound brutality lies in the story of an angry, inarticulate man's struggle to find a few grace notes in an otherwise savage existence. But however you read *Raging Bull,* it is manifestly a movie that gives, and asks, no quarter. Thereafter, no critic could fail to see Martin Scorsese as anything but a major film artist.

He's had his flops, of course, and his misunderstandings with the critics and the audience, and even his common-consent critical successes have not always been rewarded as richly as they deserved at the box office. But the range and intensity, technical and emotional, in his work have made him, in the minds of many, the Great American Director of his age. He's not so sure about that. And neither am I, largely because it is a critic's duty to resist the superlative. In any case, history has yet to have its say, and we are both historians enough to want to await its judgment—not that either of us will be around to discuss it.

Not that we were discussing much of anything after *Raging Bull,* either. I sometimes saw Marty around in New York, usually in Jay's company, and we would exchange pleasantries. But that was it. I admired a lot of his subsequent movies—*The King of Comedy, Goodfellas, The Age of Innocence*—and I thought that his documentaries about the American and Italian cinema were great works in their field. Even in his more problematical movies I saw the impatience and restlessness of a man who was easily bankable in the eyes of the studios only when he was making crime stories. Even given the admiration he has enjoyed, he has always struggled, as directors of comparable stature have not, for backing and trust from the powers that be.

This struck me, strikes me, as ludicrous, especially since his work outside what people thought was his main line—*After Hours, Kundun, Bringing Out the Dead*—was often more interesting to me than, say, *Cape Fear* or *Casino.* After 1986, when I left New York for Los Angeles, this was an opinion I had not even a wan hope of sharing with Marty. Or so I imagined. But by the 1990s I had begun writing and directing documentaries almost full-time, specializing in films about movie history, and I began turning to Marty as an interviewee on these programs. At which point some sort of sparks were beginning to leap the gap between us.

And some sort of relationship began to develop between us. It's not too much to say that he became my favorite talking head, because his knowledge was so boundless and expressed with such riveting passion. We always exceeded the bounds of our ostensible subject (and the planned length of our talks). Everyone knows from Marty's many appearances on television and on DVDs that he is an explosive, free-associational talker about movies. But what I was at first unprepared for was his self-deprecating humor. He's onto himself. He knows he's an obsessive. He knows that he's quite capable of driving people crazy with his attention to minute details, not just about the making of his own movies, but about everyone else's movies as well. Off camera (and sometimes on), he was always shaking his head over his behavior—not that he shows the least sign of self-reformation. Eventually, these sessions led to my making, in 2004, a film, *Scorsese on Scorsese,* about his career, which in turn led to the series of conversations that comprise this book.

Most of these talks took place in an apartment at the Waldorf Towers in New York, where Marty and his family were living while a house he had purchased was being renovated. We would start in at eight or nine at night and I would stagger out around 1 a.m., exhausted and exhilarated by our exchanges, very much needing the long walk back to my hotel, through the deserted midtown streets, to decompress.

But even if Marty's days had not been filled with preproduction chores on *Shutter Island,* work on his documentaries and on film preservation, I suspect we would still have chosen to meet in the deeper reaches of the evenings. For he's a night bird—always has been; his boyhood career as an altar boy was cut short by his struggle to get up for the 7 a.m. mass.

No one can explain someone's else's circadian rhythms and I'm not going to try. But as the day's activities faded from his mind, as the city far below us fell into fitful sleep, Marty's memories grew more vivid and freewheeling, including everything from his almost demonic early moviegoing to his grapplings with faith and family matters to his childish attempts to create movielike narratives through drawings to his embrace of professional moviemaking even before he graduated from what would become NYU's film school. Eventually, of course, we talked in some detail about all the movies he has made in the years since.

Every time we met, we vowed to try to keep our conversations on a rough chronological track. Every time we failed to do so. He's as breathless and excitable off camera as he is on. At some point every night we would just give up on chronology and go with whatever flow had arisen out of our exchanges. These resulted in quite amazing transcripts—full of repetitions and false starts, to be sure, but also full of fascinating autobiography and astonishing detail about the choices he has made over the course of a career that now extends well over forty years. These were never easy to edit, but they were never tiresome, either.

Like virtually every good director I've ever known, Marty is not entirely comfortable at explaining his motives, why he may opt for one project over another— or, for that matter, one shot or edit over another. Movie directors are as instinctive as any other kind of artist except that they have to marshal and control far more numerous and often more recalcitrant collaborators than someone working alone—a writer or painter, say. There is, as well, something hypnotic and addictive in the filmmaking process, something that drives its practitioners to immerse themselves in the work to the exclusion of all else. And it's quite a long process. Preproduction, production, and postproduction cannot take less than six months. Sometimes, as in the case of a difficult project like *The Last Temptation of Christ* or *Gangs of New York,* it can take years, decades. You have no choice but to embrace this addiction—there is no twelve-step program that can cure you—else your picture will fail and eventually your career will fail as well.

You get the sense, when you're around someone like Marty, that directors are not fully alive unless they give themselves over entirely to the proffered obsession. It may even work the other way. I sometimes think the reason directors occasionally embark on movies that are not up to their highest standards is that the need to obliterate themselves in a project also obliterates commonsense caution. Putting that point less melodramatically, it may, in Marty's case, account for the fact that he meticulously draws out on paper every shot in his movies before going on set to make them. It's not quite actually shooting the thing, but it is as close as he can come to that limbolike state that occurs while he is impatiently awaiting his start date.

This is also a reversionary state. It is exactly what he did when he was a kid, not even consciously knowing that he wanted to become a director: drawing his little movies on sketch pads and showing them perhaps to a single friend. I suppose, indeed, that the most important thing I learned about Marty—or at least had powerfully reinforced—during the course of these conversations was the power that his past exerts on his work. I'm not just talking about his drawings. Or about the films like *Mean Streets* or *Who's That Knocking at My Door*, which so clearly contain autobiographical elements. I'm talking, for example, about the way violence presents itself in his films. It appears so suddenly. There is rarely much buildup to it, no hint of gathering menace. Some guys will be kidding around in a bar or on a street corner and suddenly, bam, someone is hurt. Or dead. That's how Marty observed violence when he was a kid. That's the way he presents it as a grown-up. His deadly confrontations are only rarely blood-drenched. They are more often over before we sense them starting. He wants us to be as shocked—and as wary—as he once was. It is the inbred signature of his sensibility.

I'm also talking about what I'm afraid I have to call his spirituality. In the pages that follow the reader will find much about Marty's struggles with questions of faith and belief when he was growing up. One thing people with only the most superficial knowledge of Marty's personal history know is that he "almost" became a priest. That is not true; to his chagrin, he found that he could take only the briefest steps along that path. For some time he counted it as a major life failure (though he seems no longer to feel that). It has also led some people to see his passion for film as a substitute for formal religious belief, which is far too easy an explanation for this career. But just as the kind of violence he observed as a kid is present in his movies, so are his youthful yearnings for belief. It's obvious, of course, in pictures like *Kundun*. But there are hints of those aspirations, a longing for some kind of transcendence, or, at the least, relief from reality's harsher limits, in so many of his secular films. It's obvious in such early films as *Mean Streets*, less so in films like *The King of Comedy, Goodfellas,* and *The Age of Innocence*. But in one form or another, in small ways and large, his concern with matters of belief is nearly always present in his work.

So is his concern with betrayal. The picture for which he won his too-long-delayed Academy Award, *The Departed*, is a kind of festival of double-dealing, with Matt Damon's and Leo DiCaprio's characters acting as spies—one in the cops' camp, one in the criminals'—and a rich variety of subsidiary characters joining in the deadly game the film portrays. Something similar occurs in *Goodfellas*. In a film as relatively minor, yet darkly farcical, as *After Hours*, a square young uptown man ventures into downtown New York persuaded that he's going to get laid by an attractive pickup he's met in a coffee shop; he nearly gets killed by her and her self-absorbed and heedless friends. And when you come to something like *Raging Bull*, Jake LaMotta's suspicion that his wife may be betraying him—she is not—drives much of the story, and a large portion of its violence.

I don't believe that Marty is himself particularly paranoid—though he does have mirrors up in the "Video Village" from which he operates on his sets and in his editing room, so that no one can catch him unawares, from behind his back. And he does speak of being taught, as a kid, not to react to the suspicious behavior that went on around him. Eyes front (and blank), lips sealed—that's how he passed many of his years in Little Italy. Where he grew up, almost all the deadly behavior he observed stemmed from someone betraying or attempting to betray someone else, whether the business at hand was criminal, familial, or something as simple as an attraction to a pretty girl (see his first feature, *Who's That Knocking at My Door*, which seems to me underappreciated, especially by Marty himself).

Finally, there is this irony to contemplate: Marty is obliged to make his living in an "industry" controlled by people who have always wanted to impose rationality on their enterprise, have always tried to tame its wild children. Or ostracize them. Or break them. The idea that making movies at the highest level can ever be a fully reasonable activity has always struck me as laughable. But forget that. The point I am making is that the studio and the filmmaker have different motives and that the relationship between them is bound to be mistrustful, therefore rife with the possibility of—yes—betrayals. There's this cliché about Hollywood— "It's high school with money." But you have to wonder: What if it's actually Little Italy without gunplay?

If that's the case, it becomes possible to imagine that what Marty observed and learned in his formative years was the best possible preparation for the career he later took up. Which, in turn, is a way of saying that in a fairly deep sense he is an autobiographer—not so much an anecdotal one, but one of his inner life, his yearnings, his feelings, his fears in his formative years. Nor is that impulse limited to his portrayals of criminal life. To give just one example that came up in the course of our talks, he observed that the codes of conduct enforced by New York's upper classes on Newland Archer and Ellen Olenska in *The Age of Innocence* are as harsh and unforgiving as any administered by the modern-day Mafia.

His is not the only way to make good movies. There is much to be said for the show of calmness in a line of work where the pretense that reason rules may be the nuttiest idea of all. But I'm here to tell you, there's also much to be said for sitting up half the night listening to the spiraling enthusiasms—and the occasionally drowned dreams—of a man who cannot help but make the kind of commitment Marty has made to every aspect of filmmaking.

In a sense, Marty's passion is his saving grace. It is so intense that when you're in its presence you have only two choices: embrace it or flee it. The former course is, for me, at least, infinitely more rewarding. You can learn so much from him— not just about old movies you really ought to see, or re-examine more thought- fully, and not just about how to achieve all kinds of potent movie effects (how to stage a scene or fire up an actor or find a solution to a technical problem). Some- how, as I've grown closer to Marty in recent years, that famous formulation of Henry James's keeps tugging at my mind: "We work in the dark—we do what we can—we give what we have. Our doubt is our passion and our passion is our task. The rest is the madness of art."

It would be nice someday to apply that grandiose sentiment to a mere movie- maker without feeling a twinge of embarrassment. But there it is—it fits this case. And the case continually redeems himself by knowing what an absurd figure he can sometimes cut. He is also, in my experience, a courtly man—impeccably dressed in his European suits, a generous host, a man widely read in Greek and Roman his- tory (some of those sketch movies he made as a child were epics about the classic age), and in the writings of men and women who share his need to lift himself out of the quotidian, to find something more than the brute reality of everyday life.

"I'm not an animal," Jake LaMotta murmurs to himself when he finally touches bottom in a jail cell. And he is not the only such figure in Marty's films. They may be full of "animals," but for the most part these are balanced by figures who, fol- lowing dim and enigmatic instinct, aspire to transcend their ignorance and their circumstances, to find some touch of grace in their grim and circumscribed lives. But there never has been and there never will be "a triumph of the human spirit" in a Scorsese film. He's too intelligent for that. And too sternly moralistic. What I respond to most in his films is not just that they are unsettling, but that they gener- ally remain unsettled. His stories reach their firm narrative conclusions, but they remain open-ended. You are always left wondering what might happen next to his survivors. And thinking that probably their fates will not be entirely contented ones.

To consistently achieve that effect, especially in a society that, at least in its entertainments, is devoted to optimism, to the unambiguously happy ending, is no small matter—the onetime altar boy as existentialist. But you get all that, I'm sure. It remains for me to say only that I feel privileged that he has allowed me to hear and record his reflections on his long and still unfinished journey. It has been a pleasure, sir.

—R.S., July 2010

Conversations with Scorsese

LITTLE ITALY

RICHARD SCHICKEL: Let's begin with the basics: Where and when were you born?

MARTIN SCORSESE: I was born in 1942 in Corona, Queens. My parents had moved there earlier from the Lower East Side. The idea was to leave the old neighborhood, for them to better themselves, as they used to say. I loved Corona. We lived in a two-family house. There was a little yard in the back, a little tree. You could go to a park—I saw the trees, I saw something. But then my father got into big trouble with the landlord, and we had to move back to Elizabeth Street, in Manhattan, which was, in a sense, a humiliation—back literally into the same two and a half rooms where he was born, to live with my grandparents, until we found rooms down the block at 253 Elizabeth Street.

RS: It was obviously a trauma for your family. What happened? I mean, Corona was kind of Edenic for you.

MS: Oh, it was wonderful.

RS: What exactly happened with the landlord?

MS: Well, Nick Pileggi and I worked on it in a script that I'd like to do.

RS: Really?

MS: Yeah. I don't know if I can bring myself to do it. It's complicated. If you're not educated and you're working in a certain area, your fealty is to a certain group. There were different families. It was not part of the culture to go to the cops or a bank. My father was assisted by a certain family.

RS: He was not a criminal, but he was a—

MS: A friend. They made it possible for us to have the house in Queens. But my father had many problems with his brother Joe. From what I understand, he had "sitdowns," where he tried to make sure that Joe wasn't killed by the Mob people.

The landlord was a guy who had a vegetable truck in a garage next door. He didn't like my brother. And he had a chicken. The guy grabbed the chicken and just wrung its neck in front of my brother, and made the kid run and cry, you know. And he started to resent my father, because my father became friends with the landlord's brother. He took the brother to get a suit in New York.

Anyway, the landlord may have felt that my father was involved with under-world figures, which he wasn't really, but he behaved maybe a little bit like that; my father always liked to dress, you know. And this guy was a man of the earth, so to speak. And I think also his wife liked my father. So all this resentment was building up. And then there was a confrontation. Probably my father used some language he shouldn't have, because I remember he apologized for it. That led to the fistfight, and the landlord picked up an ax.

RS: Oh, God.

MS: And my mother's younger sister literally walked out there and pushed him aside and said, "Stop that. Don't pull an ax. Don't do that to my brother-in-law." And he stopped. [*Laughs.*] You talk about *The Quiet Man* [the John Ford movie that contains a similar scene]. I mean, the women just stopped it. And that night there was another fight on the corner. I saw the two of them fighting at the bar. And I came back in and told my mother, "They're fighting." And she was ironing clothes and said, "I know." And then the next thing I knew we had to leave.

We moved back to the apartment my father was born in, 241—it's still there—living with my grandmother and my grandfather. My grandmother, my father's mother, was very tough. My brother had problems there, fighting with my grand-mother. There were like seven people living in three rooms, until we got rooms down the block at 253. It was tough leaving a nice place that was idyllic, or at least in my mind was idyllic.

The Lower East Side was pretty rough. You've seen it in the old movies in the thirties and forties and fifties — the Dead End Kids, it was pretty close to that. Kids ran up and down the street. You played with what you had. You know, you had a garbage can, and the top of it became a shield. The orange crates — you'd rip off one of the pieces of wood and it was a sword. A lot of cars. A lot of everybody living on top of each other. And a lot of tension. I was living virtually on the Bowery, which to this day has marked me in a way. *Gangs of New York* — I couldn't even get it close to what I saw on the Bowery.

Marty, age seven months, takes the rooftop air with his mother (left) and Aunt Lena and her son, Anthony (right).

I had gone to a public school for two years, but the next thing I know I was in a Catholic school, being taught by the Sisters of Mercy, Irish nuns, at the St. Patrick's elementary school, which is still there. Irish nuns in an Italian, Neapolitan, Sicilian, neighborhood. There was conflict. But the school introduced me to the church, which was St. Patrick's Old Cathedral on Mott Street. It was the first Catholic cathedral built in America. And I found some peace there, and a little bit of protection.

In Queens, the house had bigger rooms, and you could always hide out a little bit, kind of disappear. Here you couldn't disappear. Here I was in the room. And I couldn't say anything, because I was the youngest. So I'd go in the church, and I became fascinated by the rituals of the mass. It was 1949, 1950, and the image of the Catholic church was the one from *Going My Way.* Barry Fitzgerald. Bing Crosby. Ingrid Bergman, *The Bells of St. Mary's.* You know, it was a pretty good image. And inside that cathedral — the sense of peace. It was quite, quite amazing.

And then, of course, my father didn't know what the hell to do with me. After working in the garment district all day he'd go to my grandparents' and deliberate with them about family issues at night, and my mother didn't like that very much. And then he'd come back around eleven o'clock, having picked up the tabloids, the *Daily News* and *Daily Mirror.* They'd argue it out a little bit, and then everything was fine. And the next day he'd go back to work. So I didn't see him much. But he was forced to take me to the movies; he took me to the movies all the time.

RS: Relating the movies to the church, was there something in the movies that was ritualistic, that appealed to you that way? An analogy between the big picture on the screen and the gorgeous altars of the church?

MS: I think that's a good point. My asthma isolated me from everybody else. And so in this isolation, I was made to think that I couldn't do anything physical. I had to be very careful, and be sort of coddled in a way.

So the ritual of going to the movies with your father—it didn't matter what film you saw—became important to me. It was a matter of going to the Loew's Commodore on 6th Street and Second Avenue, which is now part of New York University, by the way. (In the sixties it became the Fillmore East.) And going to the Academy of Music, which is gone now, on 14th Street. We were always walking into the middle of the film. There was a sense of peace there, too; there really was. You had faith when you went into the church. And you had faith when you went into the movie theater, too. Some films hit you more strongly than others, but you always had that faith. You're taken on a trip, you're taken on a journey. The posters outside sell you dreams, you know. And you go in there, and the dream is real, almost. And then if you're sharing these very strong emotions with your father, whom you don't really talk to very much, this became the main line of communication between us.

I mean, he took me to see *The Bad and the Beautiful*—the first movie I saw

Marty, happy in Queens, plays Indian without a cowboy in sight.

about the process of filmmaking. I loved westerns, so he used to take me to westerns. *The Day the Earth Stood Still* was one of the great theater experiences: a Sunday afternoon at the Academy of Music, a couple of thousand people reacting to that picture. Or *The Thing*—Christian Nyby and Howard Hawks—that was an amazing experience, the shock of it, the humor of it, the overlapping dialogue, the moment when they open the door, and James Arness [playing the monster] is standing right there—you ever see two thousand people jump at once? That was an amazing experience.

RS: Movies in those days, because the Code was in place, were judgmental, or, shall we say, moralistic? I mean in a certain sense there is an analogy between the church and the conventional morality of movies. I wonder if we could explore that a little more.

MS: Around 1954 you started to get the United Artists films — *The Big Knife,* even *Autumn Leaves,* with an extraordinary performance by Cliff Robertson. And you have Otto Preminger, Stanley Kramer, producing and directing. One way or another their pictures were addressing serious social and psychological matters. And all of a sudden the whole Code is breaking down.

RS: Did you like those Stanley Kramer movies? I mean, try and think back to then, not what you may feel now.

MS: Sure, we went to see them. They were pretty strong and shocking, you know. I don't know if they hold up over the years. I liked *Judgment at Nuremberg* a lot. And I'm talking about Kramer's productions, too, like *The Men,* Fred Zinnemann's picture, and *Home of the Brave* and *High Noon,* to a certain extent. I prefer the Ford and Hawks westerns. But still, there's something about Gary Cooper and that music and the editing that's just remarkable. There's so much tension in the way the film is developed. [It is about a sheriff forced to capture an outlaw gang alone, when no one in town will aid him.]

RS: But Cooper was in and of himself a remarkable figure, don't you think? I mean, he was such a great minimalist movie actor.

MS: Oh, you're absolutely right. In the forties he went into a dark period, like James Stewart had with Hitchcock and with Anthony Mann — I think of films like *The Fountainhead.* But primarily there's a film, a very lurid melodrama called *Bright Leaf.* Do you know it?

RS: I ran it just recently.

MS: I saw it at the age of about ten. I have been affected by that picture.

RS: How so?

MS: The hysteria of it, and his destructive character. And the sensuality between Patricia Neal and him and Lauren Bacall. And the whole way it develops, with him killing his father-in-law, Donald Crisp. And, of course, the whole film ends in a conflagration.

RS: Yeah, and what's interesting about it is that it takes you about half the movie to realize he's nuts.

MS: The fact that the film was glorifying the making of cigarettes has nothing to do with it. Right? It has nothing to do with it.

RS: Right [*chuckles*].

MS: There's something about this crazy character that was terrifying, and very interesting.

RS: Because, after all, this is nice, heroic Gary Cooper.

MS: You know: Come on, what's happening here? It was shocking. It's not a great film. But it was a very surprising one.

RS: He was an amazing actor. I mean, I don't think he ever consciously acted a second in his life. But there was something in him that could bring you close to tears sometimes.

MS: I'll never forget him writing his last will and testament in *High Noon*. And the last shot, I went back home and I drew a scene from the film. You know what I drew?

RS: No.

MS: I drew his boot and the star next to the boot, his sheriff's badge when he threw it on the ground. Just that. That represented the film to me. Because that boom out [a huge camera pullback, isolating Cooper from the rest of the community] made me understand a little about effective imagery on the screen. Why was that so effective when he was so small in the frame? I went back and studied that one.

RS: That boom locks him out of the town that has betrayed him.

MS: And the betrayal idea for me was very powerful. I mean, it always has been, and I still explore it in the pictures I make. So that's why that image of the star in the dust by his boot was so strong for me.

RS: It's funny, it's a movie that in my head I don't like, but when I see it, it takes me up in some way. Finally, I think it's a western for people who don't really like westerns—I mean westerns that take up more conventionalized stories. This one offers an unmistakable McCarthy-era metaphor for them to chew on.

MS: And then you had *Baby Doll* [a comic Southern Gothic film about a virgin bride, her dimwitted husband, and a sexually avaricious neighbor], the Elia Kazan movie that was condemned by the church from the pulpit, which I never got to see then because I always used to check the condemned list—I was a good kid trying to behave. The C list [it stood for "condemned" by the Catholic Legion of Decency] was always filled with titles like *Le Plaisir* [Max Ophüls's three-part film examining three aspects of pleasure—in youth, in the pursuit of purity, in the waning years of life], and *Letters from My Windmill* [directed by Marcel Pagnol, it is also an anthology film—warm, gently sacrilegious, featuring tipsy and devil-tempted priests], and any Ingmar Bergman film.

There was this contrast between the movies and the place I was living. Where I came from was a Sicilian village re-created on the Lower East Side. You know, in Sicily you don't trust anyone. It's not very evolved, but the reality is that on a certain level you grow up full of mistrust. And I'm sorry, it was pounded into me. It

Elizabeth Street in Little Italy. The photo, taken by Marty, was shot from the fire escape outside the Scorsese apartment.

really was. My parents were good people, hardworking people, weren't in organized crime. But there was that attitude toward the world. If you see that film, *Golden Door,* [Emanuele] Crialese's film [about Italian peasants immigrating to the United States], those are my grandparents.

RS: I've seen it. I understand.

MS: There's a woman in it who's a healer, could have been one of my grandparents. Now I didn't say my grandmother did that, but I know a guy who did that. Basically he was the same age as my grandparents, and he was a healer. And if you had a headache, you had something wrong with your stomach, you would go to him. Women would go into his room and he would do things to them. I mean, my mother said, "Yeah, he was a healer," and she'd wink. She was growing up American.

But the old ones, I was raised by those people. I was raised by the people you see climbing the mountains in *Golden Door.* In the fifties, it was very interesting trying to be American and trying to buy into something American. I mean, for instance, I just could not reconcile the nature of authority—of, let's say, Eisenhower playing golf every day—with my own experience. I came from a world where the reality was "Yeah, sure. Just be careful."

And so what happened with *The Departed* is that what it came down to, dammit, was the same story, the fathers and the sons. I was shooting the scene with Jack [Nicholson] and Leo [DiCaprio] where Jack is at the table and Leo is in the room. We had done the scene, a seven-page scene, the night before, and it was very nice—four takes, maybe, two cameras. But I said to Leo, "There's something there. I don't know what it is. Something is not quite pushing it yet." This was the turning point in the picture for me. I can't get into how I work with Jack, or how he'd

9

work with me, but there was something about just being around him and making it easy for him to go to certain places. So I just said to him, "Jack, we're going to do the same scene tomorrow. We've got the whole thing. It's just two angles. But anything you could think of to put him on edge—"

And then the next day Jack came in, and told me, "I have ideas. I've got some ideas." I said, "Don't tell me, don't tell me. Let me see." And so he sat down. Leo sat down. And the first thing Jack did was sniff the glass and say, "I smell a rat." If I was that kid, I couldn't imagine the guts you'd have to have to sit there. And then he pulled a gun on him. He didn't tell me he had a gun. It was great. And he had all these other ideas. We took a lot out, but Leo's reaction is in real time. So I said to him, "I don't know what's going to happen to you. And he's capable of doing anything. You have to work your way out of it. You have to make him believe that you are not the rat. And you are the rat." As we were doing it, I thought it was wonderful.

And suddenly I looked around and I said, "I've done this scene before." Looking back now I find that theme in other movies I've made—*Mean Streets, Raging Bull,* all the way up through the other movies. They usually have to do with fathers and sons, and what a father owes his son, and what a son owes his father in terms of loyalty. It has to do with trust and betrayal. Growing up in that world, the worst thing you could do was betray. And I felt excited, I'm even excited telling you the story now. I think I should go and make the picture again! I probably will!

RS: You can make all the gangster pictures you want as far as I'm concerned. But my point is, people say, Well, he could do that theme and they could be two upper-crust guys from Long Island betraying each other over a Wall Street deal.

MS: That's true. That's true. Take something like *Casino*—there's betrayal there. And there's the downfall. It's interesting that the downfall in *Casino* is always looked at in terms of people who are of a different nature, so to speak, than we are. But to me they're just human beings—a downfall in the underworld is just as valid to me as the downfall of a president.

RS: It doesn't make any difference at which level of society the betrayal takes place. The interesting thing is that a betrayal takes place and the betrayal doesn't necessarily mean great matters of state, or even money that the gangsters owe each other.

MS: No, no.

RS: Betrayal has to do with—well, you say what it is.

MS: Well, it has to do with love. It has to do with love between people, and how it's betrayed. Because there is a bond between these people. Otherwise they wouldn't

Charles and Catherine's wedding photo.
The bridal couple are attended by her sister
Frances and his brother Tony.

really be affected so strongly. I think that has to be it. Maybe I'm just repeating the same ideas and the same things in the end. But—

RS: Look, every artist repeats themes. Isn't Hitchcock always making the same movie?

MS: Oh, that's true. Yeah.

RS: I mean, there are different settings, different people, but in the end they are variations on a theme.

MS: You're absolutely right about finding those themes. But I found that in *The Departed* it was more incestuous in a way—we don't know what Frank Costello's relationship with Matt Damon's character was as a boy, raising him. [Nicholson's Costello is a kingpin in Boston's Irish Mafia who places his surrogate son in the state police, where he acts as Costello's spy as the cops investigate Costello.]

If you read any of the books based on the real characters—it's very dark, and it has a lot to do with the sex and the violence. That's why the sex, the obscenity, is up there in front. It has to do with getting thrills that way. The more we read, the more ideas we got. And, sure enough, the human monster emerges, so to speak.

RS: But here's my question. My experience is antithetical to yours: no mortal betrayal has ever occurred to me. But when you talk about this film, you immediately go back to that childhood of yours. So the question arises once again, about Sicilians, and their apparently naturally suspicious natures—

MS: Not all Sicilians but, yeah, suspicious.

RS: It's amazing to me that you took from that experience something that has been so controlling in your life as a filmmaker. What is it? I mean, okay, you were an asthmatic little boy and you needed special attention, but you got it from your obviously adoring parents.

MS: Yeah, I got it from my parents, who were great with me. But it was a little tough. The household wasn't easy. That's why *East of Eden* is such an important movie to me.

RS: Stop right there. Why is *East of Eden* so important? You've never mentioned that to me in this context.

MS: The struggle of the father and the son. The good brother and the bad one. And the good brother is—

RS: The good brother is a schmuck.

MS: Yeah, I know. But the thing was—

RS: And we don't like him.

MS: In my household, the conflict was mainly between my father and my older brother, Frank. I was supposedly the "good" one. But in reality, when I was watching *East of Eden,* I realized that I felt like the bad one—the James Dean character. I had the same feelings as the bad one.

RS: Go into that a little more.

MS: The thing I felt was what all adolescents felt when they saw James Dean in that movie, whether or not the performance still holds up.

RS: I'll reluctantly stipulate, for the purposes of this conversation, it's a great performance.

MS: Dated at times, though. But it's about wanting his father's love—that tension. Somehow I read into that what was happening in my household, with an older brother and my father who had problems.

RS: These were really angry confrontations? Big, loud ones like there are in *East of Eden*?

MS: Oh, yeah. Basically, there was a period in the fifties, before my brother got out of the house and got married, when pretty much every night there was a confrontation.

RS: Over what?

MS: Over how to live. How to behave. Or how to be a man. I'm not saying one's right or wrong. And the quiet one, the sickly one, me, had to take it all in and couldn't say anything. And I was getting pretty angry about it.

RS: Angry on whose behalf?

MS: I think it was probably against my father. But I also wanted to love my father. And I know he loved me. But he had to be very stern. He had to be very tough. Besides which, of course, he had to be making a few bucks a week and making sure we were fed, and making sure we went to school, and making sure he took us to the doctor. I mean, you know, that's what you do as a parent. And it's amazing the stuff that they did that I haven't done.

RS: You've mentioned it before to me, and with considerable love and respect. Because these weren't rich people, every doctor visit had to represent a sacrifice of some kind. And yet they did it.

MS: Yeah, and there was nothing outside, only an extended family. My father was one of eight or nine children—I keep forgetting, maybe seven or eight. My mother was one of seven or eight also. So there were lots of aunts and uncles and cousins. And then there was his respect for his parents, who lived down the street.

Basically every night, after coming back from the garment district, having dinner, the fighting would start up. Some nights it was okay, but most of the time it was conflict over my brother, whatever the reasons were. He was doing things that my father didn't think were right, and he was asking himself, "Why doesn't this kid listen to me?" And he was very excitable, because he had his own problems in the garment district with people he was working with.

And, finally, at a certain hour, about seven o'clock, he would go over to his mother and father down the street. And they'd convene about the family. His older brother would come over, sometimes the other brothers, and everybody would talk—this shouldn't be, that isn't right, going back and forth. My father's mother was extremely matriarchal. And she didn't speak English. She was loving, but she was scary.

My grandfather was very quiet. But apparently in his day he was pretty tough with his kids. There was no such thing with them—with all those children living in two and a half rooms or three rooms—as an independent character of any kind. You know: We just had another baby, you take care of it. You're the eldest daughter, the eldest son—move. You come and dig ditches for me at Con Edison. That's it. You can't be a CPA. And so with that kind of harshness—the conflict with the New World, the conflict with America—they didn't know how to take advantage of opportunity. They didn't know.

But with me they kind of saw a little something. But they didn't know what the hell to do with me. The problem there in the house was something I've been dealing with ever since. It's very hard for me to talk about, but I put it on film in different ways. It's in *Raging Bull,* it's in *Mean Streets.* The whole picture of *Mean Streets,* it's really him, my father, not me. I mean there's a part of me in there, but . . .

RS: Which part?

MS: Well, Harvey Keitel signing the notes for Johnny Boy. [Robert De Niro's character is a wild, oddly lovable kid who needs protection by his more responsible peers.] I didn't sign any notes, but I had a close friend who, every now and then, vouched for a friend of ours whom we loved, and he got into a lot of trouble. But he was a nice kid, and he survived. He's still around, but not in this state. In my world, if you borrowed money from somebody, you had to pay it back. Now if you borrowed it from a bank, there was some leeway. But when you're borrowing it from a fellow on the street corner and he's a friend of so-and-so's, and there's a crime family down the block, you have to pay it back, or at least you have to make an attempt to pay it back. And you have to be well-connected so that powerful people—Mob guys—could talk for you. I've heard stories my father told me, I've seen things happen. It's what happens in *Mean Streets.*

It's about the respect issue. It's a point of honor, dealing with this sort of thing. And even if you have nothing, there's still got to be the honor of your name. So you can walk in the street. Because there are no other streets. You can't get on a plane and go to Paris. You've only got the streets. There's about eight blocks, that's it. And you're not going to go to the West Side, where you had actors, you had mimes, you had writers, you had intellectuals. There's no such thing on the East Side. What you had on the East Side was the Bowery, the bums who were dying in the street.

But we're getting off the subject. Besides my brother, my father's youngest brother, unfortunately, was getting in trouble all the time. And the rest of the family sort of threw their hands up, so my father, to the end of his days, had to go and finesse the issues with different parties and different groups of men. And it was very serious, very serious.

RS: In other words, your uncle was constantly in danger.

MS: All the time. But I loved him. He was on the second floor, we were on the third floor. And he had a great sense of humor, he was very funny. But he was also a very dangerous man. Every time there was a crisis, my father would run it with my mother and discuss it and the reasons why my uncle had to behave a certain way, and the reasons why my uncle had to find the money to pay this or that person. And my mother would say, Don't do it. How many times do I have to tell you? Don't lend him money. He was in and out of jail. I couldn't say anything because it was none of my business. You're the son, you keep quiet. It wasn't until after my father died in 1993 that I realized *Mean Streets* was really about him and his brother.

RS: Obviously, now that you mention it.

MS: If you borrowed money from certain people and didn't pay it back, they were dangerous. They weren't banks. It would be a matter of serious leg-smashing, head-smashing, or whatever.

But in any event, my father was dealing with my uncle until he was in the hospital and he was getting his second heart operation; he had to sign a check for my uncle for $200—with my mother and my brother telling him not to do it. He goes, It's my brother, what am I going to do? And my father dies, is laid out in the church, and my uncle is there the night of the funeral; the mass was in St. Patrick's Old Cathedral. He gets a heart attack. They take him to the hospital and about a month later he dies.

RS: My God.

MS: Yeah. Yeah. But that's the nature of the bond. I'm sorry. I was impressed, and it hasn't gone away.

RS: And yet you loved your father unconditionally, at least as you talk about him now.

MS: Absolutely. I don't belong in any other place. I don't belong in a world of writers or whatever. I've found that over the years I don't want to think of myself as anything other than what I am.

But things were so overwhelming when I was a kid, a little kid growing up down in that place, in those times. The only place I could burst out, I thought, was with stories, drama, ideas.

RS: So you did a lot of that?

MS: Constantly.

RS: As a little kid?

MS: As a little kid. I would fantasize a lot about that. And I would draw my own movies.

RS: Really? Little storyboard-like things?

MS: Yeah, they were storyboards. They started out in 1.33 aspect ratio in black-and-white, standard movie size. When I was quite a little kid I liked *The Little King* comic strips. And I would draw my own comic strip.

RS: Otto Soglow was the cartoonist. That was a cute strip. Yet it was very visually pure, almost austere.

MS: I remember doing them when we lived in Corona. That was like a movie for me. I must've been five or six. And then, when I was in Manhattan, in 1950, when I was about eight or nine, I would watch other shows on TV and try to do my version on film, in drawings. And I'd make drawings, and I'd paint them with watercolors. I had a whole bunch of them. And I actually finished them. But then my father saw me one day playing with them and I hid them. He didn't like the idea. He didn't know what I was doing, you know. He thought it was too secretive. And so I guess I got embarrassed and threw them away.

RS: There are none of those left?

MS: No. As I said, everybody was on top of each other in those three rooms, you know, and I felt ashamed of it, I guess. And I threw them away. And then, a year or two later, I said to myself, You know what? The hell with them, I'm going to do them again.

I never finished them, though. By that time I was turning into a teenager, and things were changing. And by that time, too, I was going wide-screen. They were like big Roman epics, one of which I called "The Eternal City." I got into gladiatorial combats. And then they got kind of decadent, I guess—my drawn frames expanded to 75 millimeters, wide-screen; 70 wasn't enough. Roman epics, you know. The Roman epic I never finished. But a few of the others I finished.

RS: So you were drawing in little notebooks.

Marty's childhood "film," one of the many epics he drew in what amounts to storyboard form. He pulled the images, one by one, through a little theater he had constructed. His audience was a single boyhood pal.

MS: They were drawn on pads. And then the strips were cut out, and were put into a little screen. I would only show them to one friend—I didn't show them to anybody else. I hid them in the apartment.

RS: At what age did you start doing that?

MS: Oh, I must've been about eight or nine until about twelve, or maybe thirteen. They're in some of the books about me, some of the Roman drawings. But the other ones I don't show. And some of the early ones I guess I threw away. But I would show them to this one friend of mine because he was a very sweet kid. He was sort of the intellectual of the group. And he would insist, "Marty, these don't move." I said, "They all move. See, from one frame to the other." "Oh, yeah, but the drawings are not moving." I said, "Why do you have to be literal about it?" But he was an avid reader and he taught me to read, too. Read books. We'd go to the library together.

RS: At what age did you start doing that?

MS: Oh, I guess ten or eleven.

RS: What kind of books would you take out? Kids' books?

MS: I remember taking out *When Knighthood Was in Flower.* That was enjoyable. Then some other books written for young high school students, I think, about the Revolutionary War and that sort of thing. I don't remember getting through them that well. I found it was very hard, I didn't know how to read a book, I didn't know how to live with a book, or read fast. I still can't read fast. The biggest revelation was when I forced my father to take me to see *Julius Caesar.* He didn't want to see it, but he would take me to see anything I wanted to see. And it was the Mankiewicz version. It was Brando, James Mason, John Gielgud. Mason is fantastic.

RS: It was a little stodgy as I recall.

MS: Very stodgy.

RS: And a little underpopulated. There are not enough people in the crowd scenes.

MS: Yeah, yeah. You can see it now, when the camera pulls back. But as a kid I was fascinated by Ancient Rome because of the church. And I liked *Quo Vadis* when I first saw it. But *Julius Caesar* was black-and-white and it was Shakespeare. I went with it. It was fun. And I was so taken by the story that I found the book in the library, illustrated by Rockwell Kent. I took it to class. And that particular year the nun who was teaching the class had to leave, so they had a lay teacher in, a woman. And I said, "I saw this film, and I'd like to put the play on right now." And so I assigned the different roles to different friends of mine in the class that day. I think I got halfway through act one before my friends started walking off. They'd had enough. But I would hand the book to the next person for his part, and the next and the next and so on. I thought it was so amazing.

And then there was Orson Welles's *Macbeth* on TV, which I saw repeatedly on *Million Dollar Movie* [a local TV series that ran old movies every night]. And Olivier's *Hamlet,* which I saw when I was six years old. My brother took me; basically, he said, it's got ghosts and sword fighting. We sat through the whole picture.

RS: It must've been around that time that I went to *Henry V*—a school assignment.

MS: Oh, I got to see that one later. We got to see it at the New Yorker theater. I think it was the first film shown at the New Yorker. But the library was so important, because it, too, was quiet.

RS: You keep coming back to that.

MS: It was pretty quiet—not quite like the movies, which sort of induced a pure dream state.

RS: Except, I guess, if the movie was lousy, and all the kids started hooting and hollering.

MS: Making noise on a Saturday afternoon—yeah. But this was a refuge. Along with the church, the only place where there was some hope.

RS: You had to get away from the pressure.

MS: You had to get away from the

Marty with his brother, Frank.

pressure, and there was no place to go except the church. There was one priest, Father Principe—it was his first diocese, he was twenty-three years old—who was the one who presented the idea of thinking ahead to me and my friends. Prior to that, there were some other priests, very nice priests, but they were Italians and Italian Americans who were dealing with the older Italian community. So there was a disconnect with the younger people who were growing up in the mid-fifties to the late fifties. And this young man, he looked at us and he would say, "Look, you don't have to live like this." He started to make us listen to certain kinds of music. He was a great film buff. Of course, he liked certain kinds of films that had messages, you know. But he also loved westerns, although he disliked *Johnny Guitar.* I'll never forget when he came back and spoke out against *Johnny Guitar.* He said it's an impossible film. [Nicholas Ray's hysterical western has become a cult favorite. Joan Crawford stars as a saloon keeper fighting with Mercedes McCambridge for control of a town.]

He kind of liked *The Searchers,* but got a little disappointed with John Wayne's character. But we understood that character—you know, the darkness . . .

RS: And the towering rage.

MS: That was the thing. When I saw Wayne in *Red River*—maybe I was six or seven years old—I think that connected with whatever was going on in me, something that connected with my father.

RS: I can see that—very much.

MS: You know, with me, in my situation—it was like a force that overwhelmed me.

RS: *Red River* revolves almost entirely around a father-son theme—love, hatred, reconciliation.

MS: That was it. When he and Monty Clift separate, when the kid breaks away and Wayne says, you know, you turn around, I might just be there.

RS: Meaning he intends to stalk and perhaps kill him. But there must have been dozens, hundreds of little boys in Little Italy in something like your situation: having intense family relations, struggling to resolve their spiritual lives and their secular lives.

MS: I know.

RS: Yet, you're the only one who went on to make art out of that experience. Again I wonder, what's comparable between moviegoing and churchgoing?

MS: I wouldn't know. I don't have any other experience, really. Certainly not sports. I couldn't play sports. I would get asthma, I'd cough and, you know, turn blue [*laughs*]. Then they'd have to take me to the doctor.

RS: Later, when you went to Cardinal Hayes High School, did you go to the basketball games or any sporting events?

MS: I went to a football game once.

RS: [*Laughs.*] I see.

MS: It was cold. It was Thanksgiving Day. And I found that I didn't like the, the—

RS: The violence of it, perhaps [*laughs*]. Which is a funny thing to say to you.

MS: No, the violence was all right. But there was something about the bravado I saw in the jocks that was similar to what I saw in the streets—bullying from guys who were bigger than you. Or more popular. So I was always the outcast in that way.

But, really, it's all about the church, my relationship with the church. I went in there, I bought in. And now, at this stage of the game, at my age, it's almost like you have to apologize for saying, Yeah, I believed in certain things. There are no illusions now.

I finished this book last week by Marguerite Yourcenar, who wrote *Memoirs of Hadrian*—do you know it?

RS: Yes, I know it.

MS: This book is called *The Abyss*.

RS: I don't know that one.

MS: It's extraordinary. It takes place in the Middle Ages, and deals with an alchemist-philosopher-doctor named Zeno, who's based on a number of people at the time. And it's a remarkable book about knowledge, and about ignorance. Particularly the way she lays out the church's treatment of these intellectuals. And there're just remarkable things in the book about the love of knowledge and the depth to which the character surrenders to the art of knowledge, so to speak. And embracing and finding himself in the abyss, where we all will go [*laughs*], and we all come from.

I mean, I can't do it justice with the words I've just said, because it's quite enlightening just in the way she handles the history of it. It doesn't read like it's written by someone looking back at that time. It reads like it's somebody *in* that time.

RS: In talking about that book it sounds as if what you were saying about your childhood is that you had a similar lust for knowledge. When you mention your trips to the library it's as if you're saying the difference between you, or the potential you, and the yabbos on the street is your quest for information, for knowledge, or wisdom, whatever you want to call it.

MS: I saw it in certain films, too. I saw characters survive with their knowledge. And I remember that priest, Father Principe: he'd get so fed up with some of the kids sometimes, they'd do such silly things. In my case, he even tried to force me to do sports. I wouldn't do it. And he'd say, "This is good for you. Team sports." I wouldn't do it. I couldn't. I mean, reading about Teddy Roosevelt now, I should have [*laughs*].

RS: Not necessarily.

MS: The thing about the asthma—I think if you're told you're sick long enough, as a child, you begin to take it seriously.

RS: You mean, you think the more people talked about it, the more you embraced sickness?

MS: It could be. When a child is sick he gets attention.

RS: Sure.

MS: But I really was sick. I almost died at two weeks old. I was brought back to life by a doctor, from whooping cough. It was an epidemic or something. It was Dr. Vogel, from Jamaica, Queens, a very nice doctor. I remember him very well because later I was going to his house all the time, every week, for injections for allergies and asthma and that sort of thing. But the asthma—at the time, working-class people didn't know about it. It was scary to them.

RS: So you were born asthmatic?

MS: I don't know. But I had my tonsils taken out at the age of three or something, and from that point on the asthma showed up. Maybe for me it came out of the lungs that were wrecked from the whooping cough. One problem was, you couldn't really enjoy yourself. Whenever I would really get into enjoying myself— laughing, for example—I couldn't catch my breath. And a terrible attack of wheezing would start. I laugh a lot now, and I think that's one reason I do. But as a child you start to pass out and you don't know if you're going to take another breath. You just don't know.

So you're frightened. They put me in one of the bedrooms, with me in a tent on a bed. And there was a little vaporizer inside the tent. People would come and open the tent and see how I was doing, and close it.

But look, what can I say? That's where I come from, it's who I am. A lot of time, in my earlier films I was talking about myself, but in those days, in the 1970s, I really couldn't say certain things. By the time I did *Raging Bull*, I didn't care anymore in terms of being silent about where I came from or hiding certain things. Because that world was disappearing and it's gone now, but what remains in my memory was its atmosphere of fear. That's something I tried to get at in *The Departed*.

RS: Fear of what?

MS: Powerful people. Who were above the law.

RS: You mean gangsters?

MS: Yeah. They were like, well, anything could happen. You couldn't say anything. You couldn't do anything. You never knew when they might lash out—over things that seemed completely innocent to you.

RS: Because they controlled the neighborhood in all the important ways.

MS: Yeah. Though I was around a couple who were very nice to me, actually, very sweet to me. One of them—he died in 1968—was a very powerful man who was much feared, and rightly so: he was a killer, a real killer. But he was a very nice man—to me.

The guy was sort of the one the uncle in *Mean Streets* is based upon. I was friends with one of his nephews—hanging out together and playing. We were always there, and to a nine-, ten-, eleven-year-old kid, he was fascinating, because of the power he wielded in that area. The way he moved, what happened when he came out of his doorway—it was the parting of the Red Sea.

One day some young kids who were really sweet were having a basketball game, and a young kid called Moon—nice kid, never any trouble—got into a fight with the other team, from another parish. It was a heated thing, and the police came around. Nothing happened; it was just kids. We went into a bar, and this guy the uncle was based on came in and went in the back, and we all knew that he was there.

So the tone of the room changed. And one of his guys came up and said, "Where's Moon?" He says, "Come here." And he took the kid in the back. And the guy looked at him, and he said, "You're Moon?" And he says, "Yeah." "No more trouble." Moon says, "Oh, okay." It was not like a young wiseguy who was trying to get into the Mob or anything; it was just, You caused a fight at the basketball game, you brought the police down here, we don't want the police here. We have our own lives here. Just no more trouble. Not mean, not threatening—just be nice. So that was it! There were other kids who didn't get that. Other kids got shot. It was just, you know, we run this place. We want it nice and quiet. We don't want people coming down here and checking out what we're doing.

So there was always an atmosphere of fear. In that, if anybody asked you anything, you always said, "I don't know what you're talking about. I don't know who you are. I don't know, you must have somebody else in mind."

RS: So, this notion of silence—it's a big deal in the Mafia, *omertà* and all that.

MS: You just pretend not to know anything, see anything, because you have family too and family gets attacked. But it affected me. Yeah, it affected me.

RS: Later, making movies, did you want others to see into this hidden, secret world?

MS: No, not really. I didn't want anybody to know. I didn't even want anybody to know I came from there. That's why I think by the time I did *Raging Bull,* after having gone through my own difficult period in 1976 and 1978, I didn't care anymore, because I thought it was my last film anyway in that style. And I figured it didn't matter. It's who we are. And when I moved to California, I thought I could be more Californian—a movie director in the old Hollywood style, making genre films at a rapid pace. But the old Hollywood was dying.

And we were looking around, trying to collect things, me and Steven Spielberg, and all these guys, trying to collect memorabilia to keep the old Hollywood alive. But it was a transitional time. It wasn't like what people said: Oh, well, you kids

Catherine and Charles Scorsese on set. Both of Marty's parents appeared in small roles in many of his films.

looked at movies, that's all you know of life. That's not so. It's always with me and never will go away—the way I grew up. That world is always in here. I mean, when I see the world the way it is now, I don't see much difference from where I came from.

RS: You mean in terms of brutality, stupidity?

MS: Ignorance, and how attitudes, emotions, could switch around in an instant. But the thing about the fear is interesting. An old friend of mine once said it was like being in occupied France. He said if you were asked a question, you were afraid you'd be taken to the Sûreté to be questioned. You couldn't say anything.

RS: I imagine your parents were saying, Don't look, Marty; don't talk, Marty?

MS: Constantly. Constantly.

RS: In other words, you were supposed to be of this world, but not really in this world.

MS: In fact, it was, Please get out if you can. But be decent, be basically a decent person, like my parents were. And, by the way, that's the reticence I think you see in my father in the first half of *Italianamerican* [the documentary Scorsese made about his parents]. We just don't talk. We don't talk about anything. Though sometimes my father did. He couldn't resist complaining about how many Irish bars there were in the neighborhood [*laughs*].

Sometimes Irish people laugh when they see *Italianamerican*. But when Nicholson's character says, "I smell a rat," that's what I'm talking about. That's when I suddenly got chills. Even telling you about it, I still get chills. It's so real to me.

RS: So you lived in a world where everybody smells a rat. Is that what you're saying?

MS: Well, I lived in a world where if you did the wrong thing or said the wrong thing, you didn't know what would happen. I mean, I saw things happen. I saw people be censured. Not censored: censured. I saw people being slapped, which is worse than being hit.

RS: There's a lot of contempt in a slap.

MS: And it's done in front of a lot of people. And that's the worst. And then I saw people lose their minds. I saw people, good men, turn into complete human wrecks by the end of their lives, because they couldn't make it in the street. People's lives just imploded.

I don't want this ever to be about this me as some sickly kid observing from the sidelines. I'm just saying this is where I come from. It's the reality. I saw some tragedies. At least, I thought they were tragedies.

RS: You mean, like, a boyhood chum who—

MS: No. Older, older—my father's friends, people for whom the last twenty-five years of their lives was one bad day after another. The humiliation of it . . .

I saw a couple of cases where over the years they just came apart. Because before I was born, something happened. They aspired to a kind of street life. They were in the rackets, they were in with the wiseguys. But they didn't have it in them to hurt somebody. Didn't have it in them to use their heads a certain way. When the time came for them to do what they had to, they couldn't do it, and they were humiliated, constantly.

And yet, my father, out of loyalty, stayed with them and took them in as respected people. And so there was that constant discussion: How could you embrace this person, how could you still take this person seriously if no one else took him seriously? My mother didn't say it, but I heard other people say it. And my father would say, So-and-so, he's related to so-and-so, he was an old friend of mine, he was loyal to me, I'm going to be loyal to him. And that was it. Until the end. I was fascinated by that.

It's just the nature of the world I knew. And, as I said, I get excited again to even tell you the story about that scene in *The Departed* that deals with those issues, a man coming apart who has a lot of power.

But I think who I turned out to be has a lot to do with Irish Catholicism. When I first started bringing books home, one of the first ones I got my hands on was *Portrait of the Artist as a Young Man.* James Joyce. The sensibility of that novel—I was right into it. It was fine with me [*laughs*].

RS: I probably read it at the same age you did.

MS: I was about fifteen.

RS: Me, too. It reinforced for me my growing atheism—although that sermon about the length of eternity is a great piece of writing.

MS: Oh, it's wonderful. In *Mean Streets,* we put Harvey Keitel's hand on the flame of eternity—that probably comes from Joyce. But we did hear sermons like that—the sermons about sex, for instance. That's what we heard in some cases. Other priests, not. There were some priests at Cardinal Hayes that were not that way.

RS: It's interesting to me that your parents were not particularly religious.

MS: They didn't buy into it. It's maybe partly a reaction to the peak of the American Catholic church of the fifties. I mean, you're coming off of *Going My Way, Bells of St. Mary's.*

RS: But they're Irish versions of Catholicism. Isn't that a conflict?

MS: Yes. In fact, the nuns who were teaching us had Irish brogues. And that caused some tension.

RS: There is a difference between Irish Catholicism and Italian, isn't there?

26

MS: I'm glad you asked that. Because last time Father Principe came to my house he started talking about the difference between Irish and Italian Catholics. I didn't

Marty's second-grade class photo. He is second from the left in the back row, against the wall.

see any of this at the time, but I think that's one of the reasons I was so attracted to *The Departed.* There's something about [screenwriter] Bill Monahan's Irish Catholicism, the fatalism of it. And the humor. The nature of how people feel about themselves. I think I was more exposed to the Irish Catholicism because of the elementary school and also Cardinal Hayes.

Father Principe was the one who finally, when he saw *Taxi Driver,* actually summed up my career. He said, "I've always told you, 'Too much Good Friday and not enough Easter Sunday.' " That's it.

RS: That's pretty good.

MS: That sums it up. And I think it has a lot to do with Irish Catholicism.

RS: I suppose, just as your spiritual and intellectual life in this period was changing, so was your taste in movies.

MS: When I started to go to high school, I realized my interest in movies was in more than just American films, because having been exposed at the age of five to the Italian neorealist films I also was very, very closely tied to the European sensibility. Obviously, I'm not European, I'm American. But I had Europeans around me all the time, and so I was always pulled in that direction.

Sometimes I would see these films on television when I'd come home from school—*Diary of a Country Priest,* Jean Renoir's *Diary of a Chambermaid,* which was in English, of course, and *The River* by Renoir. But *Beauty and the Beast*—

RS: I just think it's wonderful.

MS: It's something.

RS: I don't like fantasies much in movies. But it's one of the rare fantasies I love.

MS: Boy, that works. So what happened was that when I was going to high school, I would get *Cue* magazine and I would see these movies that were mentioned. There was *Alexander Nevsky,* and I would go to this theater called the Thalia.

RS: You didn't know what you were going to get.

MS: No, I didn't know what I was going to get. In a way I was aware of the Bergman pictures; *The Seventh Seal* was the one that was a revelation. I wanted to see it, and I was mesmerized by it; I kept going back to see that. There was *Smiles of a Summer Night,* and it was condemned. And so I had to ask the priest in confession if it was okay. And he said, "Oh, you're studying film, it's all right." It didn't do any good because I didn't understand it. I was too young, much too unsophisticated. And then I saw some of the other ones, but of course I was not able to understand them, either.

And then there was a rerelease of Renoir's *Grand Illusion.* Around 1958 or '59, an intact copy of the film that the Nazis hadn't burned was discovered. Renoir's name was very important to me. I knew it had something to do with a painter—his father. When I was a child I saw some of [Pierre-Auguste] Renoir's paintings in the museum. I'd go to the museum a lot. But I've never forgotten *The River* [Jean Renoir's coming-of-age tale, set in India, about three girls falling in love with a former soldier] on that big screen. I was eight years old, nine years old. It was an astounding movie to me, and it still is. In fact, I showed it to Wes Anderson about four or five years ago. And I just spoke to Wes two days ago, and he said, That's when it began, his film *The Darjeeling Limited.*

RS: Really?

MS: Yeah. He said, while he was watching it, he said to himself, I think there might be something here. And then it opened him up to Satyajit Ray films, and the Merchant-Ivory films they made in India. And so it's there.

RS: And neorealism? I think of *Mean Streets* or a picture that I discovered more recently and like quite a bit, *Who's That Knocking at My Door.* They're both in the neorealistic manner. [The latter is about a young man who falls in love with a woman who has been raped and cannot handle the notion that she has been "ruined."]

MS: Uh-oh.

RS: No, it's good, Marty.

MS: Well, it's a rough sketch for *Mean Streets,* really. If you see them both, you have an idea of what my life was like in those days. Those Italian neorealist films were shown on TV, in 1949, or 1948.

RS: Imagine that.

MS: Yeah, every Friday night they had an Italian film with subtitles: *Shoeshine, Rome 11:00, Anna, Bitter Rice.* My grandparents were sitting around crying, but it was not nostalgia. It was a hard, bitter truth for them. And the solemnity with which these films were viewed, the solemnity with which they were discussed, by the different generations, made me realize that that was the real world. What I was seeing in those pictures is real. The human condition is that.

But something else was happening in those pictures. I didn't understand the war. I didn't know from partisans and fascists. I had no idea. But I did understand the extraordinary communal experience around that little TV screen, watching those scratchy black-and-white images. We had compassion for the people in those pictures.

RS: So that was in your bones when you started to make your first features?

MS: Yes, but what was also in my bones was *Singin' in the Rain.* A great experience. My brother and I went to see that in 1952. And at nine or ten years old, we were picking up on all the satire. It's just so well done, so deftly put together—[Gene] Kelly, and Donald O'Connor and Debbie Reynolds, that was extraordinary. My favorite scene—it's really about what a director does—is when the director is trying to explain to the actress to speak into the microphone: It goes through the wire and comes through here, and we put it on a disk. But you have to speak into the microphone. It's also about that extraordinary quiet that you have to have as a director—knowing when to speak and when not to—which goes back to when I was a kid.

Because of being the youngest, whatever conflict was going on, I couldn't say anything. And I find that in directing: I have to keep my feelings hidden from key crew members or, in particular, from the actors. Because my feelings are uncontrollable. Or can be. So I have to pull back. And it's an excruciating experience for me.

But there's the humor in it, too, the humor of being in this situation. Maybe that's why I loved *Sunset Boulevard,* because nothing is held back in it. There was nothing like seeing that picture in 1952, when I was ten. To me it was a horror film. An extraordinarily, madly funny horror film. Burying the chimpanzee, and the poor woman in that room with no locks on the doors. William Holden in the pool.

RS: How does that get into something like *Mean Streets*?

MS: It probably doesn't—not directly. But by the time I was maybe twelve, thirteen, fourteen, I was asking myself why some film was affecting me, like *Force of Evil,* which I saw on *Million Dollar Movie.* Why did certain scenes in that film affect me so strongly? And because it was on *Million Dollar Movie,* I could revisit it every night for a week. *Force of Evil* was the big film.

RS: I have a little bit of a problem with that movie. I kind of appreciate it without fully feeling gathered in by it.

MS: Interesting. It was depicting people that we kind of knew, but in a Hollywood way. It was about the numbers game. And everybody ran the numbers. I used to take the numbers back and forth in paper bags. Somebody would say to me, Hey, take this, go over there and get that, and bring it back. So you'd do it.

I was ten years old and that was basically a way of life. Everybody talked about the numbers they dreamed of. And the number they played. What was the Brooklyn number? What was the Manhattan number? It was easy for us to feed into it, it was like a film being made about people we knew. It didn't have to win us over. And, of course, John Garfield could do no wrong as far as we were concerned. [He plays a Mob lawyer trying to force his brother into playing along with a scheme to consolidate the numbers racket.]

RS: Well, putting it that way—no wonder it appealed to you more than it did me.

MS: I was trying to figure out the other day: Why does one remember a scene? Like the scene in *Force of Evil* where Thomas Gomez takes his friend who is ratting him out to a restaurant late at night to have coffee.

RS: It's been a while since I've seen that movie.

MS: You have to watch that scene. Part of its power, I realized, came from David Raksin's music in the background. And the extraordinary power of the dialogue with Gomez, realizing that he was ratted out, and saying, "What have you done to me?" And as they pick him up, the two guys who are thugs suddenly begin to see him crumple because he has a bad heart, and they go, "No, no, take it easy, take it easy, old pal. It's okay. We're just taking you with us. We're not going to harm you." And they begin to feel sorry for him, the music building. And then the rat, the guy with the glasses, panics. He trips and he falls. And one asks, "What do you want to do with this one?" And the other says, "Shoot him, kill him, kill him. He knows me." And the guy screams. It's a close-up, and the gangster, the thug, fires a gun right in the camera. And it's a series of cuts and camera moves. But most is achieved with the actors and the dialogue, and the use of music. And Gomez has a great speech in there where he says, "You know, sometimes you feel like you're dying." And it's just beautifully done, because he is about to die of the heart attack and he doesn't realize it. It was just absolutely extraordinary.

RS: And you were what, twelve, thirteen?

MS: I was about thirteen years old when I saw it, yeah.

RS: Okay. So, you are already at that point committed to becoming a movie guy?

MS: No. No. This is just something—

RS: Well, what were you doing those drawings for if you weren't beginning to think—

MS: I don't know what the hell I was doing.

RS: But there's clearly some instinctive thing going on here.

MS: But you don't make movies from where I came from; you don't. First of all, movies weren't made in New York in 1959, or they were made by people in the Village, maybe.

And I have to say that as a boy I did have trouble with some genres, especially the more romantic genres. I had trouble with Douglas Sirk. I mean, I saw *Magnificent Obsession.* And I saw *Written on the Wind.* And I was counting the minutes. I'd walk around the theater, then come back and sit down. The only thing was the color. The color was amazing. Now it's one of my favorite films, of course.

But I was much more into the western genre because the West had the outdoors, in Technicolor, usually. And it had horses. Horses are beautiful. And my mother's father, Martino Capa, was in the Italian cavalry, in Sicily. So he loved horses, too, he used to like watching them. I love any horse picture made from 1946 to 1955—you know, *Blue Grass of Kentucky, The Red Stallion.* There was the texture of the color on the horses. They were in Cinecolor.

Shane was a great experience, for example. I couldn't wait to see *Winchester '73.* But when my father took me to see it, I had trouble with it, because it was more psychologically mean-spirited. It was very disturbing, almost an ugly picture of the West. *Blood on the Moon*—my parents took me to see that. That was an experience, because of the look of the film. The way they were dressed, it had an authenticity to it, and there's an extraordinary scene in a bar where Robert Mitchum fights Robert Preston. They're wearing these heavy coats and the fight is not the traditional cowboy fight that I was used to seeing—the darkness, the low angle, these men sort of tumbling on each other, it was humiliating for the two of them. But it had a truth to it, and it was great how this noir aspect to the movie was really effective.

What was happening was that the noir stuff—mostly set in the cities—started to sneak into these other genres. And I connected with that. In 1953, *Pickup on South Street* was on the bottom half of a double bill. And the expression in that film, the way it was shot, the way the characters were relating to each other, the extraordinary opening sequence with Jean Peters and Richard Widmark on the subway [where, as a pickpocket, he dips into her purse and comes up with microfilmed secret documents she's—innocently—carrying to Communist agents], and the fight scene where he hits her—it was pretty shocking, and it stayed with me.

RS: Okay. Let me go back to something I raised before. There must have been dozens, hundreds, of young boys like you, living in places like Elizabeth Street, in situations comparable to yours. How come your situation affected you so powerfully, taking the form of a sort of quiet, unacknowledged rebelliousness?

MS: I don't know where it comes from. I don't know whether it's weakness, or whether it's strength. I don't know why that affected me that way. But I really did believe that there could be a transcendence. I hate to use words like that, but the idea is that there is a part of us that would yearn for something that is—

RS: Some of us, not all of us. A lot of people yearn just for what they've always known.

MS: Yeah, but I thought, There are some great Catholic artists. For example, Roberto Rossellini and his film *Europa '51*. That for me was something that had hope. It has to do with the teachings of the New Testament. I really bought into it, because of what I saw around me. I thought this is the right idea: feeling for the other person and giving something to the other person. Compassion, maybe that's it.

RS: Well, let me put it another way. Little as you were, and powerless as you were in the situation, there must've been some part of you that said, Oh, Christ, Dad, let him alone, referring to your brother or your uncle. Let him be what he wants, let him do what he wants.

MS: Oh, absolutely. Let it go, yeah. But I also knew what he meant. He was afraid that certain things could happen to them. And invariably he was, you know—

RS: Half right, at least.

MS: He was half right. But it's hard, how you approach the issue. You can hammer it too much, and then they're not going to listen to anything, you know.

RS: The only direct knowledge I have of your father is from *Italianamerican*. He's almost cowering away from your mother. It's like a Thurber cartoon.

MS: I know. But he wasn't really that way.

RS: But he's very reserved. And she's kind of pushing him.

MS: That was the balance, that was the duo. That was part of a routine they had. She was much more open. He would be more reserved. But once he felt comfortable—if you notice, halfway through the picture, they're both narrating the same story, and contradicting each other and arguing.

But in the beginning, it was hard for him to be on film, there was no such thing for him as being on film. You never show your personality on film. You're not going to show people who you are. Imagine when they saw *Mean Streets*. They were stunned.

RS: Tell me.

MS: Well, that opening night at the New York Film Festival, they were shocked. They didn't know if it was good or not, but they knew where it came from. They were surprised that that kind of stuff would be on the screen. And my mother went out into the lobby and people ran up to her and they said—I always tell the story—"Mrs. Scorsese, what do you think of your son's film?" She goes, "I just want you to know, we never used that word in the house."

Marty as cowboy.

And she was right. She was right. The four-letter word [fuck] was never used in the house. In the most heated discussions I never heard that word used by my uncles, by my brother, or by my father. But it was her first response. She just wanted people to know how my parents raised me. We didn't raise him to be that. But on the other hand, people seemed to like the film. There seemed to be a good reaction to it. And they didn't quite understand this.

RS: Obviously, there was a disconnect between the little Marty they had lovingly tended as a child and young Marty, the explosive filmmaker.

MS: Those formative years between six or seven and until about fourteen were really, really tough years for me. Because I didn't fit in that neighborhood. I mean, I couldn't really be the young person I was trying to be. I wasn't able to take [my studies] seriously enough to go to Regis High School, let's say, and take Greek and Latin. I couldn't do it. Or wouldn't do it.

Even so, my first impulse was to go to the priesthood. It was overwhelming. Especially if you were a kid who couldn't become a member of organized crime. I mean, you had to have a stone heart. You have to be a stone killer.

RS: Which, of course, your father had no intention of your being.

MS: But he was quite intense, quite intense. He made you realize that everything had a meaning and everything had to be done a certain way. Meaning that there was a reason why people lived a certain way and behaved a certain way. Even though you're kids, this is the world you're in.

RS: Whereas your mother was more live-and-let-live?

MS: Yeah, absolutely. If there was a little too much nudity in a new film, my mother would say, "Oh, come on, that's life." And my father had to say, "Well, okay." But he made you aware that there was a code, a morality, that was different from what I was hearing in the church.

RS: How different?

MS: It was more guarded.

RS: Less black-and-white, maybe?

MS: Yeah, less black-and-white. First of all, the family owes loyalty to itself, to each other. It all stems from how you treat each other in this room.

RS: So, if that room is small enough, it's going to increase the intensity?

MS: It's the table scene in *East of Eden.* I don't mean he was pompous or in any way like the character played by Raymond Massey. But for an eight-year-old or a seven-year-old kid, you hear things that are just pretty scary.

RS: And your parents are thinking, I don't know what to do with him?

MS: Exactly. My father was very concerned: The boy says he wants to be a priest. What if he's not a real boy? Maybe there's something different about him, you know.

I wasn't tough. In a way, you have to not believe in the soul. Certain people in those "mobs" had almost no choice. Some basically good people ended up doing bad things, because they had no choice. Then you have the monsters like the one that Jack becomes.

But there are others who are doomed. My friend Raffaele Donato used to talk about good people forced into doing bad things because they're uneducated, because they're stuck, because they have problems with their families. And on the feast days or the festivals of the saints or whatever, they'd be the ones carrying the saint, and putting the weight on their shoulders to take the suffering. So that's where a lot of my work comes from. It doesn't come from a desire to always show the Italian Americans in this dark way.

De Niro one time had a good answer for that. He went on for about five minutes in a meeting that I don't see it as solely an Italian-American problem. I see it as what is in us, in every one of us. And I have to face what I think is not good about myself. And it's realized more truthfully when I deal with it in those particular stories of the Italian-American world.

All this comes together and it feels almost universal to me, and ultimately it seems that I found it more comfortable, more accessible to me to do in the stories that happened to involve Italian Americans. There is one more film about it called *Neighborhood*, a Nick Pileggi film, that one day I might make. Elia Kazan always told me to make it. It's sort of a story about my mother and father.

RS: Art has to be specific. Generalizations are the enemy of art.

MS: I was thinking about it the other day, this idea of becoming a priest. Maybe it wasn't really a serious vocation after all. Maybe I just wanted to be like that neighborhood priest, Father Principe. But, as I said, my parents were not religious.

RS: Christmas and Lent Catholics?

MS: Kind of. The last time my mother went to confession she said, "That priest asked me some questions. It's none of his business." She never went back.

RS: That's funny.

MS: But, you know, what were they going to do with me? For about two years I was an altar boy. It was something to do and the priest was nice to me. But I got thrown out because I couldn't make it to the seven o'clock mass. I'm not very good in the mornings.

RS: I'm guessing that even that early you had some sort of half-formed doubts about the priestly vocation. Maybe it was too focused on you, your own needs.

MS: Yeah, and it should be the other way.

RS: And you felt that if you had a priestly vocation, it should be to help others.

MS: Well, no. I understood that you have to help others, you do things for people, you work in schools, you work in the streets. But I was only thinking what was in it for me, not for what really mattered. And that's what interests me about the Dalai Lama, about any truly spiritual or religious figure.

RS: Talk a little more about that.

MS: I don't say I believe it now, but at that time I wondered, What's the sense of hanging around here? If you die, you can go to heaven. So why be here? I mean, I put it in childlike terms—ultimately, maybe it's just a matter of marking time until you're dead.

RS: The thought occurs to me all the time. Or I'll say to people, "Well, you've got to do something between the cradle and the grave."

MS: We have to do it. I mean, I look back, I think about it a lot. But, anyway, I went to Cardinal Hayes, and in two and a half years at Cardinal Hayes I sort of straightened out—at least got focused. For what, I wasn't quite sure.

I wasn't focused on movies. There was no such thing as that. I was focused—how should I say?—on not living the way the others were living, the ones who hadn't gone to high school, the ones who hadn't gone to college. I wanted to go, after Cardinal Hayes, to Fordham, but I was in the lower quarter of my graduating class, I hadn't applied myself, or whatever.

CUTS AND ANGLES

RICHARD SCHICKEL: Was there any film, when you were a kid, where you would say, Well, that's a knockout cut. Maybe you wouldn't even have known to call it a cut. But a juxtaposition, maybe?

MARTIN SCORSESE: I think I was aware of it. There was no doubt when I was very young and I saw *Duel in the Sun* [the epic, heavily sexualized western of 1946], there were some edited sequences, spectacle sequences, not the melodramatic stuff.

RS: When they gather from all over the ranch—it's beautiful.

MS: I'll never forget that.

RS: It's one of the best sequences ever.

MS: Ever.

RS: I mean, it's a wacko King Vidor movie, from what Andrew Sarris once called his delirious phase, but boy, that's a great sequence.

MS: Yeah, yeah. And I'm trying to think. I'm trying to project myself back now: Is that something I noticed, the editing? Or didn't I? I think I did in some way,

Marty's merry Christmas.

because, you know, there's the one cowboy and then there's the two cowboys.

RS: And then there's twelve cowboys.

MS: And how about, finally, hundreds of them coming over the hill to stop the railroad.

RS: It's just classic filmmaking.

MS: Another one I remember liking when I was a kid was *I Shot Jesse James,* Sam Fuller's first film. My father took me to see that when I was about six or seven years old. That ending. And those close-ups are amazing. I remember those close-ups very strongly. But the thing is, I knew it wasn't your traditional western—a *High Noon* kind of thing. Something else was going on there. It was more intense. But I think the big one for me was *Shane.*

RS: Really?

MS: Because I was the same age as the boy. And there was something about the way the director [George Stevens] used the medium. For example, the fight scenes, the way the action erupts. And the way Shane goes for his gun—the use of sound effects and editing. And it cuts to Brandon De Wilde and his eyes open. And, of course, the fight in the bar.

It's beautifully constructed. You watch how it builds, and builds, and builds. Now, these days, I notice the music helps it to a certain extent. But, still, it's got the traditional scene, which I did in *Gangs of New York*—you know, the intimidation at the bar. And again in *The Departed* with the cranberry juice, which is [Ben] Johnson in the bar with Alan Ladd, and Alan Ladd ordering sarsaparilla.

I watched it while I was doing *The Departed.* And I liked the way it's constructed. I don't know if it holds together completely. I think there are elements of it that kind of get bogged down.

RS: Well, I have observed this a great deal in interviewing directors, where directors do not look at movies the way movie critics do, or the way the audience does. Director conversations about movies will always come down to a cut, an angle, something to do with technique. Which the audience mostly skips. They're really there for the story. And the story of *Shane* works for them.

MS: Yeah, especially at the end—I was a little boy, and Shane's the kind of father I wanted. It's the kind of father any boy who saw it wanted. In the meantime, the kid's real father, Van Heflin, is a good man.

RS: Well, Van Heflin was kind of like your dad. I mean, a dutiful man.

MS: Dutiful. And it's also about taking responsibility for yourself, I hear that again. It's hammered into my head.

I disagree with you about the audience, though. The audience is affected by, for instance, the way the level of the sound effects were raised in that movie. And the editing of the scene—technical things, even if they're not aware of them as technical. But a filmmaker may well be more aware of them.

RS: And a filmmaker will be able to talk about it later, may even be able to trace influences on his work. It's just an entirely different way of looking at movies.

MS: Well, it is. Another example: *Bonnie and Clyde,* which was, I thought, an extraordinary film. I remembered a scene where they all get shot up in a motel that they're in one night. And they get in the car, and they start to drive away. And they're firing at this other car. And I swore there was a close-up of a gun coming toward the window and shooting into the car and hitting Gene Hackman in the eyes. I could have sworn there was a separate cut. But if you look at the film, it's a medium-wide shot.

So then I'd go back to see why I felt that way at that moment in the film. And often it isn't just that moment—it's scenes that build up to that moment. And acting for me was very important. When Brando came on the screen in *On the Waterfront,* my whole idea of acting changed. That doesn't mean I didn't still like James Mason or didn't like William Holden. But for me, until Brando, cinema was the rhythm and the timing of the performers, like Judy Holliday and Broderick Crawford and William Holden in *Born Yesterday:* George Cukor directed that, and these films were plays, but yet they don't feel like plays. You know, they don't feel stagebound.

RS: George was really good at that.

MS: Yeah. I think it's the actors and the timing. Also it came from watching some of David Lean's films. I saw *Breaking the Sound Barrier* on its first release, and I think it holds up better than *Brief Encounter.*

RS: I've always loved that film. [David Lean's 1952 film about the development of supersonic flight is also a tense family drama involving a tyrannical airplane designer, his daughter, and the test pilot she marries.]

MS: If you watch it now, it is really mystical, the whole relationship between the father and the son and Ann Todd at the end. It is really a beauty.

RS: Yes.

MS: And I learned a lot about sound editing from it.

RS: Oh, really?

MS: About the plane, and the way it was landing, the way the director cuts to the plane. They hear nothing, nothing, and then suddenly the buzzing gets louder and louder, and comes right at the camera. I used that a lot in *The Aviator.*

RS: I wasn't aware of the Lean connection.

MS: But the Powell-Pressburger films are much more influential for me, of course. There was something about watching *The Red Shoes* that was all-encompassing, the excessive performances—Anton Walbrook, Moira Shearer—the makeup on their faces, it was extraordinary, the beauty of the production design. Then this very strange ballet sequence, which visually had more to do with silent cinema than anything else.

RS: I don't know if you felt it when *The Red Shoes* came out, but all the girls wanted to see it, and us hearty guys were saying, "Aw, don't wanna see that!"

MS: The guys were not going to go see the ballet. But for some reason my father took me to see it.

RS: I remember going to it and, kind of against my will, being sort of strangely enchanted by it.

MS: [*Laughs.*] But, you know, I guess what I'm getting to is that I became aware of those angles—even in something like Sam Fuller's *Park Row.* It was again on *Million Dollar Movie,* and that obsessed me. I began to really notice long takes with a crane that he used. Granted, it was a very volatile picture, and maybe it was the energy of it that grabbed me. And maybe the way he moved the crane in the scene of rioting in the streets. And it ends with him fighting with somebody at the base of the statue of Horace Greeley. There's something that was so explosive about the way the camera relentlessly kept moving.

RS: But it seems to me important to point out that you're probably the only person you knew at that age who was paying attention to that.

MS: I know.

RS: Everybody else was going, Oh, that was a neat flick.

MS: Yes. But I did have my friend whom I had tortured by showing him all these drawings I had pretended were movies. And there was my other friend, Joe—we were altar boys together, and we hung out a lot together, and we just kept seeing all these movies. And we loved Ford, we loved John Wayne in these films, and I admit we didn't really talk about technique. We talked about story and character, mainly character.

In the American cinema—George Cukor, Billy Wilder—the angles are precise, they're intelligent angles. They serve the story, the narrative. It's very, very clear. And it's a very gifted thing. I don't even know how to do that, quite honestly.

RS: So in this period, are you saying at all to yourself, I don't know how you do it, I don't know where I would go learn it, but that's something I want to do?

MS: Yes, absolutely. And you really couldn't say it aloud. That's why I hid the drawings, because you couldn't say it. Your parents would think you're mad. And then everything came together at the end of the fifties, the beginning of the sixties. The New Wave France and Italy and the 16 millimeter Eclair camera—the break away from the studios—because that camera gave you freedom. The French were using it, the Italians, the new American cinema in New York.

Yet, at the same time, we were made to feel ashamed of American films—it was snobbery. They were not very intelligent, maybe not completely worthless, but still the more important films were, of course, Bergman's, and the New Italian Wave. By the time Fellini did *La Dolce Vita,* by the time he did *8½,* you had Bertolucci, Bellocchio, Olmi, Rosi. They seemed light-years ahead. So even though I loved the westerns, and musicals, there was something happening to me, something was seeping in from the Rossellini and the De Sica pictures.

But, a little later, right around the mid- to late sixties, the much maligned, or misunderstood, auteur theory was being expressed. And Andrew Sarris came out with the *American Cinema* book [1968]. And I just looked at that list: John Ford, Nicholas Ray, Sam Fuller. I didn't know anybody else knew about these films. There were in those days very few books on film. There was Arthur Knight's *The Liveliest Art,* or Paul Rotha's *Film Till Now,* the introduction to which already had an inferiority complex about English cinema. And I said, wait a second, I love *The Fallen Idol*—

RS: Just to go back a minute, when you were a kid, maybe you weren't consciously thinking about it, but some instinctive thing was pushing you toward film—the drawings, the whole obsessive interest in just seeing movies and absorbing them.

MS: But it was a dream. Or maybe not completely a dream, because I drew them out on paper. And then with a couple of friends I did a little 8 millimeter thing that wasn't very good, a short film with my friends, two or three of us, which I shot on the roofs of Mott Street with white sheets, in black-and-white. I didn't understand lighting. I understood some camera movement, I think. And I tried to make this little film.

RS: At NYU?

MS: No, no, before NYU. A friend of mine whose father had a little extra money had a little camera, 8 millimeter. We were sixteen years old, seventeen. But I learned some things about camera angles and fooled around. And, what I did was, in my mother and father's apartment—it was a Saturday night, they went out—I invited all my friends and our girlfriends, and we wound up trying to sync music to the film with a tape recorder. The music was eclectic. It was Django Reinhardt, Prokofiev's *Alexander Nevsky*, Lonnie Donegan. It actually worked.

RS: It was really an insane kid thing to do.

MS: [*Laughs.*] But we did it!

I had, by that point, seen Stanley Kubrick's *Paths of Glory.* It gave me the sense of camera positions. And I'd also seen *Citizen Kane* many times. I was crazed about *Citizen Kane.* It was on *Million Dollar Movie,* so I saw it twice a night for a week, even though the *March of Time* sequence was edited out.

RS: My God.

MS: I saw *The Third Man* that way. *The Third Man* and *Citizen Kane* were the ones that actually made me try to direct—coupled with John Cassavetes doing *Shadows,* which has an improvisatory style. His people seemed like people I kind of knew. It had a freedom to it.

RS: *The Third Man* is—I mean, talk about angles—

MS: If Carol Reed never made another movie—*The Third Man* is a beautiful film, and it still holds up. *The Departed* just reeks of *The Third Man.*

RS: Really?

MS: Yeah. I mean, particularly the last sequence in the cemetery. I shot every angle of Vera [Farmiga, playing the estranged lover] leaving, going past Matt Damon. We went crazy shooting every possible angle. But I knew that the only angle was the one that was similar to the one at the end of *The Third Man*—not exact, but similar. And I shot that, too. And in the editing—well, I said, That's it, there it is, just do it. It was so obviously my reference, anyway.

RS: Well, in retrospect, I suppose.

MS: But there was something about the excitement of the camera positions that I saw with Welles, even though I hadn't seen *The Magnificent Ambersons* and I hadn't seen *Touch of Evil* yet. The other thing was that when I would go to the Thalia, I saw everything—*Alexander Nevsky,* a lot of Russian films. Also Jacob Ben-Ami and Edgar G. Ulmer's *Green Fields* and *The Dybbuk,* Yiddish cinema. I saw whatever seemed interesting. Some of the Mosfilm screen versions of obscure Chekhov plays were staggeringly dull, you had no idea what was happening, as opposed to Eisenstein, Pudovkin, and Dovzhenko, who was the best. And even now, Dovzhenko is the one who holds up for me.

RS: Same here.

MS: *Earth*—

RS: *Earth* is a wonderful film.

MS: And *Arsenal.* It's just a remarkable movie. It's just so moving. They sent me a print from Russia. I have it at the office. It's beautiful. We have it in 35 millimeter, silent, you know. And it was sent in these old film cans, too. It looks like the cans were made in 1929. But what I caught in *Nevsky* [about a Russian prince defeating an invading army in a famous battle on the ice; Sergei Eisenstein, 1938] was the editing. The battle scenes were amazing in terms of energy and visualization. And very often it was a mixture of silent cinema and sound cinema with a very, very crude-sounding sound track—Prokofiev on the track, very, very crudely recorded, so that the instruments sounded as if they were recorded in the twelfth century.

Catherine Scorsese's father, Martin, in his Italian cavalry uniform.

RS: I once saw that with a live symphony orchestra playing, and I didn't like it—too slick. The orchestra was too big; it dominated the screen.

MS: I became fascinated by the editing, because it seems like sometimes time stops. It doesn't flow. You're aware of different positions of people in the frame, and it becomes about something else, about forms, in a way. Not that I could intellectualize it at the time, but that feeling was something I wanted to create. And the only way I could do it was to get the camera angles and cut them together.

RS: Your first two features [*Who's That Knocking* and *Mean Streets*] seem to me to be very, very camera conscious, though not in the way of a conventional Hollywood movie—I mean, a Howard Hawks movie is camera unconscious.

MS: Well, that's the thing. Now you hit it, because the issue was this: If you look at neorealism, the camera is relaxed to a certain extent. It's not there. It's not up front.

RS: Right.

MS: Even in British cinema, except for Powell and Pressburger. The only Powell and Pressburger picture I had seen in its original form was *The Red Shoes.*

The thing was, the enjoyment of finding the angle, of seeing an image in your mind. I kind of was affected more by editing than by camera movement. And yet I loved camera movement when I became more, what's the word, cognizant of it. At that point I was seeing *The Seventh Seal,* I was seeing other foreign films. But I had been used to the American classical cinema—the seamless editing of William Wyler, John Ford.

RS: Unfairly, I think, your name is very heavily associated with gangster pictures in the public mind. But so far, in talking about your formative moviegoing years, you've scarcely mentioned gangster movies.

MS: I saw *The Roaring Twenties* on television. But the older ones that I saw in the theater, when I was ten years old, were *Public Enemy* and *Little Caesar,* which my father took me to see. *Public Enemy* is the one that stays in my mind as probably the more truthful one.

RS: *Little Caesar* is not a good movie, if you go back and look at it.

MS: No, no.

RS: I mean, there are a couple of shots in it that are great.

MS: A couple of shots are good, right. But *Public Enemy,* as I say, is probably the most truthful one. I sort of gathered that, I think, from my father's reaction to it. I mean, as I've said, he was not in with those people, but they were around him and he had to behave a certain way with them. And that conditioned his response to *Public Enemy*—the powerful man, full of hubris, attacked and then falling. The fallen hero.

But the brutality, the toughness, of the picture was something that never left me. Maybe the humor, too. *Goodfellas* kind of has both—in my mind, at least.

RS: Stop me if I've told you this, but Bill Wellman told me this story. They were all at a preview—he, Jack Warner, Darryl Zanuck, and Mike Curtis all went together. And it was a smash. I mean, nobody had actually ever seen a movie quite like it.

Anyway, it was over, and they were standing around outside or sitting in the manager's office smoking cigars, and looking at the preview cards. And Jack Warner says, "Look, I don't care. The ending in this movie makes me sick. You've got to cut it." Zanuck says, "No. It's the whole point of the movie, for God's sake. I mean, you can't cut that." And Bill says, "Come on, it's the best thing in the movie." And Warner turns to Curtiz and he says, "You agree with me, Mike, right? It's just too brutal for the audience." And Mike Curtiz goes, "Yeah, Jack, I think you're right." And according to Wellman, Zanuck reached out and shoved the cigar down Curtiz's throat.

MS: It's something you'd see in a 1930s movie. [*Laughs.*]

RS: Yeah! And, then Bill said, "Zanuck was a tough little guy. Don't ever forget that." And then he adds, "God, that's what was so much fun in those days!"

MS: Oh, imagine those guys working together. Oh, my God. William Wellman making three films a year. Yeah. What was that one, *Safe in Hell*?

RS: That's one of the strangest movies.

MS: One of the craziest movies.

RS: And it's so sort of un-Bill, you know what I mean? But the opening, that scene where the girl is visibly being called up by her madam saying, "I've got a customer for you, let's go." She says, "I'll be there in ten minutes." Pre-Code picture, of course.

MS: Yeah, it's a tough movie. But they were doing those things, knocking them out. Boy, it must've been great.

RS: There's a little book that came out recently that Bill Wellman Jr. found, a bunch of letters that his father wrote back from the front in World War I.

MS: Wow.

RS: It's a wonderful little book. It's about this kid from Brookline, Massachusetts, joining the Lafayette Escadrille, going over there, the only American, who doesn't speak any French, and all the French fliers are all bonded up and they're fine. And then every morning you strap yourself into this plane and you're so cold, you can't breathe. And you go up into the sky where you could easily be shot down in five minutes. They're wonderful letters, because he's keeping up a front for the people at home: "Oh, everything's fine over here. It'd be great if you could send me a few more bucks."

MS: I admire that. I really do.

RS: Well, Bill was, of course, a sensational guy.

MS: A film I like a lot of his that is being shown recently is *Island in the Sky*.

RS: It's strangely static, that movie. I mean, they're up there in the Arctic, they crash and they sit there.

MS: But there's something very mystical about it—especially the fellow who goes out and dies. He thinks he's miles away from the plane, and he dies right by the plane. It's very moving. I watched it again last week on television. Not a great one, but something unique.

RS: Well, I think his great period was the early 1930s when he was at Warner Bros.

MS: I have one of these films here called *Other Men's Women* I'd like to look at.

RS: Oh, that's a wonderful picture. And *Heroes for Sale* is great. *Wild Boys of the Road* is great.

MS: Yeah.

RS: And *Central Airport*.

MS: Oh, really? I haven't seen that.

RS: It's very minor, but a real pre-Code-er. You know, she goes to her room, he goes to his room. There's a door between them and, you know, he walks in and they just start screwing—no preliminaries, no sweet talk. And they're not married. But it's a good little story—you know, the cashiered-flier-seeking-redemption story.

THE FORD CONNECTION

RICHARD SCHICKEL: We've talked very little about the director I know was your favorite: John Ford.

MARTIN SCORSESE: When I was a kid I liked him because of the cavalry films, and *The Quiet Man* was very funny to us when we saw it as eleven-year-olds, twelve-year-olds. The look of the original Technicolor of that film is magical. But *The Searchers* was the key one, because of the nature of John Wayne in that. And the look of it. I saw it in VistaVision. What happened was that I realized there was one way of making a picture, which was the classical cinema. I didn't call it classical at the time. And then there were these foreign films that just seemed to erupt, almost like comics in their radical angles and their changes from frame to frame.

Three of us went to see it at the age of thirteen. We graduated from St. Patrick's. Then we went off to dinner that night at Toffenetti's, off Times Square, then on to the old Criterion Theater. We walked in in the middle, you know. And there it was up on the screen.

And we never stopped talking about the picture, because of the complexity of Wayne's character—his anger, his longing for his brother's wife, his obsessions. We didn't quite understand it, but we went with it. And then it came on tele-

Marty, in cap and gown, graduating from eighth grade at St. Patrick's Old Cathedral.

vision, and we saw it in black-and-white constantly. And we'd be having something to drink in a bar on Hudson Street, and Joe would say, "Did you notice that scene where John Wayne is standing there and Ward Bond has just talked to him, and he looks over in the doorway and he sees his sister-in-law, and she's folding his coat? I think there's something between the sister-in-law and him." I said, "I didn't notice—I'll take a look at it again." And so the film got deeper and deeper and deeper.

RS: I think Ford was so often careless, and so often sold out to the lowest popular tastes.

MS: I have a problem with *The Man Who Shot Liberty Valance.* I saw it on the giant screen at the Capitol Theater the second day after it opened. And I was taken aback by it, because there was a lack of authenticity in it.

RS: There are a number of soundstage westerns. But that's almost the worst of them in that way.

MS: But it's got great things in it, great things.

RS: It's a pretty good story. But Jimmy Stewart is playing a guy maybe thirty years younger than his real age.

MS: Yeah, it's a great story. I guess it's a great film. I just missed it, you know.

RS: I don't think it's a great film. But I do agree with you that of the three cavalry westerns, *Fort Apache* is the best.

MS: I think it is, yeah.

RS: I don't know why it is. Maybe it's because of Henry Fonda.

MS: I agree. It's that Colonel Thursday—

RS: It's an amazingly good performance by him. And it's not Fonda as we had known him before. I mean, he's this ramrod hard-ass—

MS: And he brings down total destruction on everybody. And yet there's something about him. You care about him, particularly in the scene where he has to dance with the, you know—

RS: The sergeant's wife? At the noncommissioned officers' ball. It's a brilliantly staged scene.

MS: Watch the editing in that scene and watch when he moves the camera positions as the people line up. First they come out in twos and then fours—and eventually they're all marching forward together. It's just dynamic. It's like the dancing scene in *My Darling Clementine*, which is quite beautiful.

RS: Right. Beautiful.

MS: And this is very carefully put together. But the greatest scene is his conference with Geronimo, where he has the nerve to open up that little camp stool and sit down.

RS: And he's wearing that stupid thing on his head [a kepi like those worn by the Foreign Legion in Africa].

MS: Yes, that French Foreign Legion thing. And Ford has Pedro Armendáriz in the middle. Watch the intercutting of that. It's just wonderful.

RS: Oh, that's beautifully shot, that sequence.

MS: He actually has to translate and repeat what he says to Geronimo. And ruin everything. I always find stories about pride taking a fall so interesting.

RS: Oh, absolutely.

MS: Like the Howard Hughes thing, you know. So Colonel Thursday is classic.

RS: But aside from those scenes, what I really hate in John Ford movies are those Irish guys going down to the barracks and singing all their stupid ballads.

MS: *Rio Grande.*

RS: But there's one moment like that in *Fort Apache:* they're bawling those ballads.

MS: Oh, they are? I mean, I may have blocked it out.

RS: Yes, you did. Because I did, too. Until I saw it again recently. But *The Searchers* is an infuriating movie to me.

MS: Why?

RS: Because it has greatness, and it has banality.

MS: It has problems in it.

RS: It's almost like, Oh, Jack, you're doing it, it's so great, and then—

MS: Then he has that comedy, and—

RS: And then the fat, horny Indian woman.

MS: I know, that's a problem.

RS: I mean, it is so close to being a true masterpiece.

MS: It really is. But I loved it as my favorite film, because, among other things, the scenery in that film is a character.

RS: Oh, absolutely.

MS: It's not just scenery. If you see it on a small screen, it's okay, but on that giant VistaVision screen—

RS: But those people—how much corn are they going to get out of that land, do you really think?

MS: Nothing.

RS: You couldn't grow a radish out there!

MS: Desert, red dirt, you know. And then there was a period of time where I realized, too, that the comedy may have been strained.

RS: And the romance—Vera Miles waiting and waiting and waiting for Jeffrey Hunter back home.

MS: But when I saw it again a year and a half, two years ago, I got involved with it again. And the archness of the humor actually wasn't as arch as I remembered it. I watched their faces. I saw Jeffrey Hunter's eyes. He really was so earnest, you know. I still have some problems with it in some areas. But for some reason, seeing it on a big screen in the right atmosphere, it seemed to carry itself along in a way. Even the Indian woman has her moments; when he mentions the name Scar, the music score kicks in, and she gets upset. And that changes everything. You actually see it in her eyes and her face. I'm just saying, Give it another chance, if you can ever see it on a big screen.

RS: It comes up in your very first film, doesn't it? I mean, Harvey Keitel is riding on the Staten Island ferry and trying to pick up this girl, and they're talking about *The Searchers*.

MS: Oh, yeah, because he's looking at the picture in the paper of *The Searchers.* We just didn't know what else for him to talk about.

RS: I guess that was generational. I know Steven Spielberg loves it.

MS: Steven grew up the opposite of where I grew up, and he felt that way about it. John Milius, of course, Paul Schrader—both very much the opposite of Spielberg and me.

RS: You were all at the right age for a movie to take you over.

MS: Thirteen, fourteen years old. That was it.

RS: It happens to everyone at that age—"the impressionable years," I call them. You can never get those movies out of your head.

MS: I remember Leo DiCaprio mentioning to me that *Fight Club* was like that to his generation.

RS: I never much cared for it.

MS: He's a very interesting guy, David Fincher [director also of *Seven, Panic Room, Zodiac*]. I like his pictures. But you're right about certain pictures hitting you at a certain age. There's no way to argue about them.

RS: No, you can't argue those movies.

MS: It's like you're stuck. And that's what was so interesting with Lindsay Anderson's take on Ford for so many years. I got to know him a little bit in the early seventies. And it was so clear that he rejected *The Searchers,* while it was accepted by us.

What hit us at the age of thirteen or fourteen was Wayne's character. I mean, he reflected America. We couldn't articulate it, but that was the tone of everything around us—the Cold War, the racism, all that was reflected in his face.

RS: Well, that's a good point I hadn't actually thought of. In the fifties we knew it was wrong—the racism—and yet we practiced it. And that's in that movie.

MS: And don't forget, he was a Confederate, too. Pro-slavery. He was the flawed, crazed hero of the fifties. I guess coming out of the Kazan films and coming out of Preminger's and Stanley Kramer's pictures, it was natural for us to accept that kind of character.

OF STUDIOS AND STYLES

RICHARD SCHICKEL: I know you think highly of Warner Bros.' role in American movie history, and *The Searchers* was a Warner film. Did that have any influence on your opinion of the film?

MARTIN SCORSESE: No, I don't think so. But Warners is still a great studio.

RS: Oh, it's the greatest.

MS: I love that *Mean Streets* was bought by Warner Bros. And then *Alice* was done there. And *Goodfellas* was made there. *The Departed* was made there, in the tradition of Wellman's *Public Enemy*.

See, the thing is, when I was starting out I would get excited by discovering what lens to use to create a certain feeling from another film. You had all this technique, all these choices, at your disposal. And you had to sort of figure out the ones that would tell a certain part of the story, psychologically and emotionally, more powerfully.

But in the sixties, I went against the established filmmakers, wiped them away, and said, If this filmmaker did a track in on that shot and on that line of dialogue, if I ever come across the same thing, I'll do a track out—just to see what would happen.

Well, sometimes you'd track out, and it didn't work. Sometimes it did work. So we were sometimes also finding what to do from watching films we didn't like.

RS: But you must have liked some of the kind of routine American, or seemingly at the time routine, guys, right? Surely you must have liked Howard Hawks.

MS: Sure. But I didn't realize it at first. I saw the name Hawks and I began to realize certain films I liked all had the same name on them. [*Laughs.*]

RS: It's a very unobtrusive manner of his, you know. I mean, it was never something where you'd say, Wow, I've never seen anything like that before.

MS: But there was something about the way the people behaved in his pictures in the frame. There's something about the nature of the relationship—the men, the women. And the men together. *Rio Bravo,* for example, or going earlier—*Red River,* of course, is the key one.

RS: There's something in Hawksian behavior that maybe only a steady kind of eye-level camera can capture.

MS: You can't get in the way of that. Yet you can get in the way—with wide shots, medium-wide shots. It's very hard today because everything's wide screen. You can't get that close. It's tricky too, when you can't do the American shot. You know, from below the knees and up.

But what was happening was I'd see the Hawks name showing up and I started to put it together. I didn't care what it was—if it was the crazy *Monkey Business* or if it was *Gentlemen Prefer Blondes,* I'd watch it. Even *Land of the Pharaohs.* As a kid I just became obsessed with ancient Egypt. [The film, co-written by William Faulkner no less, is about a pharaoh obsessed with building an impregnable tomb so he can take his wealth with him to the next world.] It was really silly—and a lot of fun.

RS: I have to admit, I sort of loved *Land of the Pharaohs.*

MS: I just loved it. I went to it from theater to theater. It was my favorite film as a kid. And then *On the Waterfront* wiped all that away. It didn't wipe away the love for it, but I didn't have to go see it again. But there was something about the ancient world and the way they shot it in modern Egypt that was interesting to me, using wide screen. And the sound, the music, was interesting, with Yma Sumac on the track, and it made me think of other cultures. Maybe it was all ersatz, but still I liked it a lot.

RS: I did, too. But in that period I think you enjoyed movies like *Helen of Troy.*

MS: Yes, I did. I was talking about *Quo Vadis* two nights ago. And then me making my own Roman epics from that. Discovering Shakespeare through *Julius Caesar.* And then, yes, about the same time, *Helen of Troy,* and reading *The Iliad* because of it.

RS: And, of course, *The Silver Chalice.*

MS: Yes, of course; it is wonderful. I saw that uptown at the Warners Theater. To see that in 2.55 Scope with stereo sound was great. It was astounding to see those sets—the audacity of it. Too bad about the script, but you know—geez. Don't forget that Boris Leven worked on that. He did the art direction.

So the ancient world pictures were the ones I just was obsessed with. But the ones that really gave me the impetus to make a film were the other pictures. Because I could never do anything like the Roman ones.

RS: From all you've said so far, I gather that the other genres—westerns, historical spectacles, even musicals—loomed larger in your formative years than gangster pictures.

MS: I was thinking this morning, could we mention my films that aren't gangster films? *Alice Doesn't Live Here Anymore.* To a certain extent *Taxi Driver. New York, New York.*

RS: Of course, naturally.

MS: *The Last Waltz. The King of Comedy. After Hours,* and so on. I mean, really, the majority of my films are not about gangsters. Most of them aren't even *that* violent—*Kundun, The Aviator, The Age of Innocence.*

RS: Right.

MS: The gangster films make more of an impression, I guess.

RS: Well, back when you were doing *Mean Streets,* were you saying, Look, this is what I know. This is my world. I can bring a certain amount of authenticity to it that I couldn't if I was doing a Roman epic, not that anyone would let me.

MS: No, not really. No, I didn't think it was my right. That's why I tried *Alice.* And *Taxi Driver* is very different, *New York, New York.* And that's why I embraced *Raging Bull.*

RS: Of course, sure.

MS: After *Mean Streets,* I kind of pretended that that was all past. But by the time I embraced that world again I wasn't trying to hide anything about where I came from. It was still very vivid. And at a certain point, my father said, "One day you should do a really good gangster film." He kind of liked those—they were part of his folklore.

But *Taxi Driver* was easier to finance because of the success of *The Godfather,* the first one. That's how Bob De Niro was hired. I took the answer print up to show it to Francis [Ford Coppola], and he looked at it, and the next day he called De Niro to play in *Godfather II.*

RS: Really?

MS: Yes. So Francis was very important at that time for me. But I never thought I would make another gangster film until *Goodfellas* came up. *Mean Streets* to *Goodfellas,* that's 1973 to 1990.

RS: We're getting a little ahead of ourselves. Let's go back to your teen years, when you were going to movies on your own recognizance.

MS: In my last two years at Cardinal Hayes High School, I kind of realized I didn't know what I was going to do. I mean, I took some elective courses, more to do with business, which is the antithesis of who I am and what I do. So I was miserable. But, primarily, I think, at that point, the idea was to try English literature. And I was going to go to St. Francis College in Brooklyn. I was accepted there. I remember taking the exam and going in and discussing literature. Again, as I said, I didn't think I read much, but I must have, because I was talking about Thomas Hardy and James Joyce, Graham Greene, James Baldwin, and Dostoyevsky. It wasn't easy for me to read. You know, it wasn't part of our cultural makeup, but I was ready to delve further into that.

Instead I saw this catalogue from the New York University Washington Square College, and they had this department called TMR—Television, Motion Pictures, Radio. And I saw that for the first year you were allowed to take a history of motion pictures course. Everything else was what they call liberal arts curriculum. And so I thought, Well, I'm going to see what that class is like. NYU was in the Village; it was America, and I was becoming more American. It was not Elizabeth Street, you know.

And the day I went for orientation, a member of each department got up, the English department, the French or whatever, and gave a speech. And the gentleman who got up to speak about the Television, Motion Pictures, Radio department was Haig Manoogian, and he had such energy, such passion. I said to myself, That's where I want to be, with this person. At NYU at the time, if you could pay you were in, so my father got some student loans and I just joined up there. And, eventually, by my third year, I was making a film.

WASHINGTON SQUARE

RICHARD SCHICKEL: At that point you had definitely decided not to be a priest?

MARTIN SCORSESE: I thought I might go into a seminary, but then I began to think this vocation I had was for the wrong reasons—it shouldn't be about you, it should be about others, as we discussed before. But for me, it was going to be about cutting myself off from the world, not being a participant in it.

I think I made the decision not to go when I went to my first class at Washington Square College, which had to do with movies.

RS: Really? With that on-the-spot immediacy? Though by that time it must have occurred to you that all the stuff you'd been doing, all the drawing and movie-going, had somehow brought you to this place.

MS: Well, yeah, it really was something like that. And it could have been television. I mean, they had one little television studio with two TV cameras. I did a few television plays. So it could've been television. It was still using a moving image, you know.

And radio, I did a little bit of radio. Whenever we could we did radio plays. All on that one floor, by the way, the eighth floor of the East Building on Greene

Marty interviewing his parents for his documentary *Italianamerican* (1974).

Street. And by 1960, all these other films were being made: by Cassavetes, Shirley Clarke, the French films, the Italian films. I knew something was happening with film, and I thought maybe I could get something to do in television or maybe documentaries. Because that's what Haig emphasized: documentaries, never feature films.

RS: In your recent *DGA Quarterly* interview you talk a good deal about documentaries in that period.

MS: I love them.

RS: Did you think, Well, I wouldn't dare to aspire to do a fictional film, but there are things I see around in life that I could make documentaries out of?

MS: No, I didn't feel that. I did feel, though, a power from a documentary that no fictional film could generate—a different kind of power.

RS: Were there documentaries at that time that you particularly admired?

MS: Oh, there was work by the Maysles brothers, and there were Leacock and Pennebaker. There were films coming out of France by Chris Marker. There were the older ones from the USIA [United States Information Agency] and other government agencies.

RS: Very formal.

MS: Very formal. There were pictures like George Stoney's *All My Babies.* Then there were pictures that kind of crossed between documentaries and fiction. And I responded to them—a lot of it is because it felt like it was of the street. I don't want to say "real," but it had a kind of authenticity to it.

RS: Right.

MS: Kazan's films from *On the Waterfront* on—look at the extras in the background, look at the people—*Face in the Crowd, Baby Doll,* and ultimately even *Wild River* and *America, America.* Somehow, Kazan brought it all together in a way. He was really the one who made me see the combination, I think, of the real and the fictional.

RS: Doesn't that reflect back, too, on the Rossellini films?

MS: You're absolutely right. It goes back to *Paisan.* But, you see, that was from another world, related to my grandparents and my parents; I wasn't there in Naples with the little boy with the black soldier. But it is the same impulse.

RS: I remember Kazan talking to me about *Boomerang,* the picture with Dana Andrews up in Connecticut, and saying how it was the first time he used real people in a fictional film. And that he really loved it. And then he went down to New Orleans and did *Panic in the Streets,* where he did the same thing.

MS: When I saw that on television, after *On the Waterfront,* I realized that you could even do a thriller, or a conventional genre film, a studio film, within the trappings of a real location.

RS: He also said to me, "I don't think I could have made *Waterfront* if I hadn't made *Panic in the Streets.*"

MS: That's right. But you're also right about my direct line with Italian neorealism—*Paisan* and *The Bicycle Thief,* and *Shoeshine;* real people, non-actors, in real urban settings. There's no doubt about it. They were more than movies to me. They especially hit me at that age of five or six years old, because it was so personal because of watching them with my family.

But remember, there was no school of the arts at NYU at the time. There was liberal arts. You did your first film, if you could, in your junior year. There was a course where you learned a little bit of technology—the basics of 16 millimeter. But mostly it was English courses and philosophy and French.

And, frankly, I was still involved, in real life, with the group that was in *Mean Streets.* The problem was that I could never survive in that group. I was a semi-outsider there, because you had to be somebody who could handle yourself in situations . . .

RS: You mean muscular situations.

MS: Muscular. Also, you need a kind of bravado that you also should back up. If you're going to use your mouth a certain way, look at somebody a certain way, you have to be strong enough to back it up.

RS: Otherwise they'll kill you.

MS: They'll kill you. And it was constant. At that time, you know, there were a number of kids who were killed. They were—taken out, I should say. It was shocking. And this priest, Father Principe, made some sense. He made some sense about people and about living—about what it is to be a human being. And what it is to transcend. I don't mean, you know, becoming beatific and experiencing stigmata. I'm talking about just basically living a decent life.

RS: Well, the question I have is this: In *Kundun* it's not just that the little boy is absorbed in his religion. I always see him as this kid up in the equivalent of—

MS: The window overlooking the third floor front. [*Laughs.*]

RS: —the window over the street. And he's looking through his telescope. Or he's grinding his little movie camera that will show him images of a world he's never seen personally. And it's one of the more touching qualities of that little boy that he wants to know more.

MS: And learn about the world.

RS: And so I, of course, immediately said there's some analogy here between him and you.

MS: I don't know if I took that in consciously in any way. I mean, that's from Melissa Mathison's script, from the story of the Dalai Lama.

RS: But it's there.

MS: It might very well be. But I was more interested in the young boy who was devoted to his spiritual life, as in *Europa '51,* when the woman becomes a person who tries to help people.

RS: I've never seen that film.

MS: It's a fascinating film. [Roberto Rossellini's 1951 film, starring Ingrid Bergman, traces a careless, conventional woman's conversion to sainthood.] I mean, I'm going to sound like a public service announcement. But there is the danger that if you give to somebody, you might get a gun back, get shot at. But there is something about changing that basic dynamic between people. It depends on whether you're able to give. I found it fascinating.

RS: But getting back to NYU and that first, I guess you could call it, life-changing experience of formal film studies.

MS: The first year at Washington Square College, if you were thinking about majoring in communications or motion pictures, you had to take a history of motion pictures, radio, and television. And Haig Manoogian was the one who taught that—once a week, two and a half hours—everything from the Lumière brothers to *The Great Train Robbery* to *Variety, Greed,* then finally, maybe *Nights of Cabiria* or something else from Fellini. He was a very dynamic speaker, with a magnetic personality.

He'd just get up on that little stage on Waverley Place near the main building of Washington Square College and start talking, and he didn't care if anybody was listening. He just kept going on and on and on and on. And younger people were coming in and he'd say, Okay, you don't come back, you don't come back, "because some of you kids think because we're showing movies, it's fun. Get out."

RS: That appealed to you?

MS: Well, he was very serious about it. I'll never forget, the second week, one of the young people remarked that there was no music with the silent films. Haig said, "What do you think this is, a show?"

RS: What did Haig think it was?

MS: He was teaching about film. He was showing different developments, he had so much to tell us, and it was only two and a half hours a week. And an hour and a half is a film. You only have at most an hour to set it in context—he showed one German expressionist film, and then had to talk about the whole movement in less than an hour.

You could see that he cared about this very much. And I felt the same way. So the passion that I had put into the church wound up being placed here, in film.

In Haig Manoogian's classes in 1960—I always point this out—you only had maybe a little over forty years of cinema to catch up with. Which was very doable. Besides which, only a few countries had a lengthy film tradition: England, France, and Italy, that's it. We didn't see anything from Asia until Kurosawa came on in the 1950s.

RS: It's a point I've often made, too. I believe it was theoretically possible, in the period you're talking about, for an individual to have an all-encompassing knowledge of world cinema. It's impossible now.

MS: Impossible. Especially silent cinema—it's a whole other language.

RS: It's not just that they're movies that don't talk. It's an entirely different medium. It communicates in a different way. It has nothing to do with movies as we understand them today. But when, say, you show a little kid a Chaplin movie, she won't care about how it's different from what she's used to. She just sees the funny man and the funny gags and it's fine with her.

MS: Right.

RS: She hasn't gotten so sophisticated that she realizes, Wait a minute, this is not a movie as I understand it.

MS: She asks, "Will they be talking?" My daughter asks that now, and I say, "The Tramp, the Little Tramp, never spoke. But there will be talking by other people from time to time." Especially in *Modern Times*.

RS: A little in *City Lights*.

MS: And she was fine with that.

RS: Getting back to NYU, was it a big surprise to you that there were movements—or moments—like German expressionism in film history?

MS: Yes, but not a complete one. I suspected it because of all the movies I'd seen as a kid, especially when I saw foreign films on television, particularly the Italian films. And then I saw *Children of Paradise* in French with subtitles. And other films: *Beauty and the Beast,* for example, was on a great deal in the afternoons.

RS: Forgive me for saying this, but Haig Manoogian sounds kind of like a Jesuitical figure.

MS: Maybe. But I think I may have put that on him. You know, he was Armenian and very, very passionate. He reminded me of the Greeks or, of course, the Italians. I met a lot of Greeks at Washington Square College—Greeks, Jewish kids, and Armenians. It was a great time. It opened my mind completely, and separated me from where I had come from.

I felt really, really comfortable with it. And Haig was tough. He was a very stubborn man. He was really an amazing man. But that's when it all clicked. And

Marty at the NYU film school, circa 1963.

don't forget, by that point I had seen Cassavetes's film *Shadows.* I realized that films were being made around New York that didn't depend on the Hollywood studios.

RS: Right.

MS: I would've liked to have made a film for a Hollywood studio, but it was all changing. We had *Shadows,* and, as I said, Shirley Clarke making her films, and Jonas Mekas. And the avant-garde cinema in general. That opened up a whole lot to me.

RS: Did you go to Cinema 16 [the leading film society devoted to independent cinema at this time]?

MS: I didn't go to Cinema 16, because right at that time Cinema 16 changed in a way. But every little storefront was showing film. There was Stan van der Beek or Hilary Harris, or Ed Emshwiller's films [all avant-gardists, making non-narrative films]. Amos Vogel [a leading theoretician and exponent of avant-garde cinema, and the founder of Cinema 16] would be there, and I became friendly with him, and we would just go see everything. It was an amazing time with cinema, the actual celluloid carrying the image—directly drawing on it or scratching on it, whatever. Stan Brakhage's pictures, too.

RS: Oh, those are wonderful.

MS: Yes. But I found that for me, I wanted to do narrative cinema—traditional narrative cinema. And so, if anything, I was influenced by Italian films and English films, certainly. And when the New Wave started in France, you couldn't help but be influenced by it if you were twenty, twenty-five years old—Truffaut, Godard, Rivette, Chabrol, all of them.

RS: But aside from that little technical course you mentioned, NYU didn't offer— at least in your first years—much in the way of hands-on filmmaking instruction?

MS: No. But as Orson Welles said, You can learn everything you need to know about a movie camera and a movie studio in about four hours.

RS: I've read that often. But, as you know, a lot of mystery surrounds the craft of directing.

MS: Well, what you know is, basically, This is the lens. This is a longer one, this is a shorter one. A shorter one makes it wider. If you get too close with this, you're going to have a kind of cartoon effect. But if you lean it against the wall and you go fast with it, it feels like the wall is going faster and therefore you have the corridor shots in all the Welles pictures. Welles says in a documentary I saw recently, "If I used a 40 millimeter lens at this point, and I aimed the camera that way, I knew what the effect would be." That much I knew, too. And somebody said it wouldn't work, and I said, I knew it would work. I didn't even know what a 40 is except that it's 10 millimeters less than the normal lens, the 50. I rarely use it. I use usually a 32 or something wider. I don't like long lenses, which I picked up on from the Polish films—Wajda and Polanski.

RS: It seems to me directors break down into two categories. On the one hand would be Preminger, who almost never used a close-up and didn't edit a lot. Then there are the other directors, who love to cut.

MS: I really like cutting. I think a lot of that has to do with seeing Eisenstein's *Potemkin* in Haig's class. I was fascinated by the editing. And it didn't need sound. It told a story, although Pudovkin [a contemporary of Eisenstein's in the Russian cinema of the 1920s] became very heavy-handed, especially in *Mother.* But you had to understand the audience that it was being made for, too. Many of them didn't even have electric light; they hadn't seen a movie or heard a voice on the radio.

So I became interested in the effect that these juxtapositions of images created. That sort of clashed with the classical style from Hollywood films, also with some Italian films from the neorealist period. But the choice of lens feeds into that. And the enjoyment of choosing the lens. You know, if you use too wide a lens it draws too much attention to the camera angle, and it takes you out of the movie to a certain extent. There are a lot of wonderful movies that use long lenses. Kurosawa uses long lenses. But I always feel long lenses are very indefinite. I couldn't define the actors the way I wanted to. I felt that they were like floating, dreamlike images, and I preferred to have something harder and crisper.

I didn't know what that was until I got to school, and Michael Wadleigh showed me a 16 millimeter camera in our second year of college. You were able to take two camera courses in the third and fourth semesters. You had a Filmo camera, which was the 16 millimeter version of the Eyemo, which they used in World War II. And it had parallax and everything. [Parallax is the difference between what the camera lens sees and what the viewfinder sees.]

RS: You had those little two-minute loads?

MS: A hundred feet. A hundred feet is about two and a half minutes. And so you'd do your film on that. You had to learn parallax view, which is very complex. But once you learned it and you tried it a few times, and once you got the basic ideas of exposure, you had somebody you could rely on to help you with it. I didn't really understand too much about exposures. But I began to understand more light, less opening. Less light, more opening. And then I became fascinated with the idea of very fast film and fast lenses, because I didn't like the encumbrance of the lights on locations.

That became a big deal. I didn't have that skill until maybe *Taxi Driver,* when I got a little better at that. But in *Mean Streets* we just couldn't get enough light. For *Who's That Knocking* too.

RS: There's some very beautiful black-and-white in *Who's That Knocking.*

MS: There is. Michael Wadleigh did the 16 millimeter sections. At the time I was inspired by the use of black-and-white photography by Gianni di Venanzo. And also Giuseppe Rotunno, but primarily di Venanzo. [Both were leading Italian cinematographers at the time.] I mean, I really loved to look at di Venanzo's films—there was something about the bright white southern Italy in black-and-white, the Mediterranean, those white houses, like Greece. So I tried to get that look for *Who's That Knocking.*

RS: But, since you couldn't learn it at NYU except for this little camera course, where were you beginning to learn this stuff?

MS: I'd go to the Art Theater on 8th Street [in Greenwich Village].

RS: So you were learning just by looking?

MS: Looking. Always looking. But in the second year with Haig Manoogian, at the end of the semester, we had to do a report on one film that we liked. And I did *The Third Man.* And he gave me a B+ because, he said, "Remember, it's only a thriller." So, that was it. We were at the opposite ends of the pole, in a way. He preferred *Paisan* and *Open City,* and I liked everything.

By the third semester and in the fourth, there were little exercises. You'd do something for exposures. Then you'd do something for editing. And you'd begin to understand what film is. By 1963 Haig gave a summer workshop. In six weeks you'd write a film, direct it, edit it, and print it in the lab. Now, you'd maybe have thirty-six kids join in. And he'd break them into six groups. And he'd say, Okay, you're director, you're grip, you're camera, whatever.

And people would complain and say, "I signed up to direct a film." "So where's your script?" "Oh, well, I thought I could direct somebody else's." "No. Come in with your own idea. If you don't have an idea, you're not going to have a group," he said. Another guy said, "I didn't sign up to be a cameraman." "You'll learn from the camera just by putting your eye at the eyepiece." So there were a lot of people who were very unhappy.

But what I did was write a script and get it to him as soon as possible, and he okayed it, so I was given a crew, and they all knew that they had to do what I wanted. And so we got it all set

Marty directing his first NYU student film, *What's a Nice Girl like You Doing in a Place like This?* Made in 1963, it was nine minutes long and shot in black-and-white.

up in five days, and then we shot it in six, seven days, and edited it. It was a comedy, based on camera angles and it was very technical—quite silly and childish, all about the idea of clichés, and "What's a nice girl like you doing in a place like this?" That was a famous cliché and we used that. But there are some funny things in it. It's more influenced by Ernie Kovacs and Mel Brooks than anything else.

RS: That's not so terrible. I loved Ernie. He was great.

MS: Ernie Kovacs was just my favorite. We all loved him, you know—the total surrealism on television. And pushing the limits, making innovations in television storytelling.

RS: I came to know him. When I was a very young journalist, I did a story on him. We would meet in his hotel room, and we'd get lavish room service and we'd be there all afternoon, just bullshitting.

MS: Oh, I loved him. I loved him. Anyway, my little film had all the tricks and the fun of just putting pictures together in slow motion and fast motion and stills, and intercutting with mattes the way Truffaut would do in *Jules and Jim.* It had no depth at all, but it was a lot of fun. And it won me a scholarship, so my father was able to use it for the tuition for the next year. And then that led to me doing another short film in junior year, the second semester, and that became *It's Not Just You, Murray.*

RS: I've never seen it.

MS: It was basically *Goodfellas.*

RS: Huh?

MS: It's *Goodfellas.* I did it in 1964. *Murray* was a big epic, as much as I could manage, of two guys who were friends in the underworld, from my old neighborhood. But I did it with very New Wave techniques. It was also a cross with *The Roaring Twenties,* an attempt at that sort of scale which led eventually to *Mean Streets,* which led ultimately to *Goodfellas,* and to *Casino* and *Gangs of New York*—the scale of it, the excessive nature of it. I mean, in *Murray* there's just a hint of it. We didn't have the money.

TURNING PRO

RICHARD SCHICKEL: Chronologically speaking, I guess we're coming up to graduation at NYU. And I'm sure your parents are saying, Well, what are you going to do, Marty?

MARTIN SCORSESE: Well, I was going to make a first feature. As I said, my father kept saying that I should have something as a backup, like teaching. But my parents were heartened by the new world that they were let into—the academic world and Washington Square College. They came to the events, and they met all these very interesting people. And the short films were shown in the New York Film Festival and other people liked them, people from different walks of life.

RS: That, of course, is very important to parents.

MS: The problem was, Did I have the maturity to make a first feature, the maturity to be able to say what you want to say, know what you want to say, and express it through cinema? That was the next big step. And that was the thing that they helped me with a little bit. Not money, but helping me, you know, psychologically supporting my ambitions. And then I started *Who's That Knocking at My Door,* which came out in 1969. I started shooting in '65, though. It took four years on and off. I don't think it's very good. I mean, Harvey Keitel is good and Zina Bethune is good. And the camera work is good. It was a favorite of John Cassavetes. He liked it a lot.

RS: Let's stop there for a minute and talk about Harvey, who was so important in your early career. How did you meet?

MS: He answered an ad that we put in *Show Business* for people to come and audition for a student film at NYU. I didn't tell him this, but I had a friend of mine who was a comedian, Bill Minkin, who is in a number of my films. I had Bill sit behind a desk, up on the eighth floor at the Greene Street building. And Harvey walked in. Bill says, "What are you doing here?" Harvey said, "I came to answer an ad." "What ad?" Bill says, "There's no ad. We didn't take out any ad. Who the hell are you?" And they got into a big argument. I thought it was great! That was the audition I set up, but I neglected to tell Harvey [*laughs*]. And Harvey got so mad at me. But I said, "You're wonderful" [*laughs*]. He said, "Well, why didn't you tell me it was an improv?" I said, "I just never thought about it." And so we started working together on *Who's That Knocking.* He was a court stenographer at the time. And it was a big problem for him sometimes to get free to work with us.

But it wasn't just a matter of Harvey's schedule: Sometimes I didn't shoot for three months, which created terrible problems matching scenes. Or we'd go to shoot in the building and we'd blow all the lights and then have to wait for four, five, six hours. It was a nightmare. We didn't really know what we were doing. And when the film was finally finished, I tried to get it in the New York Film Festival. They told us I was living aesthetically beyond my means [*laughs*]. Which was true, you know. But I was trying to formulate the narrative of where I grew up and I couldn't articulate the emotional aspects of the love story. I could not articulate the scenes.

RS: Do you mean articulate them to the actors?

MS: Yes. Make it a dramatic narrative. It was kind of pastiche. But Harvey became like family, like a brother. He'd stay at the apartment and sleep over on a cot. He's a lovely man, and a very sweet guy. We were also able to argue, which was a good thing, without holding a grudge for three years. He has a certain emotional strength that's powerful, really powerful. And he grew up in Brooklyn. So he came from a similar background. He was kind of the opposite of me, though, in some ways. I tended to pull back sometimes, but he would be much more comfortable around new people, or new women. He was a little more fearless. And he had forced himself to be a Marine. In 1958 he was in the invasion of Lebanon. And I told him I always admired people who had that courage. He never bragged about

Marty directs Harvey Keitel and Zina Bethune in what was Keitel and Scorsese's feature debut. At that point Bethune was a veteran TV actress. She has also had a notable career as a ballerina and choreographer. The film was released in 1969.

it. He's just a person who took the fear and accepted it and went through it, did it. And that's the same thing he did in front of the camera.

RS: Oh, sure, you can see that.

MS: The structure of his career is very interesting. He didn't stop working a day in his life. He still hasn't. He just kept working. He never bought into the Hollywood situation. He never went with the star system, he never went for the machine. He had a taste of it, and they had a taste of him, and they all decided they maybe should part amicably. But he also developed as an actor. He takes some chances, boy.

RS: That's an understatement.

MS: And he's a very, very warmhearted guy.

RS: So you're still in touch.

MS: As much as possible. I guess in analyzing what is a friend, it's simply some-body you can trust. And we trusted each other with what we wanted in film. We trusted each other to make mistakes, to try different things—to go different ways, to be outrageous.

RS: I know the first version of *Who's That Knocking* was as a student, or maybe I should say a sort of postgraduate, film, but you actually undersold that movie to me before I saw it. When I did, I quite liked it. I mean, yes, it's crude, it's pretty simple in its development, but there's something—I don't know quite what.

MS: I guess it's too personal or something. Harry Ufland, who was my first agent—he was at William Morris—saw my short films, then signed me up and tried to get me some documentary work. After he saw the feature, the first part of it, he would bring it around and show it to people, and they would say, This is the late sixties, the sexual revolution, free love, and here's this guy who won't make love to a woman because he's in love with her! People were saying, Where did this picture come from? Are you mad? But I was just being truthful to the culture I knew. It was like kids from a provincial village making a movie about it.

RS: The trouble in it is the going away from that and embracing the sexual revolution. You know, that nude sex sequence.

MS: Yeah, yeah, it's hilarious. Well, that's the only way we could get it distributed. So we shot that in Amsterdam. By that time Haig and Joseph Brenner had come in to help finish the picture with me. Haig was like my producer. And at a certain point, Joseph, who was this distributor of exploitation films, agreed to distribute it. He was trying to make a crossover at that time. You know, at the time, Brian De Palma's *Greetings* was doing well. Joe was a nice man. He had his office on 42nd Street and Eighth Avenue. It was like the worst area you could imagine. And he would release films like *White Zombie,* and even *Birth of a Nation.* He had me cut a trailer of *Birth of a Nation* for him. He did basically public domain things—*Reefer Madness,* that kind of stuff. So he was going to try to go with this new youth culture. Eventually he pointed out to Haig and everybody, "The one thing that will get this done, and I guarantee to get this

Marty's film got top billing, over a film by Jean-Luc Godard, at the Chicago Film Festival, where it was championed by Roger Ebert.

in theaters, would be to do a scene with some nudity in it, and some sex."

RS: I've been going through your stills. There's something called the Three Penny Cinema. There's a little picture of the marquee and you're top-billed above Godard, and his picture.

MS: *Band of Outsiders.*

RS: One of my favorites of his.

MS: Me, too. That was in Chicago, and that was the first run of the film, I think. And that was on the same street as the Biograph Theater, where John

Who's That Knocking at My Door could not find a distributor—until a nude scene, largely irrelevant to the plot, was added. It was shot in Amsterdam, with Marty hating the task but Keitel obviously enjoying it.

71

Dillinger got shot. One of my uncles said, "That makes two things that died on that block" [*laughs*].

Roger Ebert was the critic who came out for the picture when it was shown under a different title at the Chicago Film Festival. That was the year before we put the nude scene in. And he gave us a very nice review.

RS: The stills of the nude scene are great, by the way.

MS: Yeah, from Amsterdam.

RS: Harvey looks so blissful in those stills. And there's little Marty, operating the camera.

MS: I'm doing it, and Harvey's having a good time. And the people in Amsterdam at that time were wonderful. I was in Paris in May of '68 when all the fighting started. I was with a friend of mine named Richard Coll, who was the cinematographer of most of that film and my short films. He had taken me to Amsterdam and London to do some commercials, and I was making a little money working with him. He was one of the two collaborators I gravitated toward—along with my old friend Mardik Martin. It was a wonderful time. It was 1968, from January to June.

At that time we still couldn't get *Who's That Knocking* distributed. And Haig Manoogian said, "Look, there's this one guy, Joseph Weill. Could you come to

America?" And I said, "We can't get out of here. There's trouble. All of Europe is blowing up." And he said, "Well, what if we fly Harvey over?" And I found a

place in Amsterdam that looked like a loft in the Bowery. And I did a storyboard of the scene, and sent it back, and said, "This is what I want to do." I put The Doors music on it at the end. I had to edit it in Amsterdam, too. I had the track on one side and the picture on the other side. And I put it in my raincoat, and I got it through customs [*laughs*].

Marty takes in the European sights, circa 1974.

RS: Marty the smuggler. Who knew?

MS: I just did anything to get this stuff done. But *Who's That Knocking* was a film that was obviously in a European mode, the French New Wave, the Italian New Wave, and Cassavetes, mainly.

RS: Why Cassavetes?

MS: Well, because of the energy and the audacity to pick up a camera, a 16 millimeter camera at the time, the Eclair, and shoot a movie right here—on the East Coast, where there were no movie studios. And the excitement of cinema itself was seductive for me. I wanted to be there. I think part of wanting to be there was to be away from where I was. So, I decided, yes, if there's any role for me in American cinema, it would be the gangster film. It would be noir. It would be of that world.

RS: In *Knocking,* the guy attempts to seduce the girl with these heavy film references—

MS: That's me. I mean, I was stuck. The asthma created a complete lack of confidence, so he doesn't know how to talk to a girl.

RS: That's how you would have been?

MS: Probably. If I'd ever found a girl. But what was happening then was interesting. I think what happened was that somehow I related to the Wayne character in *The Searchers* because of the darkness of his character—how he was exposing his racism, exposing his own inner conflicts, and yet he was a hero.

RS: The darkness of Wayne's character seems to be referenced in the strange darkness of Harvey Keitel's character in *Knocking*. But when this guy is almost obsessively talking about *The Searchers* with the girl he's trying to seduce, that's you saying, at least in part, Wait a minute, American film is worthwhile.

MS: Yes. We happened to see *The Searchers* in VistaVision the night I graduated from elementary school, as I told you. That VistaVision screen, and Monument Valley, and Wayne, and Jeffrey Hunter, and Natalie Wood, Ward Bond, all of them. It's a film that my friends and I kept talking about and talking about. And then we'd see it on television, in black-and-white, and we'd say, Hey, interesting: Remember that line of dialogue? And the way he moves here, and the way that happens there.

RS: In *Knocking* Harvey falls for the girl he meets on the Staten Island ferry, and chats her up about *The Searchers,* as we discussed earlier. But this poor girl has been raped. And that means that, try as he might to understand, she's ruined for him.

MS: Absolutely.

RS: He seems to understand that compassion is in order, but—

MS: But he's bred not to understand it. He's bred not to mature, not to move ahead. Although I try to suggest at the end that it isn't quite the same with him as it is with his friends, that a seed has been planted in him that is going to make him change. It's about being selfless, understanding other people—that's what I was hearing in the church, you know.

This was the key. There are elements in Harvey's character that I'd say line up directly with Ethan in *The Searchers.* There's no doubt about it. And the guilt, whatever the hell Ethan is hiding in himself, whatever he did in that war—he can't stand himself anymore.

But I couldn't articulate what Harvey's character is going through. Harvey understood, though.

RS: Haig Manoogian, and his notion of "Don't bring a gun in here; we're not making melodramas, we're making some other kind of picture," was terribly influential for you. And yet in a certain way, you are beginning to challenge his austere principles, aren't you?

RS: Well, yes, but he came from a different world. Five blocks away from where we were editing, that's the world I was living in.

RS: So he could accept that you had to do this kind of material?

MS: He accepted it, and when I gave him the script of what became *Mean Streets,* he knew the world I was in. When I was a young student in the early sixties, he didn't know. But he got to know my parents—as I said, they were very popular around school. And I would live in Haig's house in Suffolk, New York. And he would come to have dinner at Elizabeth Street. So everybody was happy together. And Haig, by the time *Who's That Knocking* came out, began to understand that if it's a film made with Harvey and made on Elizabeth Street, that world is real to Marty. And then *Mean Streets*—he said okay. And also by that point, *The Godfather* had come out. He realized that that world also exists—on a loftier level in *The Godfather,* of course.

RS: I guess you could call it loftier. But in the pictures you've made about gangs and gangsters you are stressing the element of anarchy more than the *Godfather* pictures do. I mean, it's perfectly true that in the *Godfather* pictures there will be upsets in their smooth-running world. But it's not quite the kind of anarchy that's going on in your pictures.

MS: Well, I experienced that, too. I had a friend who was killed because he was too wild. He was twenty-one. And then family members of his were taken out. They were in some crime family.

RS: Now it's the late sixties. What else was going on in your life besides *Knocking*?

MS: Well, there was my brief adventure—or misadventure—with *The Honeymoon Killers.*

RS: Let's talk about that. How did that come about?

MS: Harry Ufland brought it to me. The script was very long and I couldn't connect with the material. I just couldn't. And it was more than that: instead of just making the film, I was trying to make a reputation. And I twisted it and turned it in different ways stylistically. I tried to make it something that it shouldn't have been.

There's something about not giving oneself over to the material. I was trying to impose my own style. I didn't have "my own style" at the time. I was trying to make, I guess, a Carl Dreyer film. I was trying to make a simple noir film into a Carl Dreyer picture, in a way. [Dreyer was the austere Danish director of such films as *Day of Wrath* and *The Passion of Joan of Arc.*]

It was a very low-budget film and I was shooting long takes. I wasn't taking any coverage. I didn't do any editing in it. I decided that it was going to be one long take. I was trying to impose myself as a master of camera and that sort of thing on this material that didn't call for it. I really didn't know how to handle a genre, or somebody else's work, and interpret it. If you're hired to do a job as a narrative filmmaker, you have to come to terms with the material. And I was fired from that after one week. And rightly so.

It was devastating, but I learned a lot from that. And they made a very good film from it. Truffaut said it was the best American film that he had seen in twenty years. Then around the same time, Haig Manoogian asked me to become an instructor at NYU—that course I told you about with the 16 millimeter film. In that class was Oliver Stone, and a number of other people. Michael Wadleigh, who photographed *Who's That Knocking*, the 16 millimeter sections, and me, and Thelma Schoonmaker, were all working on documentaries during that period. And *Woodstock* came out of that.

WOODSTOCK/ HOLLYWOOD

RICHARD SCHICKEL: Talk about the genesis of *Woodstock.*

MARTIN SCORSESE: Michael Wadleigh had this little place called Paradigm Pictures up on West 86th Street in Manhattan and we edited our films there. Mike and I were in these three or four rooms where everybody was working—Paradigm was doing Hubert Humphrey campaign films [Hubert H. Humphrey was the Democratic Party candidate for president in 1968], and Thelma Schoonmaker was editing documentaries, and we were editing *Who's That Knocking* at night. They were all very small rooms on the ground floor of an apartment building off West End Avenue.

RS: Just parenthetically, how connected to NYU was Thelma? You mentioned her briefly in that context. She became such an important collaborator with you later.

MS: The time she went to NYU was that six-week summer workshop when I did my first film. The negative was cut wrong—a complicated A&B roll negative process—and in two days she actually reconstituted the negative for me and saved the picture. I didn't even know her. But she understood edge coding [numbers on the side of each frame, vital in the editing process] and all that sort of thing, and she pieced it back together. Then I didn't see her for a while. And then she helped me put together *Who's That Knocking.*

While we were working on that, Wadleigh would work with Bob Drew, or Pennebaker or the Maysles brothers—cinema verité. So sometimes we were all editing documentaries to make a living, though I didn't make much of a living and that wasn't a good thing because I was married and had a kid. And so in the evenings we would edit my feature. Jim McBride was there, too, editing *David Holzman's Diary* in the next room.

RS: Really?

MS: And *Diary* was very successful. And then I went off to Europe and came back. Got involved with *The Honeymoon Killers,* got fired off that, and went to NYU to teach, and that gave me a steady paycheck of $55 a week.

RS: Not bad.

MS: At that time Wadleigh and I were going to do this rock 'n' roll revival show and shoot it on film, stage it for film. But in the meantime, this event called Wood-stock was happening, and I didn't know what it was. He said, "Let's go and just do a test up there." So he went up, and then we all followed him. And it became *Woodstock.* At the same time, finally, *Who's That Knocking* was being released. It didn't do very well, but as I said, Roger Ebert liked it, at the Chicago Film Festival, before the nude scene was put in. So I got this wonderful review in Chicago, and they still couldn't get it distributed. So then Haig really felt, everyone felt, let's go ahead and do it.

RS: You've always presented Haig to me as this very austere—

MS: Yeah.

RS: So what's he doing producing this thing with a nude scene stuffed into it?

MS: Well, the point is if I could have introduced it into the film more artfully, it would've been better. But I couldn't.

RS: It's just as if one movie stops and another movie starts—

MS: Or maybe I did it on purpose that way, because the reality was we had to put it in. So I just stopped in the middle of the film: Here's your nude scene, let's move on.

The whole film had a very loose structure anyway, and at the time I was influ-enced by *Before the Revolution,* I loved that. But I don't have the cultural background of Bertolucci; I just thought I should be able to make a film that had that kind of power.

But there were other things happening, too. This was 1968, and Fats Domino and Little Richard and Jerry Lee Lewis and Chuck Berry were kind of forgotten. They were being called fifties primitives. So we said, Mike and I, wouldn't it be great to do something on film. And we came up with this idea of doing this rock 'n' roll revival show in 16 millimeter—maybe six, seven cameras, whatever. Instead, he went up to Woodstock, called back and said, "This is wild. There's a lot of people, it's going to be a big deal. And the hair is being worn very long," he said.

I should probably mention that in those days he literally looked like one of the Four Freshmen. I mean, his hair was cut a certain way and he had button-down shirts. And he said, "Come on up, and we'll just see what happens." And so I went up on the assumption that I would be co-directing or associate-directing with him. Thelma came up, other people, and we wound up on the stage.

Of course, he's the director-cameraman. I mean, he's actually directing as he's shooting. I was on the side of the stage on the front. There was a lip of the stage and there was a platform for the photographers. And I was on the edge of it. So three days and nights I was assistant-directing. Because once Mike was on the

Woodstock (1970). Marty was part of the team that shot the famous documentary, and he worked on it as an editor as well. But there were disagreements with director Michael Wadleigh, and he was fired.

stage, you couldn't communicate with him. He had earphones on, with five or six other cameramen coming in and out. And Thelma was also doing her thing, associate-directing with the earphones on at the lighting board with the famous lighting designer Chip Monck, who did the best lighting for the rock 'n' roll shows in those days. He did great shows, but one problem was we needed a lot of light at night, and he would put theatrical lighting on. For example, Sly and the Family Stone—in an episode I was responsible for in the final cutting—are very dark people. And he put lavender light on them. And imagine at that time the speed of the film was slow. And Michael was yelling "Light!" into the earphones, "Light!," and Thelma was pushing and fighting with Chip to get the light. It was that kind of thing.

It just went on, and we improvised. Friday night we all realized we couldn't move. Richie Havens in the afternoon came out and sang, and then a few other people. And then by the time it got dark, there was no end in sight. It was a free concert at that point. And we couldn't even get food. You couldn't move from your spot. You couldn't go left, right, down. You were stuck. It was an extraordinary experience because everybody was, in a sense, dependent on the goodwill of the person next to him.

RS: Right.

MS: That's it. After that I started wearing jeans. Prior to that I wore slacks and that sort of thing. But I loved the music. It was an extraordinary, life-changing experience—mainly because of the way people behaved with each other. Anything could have gone wrong any second with five hundred thousand people crammed in like that.

You know, I was looking back out there and was thinking, What if one person goes crazy? What if some of the drugs don't work on these people? What if they charge the stage?

RS: A few bad trips and an audience that size can become, putting it mildly, volatile.

MS: In the meantime, you're stuck and you're helpless, and everybody else is working together around you, and you're helping them, and they're helping you, and the people are trying to get food to you. Finally, I think around ten o'clock at night, I forget who was on, it was Friday night, Arthur Barron, the documentary filmmaker, got us some hamburgers. One each, but that was enough. I'll never forget those hamburgers. By now, studio people were trying to buy the rights. And at that point, Bob Maurice, who was the producer of the film at that time, was on the phone onstage, basically making a deal with Warner Bros.

RS: That squares with John Calley's memory. [Calley was then head of production at Warner Bros.] John said, "I figured I couldn't get hurt. I figured the stock footage would be worth it, even if they never made a film."

MS: It's true. Because we were documenting an historic event. It was becoming an historic event that Friday night.

I mean, some people were just not meant for it. I'm not a country person, I'm allergic to everything. I was complaining, a lot of us were bitching and moaning. But still, it was a transcending experience.

There's a shot in *Life* magazine of Max Yasgur, giving the peace sign, and right below him, answering him, is me.

I was not shooting on the stage. I was trying to figure out which angles to get, trying to figure out what songs were coming on next.

And it was wonderful, because coming from where I come from, boy, I like seeing people happy [*laughs*]. I really do. But people have said to me, "Oh, well, they were all drugged." And I say, "I tell you, if everybody was drugged, it went along very well."

The only moment when things could have gone bad was when Abbie Hoffman grabbed the microphone. The Who was on stage, Pete Townshend. Do you know the story?

RS: No.

MS: Later, Michael Wadleigh edited The Who and Jimi Hendrix himself. He had a great time because he was up there, close to the performers. Mike started shooting The Who like that. It was nighttime, and that music was loud, and they were very aggressive, as you know, breaking their instruments. But as soon as Michael got up there, he got kicked by Pete, who wanted him—all of us—off the stage, which we all did. Everybody had their lenses right on the lip of the stage, in beautiful position. It worked, because The Who moved around a lot. And so I'm watching, and everybody's shooting, and we were mesmerized by them. It was extraordinary to be that close to see this energy.

I don't care whether it's Paganini or it's Pete Townshend, I'm sorry. I mean, people did see devils directing Paganini playing his violin. They could swear that they saw them.

RS: I've heard that—without entirely believing it.

MS: So we're standing there. And the next thing you know, they're doing sections from *Tommy.* And all of a sudden Abbie Hoffman grabs the mike, and says, You know, you people are here enjoying yourselves, smoking grass, et cetera, while

John Sinclair is in jail for two joints. He's in jail for ten years. And at that point Townshend took his guitar and hit Abbie in the neck. He was like a samurai and Hoffman went off the stage. And everyone froze, because he could have started something, because people started to hoot and holler. But Pete went right back into the music and sort of saved the show. It was the only moment of aggression during that whole time.

RS: And who is John Sinclair?

MS: Sinclair became a major cause because he was arrested for two joints. But it may not have been the right time to bring it up [*laughs*]. It was like shouting fire in a crowded theater.

RS: The unique kind of editing manner of that film—the split screens and all—did that evolve when you got back? Had you originally planned it to be just kind of straightforward, more or less conventional documentary?

MS: I don't recall. I think the split-screen idea was Michael's. They moved the editing room to another room at 86th Street, or off of 86th Street, on Broadway, that used to be a pool hall. It was the second floor of a building and it had arches. It's still there. And that's where we were doing the editing.

There was me, Thelma, Wadleigh. We had different groups of editors under us, doing different songs and different sections. I didn't do any of the documentary stuff. I did some of the songs. And eventually it was cut down to eight or nine hours. And then that was cut down further.

There was one big room with a big, white wall, and there were seven projectors, all of them in sync, so that you had seven cameramen, and you saw the whole scene in sync. The effect of running all those multiple images was so strong—usually it was three or four images at a time, not seven all together. There was something about the visceral quality of all the film going through the projectors simultaneously. And we agreed that was the way it should be cut.

When we all did *Woodstock* together we really thought of a Woodstock Nation, we really believed in it. Up until Altamont, of course [another filmed rock concert that ended in a deadly riot in 1969]. But, still, even then, I think Michael and the others really believed it. And I think they lived it. I think they were in a good way militant against the conventional ways of working, the conventional studio system.

RS: It was alternative cinema, technically speaking.

MS: That's right. And thank God they did it that way. But then, right around Christmas, they were taking the film to California to finish it there. And I was told by Bob Maurice, who was the producer, that I wouldn't be allowed to go. I was devastated. I looked at him, and asked, "Why?" And he said, "Well, Marty, this is the reality—there can only be one director."

I said, "Okay, I get it."

RS: So you were really intruding on Mike?

MS: I guess. I guess I was intruding on everybody. I think I was just overexcited, overenthusiastic, and probably taking over everything. And they finally said, You've got to go. So I said, "I feel so bad." He said, "We know you do, but you've got to get out of here." And that was it.

RS: Well, you have a credit on it.

MS: Yeah, I got a nice credit on it. And next thing I knew, I was in L.A.—got a job editing this film called *Medicine Ball Caravan,* which was a rock film.

I don't think I ever saw any of them again, except, of course, Thelma, who came to work with me much later on. By that time I was with Brian De Palma. And Jay Cocks was very helpful having me meet people. And they were right. I somehow had to do my own films in the feature film world.

RS: And Wadleigh?

MS: He's around. And I know that they've had reunions and retrospectives of the film. But I'm not in touch with any of them, except Thelma.

RS: Talk about going out to Hollywood and working there.

MS: Freddy Weintraub, who was the guy who sold *Woodstock* to Warners, and John Calley, who was at the studio, made a connection with me. Freddy liked me, and he remembered me. Freddy was, and is, a wonderful man. He was the Harvey Weinstein of his day. And he had *Medicine Ball Caravan* and he called me and said, "Look. Why don't you come out to L.A.? Come out for two weeks, see what you can do with the picture. I won't screw you too bad. [*Laughs.*] And you'll have a nice time. See what happens."

I went out by myself, and took the poster for *Two Weeks in Another Town* and put it over the bed.

And the earthquake hit two weeks after I arrived out there.

RS: I remember that.

MS: It made me very nervous.

RS: I'm nervous every day out there about earthquakes.

MS: Oh—have you been in one?

RS: Oh, yes. I was there for the last big one.

MS: Oh, no—that's like the one I was there for in 1971.

RS: They were about the same size. And located in kind of the same area, out there in the Valley.

MS: But, anyway, I started working on this thing. And fell into a bad period in my life. All kinds of things happened. I wound up going to a doctor and got myself back in shape emotionally, but it was very hard. It was the first of the three bad times I had in my life—the first big one. And Harvey Keitel came out, too, and stayed on the couch.

RS: Were you doing drugs?

MS: No, no, no. It was just emotional.

RS: Why did it happen, looking back?

MS: Oh—end of a first marriage. I had a child. I left them. I went to L.A., had another relationship that didn't work out. The next thing I know, I'm seeing this psychiatrist, which actually helped a great deal. And I was medicated.

There was one thing in that book by Peter Biskind, *Easy Riders, Raging Bulls* [1998]. One guy who was hanging around—one of the San Francisco people in the seventies, and L.A., too—said, "Scorsese, there's something about him. We knew he was going to be something interesting, but I never liked him." And I say, "Never liked me?" Why did he not like me? I don't understand.

RS: You'll never know. But I guess you sensed Hollywood's downside even before you read that comment.

MS: I only realized how the sun set in L.A. because of *Sunset Boulevard.* I was driving to the beach and I see the sun setting. I said, "I get it. *Sunset Boulevard*!" You see, in my mind it was something else entirely, because of the movie, where Sunset Boulevard was just a kind of metaphor for the things that get me nervous about Hollywood. That *What Ever Happened to Baby Jane?* architecture, that terror of being down and out in L.A., after having been in the movie business. And the sun sets. You get it?

I could never live in one of those old mansions in L.A. For me *Sunset Boulevard* was the metaphor for the downward spiral—no comebacks allowed.

RS: I'm guessing, though, that the excitement of what you were feeling mostly overrode those dark thoughts.

MS: In the early seventies, the kind of clothes we were wearing...I loved the western films, and we used to go to Nudie's [a famous western clothing store on Lankershim Boulevard in the Valley] and get cowboy shirts. They were beautiful. When I was a little boy I loved cowboy shirts. So I was acting out the fantasy.

But ambition doesn't even come near to what we were all feeling when we finally got together as a group in L.A. and Brian De Palma took me around and introduced me to Schrader and gave me the script for *Taxi Driver.* Spielberg. George Lucas, to a certain extent, but Lucas was always more of a laid-back guy.

RS: Yes.

MS: And John Milius [the screenwriter and director], too, was part of that, although I was hanging around more with Lucas and De Palma, and Steve a lot, because of his love for movies, his audacious way of thinking and expanding on spectacle.

We were just so excited. And the one who helped me out was Coppola, in the early seventies. You know, he guided, advised, smacked me in the back of the head [*laughs*].

RS: Well, at least he would have some understanding of the Italian temperament.

MS: Absolutely. But my ambition must've been extraordinary, I think.

RS: You were unaware of it?

MS: No. I was aware of it. We were just there and it was time to do it. By the time I got to do *Mean Streets,* it was the end of 1972 and the film was released in 1973. But those two years were very tough in L.A. I wound up in the hospital a lot. I was sick. I told you about that asthma.

RS: You did.

MS: But Brian De Palma was doing *Get to Know Your Rabbit,* and they'd taken the film away from him. And George Lucas was doing *THX 1138,* and they were threatening to take the film away from him. And I was doing this rock 'n' roll documentary, just sitting there on the lot at Warner Bros., just totally depressed. But we'd go everywhere, everywhere that would let us in—any party they'd let us in [*laughs*]. But it wasn't like we behaved in an ambitious manner or arrogantly. No, we just knew what we wanted to do.

And we felt that if we got to the right ears they'd listen. And, you know, ultimately they listened, in my case when they saw *Mean Streets.* That's when they really listened. And that came about just by working through independent cinema and exploitation films, and meeting everybody. You'd never know what was going to happen.

But emotionally it was really nerve-racking. John Cassavetes helped me out and took me into his house and took care of me. And I slowly got back to myself—working every day on *Medicine Ball.*

RS: You've told me elsewhere that you had some idea of being an old-fashioned Hollywood studio director, kind of grinding 'em out. But it's obvious to me you couldn't have fit, by your nature, into that context.

MS: No.

RS: Because they didn't have room for obsession. I mean, you can read the memos that came down from Hal Wallis [in charge of production at Warner Bros.] to Michael Curtiz [the studio's prolific director in the 1930s and '40s]. "Stop laying track. Just shoot it. Please."

MS: Yeah, yeah. Shoot it.

RS: "We're falling behind."

MS: Or what Frank Capra did when Harry Cohn ordered him to do one take. He said, Okay, and he did the thing ten times in one take, without turning off the camera between the shots.

RS: Right. I've sometimes said that maybe the art of directing in its essence is knowing how to throw a terrific party. So everybody's happy, everybody's having a good time. At the same time, they are focused on trying to make something worthwhile.

MS: Exactly, exactly.

RS: It's a very delicate thing.

MS: It's very delicate. And then, too, I had an expectation about the Hollywood people who make films, the lives they lead. I'm an outsider coming in. My generation were considered outsiders. I still had many ideals about the nature of the films that were made and the way people behaved, and the way they worked together and that sort of thing. I still had this idea about "the magic of cinema."

RS: Right.

MS: And it's not magic. You have to make the magic. I didn't understand that. I didn't really even understand how the studio system had worked, quite honestly. I was surprised that a lot of those sets weren't standing.

RS: Really?

MS: I was disappointed. We had to create all that stuff.

RS: Well, actually, you were coming in the era when they were beginning to rip down the standing sets.

MS: They were ripping them down and I still had dreams that they were there. So, in a way, I guess, it was a matter of growing out of my first infatuation or passion for Hollywood itself.

RS: And giving up the notion of being a sort of grind-'em-out contract director.

MS: There is no such thing as a studio director today. It's a different kind of thing. So something had already died off just as I was beginning to realize it existed.

RS: Exactly.

MS: But I thought it was fascinating because the type of films they did seemed to fit these different directors, seemed to fit their peculiar personalities.

RS: It's odd, isn't it?

MS: And they were able to work within this extraordinarily complex system, which was dealing with a lot of money. It wasn't something where a few people would see a film. No, you had to reach the widest common denominator.

RS: And you had to do it in twenty-one days or twenty-eight days.

MS: But don't forget that in that period, especially in sound cinema, the cutting was less. The editing was less. Unless you were [director Rouben] Mamoulian experimenting with some interesting things. And that classical style of sound film—you know, wide shot, medium shot, close-up—was generally simpler. So in a funny way, you could maybe do two, three pictures a year—the style fit the system.

RS: Yet they did get personality into it.

MS: They really did.

RS: That's what was so interesting about it. I mean, it doesn't take you long to see, looking at two movies without seeing the credits, that Raoul Walsh is a lot different from Howard Hawks. And so on. But even if the studio system had persisted, I don't think you could have fit into it.

MS: No, I know that. I realized that after doing *Raging Bull*, and after doing *King of Comedy*. And when I tried to get *Last Temptation* made and I couldn't. And when I did *After Hours*. But in any event, I found that certain things that I saw

[George] Cukor do, or other directors did so seemingly effortlessly, I was laboring over.

RS: But did you think, Well, look, I grew up in this neighborhood, I went to an urban university, I'm a New York kid through and through. So really there's some part of me that will always make urban films.

MS: Oh, no, no, I never thought that.

RS: You never thought, This is my world, this is where I belong?

MS: Not at all. In fact, I lived in California twelve years, thirteen years, yet people always considered me a total New Yorker. I moved back in 1984. My mother and father were still alive. My kids were here. So I moved back and accepted the fact that I'd be on the East Coast. But I always thought I could handle different types of pictures.

RS: I'm not talking genres. It's more about settings. I mean, *King of Comedy*—it's a very urban picture.

MS: I know you're right. But I tried—

RS: It's—city kid. I don't know how else to put it.

MS: Anyway, right around this time I met Roger Corman. He asked me to do *Boxcar Bertha.* You know, 1930s, *Bonnie and Clyde* genre.

RS: What do you think of that movie now?

MS: It's an exploitation picture. Not good. But Barbara Hershey and David Carradine were wonderful to work with. And Bernie Casey. I got to meet Barry Primus, because he was Bob De Niro's closest friend, so it was a good experience. And Corman was great. And all the people who did it.

RICHARD SCHICKEL: I guess every young guy in Hollywood somehow met Roger Corman, right?

MARTIN SCORSESE: Well, my agent set up a meeting with Roger when I went out to edit *Medicine Ball Caravan. Who's That Knocking* had opened at the Vagabond Theater, under a different title—everybody kept changing the title—and he said, Would you like to do a sort of sequel to *Bloody Mama,* which Bob De Niro had been in, and I said, "Yeah. Absolutely." And then he went away for six months. I went back to editing. And I just thought nothing was going to happen.

RS: The usual.

MS: But he had gotten married to Julie Corman. And when they came back from their honeymoon, I had finished *Medicine Ball Caravan,* which didn't turn out well, and I needed work and I needed to be around L.A. So John Cassavetes put me on as assistant sound editor on *Minnie and Moskowitz,* and I started to hang around with John. And one day out at Universal around my twenty-ninth birthday, Elaine Gorman, who later married [director] Jeremy Paul Kagan and later played the mother in *Goodfellas,* got a call from William Morris for me; they were looking for me because they had a film for me to direct. And she said, "Oh, don't be silly," and she hung up. Thought it was a joke. And so a few days go by, and finally my agent, Irv Schechter, contacted me. And it was this film that Roger Corman had for me—six months after we'd met.

RS: He had a script?

MS: By Joyce and John Corrington. It was a very complex, very dense script. It was just a matter of the budget, of getting all the stuff on screen; it eventually got pared down. But the script ended that way it does on screen, with a crucifixion. I had nothing to do with that.

RS: Really? I think people probably think, Oh, there goes Marty.

MS: I know. I had nothing to do with it.

Barbara Hershey helplessly witnesses union organizer David Carradine's tragic ending in *Boxcar Bertha* (1972), Scorsese's first Hollywood film, made for Roger Corman, mentor to a generation of soon-to-be-great filmmakers.

RS: One of the things that I flashed on when I saw it again recently was that notion you had of doing the Christ story in Manhattan.

MS: That's right.

RS: Somebody ending up crucified in some unlikely place.

MS: Well, on the docks, where the West Side Highway was, with the cobblestones. It was so beautiful, the old New York.

But the thing was, *Boxcar* was very important for me. It came in the period of the doors being closed—the *Honeymoon Killers*—where I didn't bring the right spirit to the material. Whereas, with *Boxcar,* I was able to take something that was abstract and design it on the page in drawings. I was doing what was required of the material, and I was not taken off the picture after twenty-four days. That was a big, big achievement.

RS: You finished it!

MS: We finished it on schedule. A lot of troubles. Three operators. But the director of photography was very, very good. The rest of it was having met [the actors]. I had a good time with them. They were really nice. And a lot of it was Corman.

RS: You were shooting down south, right?

MS: We were shooting in Camden, Arkansas. There was more to it than not getting fired. It was also a learning experience which gave me the crew for *Mean Streets*. Without that, without having made *Boxcar*, there was no way I could've made *Mean Streets*. No studio was going to make it. So I had to find the independent element in L.A. New York independents were not going to make it. We tried that. The independent cinema was out there, and it was doing all the kinds of movies that nowadays you can actually see on TCM [Turner Classic Movies], underground movies, that sort of thing. That was the group I had to be with. And that's why out of twenty-six days of shooting *Mean Streets,* only about seven were shot in New York. The rest was in L.A.

RS: Using people you had met.

MS: Literally. Paul Rapp, the production manager, who was the associate producer on *Boxcar,* and the cameraman he introduced me to, Kent Wakefield.

RS: Does the movie mean anything to you except as a learning experience? Did it have any, how shall I say, Scorsesean values to it?

MS: I did a rewrite of the script. Not a lot. Not a great deal. But I tried to add some elements.

RS: Well, it's a movie with violence in it. And people always equate violence and you.

MS: Yes, it's violent. I mean, that was the exploitation element at the time, you know. Also there had to be nudity or the suggestion of nudity every fifteen minutes. Read the script. [It's a story about a union organizer and his lover trying to take revenge on the exploitative management of a railroad.] And the Depression, which is the time it's set in. *The Grapes of Wrath* was something I liked a great deal. And of course *Tobacco Road* and other Ford films.

RS: *Boxcar* was more like *Tobacco Road,* I'd say.

MS: I really like it. I think it's an underrated Ford picture.

RS: It's one of his best movies. It's very funny.

MS: And it's sad.

RS: [*Imitates accent:*] "Get out the way, you dang fool!" [*Laughs.*]

MS: Remember that? [*Laughs.*] Yeah, right. The son with his car he doesn't know how to drive, and banging on the horn—a lot of that spirit wound up in the picture, there's no doubt about it. The challenge to me was: Can I create that world convincingly?

RS: Did it give you a little more security? You know: Okay, I can, if need be, efficiently do a commercial, exploitation movie.

MS: Yeah, that's what I mean about having finished it. The security is what it was about. And also the security of how I was doing it—directing scenes, camera movements, designing them, even taking extra angles for cutting later that I wasn't normally doing before. All sorts of things. Balancing the traditional way of doing as opposed to a newer way. For example, using handheld a certain way when it's not supposed to be used. At that time they used handheld a great deal for action scenes or fight scenes. But I was using it for scenes that had more emotional turmoil, dialogue scenes.

RS: Well, sure, that makes sense.

MS: There was a lot that we put into the movie, thinking back now. Every location was very specifically chosen. The idea of places where parties had been held which they'd missed. Churches that they missed. Everything that they keep missing in life. They're the outsiders.

And the huckster, the urban guy played by Barry Primus, I loved a lot because it was sort of like *Night and the City*—Richard Widmark trying to talk his way out of things or into things. And just getting outsmarted, and getting killed. All this is something that I really liked. And then, of course, the last sequences: I liked when she came back and found David older, and then he gets taken and he gets killed on the train, and she follows him on the train as he's crucified and the train takes off. Every shot was very, very specifically designed, every one of them. And we got them all, pretty much every one.

RS: Is it true of Corman, as I've heard, that once he decided on a director he'd be hands-off?

MS: He did come to Camden with Julie. I was in this motel room and was working on these shots. I still have them. And I drew three to four hundred pictures. And he said, "Do you have your preparation? How do you prepare?" And I said, "Well, I'll show you." And I started showing him these pictures. And then explaining, "This cuts to this, and this goes this way, and this is just normal coverage, but then there's a move this way." He said, "Wait a minute. Do you have this for the whole picture?" I said, "Yes." He goes, "I don't have to see any more." That was it!

And all he did was push Paul Rapp to make sure we stayed on schedule. These were very long days sometimes. But he had the kind of people who worked on low-budget U.A. [United Artists] films in the fifties, even some who had worked on some Ed Wood films. They'd been put through a lot. But we were in the middle of nowhere. Nobody could check on us. These people were on the fringes. They needed the work. So you know—

RS: Well, that's the way Roger operated—he used people so young they had nothing to lose, or people so old they no longer had anything at stake. But everyone I've talked to who knew him back then, they all kind of loved Roger.

MS: Me, too.

RS: Because he was straight up.

MS: Yup.

RS: This is the time you have. This is what you must do. Other than that, you can do kind of anything you want. Was that it?

MS: Exactly.

RS: But you had to make your schedule, you had to make your budget.

A rare tender moment between David Carradine and Barbara Hershey, who plays *Boxcar Bertha*'s title character. It was on this shoot that the actress gave Scorsese the novel that became the basis for *The Last Temptation of Christ*.

MS: Yes. He would come into the cutting room. I thought I had all the time in the world to cut it. The credit isn't mine because of the editors' union. [Scorsese was not a member.]

RS: Right.

MS: But he had to tell me, "No, you have to finish this now." "Oh, I see. Okay, I hear you." He thought I was being willful. I didn't quite understand that you pay a certain amount for the editing room, for the assistant. So he needed for us to get it done.

I had cut a ten-minute promo. Then when I showed him the first cut of the picture, which was about two hours, Roger looked at me and he goes, "You know, the energy you had in that promo reel? That's what this needs." And that was the only thing he had to say. Within a week and a half or so I had it all cut down to less than ninety minutes.

And that was it. I worked as an editor on other films for him. He would sit there in rough cuts and say, "Two more frames on that."

RS: Really?

MS: Yeah. "One more frame. Cut that, that's a little too long. The picture's too short here, we have to add something."

RS: That's the kind of thing I say when I'm editing.

MS: Me, too.

RS: But you don't expect it from somebody like Corman.

MS: No. But don't forget I met him in 1970 or 1971. And he was directing his last picture, I think it was *Gas*. But the cult around Corman had really culminated by that time. Because the Poe films were really quite beautiful. *The Tomb of Ligeia,* based on the Edgar Allan Poe story—

RS: Oh, beautiful.

MS: —was one of my favorites, a beautiful film. Moving and interesting, and provocative. And atmospheric. *The Masque of the Red Death* [also based on a Poe story] to a certain extent, too. And *The Trip* [about a bad LSD experience] I also liked. Because it was like an experimental film. And he was dealing with it in a very serious way. Yes, it was exploitation, but—

RS: Well, I think for all the kind of weird stuff he's put out in his life, he's actually a serious man.

MS: Yes, I know. I was very surprised when I first met him.

RS: Would you say working for him kind of took away the sour taste of the pictures you'd gotten fired off?

MS: Oh, absolutely. But this was a different situation. You only have a certain amount of time, and it's got to get done. This particular company says you can put your own elements into it as much as you want, but you still have to deliver this package to the marketplace on time. And it has to have these elements. The next was *Mean Streets,* and it was so different. But, as I said, there's no way I could have made that without having gone through the school, so to speak, of what Corman taught me.

RS: It's funny, people always use that term about Roger: the School of Corman.

MS: It *was* like a school. His persona was that way, as if he were a professor in a way. He was very firm, but he also had a kindness about him. So it was a more gentle introduction, rather than having to do a B film, let's say, or a low-budget film, in the studios, in a much harsher situation. I was lucky in that. I brought *Mean Streets* to him first, but he suggested doing it all African-American.

RS: Really?

MS: Because he said, Gene Corman, his brother, had just released *Cool Breeze,* I think it was called. It was an African-American remake of *The Asphalt Jungle* set in Harlem. And he'd made a big hit with it, and Roger said, "My brother's just had a very good reaction to his film. And I read your script. I can give you a hundred thousand dollars, you could shoot it in New York, if you're willing to swing a little bit." I said, "Yes?" "Would you think of doing it all black?" I said, "I'll think about it." [*Laughs.*] Of course, I never said no . . .

RS: Well, how could you?

MS: You couldn't walk on his psyche.

RS: It's about being an Italian guy!

MS: An Italian American.

RS: On the Lower East Side!

MS: So then he offered me *I Escaped from Devil's Island* with Jim Brown. And that was going to be done in order to capitalize on *Papillon.*

Again, it was a very dense script. And, I said, No, I'm not going to do it. There were two people who gave me advice to be realistic, to do it. One was Freddy

Weintraub. He said to me after *Boxcar,* when I was saying, "No, I've got to try to raise the money on *Mean Streets,*" he said, "Take this other picture. You've got this picture, it's real, and the other thing is not real. It may never happen. Go with this. This is a good thing." And I refused.

RS: It's sometimes very, very hard to say no.

MS: I know.

RS: Because, you know, you're kind of running out of dough—

MS: Exactly. That's what he was telling me. Be realistic about it.

RS: You've got a check. You can cash the check. And it's tied in with what we'd now call "family values." When I was twenty-six, twenty-seven, these older guys would kind of clap me on the shoulder and say something like, Say, young fellow, isn't it about time you started thinking about family, wife, children? And I'd kind of go, "Oh, yeah, I'm definitely thinking about that." I mean, they all wanted to get you a house on Revolutionary Road.

MS: Exactly! They didn't even know where I came from, man—certainly no house on Revolutionary Road, I can tell you that. I read Richard Yates later; boy, it's rough, it's strong—very disturbing.

RS: Well, there I had the advantage over you, because I'd been brought up in a suburb, which was very pleasant, but also very stifling.

MS: There was one other man. I don't remember his name, but he was the head of the CBS News editorial department. It was 1966 or '67. I had worked six weeks there as an assistant editor. And I liked the job very much, it was wonderful. And I met some very interesting men and women there, editors, news producers. One was a producer who was really tough. People would have to wear helmets when they were screening their rough cuts for him. He'd throw things.

I mean, it was really quite something. But I was doing the editing, and I did it as best I could. And this older gentleman took me into his office one day, and he said, "We'd like to have you stay on." And he offered me a job as assistant editor and also, eventually, as an editor. And I said, "Well, you see, I have it in my mind to make features." And he was very sweet about it. He got up from his desk, he looked at me and he said, "Look, you're young yet. And many things in life you may want when you're young, you may not be able to get. And I'm giving you something very tangible here." He basically said, People have dreams but they don't come true a lot of the time. "I hope it does in your case," he said, "but it may not. Know that."

Then later, after *Boxcar*, I took a job editing *Elvis on Tour*, and I was having too many meetings with actors for *Mean Streets* and I had to be taken off that, too. The editor of *Elvis* was Sid Levin, who was working with the producer-writer Robert Abel. He has credit as editor on *Mean Streets*, but I edited the film. He helped me along. They were friendly, but they were pros; it wasn't like a family, like the *Woodstock* situation. And basically they told me, We have a schedule, we need you here on *Elvis*, and if you can't be here we've got to take you off the picture. And I said okay. So then I started doing *Mean Streets*. I asked them right away, Can I cut it here? And actually I wound up editing *Mean Streets* in their room.

RS: It's funny: Even though our lives are so different, we've both faced the same issues. Lots of people offered me jobs back then, right after I sort of began making a little name for myself reviewing for *Life*. "Come to *The New York Times*. You can start as the second-string film critic but, you know—" Harrison Salisbury, the managing editor, said, "Mr. Crowther, there"—he pointed at Bosley, who saw me sitting there in the newsroom—"is our film critic. Not, I hope, for very much longer." And you kind of go, Geez—

MS: Was that around the time they hired Renata Adler?

RS: It was just before that. But Bosley was on the skids a little bit already. And then *Bonnie and Clyde* came along and he kept attacking it and that was that.

MS: What this gentleman was offering was basically a job for the rest of your life.

RS: What he was offering was, at the end of the line, a pension. It was: Fifty years from now you'll be glad you did this.

MS: You'll be glad if you do it because you have a family. I had a wife and kid. People said to me sometimes, "Don't you realize your responsibility?" I guess I didn't.

RS: No, your responsibility was to *Mean Streets*, which you'd been writing, off and on, for something like six years, I think.

MARTIN SCORSESE: *Mean Streets* was done at the urging of John Cassavetes, because he liked *Who's That Knocking* a lot. He said, Don't do those other movies. He didn't like Hollywood films. But I loved them. And I figured, well, *Boxcar Bertha* is like a genre. And gangster films, and musicals, and westerns—I want to do all of it. And he said, No, no, no—*Who's That Knocking,* you should do pictures like that. And he forced me. He said, You just spent a year of your life making a piece of shit. He said, The actors are good. I can tell you liked the actors. It's a lot of fun. But you shouldn't do that kind of picture. After *Who's That Knocking,* you've got to do something you really feel. Do you have a script? And I said, Yeah, I have this script I keep working on. He says, Do that. Within a year, I had it done. And so that got me the introduction into the studios, and also a critical reception, which was good.

RICHARD SCHICKEL: Let's talk about how the picture got going, practically speaking, I mean.

MS: Paul Rapp, who was working with Roger at the time, gave me the idea of how to do *Mean Streets* in the Roger Corman style, in terms of production. He showed me how to do it, if I did most of it in L.A. And so it was really thanks to Roger and his group, but mainly Paul. I did the first six days and nights in New York, and

the rest, twenty days, in L.A. We flew people in from New York for no pay. De Niro fired the gun at the Empire State Building in New York and it hit a window in L.A. [*Laughs.*]

RS: Well, that makes sense, albeit it in a crazy sort of way.

MS: That pool hall scene, where that big fight occurs—it's a big, epic scene and you've got to shoot it in one day. I mean, I laid it out not only in drawings, but with lines and arrows showing where everyone would move. And they just went with it, because we had to get out of there. It took about sixteen hours shooting nonstop.

Marty on the set of *Mean Streets*, his breakthrough film of 1973.

I did have to shoot certain things in New York that you could not replicate in L.A. I couldn't find the hallway where Harvey and Bob had that big fight at the end.

That was on Mulberry Street. And we just couldn't find a hallway like that, so we shot that climactic scene the fourth day into shooting. And then when we got to L.A., the first night we shot in this Skid Row area, Wall Street, downtown L.A. And we shot the way Corman had me do *Boxcar Bertha,* which is about trains.

RS: Tell me about that.

MS: Well, a train is one of the hardest things to shoot, because when you do a second take, you've got to wait for the train to come back.

So after Corman saw I had all my drawings worked out, he said, "You did all this? You'll be fine." Then he said, "For the first four days, you do all the train scenes." I said, "The first four days?" He goes, "Yeah. Get the worst over with first." And he was totally right.

But on *Mean Streets* the six days and nights in New York were like a student film. I mean, for example, the scene in the car on 8th Street, with De Niro and Keitel and the gay guys in the car, some of the coverage of De Niro was lost because the kids just forgot to bring it to the lab.

Anyway, when we got back to L.A. the night of my thirtieth birthday, November 17, 1972, Paul Rapp decided to do the car crash, which comes at the end of the picture, to do the hardest part first. And that's what we did.

RS: The music in *Mean Streets* strikes me as predictive of your use of it in many of your other movies—I'm talking about found music, largely about pop music.

MS: Pop music, some Italian folk songs, and some opera. The music was very important in *Mean Streets*. And also the cutting with music. It was all designed.

This was one of the first times, I think, that music was used this way. I had no choice. I didn't see it and I didn't hear it any other way. Stanley Kubrick gave me the validation to do it because of his use of music in *2001*.

RS: You've mentioned Harvey Keitel's character in *Knocking* feeding into his character in *Mean Streets*. And, of course, there's De Niro, since this was your first picture with him.

MS: I met De Niro through Brian De Palma.

RS: He'd done a picture with Brian.

MS: *Hi, Mom!*, yeah. And Jay Cocks. There was a Christmas dinner at Jay's apartment, a walk-up in Manhattan. And Brian thought that De Niro should meet me, because of *Who's That Knocking*. Brian was a big supporter of that film.

RS: I've told you, I like it a lot, too.

MS: I know. I'm sorry, I'm embarrassed because I know now—I knew after *Mean Streets*—what I could've done better in that film. But in any event, they said I should meet Bob, and Bob should see my film. He was getting some notices at the time. He was in plays. And after dinner, we—

RS: You know, I really first noticed him in that baseball movie, *Bang the Drum Slowly*.

MS: We're getting to that, yeah. I think this was 1972.

RS: He was wonderful in that.

MS: So he was sitting there after dinner, and he looks over at me, and quietly—he was always very quiet—he said, "I know you. I know who you used to be with." And he mentioned certain names—Joey, and another guy named Curty, and a couple of other guys. I asked, "How do you know that?" And it turns out that when he was sixteen years old, he used to be with a group of young guys from Grand Street, or Hester Street. We didn't necessarily frequent each other's bars or hangouts or whatever. In fact, there was always a little bit of frisson with these guys. But he always stood out in our heads. I was sixteen years old, too. He was always the nicest one, the sweetest one. Not that he said much, but he was always with them and he was always a nice kid. He looked different, of course, by the time he did *Hi, Mom!* So then, after that, he got to see *Who's That Knocking.* We had a screening for him at William Morris Agency. Then he called me, and he told me that he really liked it because it was accurate about the people he knew when he was growing up in that area. It wasn't until the 1970s, or maybe even after doing *Raging Bull,* that I realized that his father was a fine artist. I had no idea of his background, none.

And so I'm editing *Unholy Rollers* for Roger Corman. And I'm talking to Bob, who's in Florida doing *Bang the Drum Slowly.* And I was trying to line him up for the part of Johnny Boy [the film's antihero-victim] in *Mean Streets.* And actually Bob wanted to do the other part. And I kept telling him, "No, no, you're perfect for Johnny Boy." And he kept saying, "Oh, really. Maybe I should really do the other part. I don't know." I'll never forget talking to him when he was on location shooting *Bang the Drum Slowly.* And, sure enough, we finally got to make *Mean Streets.* The title comes from the Raymond Chandler quote, which Jay Cocks suggested. Both pictures came out at the same time.

RS: I'd forgotten that.

MS: I think *Bang the Drum Slowly* came out about a month or two before. By the time we did *Taxi Driver,* we were very close. He said less than, say, Harvey and me—we would talk for hours. But he knew specifically everything that I knew when I was growing up. And so to this day, it's beyond finishing each other's sentences. It's like, we just look at each other, and shake our heads sometimes and move on.

And yet he could be extremely articulate about other things. So it became the three of us—Harvey, Bob, and me—up through '76, '77. We were almost the same person.

RS: No rivalries, no jealousies?

MS: As I said, I was writing *Mean Streets* for Harvey. And he was wonderfully patient about the project.

I had to do some shooting of the San Gennaro festival, which took place three days before the main shoot of *Mean Streets* started. The heads of the festival had my father pay a certain amount of money to them. My father was furious. He knew it wasn't necessarily the San Gennaro Society that would get it.

At the same time, there was a possibility that a big actor at the time was going

Marty directs Harvey Keitel and onetime swashbuckler Cesare Danova, playing an avuncular mafioso, in *Mean Streets*.

to play the part. He took us right to the wire. Harvey understood that if this actor would agree to be in it, that if I'd gotten a name of that level, it would have probably guaranteed distribution of the picture. Harvey was willing to take another part in the movie.

The other actor was a very nice guy, and he wanted to be in it, to help us. But he just couldn't give us an answer, and we had to start shooting. So I made a call and he gave a definite no. I said to Harvey, who was waiting on the set for the phone call to be finished, "Here's your coat," and bang, he walked out onto the street and started filming.

RS: Wow.

MS: He was that loyal.

RS: That's a touching story.

MS: Yeah. He was just waiting, and we were on a roof. I said, "Harvey, here's your coat. Go down. Let's follow him in the street, in the festival."

RS: I have to tell you: Of all your movies *Mean Streets* remains the hardest one for me to come to grips with.

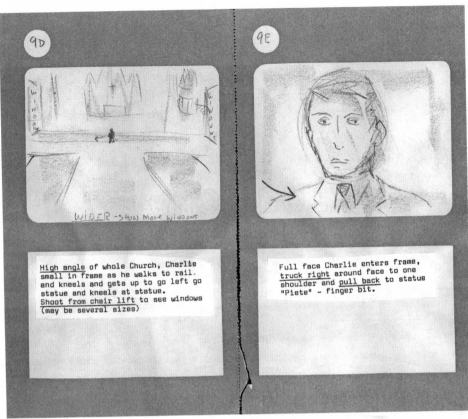

One of Marty's storyboards for *Mean Streets*. He draws nearly every shot in every film he makes.

MS: It's an aggressive film. I didn't think anybody was really going to see the film. Jonathan Taplin produced it. A young man named E. Lee Perry gave us the money, and I just thought it was going to be a film that ultimately might be on a shelf. But we thought it was a pretty accurate portrayal of that way of life—not on the upper levels, like *The Godfather,* but on the street level, what I knew and how I lived.

But it's tough: People would get up in the middle, saying of it, "Please stop the screening." And walk out. "I hate pictures like this," they would say.

RS: Harvey, on the one hand, seems to want to be with these tough guys, he wants to be as tough as they are. He is as tough as they are, in a way. At the same time, he's always going back to the church—there are those wonderful shots of him in the church. And the church is so beautiful and, as you said before, peaceful. It seems to me he's projecting the conflict you felt.

MS: After about six years of working on the script and story, that's what I channeled into it.

I had three different groups of friends. One group went to Fordham, and are now lawyers and bank presidents—good guys who made good lives for themselves. I had another friend who was more the intellectual of the group, and a loner, and I'd go with him to see Broadway plays. And then I had another couple of guys who were more street toughs. I was split among the three. When I went to NYU, in 1960, when I walked six blocks down Houston Street, it was like going to Mars. I had seen movies like *Twelve Angry Men,* showing the American process, and I was living with people who were not part of that.

People complain about my depiction of Italian Americans. But I can't help them with that. I'm sorry. It's just that it's my perception of what I know. There are guys, as I say, who are upstanding members of the community. They're doing fine. There are guys who are out of town, who can't come back. There are guys who are dead. I was in the middle of it. In a way, I was trying to understand how one should behave in life. What is the moral code? What is right, and what's wrong?

RS: Harvey's character has a little bit of you and a little bit of your father in him, doesn't he?

MS: Well, Harvey's character is named after my father, Charlie, who is trying to live morally in a world that's not moral, in a world that's primal. But there are two things going on. There's his relationship with his uncle, in which he can be elevated to a certain extent in that community. And I had him going to college at the same time, though he doesn't have enough in him yet to utilize the American opportunity education provides to get the hell out of there. But he can, because he is generally a decent guy, work with his uncle and make a good living, and have a sense of dignity in that world.

He's not a street tough. I mean, he hangs with them. But he tries to bring reason to all of this. And, ultimately, because of his relationship with Johnny and his girlfriend, Teresa [who is an epileptic], his chances are destroyed completely. He should have been killed, because he has nowhere to go. There's no way his uncle could work with him now.

He's messed up because he has this sense of love for the both of them. And he has to leave town and go to Texas or Florida or somewhere.

His love for the both of them, for Johnny and Teresa, is interesting, because for me it has religious implications, in that, for whatever reasons, this guy is just filled with guilt. Why he's filled with guilt, that's something else. There's a kind of deep curiosity in him. He's not part of a world in which he can go off into the desert, let's say, and be a monk and a hermit: he's got to deal in a rough world, a primitive world, a savage world. Can you still be a good person? Can good still happen? I know there's no justice, but can it be worked out? And so that, along with his own feelings about leading a spiritual life, he calls down upon himself a kind of suffering.

RS: Is that what the girl represents—loss as a form of penance?

MS: To a certain extent. But mainly it's Johnny. Because he says in the bar, Here comes my penance. Ultimately, I think Johnny senses something. Because at the end of the picture he says to Harvey, You're doing it for you, not for me. So that you can feel better spiritually.

But he's caught. He's caught. In that world, they're not dealing on the spiritual level. It's fate. He has transgressed, and he's going to have to pay for it.

RS: I don't understand why the uncle is so dead set against the girl, who's perfectly nice—

MS: She wants to move out. She wants to move out of the neighborhood. She's different. She's a troublemaker. She threatens the value of the family: to stay together and support each other.

RS: Let's talk about De Niro. He comes on—

MS: —and he just inhabits the role.

RS: It is certainly the beginning of the Jake LaMotta character.

MS: Yeah, it is. It's the same picture, really.

RS: The main thing, I think, is that Johnny has no sense of consequence. He has no sense of being able to look ahead.

MS: Why should he look ahead? He's got no place to go. He doesn't have the education. He doesn't have the temperament. And he acts out against these people, knowing to a certain extent that his youth will help him. He is all anarchy at that point.

He says, You want to stick with me, you're coming down with me. It's not just about how much you love me, and how much you want to take care of me. There's a lot going on with you. You don't even know what the hell you want out of life, he tells Harvey, in effect.

I thought what was going on between Harvey and Bob was great in those three and a half weeks of shooting. They understood that, ultimately, the relationship is based on loving each other, but that one was getting more out of it than the other. It was something that, in Charlie's mind, was a more spiritual thing. But they're all of them damned at the end. None of them die, which is worse, because they might as well die. The worst thing that could be—and it happens to all the characters at the end of *Mean Streets*—is that they wind up humiliated, not killed. Humiliated.

And so it was very real. In *Mean Streets,* the shooting in the car at the end was based on something I experienced. I was at NYU when it happened. I got out of a car with a friend of mine only a half hour before a shooting like that occurred. On the weekends I'd hang out with my friends—at after-hours clubs, the backs of tenements, that sort of stuff. This kid had a car, and he was going around for a ride. He was a part-time cop, had a gun. And so we went with him in the car a few times.

And then on Elizabeth Street one night at about two in the morning, we realized he was acting with bravado, in a way that we pulled back from. So we told him we were going to go home. So, all right, he drops us off. On Elizabeth Street you had cars parked on both sides. And he's driving down the block. And there's a red light, and there's a car in front of him. And the red light changes to green, and the car doesn't move. A guy comes over and starts talking with the driver in the first car. Our friend blows his horn. The car in front of him doesn't move. The guys are talking. He blows his horn again. The guys continue talking. He gets out, walks up to them, he takes his gun out or his badge. He says, "I'm a cop. Move this car." The guy says, "All right." He moves the car.

The next morning, we heard our guy was driving on Astor Place. He looked over at a car next to him and the people in that car started firing shots into his car. There was another kid in the car who got shot in the eye. And it was because he talked to the wrong people the wrong way.

And that became something that was very important to me and my friend, who had left the car an hour or two earlier. Because we could have been killed. *Mean Streets* had to be made because I was in the car that night. I went backwards from that. How the hell did he get into a situation like that? We didn't even know the guys. And I said to myself, That's the story to tell.

It made you stop and think—the kind of world we're in, the society we're in. So, anyway, that was a major moment in my life, and that's what *Mean Streets* comes out of. And it has to explode like that. I've seen it happen, a lot of times. It's just the way things work. So that's why the chaos is there. I was almost a victim of it. Another friend of mine was killed, taken out because he was a wild cannon. But by that point, I was moving to California, you know.

You get a touch of that sort of thing in *Goodfellas*—the poor kid who gets shot first in the foot and then in the chest. When the kid is shot in the foot, why the hell does he come back the next week? Why? Because he has no place to go. Can't get on a plane. He doesn't know anybody. He doesn't have the education. And it was

Marty directing Robert De Niro in *Mean Streets,* the film that announced both of them as stars in the making.

just one of those things. He came back. He came back and he said one word too many. You know? And that was it. It happens.

RS: One other thing: Right here at the beginning of your career the violence seems to me so characteristic of what we'd see later. It just occurs. There's not a lot of motivation. It almost comes out of nowhere.

MS: Well, that's the way it was. That's the world I was in. The violence is always in the background. I'd go into a place, even in a movie theater, I always had my antennae out all the way, because I had to watch if somebody said something wrong to somebody else. Some complain that the films denigrate Italian Americans. But I'm just telling it from my perspective. That doesn't mean that other friends of mine see it that way. But my experience is that there are certain groups of people who are aligned with certain families. I didn't know they were called families at the time, but there were certain people with power, and if somebody hits somebody, or does something, not just on the street level, not just kids, the settling up is done, usually, in the old way, between the different groups. Lives were run that way. It's a very tough way of living.

RS: Is that violence explicable if you really, really connect it to the Mob? And it's only to somebody like me that the violence seems almost totally inexplicable?

MS: I don't want to seem to contradict what I said before. But, no, at least in this world, it's always explicable. People criticized the film for pointless violence. I said, No, there's no such thing as pointless violence. It comes from something. In that world we have to be very careful as to who insulted whom, who brushed by another, who said something a little in a nasty way. In *Goodfellas,* where Joe Pesci and Ray Liotta are playing a game, and joking around, and all of a sudden Pesci is saying, Why do you say I'm funny? Well, says Ray, because you tell a funny story. Do you think I'm a clown? No, I didn't say you're a clown. What did you mean then? And somebody starts to speak—No, he's a big boy, he can talk for himself. And it changes on a dime. You could be killed. You could get into a fight, not be killed, but get beaten up pretty badly if you didn't know how to handle yourself.

I mean, there was always tension. None of this business of the happy immigrants jumping and dancing and doing tarantellas. It's *Los Olvidados.* It's *Journey to the End of the Night* by Céline. That is the closest of anything I ever read to the reality of the people in those Lower East Side buildings.

RS: So all of that fed into *Mean Streets*?

MS: *Mean Streets* was based on myself and a couple of friends I had, but particularly two guys. One of them thinks the Johnny Boy character is really about him, and in a way it was, but not fully. He no longer lives in New York, but he always felt angry about that.

After my father died, I realized what the hell the picture really was about: my father and that brother of his who we've talked about; a lot of money that was owed, a lot of sit-downs. Every night I'd hear the drama. For twenty, twenty-five years, that's all I heard. About what's right and wrong and you're in a jungle. It had to do with the dignity of the name, and respect—walking a tightrope of respect, not being a wiseguy. *Mean Streets* was about him and my uncle, but I couldn't verbalize it until after '93 or '94, when it really hit home.

ALICE DOESN'T LIVE HERE ANYMORE

RICHARD SCHICKEL: And now for something completely different—*Alice Doesn't Live Here Anymore.* How did that come about?

MARTIN SCORSESE: John Calley at Warner Bros. said they had a terrific script called *Alice Doesn't Live Here Anymore* by Robert Getchell. He said they all thought I could only direct men. But, he said, this is all women, and you should really do it. I read it and liked it. He said, Let's go. At that point, there was a part of me that wanted to erase everything of where I came from. *Mean Streets* was the acceptance of all that. It was said once and for all, and that was it.

I had a feeling that I had escaped. I was wearing those cowboy shirts. Our hair grew a little longer. And it was 1973 or so. It was really good.

Alice was a way of trying to find another way, really—could I make genre films in Hollywood? It was something like a vehicle, like a Bette Davis vehicle, or a Joan Crawford vehicle. I enjoyed Bette Davis films, like *Mr. Skeffington.* So I felt this would be a way of embracing the genre.

I knew Ellen Burstyn as an actor, and Diane Ladd, and all the other people in the picture—they were of the New York school of acting. It was very close to what Harvey and De Niro and I had been working with. I felt, after meeting her, that we could deal with improvisations within Getchell's work, but also at times out of it. Again, it was very inspired by Cassavetes's pictures.

RS: Really? Superficially, it doesn't seem to have his kind of improvisatory roughness.

MS: But it does—very much so. Especially the last third of the picture: a lot of improvs, between Ellen and Kris Kristofferson, and Diane Ladd. It's a problem, because people don't understand the interplay of improvisation and script in some films. Getchell's work was great in it. But there were times we were able to open up and take off, and then come back.

Ellen Burstyn visits Marty on the set of *Taxi Driver* in 1975.

RS: A lot of your characters in one way or another are kind of obsessive folks. And she, in her little way, is kind of obsessive. She really wants to be a singer. Then you hear her sing. Well, she's fine, but she's not great.

MS: No, but for a lounge singer, she's not bad. For lounge singing, it was, you know, better than whatever the hell else she was doing, she felt. And she had this dream to get in a car and take off. The first meeting I had with Ellen, we talked about the possibility of her divorcing the man.

And then I said, Well, no, if you divorce him, you've already made a step. You've already expressed yourself consciously. Here God comes in and takes him away. Now what do you do? Well, you have the kid. Okay. You can still deal with the kid, to a certain extent. But do you want to stay in this town? There's nothing for you in the town. You might as well leave.

RS: Her relationship with her little boy is very funny and charming.

MS: I loved that.

RS: Was there a certain amount of improv in that?

MS: Not really. The wonderful script was there. Alfred Lutter, the young boy, was also pretty good. The main improvisations were with Kris, and with Diane and Harvey a bit. And there's a little bit of my past in that relationship. My mother was very funny. She had a good sense of humor. I was very close with her, and so a lot of that reminded me of my own relationship with her. She was more Old World, but she had that kind of humor, and irony. Constantly making wisecracks. Constantly hitting your ego. And her own ego—deflating it. You can see a little bit of it in the documentary, *Italianamerican:* My father's much more stern and trying to retain a certain dignified air, whereas my mother is very ironic and funny with a lot of warmth. That was the key thing, I think, that drove me to the picture.

RS: What's with you and Kris Kristofferson? He's not only in this movie, there's that record by him in *Taxi Driver.* What does he represent to you?

MS: The record in *Taxi Driver* was in the script—that's Schrader—"Silver Tongued Devil," right? But Kristofferson at the time had the ability to express what he felt in his songs. He was a new voice coming in America. And his performance, he had that gravelly voice, he had a tough voice, but also he had a dignity about him. He had a dignity about him that helped me a lot in *Alice.*

We got into some interesting situations where people wanted us out of the buildings where we were shooting, and he would always say, "Having any trouble, Marty?" And I'd say, "Oh, just a little, bunch of people screaming." And then, they'd say, Well, for you, Kris, we'll do it. He just had a calming influence on all of us.

RS: Is he a kind of male that you had never encountered before on the mean streets?

MS: Well, that's one of the things, too. Because you know, seeing those western films as a child, and then listening to country western music—that was a direct line to his work, by way of Dylan, of course, and The Band, to a certain extent. I liked being around him. And I liked watching what he did, how he behaved, how he reacted in life. It was very different from the way I reacted.

When we first met, he really liked *Mean Streets,* because he had a relationship with a friend of his like the one Keitel had with De Niro. He just wanted to work with us.

I loved him, of course, in *Pat Garrett and Billy the Kid.* I got to see that—a rough cut—along with Jay Cocks on a Sunday afternoon, with Sam Peckinpah. And Pauline Kael came into the screening room. The picture was then taken away from Peckinpah. And it was re-edited to a ninety-minute version. But I loved what I saw that day on that screen. And, luckily, the editors somehow kept the original cut. And that's what you see now on DVD, and on TCM.

I thought it was a masterpiece, and I thought Kristofferson was extraordinary in it. He inhabited that film as if he really lived it. He's just shot the deputy and he's about to make his escape and he takes the chains off, and he's getting his jacket, or he's getting a gun or something, and he's walking around the room and the people downstairs are gathering—they're looking at the body. And he sings about what a down, ornery town it is. He makes up a song—"Never seen a town like this"—that was just extraordinary. It reminded me of De Niro in *Mean Streets:* before he gets in the car, before he's shot, he dances around the car.

So I found that kind of authenticity in him, like I saw it in Bob [De Niro] and Harvey Keitel from the urban areas. I felt really comfortable with that. And Ellen and him with those kisses—I thought that was a beautiful moment.

RS: Yes. Well, I also liked when he comes in at the end, and he's in the restaurant, confronting her, trying to force her to make emotional sense of her life. I think it's a wonderful scene.

MS: I always get a little nervous with that scene. But I think it's okay, because the picture really ends there, I suppose, though it literally ends with her walking down the street with her son. It's really about her and her son, the movie. She finds another man, and she moves on in life. It was not for feminists. They felt that because she took another man, or got involved with another man, it was undercutting the independence of the woman and the empowerment, I guess, of the woman. But that's the movie I made. And so, the last line of the picture, where she's holding the boy, and he says, "Mom, I can't breathe." That kid improvised that because she was hugging him so tight. But it's the perfect ending, as I said at the time.

Which is like my mother, at the end of *Italianamerican,* in a small apartment on Elizabeth Street, saying, Okay, come on, put this stuff back. She didn't know we were still filming. The chair can't stay like this, she says. You've got to put the table back, and all. And then she goes, "Are you still shooting this thing?" And we all started laughing, and she goes, "You'll never get out of this house alive." And I guess if you look at any family, it's amazing the kids do get out alive [*laughs*].

TAXI DRIVER

RICHARD SCHICKEL: *Taxi Driver* is not at all ethnically oriented. But yet it seems to draw on your own urban experiences.

MARTIN SCORSESE: Yes. I again have to talk about where I came from. My grandparents—coming from Sicily, basically peasants—helped raise me, too. Even though I didn't understand the Italian, I understood when they said things a certain way. They were extraordinary people, really.

My mother's side of the family reminds me of the family you see in *La Terra Trema* in Sicily, the mother who's embracing all her sons. [Luchino Visconti, 1948: Sicilian fishermen try to buy their own boat in order to fight off greedy wholesalers.] My father's side of the family was very strong. His mother was very strong, like Katina Paxinou in *Rocco and His Brothers*.

So it was very operatic, very hot-tempered. They had really strong values. When I saw *Shadows*, or Ingmar Bergman, or going to New York University, I was escaping into another world. That was expressed in *Mean Streets*. In *Taxi Driver*, when Brian De Palma gave me that script, I saw in it my reaction against the world I came from, which in a way I wanted to be rid of. I didn't want to say where I came from. The film had a rage in it that I saw in my grandparents.

Taxi Driver. Robert De Niro *is* Travis Bickle. The 1975 film is one of American cinema's most profound and disturbing meditations on the endemic violence of our culture.

With *Taxi Driver,* I was going to blast that away, so that I could be even freer. I think the immediate connection, when I read it, was with the anger and the rage, and the loneliness—not being part of a group. I was always on the outside. You grow up in a neighborhood where what a "man" is, quote unquote, is a guy who can go into a room and slam some people around and win, like in a Schwarzenegger film. But on the other hand, I heard my father say different things about what a man is; that had to do with being morally strong.

Coming from that, not being able to really fight it out in the streets the way other kids were able to do, and having to keep everything in quietly, my feelings blasted on the screen with *Mean Streets.* Later, with *Taxi Driver,* we really tapped into the idea of not being one of the group, not being part of anything. I remember Bob De Niro giving a speech at the first Tribeca Film Festival a few years ago, in which at the end he said, I've always wanted to belong, and now I feel I do. Something like that; it's a paraphrase, and it's the first time I heard him actually say that. In *Taxi Driver* we didn't have to say what it was about, why we were connected with it, why we felt we had to make this picture.

RS: Wait a minute, this guy's a psycho. Or isn't he?

MS: He comes out of Vietnam. We don't know what happens to people in a war. Give a seventeen-year-old kid a gun, get him into a battle situation, God knows what happens to him. You know, what makes a hero? Is there such a thing as a hero? I don't know. I never went to a war, never had that kind of experience.

But the loneliness, being an outsider, not being able to connect with anyone, expresses itself in the film and in the character through violence. Which is acting out the fantasy. [In the film De Niro's eponymous antihero comes to the rescue of Jodie Foster's teenage hooker by bloodily wiping out the criminals exploiting her and, ironically, being lauded as a hero for what is essentially a psychotic act.]

That's it, you've got to accept it. I mean, you have those fantasies. And then this guy crosses the line. The beauty of what Paul Schrader did in the script is that it touches on something that's very human—also filled with racism and all kinds of unpleasant aspects. But you know, these are aspects of a lot of people.

You grow up in a certain way—it structures a racism to a certain extent, and you try to come to terms with it as you get older and you see the rest of the world. And you try to say, No, that's not right. But there are certain things that are inbred that are difficult to overcome.

RS: At some point in the script, he says, I'm an avenging angel.

MS: That's right.

RS: Are we to understand him as believing that to be almost literal? Because I don't quite see any system of belief in this character other than what you just described— you know, the free-ranging psycho who can't really connect with people. I mean, how do you parse that?

MS: Well, it's why I wanted to make the film. Because it speaks to the zealousness of this kind of person, someone who will level a village because its inhabitants don't believe in the God that he believes in. He'll kill men, women, children, and animals.

This is the person who would do that when pushed—the outsider who is filled with the zealousness and the righteousness of the Lord. He shoots people who didn't do anything to him. Why? Because he couldn't shoot the political candidate who didn't do anything to him, either. It isn't necessarily explaining the act, or explaining the character. It's getting into the mindset of the character.

As I've said, I had trouble reading as a kid. My parents didn't have books in the house. But for some reason, in the late fifties I began to read, and there were three books that really hit me: *The Heart of the Matter*, by Graham Greene. *A*

Jodie Foster is the teenage prostitute, Iris, whom Travis rescues, in the process converting himself from psychopath to media hero.

Portrait of the Artist as a Young Man, by James Joyce, and the key one, Dos-toyevsky's *Notes from Underground.* These books reflected the way I felt. It turns out later that that was one of the elements Schrader worked from. The other was Arthur Bremer's diary [he was George Wallace's would-be assassin], and a few other things.

But those feelings I took away from reading *Notes from Underground* were a direct connection for me to *Taxi Driver.* You don't like the person. But in your deepest, darkest, secret self you realize that's the way you've been thinking as well. It's also from constantly being pushed aside and rejected, rejected, rejected. It's not the rational way to be, it's not the good way to be, but it is human. It's part of the human condition.

RS: Yet there's very little human about De Niro's character, no religious feelings, no political ideas, no human connections—aside from the fact that he lusts after the Cybill Shepherd character. Maybe you do get a sense of liberal impotence from the people around her. The candidate is an idiot, basically. And I love the patronizing thing he does—you know, I learn more from talking to cabdrivers than I do talking to other people. The woman—a society campaign worker—is attracted to Travis because he's so out of her league, as it were. Her Junior League, I guess. Which makes this notion of taking her to a porn movie—

MS: Oh! I know. Well, you have to remember, a lot of people don't remember now, but at that time, they were trying to make porn acceptable, with *Deep Throat* and *Sometimes Sweet Susan,* and pictures like that.

RS: I went to a few of those.

MS: It was okay to go with a girl. But Brian De Palma and I went to see *Deep Throat,* and he said, Look at the people around us, it doesn't feel right. There were couples. I said, You're right. We should be with all these old guys in raincoats. It was a wonderful kind of hypocritical thing that was happening—it opened up the society.

I'm telling you, 42nd Street, Eighth Avenue, that was hell, shooting in those places. That was like biblical in my mind—hell and damnation and Jeremiah, and someday a real rain was going to come.

RS: But that character, you know he's drawn to that. He goes to porn movies all the time. On the other hand, I guess there's a little bit of you in there.

MS: I know. It's upsetting. And it was an upsetting film to make. But we really felt strongly about it. De Niro and I never discussed it this way, by the way. It was nonverbal. It was just understood. I can't speak for him, but I know he understood certain things about the rejection, about not being part of a group.

RS: The famous scene, the mirror, where De Niro rehearses drawing—

MS: It was an improv.

RS: How much so?

MS: It's all improv. In the script, he sort of preens in front of the mirror, to get that maniacal expression on his face, to have the gun sliding in and out of his sleeve, which if you actually did it wouldn't work that well. But in the film it worked well.

He comes from a Special Forces unit, in Vietnam. I had a friend, who went to school at NYU with me, who was in Special Forces, and then became a stunt man. Unfortunately he was killed on a movie doing a stunt, a sweet guy, and he showed us pictures of these guys who were going on these special missions. Their haircuts looked to me like Mohawks. That's how we came up with the idea of that haircut. By that time, it was near the end of the shoot, and I was about five days over schedule on a forty-day shoot. That's pretty bad. We got hit with a lot of bad weather, all kinds of things.

Anyway, in the mirror scene, I really thought he had to say something to himself. I didn't know quite what. But I remembered Brando doing something beautiful in *Reflections in a Golden Eye,* in a mirror.

So he just started. It was in an apartment that was going to be torn down on Columbus Avenue at 89th Street. We were in the front apartment on the second floor. You could hear the sounds from the street. I was on the floor, and he was in the mirror. Michael Chapman had the camera, and Bob just started improvising—thinking about people coming up to him, saying things. If they said certain things he didn't like, he would have to turn and say, Are you talking to me? Because that is not a good thing to say to me. Now you're going to have to deal with me. Are you talking to me? He didn't say the words I just said, but he got the attitude.

I was forcing this into the schedule. Meanwhile, Pete Scoppa, who was the great AD [assistant director] at the time, was banging on the door between takes. "Come on," he would say, "you've got to get back on schedule." And I'm going, Give us two minutes, give us two minutes, this is really good. It was very noisy. And a couple of times I asked Bob to repeat, that's all. But he got into his own rhythm. And then got into the wonderful line where he admits that he's the only one there, so he must be talking to himself. And that did it.

RS: At the end of the movie, he seems to me to be all right. He's talking normally with cabbies. She gets in his cab, and she's sort of sweet with him. And he seems like he's not going to assault her.

MS: No, he's not going to assault her. Schrader very much liked Harry Chapin's song "Taxi." I wasn't that much of a fan of the song: the woman getting into the cab with a guy who hasn't done well, while she's done well; kind of sentimental, I thought. I had to find a way not to make the ending sentimental. So when she leaves the cab, I had him look in the mirror again, as if he just saw something happen. I wanted to give the impression that the time bomb is beginning to tick again. And it's going to happen again. Sooner or later there will be a violent outburst from him. Or, there will be self-immolation. Or God knows what. Because he wanted to kill himself in that massacre scene, but he ran out of bullets.

Schrader said he would've preferred the ending to have been more Japanese—*Samurai Rebellion* by Kobayashi, or *Harakiri,* where there's an explosion of sword fighting and violence, and the sacrificial blood is splashed all over the walls of the palaces, and finally the hero dies. I think we added the bit where he tries to shoot himself but there were no bullets. That was the right thing to do, I thought.

I didn't think anybody was going to see it. Bob De Niro, Michael and Julia

Phillips [the film's producers], felt that it would reach an audience. For me it was a labor of love, the kind of picture that should be made. Then again, I

Marty's sketch for *Taxi Driver*'s final, very ambiguous sequence.

was going to make this musical that became *New York, New York,* which, of course, I thought everyone would want to see and nobody saw [*laughs*]!

But in *Taxi Driver* we felt we could say what we wanted to say, and be as honest as possible in the picture. And it was very, very controlled—everything story-boarded, because it was a hard shoot.

RS: How bitter is the irony that Bob's character is responsible for this bloodbath and becomes a hero, and the papers write him up, and the family of Jodie Foster writes him this weird letter saying if he ever feels like visiting—they're so grateful to him.

MS: That's wonderful.

RS: Also his bland "everything's fine" postcard to his own family—

MS: Oh, that's Schrader. It was so fun, so extraordinary. And the picture of the parents, looking at the TV set as the camera goes by them. I felt that is the way of the world. People pick up on certain figures and they become very famous, they become heroes. What is a hero?

RS: Tell me.

MS: That's my question for most of my pictures. What is a man, and what is a hero? Does might make right? Or is it somebody who makes everybody reason things out and work it out? I think that's harder. Hit somebody long enough, they're going to stop. It works. For a while.

RS: Well, how much of *Taxi Driver* is really coming out of that period in New York where a lot of us who loved the city and loved living here were just disgusted by it.

MS: Oh, it was horrible.

118

RS: I mean, there was a sense of the city just spiraling down into hell at that moment.

MS: That was just beginning. But I'm a New Yorker, so when it starts to go down, it seems part of the cycle. I mean, I knew that 42nd Street and Times Square was hitting a new low. It was not a safe area. But being a lover of the city, I knew that the city was just going through a phase and it would come back.

I was more aware of, and more attracted to, this new expression of open sexuality. Where I came

Marty riding the boom on *Taxi Driver*. Exploring New York's lower depths in the mid-seventies was, Scorsese says, among the most troubling experiences of his directorial career.

119

from, sexuality was restricted and repressed. I tried to understand and tried even to join in—as a person. But I always say, when I try to be amoral, I turn out to be immoral. So it wasn't for me. In *Taxi Driver*, I didn't enjoy shooting in those X-rated areas. The sense of wallowing in it was, for me, always filled with tension and an extraordinary depression.

And the film *is* very, very depressing. The key is when De Niro tries to open up to Peter Boyle [playing a fellow cabbie]. The guy can't talk to him. He's not a philosopher. He just isn't. And Bob did an improvisation, and he said, You know, I have these thoughts, and Peter says, Oh, you'll be okay. And he said, No, I've got these bad ideas in my head. And that for me was as close as he's going to get to it. What are these bad ideas? His feelings of rage, his feelings of anger, his feelings of acting out. He did act out before, when he was in the war. But what's the next step? To pick up a gun again? Or kill someone? He's trying like hell to keep those feelings down, but they're coming out, and the guilt over that, too, is strong.

RS: So he does have a measure of what you could call moral self-consciousness.

MS: Yes.

RS: He is truly struggling with these impulses.

MS: I think so. I can't speak for Paul. I'm just saying what I felt, that he didn't want to do what he does at the end—commit multiple murders. But he does. He's driven

A very bad date: Travis seriously misjudges Betsy's cinematic tastes. Cybill Shepherd was genuinely disturbed by the milieu to which the film exposed her, and Scorsese did his best to get these scenes done as quickly as he could.

to it. It's just dealing with the human condition; that's what we're dealing with in a Travis Bickle.

RS: On the other hand, Pauline Kael did call this a comedy.

MS: That's pretty funny.

RS: Well, she liked the movie, of course.

MS: Why is it a comedy? Okay, there are some funny scenes . . .

RS: It *is* funny, in a cringing sort of way, when he takes her to the porno movie.

MS: I remember Cybill Shepherd that night got nervous shooting there. We were shooting fast and moving quickly, but she, I believe, identified with that character so strongly that she really got upset. I tried to get her in and out as fast as possible, but I couldn't. Poor kid—she really felt it, and didn't like it.

RS: Let me ask you about the character you play—this psychopathic guy talking about all the terrible things he's going to do to his ex-wife. What about him? Is he the rock bottom, worse than De Niro?

MS: I don't know. All I know is that a good friend of mine was going to play the part, but he was shooting another film. It was the last week of shooting. I had gone through all the actors I knew in New York who I liked for that part. So Bob and I talked, and the next thing I know, I agreed to do it. I don't know if he convinced me, or what. But I thought I could do it. And that's it. What came out, came out. It was honest, open—and extremely unpleasant. Also, I think, funny at times, because he got me to do a couple of things. He's very good at that. I learned all about acting there.

But it was very simple. We stopped the cab, and I say, "Put the flag down, stop here." After the rehearsal, he turned to me and said, "Make me put the flag down. I'm not going to put it down unless you mean it."

Okay. So then, the improv came. I realized, Wait a second, why is this guy not putting the flag down? I am the passenger. I have control of his life in the next fifteen, twenty minutes. That's one of the crazy things about driving a cab in the city. A passenger gets in the cab; you don't know where he's going to ask you to go, or what's going to happen. Passengers control your life.

Anyway, all the dialogue was there. And then we improvised some. But the improvs came from bouncing off Bob. It was the back of his head that did it all. I'd say something a little more outrageous and he still wouldn't move. I was getting him crazy. Because what I was saying was going to instill in him the violence. That was the idea. So I kept thinking of more outrageous things to say, and the words came out, and that was it.

NEW YORK, NEW YORK

MARTIN SCORSESE: I had a very chaotic style, on purpose, on *New York, New York.* And I found it didn't work for me. [The film is both a tribute to old-fashioned MGM musicals and a dark love story between a bandleader, Robert De Niro, and his singer, Liza Minnelli.]

RICHARD SCHICKEL: What do you mean by a chaotic process?

MS: I improvised. I tried to improvise within scenes. I had a script, but I kept pushing the limits of the scenes. Then at a certain point, I was able to improvise a scene with the actors based on the script, video it, or audiotape it. A good example of it is in *Goodfellas*—that "You think I'm funny" scene with Joe Pesci and Ray Liotta that I referred to earlier. We did four or five takes. It was typed up, I had it transcribed, all the takes. Then I constructed from the takes a scene, and had them memorize that scene. That's what we did in some of the better scenes in *New York, New York*—the ones I think worked.

Then I decided, let's go further. Let's not write down anything, let's just improvise it—whatever feelings you may have, go there. And we literally started improvising ourselves out of the sets we were shooting on. I would say, "Well, what are we going to do now? The other set isn't ready." I tried to have no idea at all what I was going to do, as much as possible, on the day of shooting—as opposed to having a fairly strong idea of what I was going to do. I was really testing the limits.

RS: That's a weird picture to do it on. You're on the street with Harvey Keitel or De Niro, and interesting stuff happens, and you take advantage of it. But this is a big Hollywood studio picture—

One long headache: *New York, New York* (1977) was a bold attempt to meld an improvisational acting style on the structure of an old-fashioned, big-studio musical, but it failed to fulfill either ambition.

MS: I know! That was the idea! The convention of the Hollywood studio film meets, or crosses with, a new style, the Italian cinema, the French cinema, Cassavetes—Kazan, of course, going back to him.

RS: So you just dumped that into a big formal setting. Maybe that's why the movie disconcerted me.

MS: I'm not happy with it. But the thing about it is that I still think the idea of mixing a modern foreground with an artificial background, like the old Hollywood, was a good idea. More than homage, it was a re-creation of the old Hollywood, even though I realized that the old Hollywood was gone. So maybe it was a way for a young kid who loved old Hollywood movies to try to hold on to it.

RS: And you've got Liza Minnelli in it—kind of a throwback personality.

MS: She comes from a Hollywood family.

RS: The picture looks somewhat like one of her father's films.

MS: Minnelli and George Cukor, really. I really tried to combine the styles and see what would happen, holding on to the old Hollywood artifice that I loved. I didn't want the old Hollywood to die. But of course we were the new Hollywood, so we were part of the demise. It was just the natural order of things.

But I didn't know that until I got there, until I was working on the picture. But, yes, and other movies like *The Man I Love* and *Blues in the Night*—and add to that Cukor's *A Star Is Born*—were certainly in my mind at the time. [Vincente]

123

Minnelli, that use of color. But primarily it was meant to be more drama with music, and not musical drama. That was the idea.

And, again, like *Age of Innocence,* it was meant to be an homage to the old style of filmmaking, meaning the studio system and the studio look of the picture. But with the influences of the newer cinema that was around me.

RS: It's a contradiction in terms, and I think it does affect the movie in an adverse way.

MS: It probably does. I was thinking lately of why I have a negative feeling about the picture. One thing is that I didn't control the improvisations the way I normally do. The best example is the moment where she and he are rehearsing, and she counts down the band. He takes her aside and says, "Don't ever do that. I count down the band." That was done the same way we did other improvisations, but things got too loose. I didn't guide them. And if I have a criticism of the film as a whole, it is that it is repetitious. I think I could have been more concise. Other people have said it's tantamount to watching a car crash, or whatever, because of the two styles together. And I said, I don't know if that's necessarily a bad thing.

So I think, ultimately, the negative aspect is that I didn't clarify or distill the drama between the two of them. It's really about the love between two people who are extremely creative, and their jealousies, their competition.

RS: But also, they are two people who don't really belong together.

MS: Right. They don't belong together. I'm not defending the picture, but our generation may be focusing on problems that won't mean anything in ten years' time.

I also have problems with the picture because of my memory of the actual work, which was very, very hard for me at the time. I don't like to think about it, so I don't really see the picture that often.

RS: When you were doing *New York, New York,* were people like Irwin Winkler, the producer, or people at the studio aware of what you were trying to do? Or did they say, Oh, Marty wants to do a musical and that'll be fine?

MS: They were aware of it. They were hoping I could pull it off.

RS: I don't know if you recall this. I think it's the first time I ever met you. You were in Los Angeles. Irwin ran the picture for me. And then we all went to dinner.

MS: Didn't I meet you before? Because I think we were in your apartment, to screen *His Girl Friday* with Jay Cocks one time in 16 millimeter.

RS: Is that true? It could be.

MS: In 1970.

RS: Maybe a little later, because I was starting to work on *The Men Who Made the Movies* [a PBS television series, consisting of interviews with the great American directors of the classic age]. But what's so vivid to me was that dinner in L.A. being so awkward because I didn't know what to say to you about the movie, because I kind of liked it and didn't like it.

MS: Your first reaction to *Mean Streets* was also not good. *Alice* was good. *Taxi Driver* I don't remember.

RS: On that one, I wrote a review and it came back from the managing editor with a note scrawled on it: "You don't like this movie as much as you say you do." He was probably right. Now, of course, he would be wrong.

MS: For *New York, New York,* Irwin was really good. He went along with this idea of combining the styles. He fought for it. He knew what I was trying to do. I was also trying to pull it from being too dark. I mean, in effect, we could've gone and made *The Man I Love.* [The 1947 film noir in which Ida Lupino's nightclub singer falls in love with a former jazz great now on the skids.] By the way, the shot of New York City that's used for the credits, that's taken from the credits of *The Man I Love.* The bridge and everything.

I'm not defending the film, as I say, and I think if I have any negative thoughts about it, it has to do with more personal stuff. But now the film is looked at in a more forgiving context.

RS: One of the things that struck me looking at it recently was the very opening sequence, where they meet. It just seemed to me it went on too long.

MS: Actually, we had it longer.

RS: I'm sure.

MS: How many times could she say no.

RS: Right. I had a feeling all along as I watched it that there was a thinner movie struggling to get out of it.

Marty attempting to turn his back on the production, something he could manage only momentarily. Its strain sickened him to the point where many of his friends feared for his life.

MS: Exactly. That's what I mean about being more specific—if I had practiced the craft better, the way I had in *Alice* and in *Mean Streets* with the actors. We were trying new things. But, still, the artifice of the old has truth to it.

RS: You know, in my mind, I may be more committed to the artifice of the old than you are. I mean, they can go on making movies like that forever as far as I'm concerned.

MS: Me, too [*laughs*]. Those are the only images I watch on TCM, the old images. If a newer film comes on, I turn it off. Even films from the seventies. I don't watch them that much, you know. But even more so for you, because you saw more films on that big screen in 1.33 aspect ratio than I did.

RS: Well, naturally I did.

MS: You're a different generation. When we screened *Out of the Past* for Leo DiCaprio and Mark Ruffalo when we were making *Shutter Island,* it was stunning. At the end of *Out of the Past,* I was wondering if these younger people would go for it. All of a sudden I hear applause behind me. It was Leo, and he said, "That was the coolest movie I've ever seen." I think he was responding to the authority of these figures on a big screen. But you were saying you prefer the artifice.

RS: If you had gone more for the artifice and less for the improv in *New York, New York,* I would've preferred it, if you had stylized the hell out of every single shot in it. That would have given it a coherence that I think it lacks.

MS: Yes, it might have. But it's interesting that younger people don't see that in *New York, New York.* They don't deal with that at all. They accept it for what it is. I still think about it as an experiment. But when you look at a musical like *The Glenn Miller Story,* directed by Anthony Mann, it has an authenticity to it that's quite extraordinary. It's beautiful to watch even on television. But he came from that period. So did James Stewart. Also, he shot it in the real places. I could have. I could've shot in Roseland. I didn't because I chose to go with the whole idea of a film called *New York, New York* made completely in Hollywood. Which was the New York in our heads when we saw it as young people. I don't think I could have directed the actors in the stylized way of classic Hollywood cinema, because I wouldn't know how to direct that.

RS: You mean, getting an actorly stylization that would match the visual stylization.

MS: Exactly, exactly—see how we could force the issue somehow.

RS: The things that worked best for me in the movie were when they were on the bandstand; all those mannerisms are so beautifully done. I mean, I remember those not from movies but from seeing those bands live onstage at the Riverside Theater in downtown Milwaukee: You know, Tommy Dorsey holding his trombone and waving his fingers as if he's directing the band.

MS: Exactly.

RS: I loved that stuff.

MS: Me, too.

RS: And yet it is a truly conventionalized romantic story. I mean, we saw that story lots in those days, you know.

MS: *The Man I Love* is more like a noir.

RS: Right.

MS: And yet there were films in Technicolor, like *My Dream Is Yours,* which had implied noirish elements in the relationship [between a cruel singing star, Lee Bowman, and the young woman, Doris Day, who is hired to replace him]. That's the film I wanted to make, trying to imply what was darker in the relationship.

RS: Oh, very dark. It's really a bummer of a movie.

MS: I know. So I wondered why they put some sort of happy ending on it. I mean, if you're going to do it, go all the way—

RS: Here's how desperate they were: It's one of the very few movies where Jack Carson gets the girl. He usually did simple comic relief.

The musical that is really like your film, in that it's more a drama with some music, yet, I think, does fulfill its implicit darkness, is the one with Ida Lupino, Jack Carson, and Dennis Morgan.

MS: *The Hard Way* [a dark show business romance of 1943, and something of a lost treasure].

RS: That's it.

MS: It's like *The Breaking Point* [a fairly faithful 1950 adaptation of Hemingway's *To Have and Have Not*]. These two are really standouts. They did lack Technicolor, though. Technicolor made such an impression on me when I saw *Duel in the Sun.* It was the first time I remember seeing it. Technicolor promised happiness, light. It promised something transcendent, an experience of joy. And yet a lot of these films that I was beginning to become aware of had elements that were darker. Living in the world that I was living in, I asked, So why can't we do that in Technicolor?

RS: But in the early era of three-strip Technicolor, I think it was very hard to do because the colors are just so glaringly bright.

MS: Some are so strong you'd have to duck. They'd come flying at you. Especially when 3-D came out. Maybe I could've done it in black-and-white.

RS: Well, you couldn't have by that time.

MS: No, by that time you couldn't. Especially accepting it as a way of doing homage to the old studio system.

RS: Well, as we discussed earlier, it's a particular homage, it seems to me, to Vincente Minnelli.

MS: Particularly *The Band Wagon.*

RS: Because his use of color was different from other people's use of color.

MS: Amazing, amazing. And we used many of the stills from *Band Wagon* as research, with Boris Leven designing. But really it was that element of Technicolor promising one thing and yet having a darkness. I wanted to combine the two. [*Laughs.*]

RS: I understand that. But I'm also not sure there's a really good chemistry between Bob De Niro and Liza Minnelli in that film.

MS: I thought there was. But I couldn't tell.

RS: There's something that doesn't quite jell, that doesn't quite say that whatever else is between these people, there is a passion.

MS: Maybe.

RS: They're acting it. They're trying. Yet—

MS: That could be because of what we did to the material. The thing we got interested in more was the competitiveness, and how that ate away at the relationship.

RS: But one of the things that's striking in the movie is that De Niro's character is much more consciously passionate about his work, his music, than she is. She's kind of a natural.

MS: That's the thing. I think, ultimately, she is a natural. And he has to work at it and work at it. And there's a resentment. And it's very unpleasant.

RS: The ambition of the movie really does come through, though. It's manifest in the way the movie is shot and staged. It just doesn't quite get translated into the dramatic action.

MS: Well, that's in the writing—in the rewriting, I should say. That's what we were trying to do with improvisation, working with Earl Mac Rauch, the writer. Other people worked on it, too—Mardik Martin, Irwin helped, Jay Cocks, a number of people. People who were experimenting to see where we could go. It was a dangerous thing because, of course, there was a lot of money involved. But beyond that, I'd come off three movies that were well received: *Mean Streets,* although it wasn't a financial hit; *Alice* was pretty well received; and *Taxi Driver* was certainly well received. So there was a lot to lose. It was a big gamble.

"The best-laid plans . . .": Marty attempts to solve his overwhelming problems on the *New York, New York* set.

RS: What is Marty up to? I remember that feeling being in the air at the time. Doing a film of a type you had done nothing like before.

MS: Maybe it was wrangling something like six to eight horses in the chariot before they just run wild. And they ran wild. And then the film was reviled for it.

I didn't go through that very well. And, interestingly enough, by the time I was pulled back together and we were doing *Raging Bull,* articles were coming out asking, Will this be his comeuppance?

RS: And you thought, I've already had my comeuppance.

MS: And if I hadn't, why would I have to have a comeuppance anyway?

RS: Well, that's an interesting point: If you do pretty well, whatever you do, directing movies, writing books, whatever, there are a lot of people out there—

MS: Waiting.

RS: —who really want you to have a comeuppance.

MS: They're waiting for you.

RS: Some don't even want to say it.

MS: No.

RS: But they do.

MS: Yes.

RS: I mean they say, in effect, Oh, screw him. He thinks he's hot stuff.

MS: And often the stuff that is reviled or soundly trounced is years later revealed to be something more interesting. It's fashion, I suppose.

RS: No, I think it's more than fashion. I think there's active resentment out there.

MS: I don't know. For me this goes back to the family, my expecting the world to be like my family. But that is not the case. For instance, your collaborators are there, and you collaborate very well, but there's a limit.

RS: That's true.

MS: Loyalty only goes up to a certain level in this kind of work. And the sooner you get to know that, the better it is. People very often have to take stands that might be against you or hurt you. And other times they may take stands at the wrong time.

RICHARD SCHICKEL: *The Last Waltz,* your first full-length music documentary, was kind of squeezed in between *New York, New York* and *Raging Bull.* And it's very different in tone from your other music docs.

MARTIN SCORSESE: It reflects a totally different mindset.

RS: Sure. But how so?

MS: Because *The Last Waltz* was really a last waltz. [The Band was breaking up and the film is, among other things, a record of their last concert.] They stopped playing. The group broke up. It also gave us a chance, although I didn't realize it at the time, to look back on something that was definitively ending by 1980, '81, maybe even earlier. I was kind of seduced into it by Jonathan Taplin, the producer of *Mean Streets,* who called me when I was doing *New York, New York* and said a lot of the rock people were watching the film, and a lot of younger actors. He said he wanted to have a screening for a few friends, including Robbie Robertson.

We loved the sound of The Band. No one has ever equaled that sound. It incorporates so many different facets of American music—the South, Canada, the Southwest. And influences from all over the world, too. There's a character they created with their voices, like in "The Night They Drove Old Dixie Down," which was a song that went against the grain at the time, don't forget.

These guys were coming out against the hippie movement. It was a special sound, different from Dylan, different from everyone else. And it was almost as if they didn't give a damn, either. They had placed themselves in a special place. So to go back to Woodstock for a moment, it was a big event. I was delighted, though The Band were really angry to be at Woodstock.

RS: How come?

MS: Because Woodstock was the place where they worked and lived. What were all those people doing there? It had become hippie heaven suddenly. It was a revolution. And they wondered, What is this shit?

They didn't allow the film onstage. The lenses had to be on the lip of the stage, rather than close to them. They gave a look to the audience which said, Do not come near us, especially you guys down front. Don't come up on the stage. We said, "Okay." We loved them so much that even if we couldn't shoot, we were happy just to listen. They wouldn't let us say anything. They weren't ruffians, but they had a determination about them: We don't want to play, but we're going to play. It was too bad they didn't get into the final cut of *Woodstock*.

Anyway, I met Robbie the night of the screening of *Mean Streets* at Warner Bros. and said hello, and he said he liked the film. So when Jonathan called me, saying there was going to be this farewell to The Band, and they wanted to get special guest stars, and would I want to shoot it, I was open to the idea, especially when I heard the people who were going to be there—Muddy Waters, Bob Dylan, Joni Mitchell, Neil Young. So over a series of dinners—Robbie had a way of seducing you into it—I decided to shoot it just for archival, in 16 millimeter. And then one thing led to another and I said, "You know what? Why don't we do a film like this in 35 millimeter? Nobody's done it before in 35 millimeter."

I didn't think it was going to be a film until I saw the first day's rushes on the editing machine. And I said, "There's something special about the look of it, the way they are on the stage." I had designed it very carefully, because they didn't move very much—as opposed to the Rolling Stones, where there's a lot of movement. It became, over a period of two years, a film we were doing on the side, because I was trying to finish *New York, New York*. But it developed into an exploration of American music, ultimately culminating with them and Bob Dylan onstage. We didn't know we were doing that, but that's what happened.

And later on, interviews were put in the picture. Robbie just said, Let's do some interviews, because people wanted to know about The Band members. So it became more of a view, a vision of an era.

Marty directing *The Last Waltz,* his documentary about The Band's final concert. It is widely recognized as one of the great concert films.

We wanted to record it, get it down. These people were important historically. But the film became something lyrical, I thought, and quite beautiful the way it was edited. It became elegiac in a way, and it took on more import than we thought it might at the outset. The form of it was important to me—the camera movement to music, the editing, capturing the live performances.

RS: You feel you broke some new ground with that film?

MS: I kind of thought we did. After 16 millimeter cinema verité in the sixties, culminating in *Woodstock,* this was rather different. This was staged, more studied in a way, much more planned out. And when the footage came on the screen, it revealed something else that was much more powerful than I thought it would be.

RS: Which is what?

MS: The presence of the performers, of the way they handled their instruments, the nature of so many of them singing those lyrics for the last time together. And Muddy Waters up on screen—he was not part of the band, of course, but it is great when he comes on: suddenly there was a special glow to the film. We felt it onstage.

RS: But you feel it was more intense on the film than being there?

MS: On film, absolutely. When we saw the rushes, we knew it was a movie.

RS: Isn't that interesting.

MS: Something happened. It just clicked.

RS: It's a gigantic version of that notion that the camera loves some people and some people it doesn't.

MS: Whether you like that kind of music or not, you cannot deny that there's a relationship of the performer to the audience. You don't even see the audience, but you can feel it.

RS: That's what's interesting in that film. Usually you pull back and you see audience.

MS: Like in *Woodstock*. Michael Wadleigh and Thelma, they edited that picture so there was a lot of audience. The audience, the event itself, was as important as the music.

RS: They made the right decision.

MS: They were absolutely right. But with *The Last Waltz* I thought to myself, We've seen the ultimate audience movies in *Monterey Pop*, and certainly *Woodstock*. What do we care? We're the audience. *The Last Waltz* is for everybody, and let's just go with it.

RS: You've mentioned you were busy with *New York, New York* at this time.

MS: I was editing it and simultaneously supervising *The Last Waltz*.

RS: Kind of a high-pressure moment for you there?

MS: Very. A year later we shot the interviews, after they had broken up. What you feel in those interview scenes, I think, is real tension—maybe among themselves, or the situation made them nervous.

RS: I think it's what makes the film unique.

MS: They were being very nice to each other because I was there.

RS: But you get that feeling of edginess, unease. It makes the movie more interesting.

MS: It's constant. There also was an interesting edginess and unease during the actual show. When Dylan got onstage it was very tense.

Bob Dylan joins The Band in *The Last Waltz.*

RS: Really?

MS: Very tense. I didn't know this until years later, but apparently backstage something happened and he said he wasn't going on. All I know is he finally came on and we were told not to shoot certain songs, which we didn't. And I was told by Bill Graham, "Shoot it, don't worry about it. Shoot it. He comes from the same streets you do." That's what Graham told me [though, of course, Dylan came from Minnesota].

RS: I don't think so.

MS: I don't think so, either. So I didn't shoot it; everything had gone so well, I didn't want him to walk off.

RS: That does happen in documentary shooting. You push it that one extra step. That's the edge the filmmaker has: it's his choice in the end.

But let's talk for a minute about documentaries in general. Unlike most directors of your stature, you have what amounts to a full career in that genre.

MS: Well, the Italian cinema documentary I did with Thelma, Kent Jones, and Raffaele Donato [*Il Mio Viaggio in Italia*]: it was an example of something that kept me alive creatively. Because I kept experimenting with it—with the form, especially the first hour and a half—trying to find the thread.

RS: What's wonderful is I've never seen anybody play clips so long. I mean, those were real scenes.

MS: That's something that Thelma and I tried to do. If I was experimenting in the feature films, I'm not in a position to say if they worked or not. Obviously, at the time I felt they worked. But everything has been done, so I'm not sure it's really important if it works or not. But the documentaries gave us more freedom. I think it started with *Italianamerican*. It burst through. Sometimes all the plans are wiped away, and a truth, or an emotional power, comes across that you never planned.

RS: It's a very strange thing, but I think I'm a better interviewer when I have a camera over my shoulder.

MS: Over your shoulder?

RS: Behind me as I'm interviewing. It's because it feels like there's something really at stake there.

MS: Yes. You've got to get it on film.

RS: You don't know if when you get to someone's house, he will have just had a fight with his wife, and everything is chaotic, and you're just standing there. And it's your only opportunity to film him. Whereas in a fiction film you can make your own reality. I don't care how simple a documentary seems to be, it's always difficult.

MS: Agreed.

RAGING BULL

RICHARD SCHICKEL: You spoke earlier about the limits of friendship and loyalty. Yet around this time a friend did come through for you. I'm talking about Robert De Niro and his determination that you make *Raging Bull.* This was coming at a time when you were very ill and were, if we're to believe Peter Biskind's book, *Easy Riders, Raging Bulls,* part of a fairly heavy drug scene.

MARTIN SCORSESE: The only good thing about the drug use is that it was very obvious in my case. And I just had to go to that brick wall. Nobody was going to tell me otherwise, whether it was a rock 'n' roller, or a studio executive, or an actor. People can try to guide me, but I always have to go my own way.

RS: The only reason I bring it up is because it's part of the public record of your life.

MS: Right. After *New York, New York* I was exhausted to the point where a number of people were worried about my health. I said, "Don't worry, I'm fine." And then after the Labor Day weekend in Telluride, at the film festival, I got back to New York and suffered a total collapse.

That's when I finally went to the hospital, and that's when De Niro came to

A still from *Raging Bull* (1980), a film that strived for new levels of realism in its brutally stylized manner.

visit and asked if I wanted to do the film. Really, we had been working on it since *Taxi Driver.* I realized I had nothing else to do. I had exhausted all the possibilities. Even my friends were all going off on their own. I was alone. And it was time to go back to work. And what I discovered—it's in *Raging Bull* and it's in the other pictures later on—is that I had to come to terms with something.

RS: What did you come to terms with?

MS: The fighting with myself. You get to the point where you just get used to yourself: that's who you are, just get on with it.

RS: Stop there. What were you fighting in yourself? I mean, you were a talented kid. You had done pretty well for a young guy.

MS: I have no idea. Really.

RS: Were you fighting the past in some sense?

MS: Probably the past, I guess. I didn't trust myself. I'm not talking about art; I'm talking about myself as a person. I've surprised myself too many times in the wrong way.

It's how you treat people around you, how you treat yourself. And then you say, If you make a little bit of peace with yourself, you might be better with the people around you, too. That's all it is. Maybe it's maturing to a certain extent, but I don't think I did. You just get older; you're a little more tired.

RS: Was this tied in to people firing you, or saying you were too damned ambitious? Was it pushing yourself to succeed when people thought you already had, given your age, your experience? Or was it that you were pressing against their low expectations for you while you had high expectations?

MS: I don't really know. I mean, I just wasn't comfortable with myself, who I was, what I was trying to be. Was I trying to be a movie director, or a filmmaker? A director in the style of Hollywood, or a filmmaker in the style of Europe? I mean, I didn't fit either place. I still don't. It's about how you're trying to express yourself. You've got this need to do something, and sometimes it's crazy. People say, Oh, you're taking yourself too seriously. But I can't help it. Out of the seriousness comes the humor, too.

RS: It's perhaps not so apparent to the people around you as it is to you.

MS: Maybe, but it is absolutely hilarious at times to me. The gambles I make— I seem to have this need. I try to do other things. I wish I could do many things— like write music. But making movies is the only thing that there seems to be a need for on my part.

RS: *Raging Bull* seems to be your common-consent masterpiece.

MS: I don't know.

RS: You don't think so?

MS: I don't know. I really have no idea.

RS: Set aside its masterly qualities for a minute. There's no doubt you were coming back with it, so to speak, even though most of us didn't know you'd been away.

MS: I *was* coming back. But I collapsed on that movie, too, during postproduction. And that wasn't from drugs. That was just from exhaustion—walking pneumonia, apparently. Later, on *King of Comedy,* Jerry Lewis would make me laugh, which made me cough, and then the bronchial asthma would start. Then he would say, "Would somebody get a goddamn ambulance over here," and make me laugh more.

I was dragging myself through each day on *King of Comedy.* But I kept pushing, pushing the envelope, seeing what would happen in terms of the work.

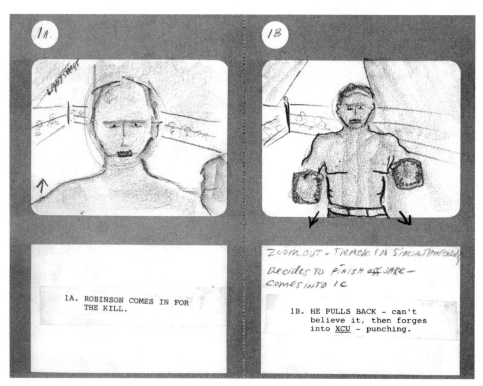

Marty's sketches for the final confrontation between Sugar Ray Robinson and Jake LaMotta.

RS: Did it do your work any good?

MS: No, I don't think it did. And I don't look at it as heroic. I just woke up one day and I had survived. That's it. It's nothing to be proud of.

RS: It obviously didn't do your health any good.

MS: No. But, as you know, my whole life I had been reliant on asthma medication. My whole speech pattern is based on that. It's very fast, and there's no breathing, the breathing isn't right.

RS: Does the asthma medicine juice you up?

MS: Not really.

RS: You're saying medicine, doctors, were second nature to you, just part of your life.

MS: I have friends who say, I'm not going to a doctor, I don't care what a doctor says. Me, I went to doctors all the time. I felt doctors were interesting.

RS: Let's look at the specifics of *Raging Bull*. What I love about that movie is its utter refusal to explain Jake LaMotta. I mean, with your first glimpse of the film, you think it's a genre movie, that it's going to be like *Somebody Up There Likes Me*.

MS: I didn't know anything about boxing. On TV, or in the movie theaters, where they'd show the fight on the weekend, the fights all looked the same. All from one camera angle. I didn't know what the hell was going on. I didn't understand it. It was sports, which took me out of the picture.

RS: What I mean to say is that it's a modernist film, even though it looks like it might be part of a classic Hollywood genre.

MS: I never thought it was genre.

RS: There never is one of those explanatory scenes—where we learn his father beat him or his mother didn't like him.

MS: I saw too many of those films that came out in the fifties, or late forties, when Freudian psychology was coming in, and every movie explained everything. *Knock on Any Door* [a tragic 1949 history of a juvenile delinquent], and there's Nick Romano.

You can't explain a human being with one Freudian term. On *Raging Bull*, I said let's take all that out. I don't want to do any of that.

As you know, I was totally resistant to that picture. But Bob seemed to know that it was a picture that was very appropriate for me to do. My old friend Mardik Martin, a very sweet guy, was working on the script, but I gave him no supervision. It was a very traditional script. We went about it in a very conventional way. Jake starts out as a young man, goes through his whole life to the end. And I wasn't satisfied. I had no intention of making that picture, none. And I was having my own problems at the time, too; I was finishing *The Last Waltz*.

Yet De Niro was very, very persistent about *Raging Bull*, despite my misgivings. I had had a lot of problems with myself on *New York, New York,* and I wasn't even sure I should work with him again at that point. It wasn't a matter of what he did, it's a matter of how I was feeling about the whole actor-director process. I had wanted to do *Mean Streets, New York, New York, Taxi Driver.* And the next picture I felt strongly about was making *Gangs of New York.* And so I felt, Can I do this? Can I go through this process? But I tried to do another version of the script, and it still wasn't right. Eventually, we agreed that if anything could come of this, Paul Schrader was the one who could write a script for us. Paul, to his credit, accepted the challenge one night over dinner. He said, "I will give you six weeks. I will give it to you in six weeks."

Paul, of course, had his own career. He was about to go shoot a big movie; I think it was *American Gigolo*. He had come off *Blue Collar*, all these really good films. And *Taxi Driver* won the Golden Palm in Cannes. De Niro and I may have gotten more attention out of it than Paul did. At least I think Paul felt that. These things get a little touchy at times. He didn't have to do this for us.

RS: I understand.

MS: But it was just what we needed in terms of structure. He started the picture in the middle. He had the scene at the end in the jail which was very interesting, he did a whole thing with masturbation in there. I thought that was interesting. But I still was not determined to make the movie. There was a meeting with Irwin Winkler and me and Paul and Bob. They got into an argument, because Paul was going away. He said, "Look, I did this as a favor. I've got my own things to do." Rightly so. "I'm not doing the second draft." By that point I was sort of watching from the side. Irwin somehow worked it out. There were a lot of things in the script that I still was not focused on, though; I was still having my own emotional and physical problems. So I wasn't at the top of my game. And, quite honestly, I wasn't that enamored of the script, though there were two or three scenes I really liked. Bob had his own feelings about the script.

It wasn't like *Taxi Driver*, which Paul delivered finished, complete. You hardly had to do anything with it. Amazing. This was something different, something he was doing for us as a favor. So we had one more meeting with him, and he said, Look. Go ahead, do it your way. Rewrite it yourselves. You should try this, you should try that. Or he would say, I would suggest doing this, combining two characters, making them one. But do whatever you want. And so, basically, that's what we did. The whole sequence of events is very different from the original script that Paul gave us. But the structure is there. What Paul did was blast through that logjam.

Then Bob came to say, "Look, we got the script. Let's work on it." He took me to Saint Martin for, like, two and a half weeks—and we wrote ten pages a day, improvised together. I wrote it all in longhand on yellow pads that I still have. Since then, he's said, You know, there is no script. But there is a script, and it was used by the studio. It's referred to in the book *Final Cut* by Steven Bach.

Everything in that picture was worked out between me and Bob on a little audio tape recorder on the island. We even had an assistant with us, and she would type out the pages at the end of the day. We would work it out in the morning. I'd write pages in the afternoon. She would type them. And we'd go have dinner. There were no phones. It was total concentration. Everything was done at that little table with that silly cabana umbrella, and we're looking out at the ocean.

We had a little golf cart, and we drove into town to have dinners at these small places, and we just talked and talked and talked and talked and talked. And we were totally alone. We saw only two people that we knew while we were on this island. One night we're having dinner and [*New York Times* film critic] Vincent Canby is sitting over there.

RS: No kidding?

MS: [*Laughs.*] I said hello. We were just waving. Another day, who's walking on the beach but Marco Ferrari. I said hello to him, and that was it. For me it was sort of like a spa, like *8½*, where I completely cleaned out. I was in good shape, given a clean bill of health by the doctors, finally.

And I thought, Okay. You know what? Maybe Bob's right. Maybe this is the right picture to make. Let's go.

RS: Now let's talk about the film you made.

MS: As I said, when Schrader came into it, he started the film right in the middle, with a man who wanted the title, and couldn't get it because he wouldn't play ball with the wiseguys—not necessarily because of any moral indignation, but because he didn't want to share his money with them. He's going to get hit in the ring and these bastards are coming in and taking the money. They do it with everybody, the character thinks, but why should they do it with me? I'm tougher than they are.

What can you say about a guy like that? You're not giving the audience any reason to like him. He's not being magnanimous, he's not being enlightened about it.

RS: It extends everywhere else. He doesn't see the world clearly. It extends to the woman he apparently loves. It extends to his brother, where he makes these horrendous accusations that he's slept with his wife. Does that come not out of this particular familial situation but out of the fact that life is so tough that no explanation of it can possibly suffice?

MS: That anger and that rage was at the level of my grandparents.

The essence of *Raging Bull:* The most visceral—and sometimes sickening—boxing sequences in movie history.

They didn't know how to take advantage of the American way. All they could do was try to have some dignity and respect within the neighborhood. And that was the struggle of my father, too. My father always wore glasses. He finally told me why. He said his eye was bad because his father slapped him in the head when he was about five or six. I asked why. He said: "I said something that lacked respect."

So they were just lucky to get where they were. And that's the nature of poor people. It has to do with simply trying to hold on to those old values. But Jake's a character who can't hang on to those values because of how he feels about himself. He's in the dressing room and he says something like "I did some bad things in my life." It's this extraordinary guilt that he has, and this anger he has, that he acts out of. We did it as honestly as possible. And it had aspects of my family in there, yes, even though I couldn't fully explain it.

Raging Bull also represented something new to me: an acceptance of where I came from. Having made *New York, New York,* a film that was not received well, I went through a rough period in my life. I came out the other side, and I said to myself, Wait a minute, I can't deny who I am or where I came from. So I embraced my parents again, and they became a part of my life in the films, too. My father's in *Raging Bull.* My mother acted in a lot of the films. They were on the set to help me remember who I am and where I'm from. So I'd been harboring a lot of anger and rage, and I think it just explodes in *Raging Bull.*

RS: In other words, *Raging Bull* is perhaps an expression of not just your own rage, but all that Italian immigrant anger and misunderstanding and desperate struggle to move up. All that is sort of coalesced in this figure?

MS: I think so. I mean, Jake's job is to go into a ring and beat people up while getting beat up. And then there's his own masochism of getting beaten up because he feels so bad about himself. Somebody once wrote that Jake LaMotta fought like he didn't deserve to live. That's it.

RS: Is that at least a little bit like the way you were feeling when De Niro came to visit you in the hospital?

MS: Maybe. I couldn't understand Bob's obsession with it until I went through that rough period of my own. Ever since then—like they always say, but it's true—every day is special. You always have to remember that every day is kind of a gift.

So through Bob I was able to find something about myself again—the difference between the genre director and the director who is trying to be a filmmaker. We worked it out in a sort of unspoken way, meaning that we were never articulate about it. We talked about feelings, we talked about a sense of impotence, about how you couldn't change some things in life, and about trust and what happens when there is a betrayal of that trust.

Up to a certain point in life, you'll kill everybody around you. You're killing yourself. And that's ultimately what I saw in the picture. *Mean Streets* and *Who's That Knocking* are about who I am and where I came from. *Raging Bull* was a break from everything else, and sort of a new beginning—an acceptance of everything.

RS: That's the most enigmatic thing about that movie, the end, when Jake retires from the ring and puts on sixty pounds and does the worst standup routine I've ever seen in my life.

MS: It was based on his actual routine.

RS: And at the end, when he's doing recitations in a little theater—

MS: Which is based on reality, too.

RS: And he's doing—

MS: *On the Waterfront.*

RS: Brando's "contender" speech. We think, Oh my God, he's finding redemption in show business.

MS: Not necessarily show business. No, not at all. I don't know if I had experienced it myself, I don't think I did, but I was hoping that by that point in time Jake would be more accepting of himself. That's all. He's more gentle to himself and to the people around him. If he gets that far in his life, that would be good. It's like the line from *Diary of a Country Priest:* God is not a torturer; he wants us to be merciful with ourselves, just take it easy on ourselves, really. And Jake kind of gets there.

Originally we were going to do one of the speeches from Shakespeare that he was doing in his act. But Michael Powell read the script and said, Shakespeare's all wrong for him. I said, But that's what he actually did. And Powell said, Well, it doesn't mean anything if he actually did that, not for a film. Bob felt that we should tackle the *On the Waterfront* speech because that was our iconography, not the Globe Theatre.

RS: However, it is significant that between the standup routine and "I could have been a contender" he beats his head against the jail wall in an astonishingly brutal way. Is that finally knocking something out of himself, whatever it is?

MS: I think it's the old story of having to reach the lowest level with yourself. I always think of the great Bible story of David having to put his hands on the Ark after reaching a point where he can't get any lower. And then God comes and lifts him up. I felt that was what was happening. We never said that, though; I'm just thinking of it now, because I love the story of David. I always reread it and I'm fascinated at how he could have done so many bad things. He sends Uriah out in the front lines to get killed so he can have the guy's wife. I mean, it's an incredible story, and still he's one of the anointed of God. It has a lot to do with what I feel about humanity: If you're lucky, there's some grace. Whether you make that change yourself, or whether you believe in a supreme being, that's up to you. A lot of it has to do with how you treat yourself.

I think that's what happens in the jail scene. That's why De Niro wanted to hit his head on stone walls. There were all kinds of things we were talking about doing in the jail cell, but he felt that he wanted to do that. Jake had described that to him, acted it out. As I said, Schrader originally was thinking of having him masturbate in the jail. Bob felt that the character wouldn't do that. By the time it all worked itself out, a lot had changed from the draft that Paul had written. It became a really collaborative experience, all of us working together. Bob slamming his head against the wall that way seemed to have the most power. As did his expression, "I'm not an animal. *I'm still human. I'm still human.*"

What he meant, I think, is an animal doesn't have consciousness, is not aware that it's alive. I have a friend who, unfortunately, may have to go through a heart operation. He said, It's like a machine. The machine breaks down, they have to go in there to fix the machine. The only thing is, there's a spirit attached. You're a much more complicated creature than just an animal.

RS: I've only met De Niro once or twice. He seems like a very shy guy. Is he with you?

MS: It depends on the day. It depends on the frequency of our meeting, or the frequency of being around each other. By the time we were doing *Raging Bull* we were like brothers, in the best and worst senses. You know, we had the same trust, but at the same time, there were annoyances: "Is that your jacket on the floor? Would you pick it up?" I have a brother, and I keep projecting that into all these relationships.

Now it's a little different. But in those days he'd be very articulate and get right to the point. "This scene I have a problem with," he'd say, or "I want to try something here." Or "What if he moves a certain way?" I'd say, "Well, show it to me." He'd get up and do it. A number of times I wished I had the camera. I would've shot it immediately if I'd had a camera.

I would say, "The language is the body. The language is right there." I'm thinking particularly of one scene in the jail at the end of *Raging Bull.* We were discussing what Schrader had put in, and he said, "I had this idea." He showed me how he was going to hit his head against the wall. And how he would hit the wall with his hands, punch the wall, in a very slow way. He had done that once before in a room at the Pierre Hotel, but I wasn't really focused on it then. On the island he got up and did it again. When I looked at it there, I saw the scene, I saw the shot, what you see in the film.

The key to that scene, by the way, is how he's forced into the jail cell by those two guards—those are real guards, incidentally. And when we said, "Action," the guards weren't prepared for his ferocity. They got frightened; that's quite real. They toss him in, and the language is over the top, but it's because the anger is so strong, the rage is so strong. We just started rolling the camera without him knowing. Then he calmed down—right before he gets up and hits the wall, I think, right after he sits down. [Cinematographer] Mike Chapman and I, we had two cameras. It was just on a little set, and the wall was treated, of course, but still it was very painful what he was doing. But we had total trust between us at that point. He knew I would turn the camera on at the right time. I just felt it from knowing what he was going to do.

Socially, Bob's usually very quiet. If you're in a meeting with him, it depends on the people. In some cases, after an hour he'll open up and say something. I've

In the arena: Cinematographer Michael Chapman stands at Marty's left hand.

seen him in meetings be eloquent on certain points, defending certain issues or people in a very strong way. Not like a firebrand, but very articulate and very soft-spoken: You know, that's the nature of this character, that's who he is, that's what he knows. I've seen that happen a lot.

Very often when we meet, it takes about forty-five minutes to get into the real stuff [*laughs*]. Usually, he meets me for lunch and it turns out to be three hours. But, finally, *Raging Bull* had a lot to do with trust, even in the editing.

RS: Did Bob remain involved at that stage?

MS: That process has changed in recent years. Now we may run a rough cut of a picture eight or nine or ten times. In those days it was two times and basically the picture was done. I had one cut of *Raging Bull* and I looked at it with Thelma. I knew what to do. We did it. Then we showed it to Irwin Winkler, Bob Chartoff [Winkler's producing partner], and Bob. They looked at it. They had a couple of comments, that was it. Then we screened it one more time.

I think after one screening Bob saw with Irwin, Bob suggested using another take for a certain scene. I didn't think it was right, but I tried it. I still didn't think it was right. Then later, when we were in California, he asked, Do you mind if I look at the takes again of that particular scene with you before you lock the picture? It was the *On the Waterfront* monologue at the end. We did nineteen takes. He still wanted to make sure which one he liked better. He made a case again for the one he liked. So we screened it in a big screening room at Warner Bros.—Stage 25, a giant room. There it was up on the screen. It's the end of the movie. Bob is saying dialogue from an iconic moment in cinema history immortalized by Brando. I had certain ideas about it. Bob leaned to the one that was a little more expressive than the other. We looked at the two takes. I turned him and I said, "I still think the take I have in is the best." And he said, "All right, let it go!" And that was it. You can only have a conversation like that with somebody you trust, because the bottom line is the actor could say, You've got to use that take I want, because the picture was made because of my name.

RS: Right.

MS: That's a big issue. You don't have to work with that person again maybe, but, right now, in the present, on the picture you're working on, anything can happen. So I always use that example as a way of working together, because I do like it when the actor brings something to the table.

RS: Steven Bach, at the end of *Final Cut,* his very good book about the last days of the old United Artists, tells quite a wonderful story about your screening the picture for Andy Albeck, the studio chief, who was about to lose his job over *Heaven's Gate.* He turns to you at the end of the picture and says, "Mr. Scorsese, you're an artist."

MS: That's right. My father was there, too; he came up the aisle and heard that. I remember he was standing next to Albeck, who was very nice to us. It was very interesting, because my father was rather shaken by the film. Albeck, at Cannes before the shoot, said disapprovingly about the script, "The guy beats his wife." We were just dealing with who this character was, and what his world is. There is domestic violence. It was the way it was.

You know, a man goes in a ring, fights, that's his living. He comes out of the ring and he gets into a fight. I mean, that's what he does for his living. How do you expect him to behave? There are certain instincts that are nurtured and move him. I'm not excusing it, this was the world he came from.

My friend Raffaele Donato gave me the novel *Journey to the End of the Night* by Céline. The way he deals with the poor, and the people who live in tenements, it's very accurate, very true.

RS: As far as I know, though I know nothing firsthand about that world.

MS: That's the way people were. I'm telling you, some were very nice, but a lot were like that, the way it's described in that book. When we did *Raging Bull* and *Taxi Driver* and even *Goodfellas* and *Casino,* that is the world we were depicting. It's harder now to make a film like *Departed,* which is insulting to a lot of people. It uses language that's offensive. And it's violent. Maybe ten or twelve years before I made those films, it wasn't that way. Maybe we were a little closer to something like a brutal reality. Or, to put it another way, if you were going to make *The Last Temptation of Christ* today, you'd be more aware of what the reaction would be.

THE KING OF COMEDY

RICHARD SCHICKEL: Is there any way you can relate *Taxi Driver* or *Raging Bull* to *The King of Comedy,* which is ostensibly less terrifying—though not necessarily to me.

MARTIN SCORSESE: It's about violation. It's the way paparazzi shoot pictures of you—not me, but certain actors. It's an attack. The flashes and the shutters of the cameras are bullets. You see that in *Raging Bull.* The ring is like a bullfight. There the fighter is. Everything is being photographed.

King of Comedy was really scary. Bob De Niro gave me that script when I was doing *Alice,* I think, and I didn't get it. I just thought Paul Zimmerman, who did the script, was a wonderful writer. The script is hilarious. But I thought the movie was just a one-line gag: You won't let me go on the show, so I'll kidnap you and you'll put me on the show. Hmm. After I took *Alice, Taxi Driver, New York, New York,* and *Raging Bull* around the world to different festivals, I took a look at the script again and I had a different take on it. I began to understand what Bob's association with it was, what he went through after *Mean Streets,* certainly after *Godfather II*—the adulation of the crowd, and the strangers who love you and have got to be with you and have got to say things.

I once wrote Elia Kazan a note asking if I could be an assistant on his set of *The Arrangement.* I got to meet him for two minutes, because he had come to NYU to speak. He said, No, I don't take assistants. It's a good thing he didn't. I would have been thrown out the first minute. I would have asked, Why are you doing that? Can I see this? When I got to know him later, it was all measured and proper.

RS: Is what you're saying that admiration can quite easily cross the line into a dangerous sort of identification and intrusiveness, the whole sad, sick side of our dysfunctional celebrity system?

MS: The person you identify with, admire, and love—at a certain point, the adulation goes past all bounds. It goes to a level that could go any which way. It can go violent. They can embrace you. They could take you home. That's what I think Bob was understanding.

RS: I think it's among your most disturbing films.

MS: It's very upsetting. It was really unpleasant to shoot, in part because I had pneumonia when I finished mixing *Raging Bull.* My intention was to make *The Last Temptation of Christ.* Then Bob said, Let's do this. We can do it fast in New York. I said, Yeah, I'd really like to do it, I understand it.

By the time I got to shoot it, I found that I didn't like dealing with the story; it crossed so many lines that normally divide private and public lives. And I wasn't a pro. Michael Curtiz could do a picture in four weeks, five weeks, Sam Fuller could do it, Ida Lupino did it. But these were real pros, besides being, I think, some of the most extraordinary artists. Every day they'd be there at a certain time, they'd be there before the crew, they'd be there before the actors, fighting through whatever problems a shot or scene presented. I found I couldn't do that.

I learned a lot about what a pro is through Jerry Lewis, who explained it to me. Immersed in the subject matter, and seeing how much it was going to affect me, I couldn't bring myself to really move quickly. The first night of shooting was the scene with Jerry coming out of the stage door, being mobbed by fans and winding up in a car with Rupert [De Niro]. Two nights go by, I don't use Jerry. I got bogged down in other things, was dragging my feet. On the third night, I got a message that Jerry would like to talk to me. I had said a couple of things to Jerry the night before—asked how he was doing and that kind of stuff. But he was pretty much in his trailer from eight at night until seven in the morning, and I couldn't go in his trailer, he always smoked at the time. So he came to mine. He said, Listen, we're about to do the scene. I know we'll probably get to it tonight. I'm the consummate pro. You tell me to be here at a certain time, then you want me to wait, I'll do that. You're paying for my time. The only thing is now, after two nights of it, I have to ask you, If you think at a certain point in the night that you're not going to get to me, could you let me know? I mean, I could go home early then. I said, Of course. I never thought of it. I had been completely selfish. I had wanted all my toys so I could play with them. And here was this pro.

I'm not saying Bob De Niro was not a pro. But the thing about Bob and me, we were kind of like siblings in a way. What we did was make movies together. By extension, I just thought we were making my movie, and everybody would wait on me—a complete megalomaniac.

RS: In that film there are a couple of scenes that I call cringe scenes. Actually, I have to stop the film, go and get a cup of coffee, and then come back to it. One is where he—

MS: Shows up at the house.

RS: Well, that's the big one. But there's also the scene with Jerry's assistant in his office. You know, "You can just leave the tape," she says. "No, I think I'll stay," he says.

MS: Shelley Hack, who does that, she's great.

RS: She is the woman we run into every time we go in to pitch a book or a movie or whatever.

MS: But she's right. Within the context of what she's doing, she's right. The kid doesn't understand it, and he won't take it. De Niro and I had been mining each other for years, maybe not understanding it, not being articulate about it, but by the time we were into *King of Comedy*, we didn't know where to stop mining. So there were sometimes twenty-five, sometimes forty takes. For me it was a comedy of manners, walking the fine line between love and hostility. The key line is when she says, We think it's interesting. What you should do now is go home, work on the act, get it edited, do some more work, and then bring it back.

And De Niro says, Well, what about Jerry? And she says, I'm telling you that that's what you have to do. She starts to go, and he stops her and says, Excuse me, are you speaking for Jerry? It took twenty-six takes. One had more hostility between them. One was not hostile at all. One had smiles. One was without smiles.

We found it excruciating in a way. We also drew upon a lot of things. There was some improvisation in the picture, like between Margo Winkler, Irwin's wife, as the receptionist. We thought it was like when you're younger and you go to the William Morris Agency, and you become friends with a receptionist. And they had a rapport, so we improvised with that. Then, when he gets thrown out by a security guy and the embarrassment, the humiliation of that.

RS: Some of it really is grotesque.

MS: There is a part of it that's grotesque, you're right about that. But I was trying to capture something. As I was making the film, I realized that a part of me was in that story, and I was forced to confront it. I look back now and I realize why I couldn't make *King of Comedy* back in 1975 when De Niro first gave it to me. I was too close to it. I didn't understand it. And I haven't seen it since I made it. It's too embarrassing.

RS: "Embarrassing" seems to me like the wrong word.

MS: Not embarrassing. It's—

RS: It gives you the creepy crawlies.

MS: Yes, it's very unsettling.

RS: At the risk of repeating ourselves, I've got to say that's really true of that scene with Irwin's wife, Margo, playing the receptionist, not letting the young comic past the gates.

MS: That scene *is* great. It took days. I just couldn't get through it. It took six, seven days to shoot. It was scheduled for two and a half days, and it could have been done in that time. But there was something . . . For example, in the case of the receptionist relationship: If you're trying to get to see Jerry, you have to get past the elevator operator. And then the receptionist and then Jerry's assistant.

RS: What you're saying, I guess, is that there are a lot of subtleties in a seemingly simple scene, a lot of undercurrents the characters themselves aren't fully aware of.

MS: It was so sad. The poor guy wants to get in there. He can't get past her. He tries to make himself likable and yet there's all this extraordinary violence and hostility in him. I can articulate all that now. I couldn't articulate it then.

RS: I can imagine why it was very difficult for you to do.

MS: Oh, it was awful for me, as I said.

RS: But it's interesting, that he, too, like Travis Bickle, gets rewarded for his anti-social behavior.

MS: Turn on TV. That's part of our culture that is just totally accepted. People have a hard time with drugs, go to rehab, then it's all over—forgiving magazine covers and everything else. Our values have gotten skewed because of "forgiving." It's insincere with values like that. I don't feel comfortable anymore—and probably never did—with the values of our society.

Psychotic fan Rupert Pupkin (Robert De Niro) finally fully entraps Jerry Langford (Jerry Lewis), the star he's been stalking in *The King of Comedy* (1982), Scorsese's thoroughly creepy meditation on the celebrity system.

I find that I miss those values where there is a firm line drawn between acceptable and unacceptable behavior. Maybe I'm just getting older and more conservative [*laughs*], but I think in the early eighties, I began to notice the cult of celebrity. And I like making fun of it. It's why I like the *Letterman* show, for example. It has a great deal of tough, ironic humor.

RS: The scene where they invade Jerry's house, I mean, honest to God, for a minute there I thought it was going to be a fantasy scene. It took me a minute to realize it was actually happening.

MS: It's important you say that. You know why you feel that way? Because I made a clear decision when I decided to make the picture to create no difference between the fantasies and the reality. Because if things are going on in your mind, and you can't go to sleep, and you're going over discussions and arguments, it's real. It's really happening. You can rewind. You can erase. The fantasy is real. You want to be a filmmaker, you want to be an actor, you know, it's palpable. It's there. It's tangible. It's not a ripply dissolve.

RS: Was that hard to do, that scene?

MS: Not for the actors. I was the one who was not getting up to speed. The scene was only scheduled for three or four days and went for seven, because there was something so grating and so upsetting, and so irritating and so embarrassing, I just couldn't do it. Luckily we had some very understanding producers.

RS: As I say, I can watch Jake LaMotta, because I never met Jake LaMotta, know nothing of his world. But I do live somewhat in the world of the Rupert Pupkins and Jerrys, and those people. So I have an instant kind of embarrassed understanding . . .

MS: I also was interested in television in the 1950s—*Broadway Open House,* Jerry Lester and Dagmar. The great Steve Allen, who would have amazing guests on, or then Jack Paar, along with *Your Show of Shows* with Sid Caesar and Carl Reiner and Imogene Coca. It was a golden age, I thought, of American television. And we possessed those people. We loved them. If we saw them on the street, it was as if we'd been conversing with them all our lives. And a couple of friends of mine who were students at NYU were also into that world; they worked on the Paar show.

I used to try to get into television with them, and do some game shows and things like that. I soon realized it wasn't for me professionally, but Jack Paar's psyche out there at night, though it lacked the drama that was going on inside that man, was still fascinating. I was very much into that world, and we'd talk about it, and that's why we ultimately came to the decision to cast Jerry Lewis if he would do the picture, because who'd better represent the night talk show host? The thing about it, of course, is that Jerry is the comedian, the actor, singer, cabaret performer, director, talk show host, guest—he did everything in that era.

RS: It's a very nice controlled performance.

MS: It is, but I'm afraid I tortured the poor man. I used to be notoriously late until I realized that no matter what time I got there, I still had to deal with whatever I didn't want to deal with. But I would never be ready until two thirty in the afternoon. The last time I saw Jerry was in Venice. I said, "We should get together more, I'm on time now." He laughed. I finally got a laugh out of him!

But *King of Comedy* is my coming to terms with disappointment, disappointment with the fact that the reality is different from the dream.

RS: I think I know what you're saying, but can you try to distill it? Are you saying that you, Marty, had a similar infatuation about movies, about being famous and all that stuff?

MS: It's like Rupert going to Jerry's house, and his girlfriend says to him, "Well, what are we going to do? What are we going to talk about?" Rupert answers, "These people don't speak the way we speak. They're very witty. They have wonderful things to say all the time." That was his dream of the celebrity life. When I first went to L.A. in 1970, there was a little bit of that need in me—to buy into, participate in, the dream world of celebrity.

RS: Sure.

MS: It's almost as if they are like gods and goddesses—that's the impression they make on you from when you're four or five years old. That's the old story. I hear a lot of actors talk about this, where people come up to them and talk to them, and finally the actor gets mad and says, Please, leave me alone. Then the fan thinks, Well, actors are a different kind of person, and also, What do you think I am? I am a person, too.

RS: That's just grotesque.

MS: It's embarrassing now to think about it, being in a way a part of all that back in the 1970s. We did it to so many people. I guess meeting Peckinpah was quite different from meeting King Vidor, let's say, or George Cukor, who was so encouraging. He and Peter Bogdanovich and Sam Fuller signed my DGA [Directors Guild of America] card.

AFTER HOURS

RICHARD SCHICKEL: You've said to me that you thought *After Hours* was your most Hitchcockian film.

MARTIN SCORSESE: The picture has direct references to Hitchcock's style, but as a parody. I also mentioned a connection to Kafka, and I got pummeled for saying it. The picture was torn apart by some.

It was a parody of the visual interpretations of Hitchcock—how guilt plays out a great deal in the camera moves and the cuts.

RS: Can you explain that?

MS: Well, in *After Hours,* when the character walked into a room and it was dark, and he turned on the light, it was important to take a close-up of the light switch turning on—click—as if you expected something to happen but it didn't. It created a sense of foreboding—until finally he screamed out into the street. He just wanted to come downtown, he just wanted to make love, did he have to die for it? Yes, he did. [*Laughs.*] He had to die for it.

Maybe it has a lot to do with me. It's about guilt; even if it's something that I reason out, I still feel bad. So the only thing is to deal with it and just move on. You can't run away from it.

Marty directs Griffin Dunne in *After Hours* (1985), an underrated black comedy which turns lower Manhattan into the Lower Depths, as a mild-mannered clerk looking for a little sexual action is almost killed by the forces of anarchical modernism.

I think there was a lot that wasn't said in the film about that. All the camera moves are reflections of the character's own dread and guilt. I keep getting drawn back to Hitchcock movies like *The Wrong Man,* which I used as an example for [cameraman] Michael Chapman and everybody else on *Taxi Driver.* The way Henry Fonda is in the line at the insurance office, the way the camera moves as a woman sees him and he reaches into his coat. She thinks it's a gun, but we know it's an insurance policy. It's the way the camera moves and it's the way he edits.

I had the cast and crew look at it again for *Aviator,* for the scenes that have to deal with Howard Hughes's obsessive behavior. It's when Henry Fonda sits in the cell the first night. You see the corner. You see the ceiling. You see the lock. It's the nature of the framing and the pace of the cutting.

RS: Which gives it such a powerful sense of entrapment. I recently did a DVD commentary on *The Wrong Man* and I had forgotten how much religious iconography it contains—but almost casually referenced. It has to be Hitchcock's most overtly Catholic film.

MS: It probably is. I was just going to say that I'm probably attracted to his work a lot because of the Catholicism. It's not overt to me, but it's there.

Actually, I like some of the minor films, like *Dial M for Murder.* It's theater. The actors are sitting in a room talking, but yet at a certain point in the dialogue the camera angle changes very slightly. I always tell film students to study that, to look at where the camera changes. How does it change? What's the image size? What does that mean psychologically and emotionally? What does that make the audience feel? The audience doesn't seem to notice it—but it makes itself felt.

Again, one of my favorite scenes in *Psycho* is when Martin Balsam is interviewing Anthony Perkins. There's one shot that's sort of strange, where Balsam tells him to lean over and look at the name in the book, and the camera is sort of suddenly looking up at Anthony Perkins's throat as he leans over. Watch the angle, watch the way he cuts, on which line of dialogue, and where Balsam begins to figure out there's something funny in the story, and where Perkins starts to realize the guy knows there's something funny.

Even the business about turning on the switch of the Bates Motel lights. Balsam says, But your lights aren't on. Perkins says, Oh!—then click—you see the lights come on. The insert is less than a second, I bet you, but when the lights come on, it's like a slap. The repressed violence there is in that turning on of that light switch. I find that kind of thing both interesting and entertaining.

RS: I saw *After Hours* first, I think, in a screening room. There was a fair-sized crowd. It was a very jolly experience. But I found that when I watched it alone at home I wasn't laughing so much. It seems like a comedy, because a lot of truly unexpected stuff happens that makes you laugh—but it's not really funny because what's happening to the main character is really pretty damned dire. I think when we talked earlier, you called it a descent into hell.

MS: Yeah, yeah. [*Laughs.*]

RS: I guess he is someone who's kind of on the edge—I mean, he's got this dull little job and he'd like to be something that he isn't. He goes into this place where he thinks maybe he could be transformed. But he isn't.

MS: Transformed into what, though? That's the thing. There's an emptiness there in that world that he's discovering, and there's a desperation. In my mind, it's reflective of what's all around us, the menace we don't usually notice. Looking at it as a black comedy, I was thinking, This could happen to me. Maybe it has.

I did a commercial for American Express, where I'm complaining about snapshots I took at a kid's birthday party. My associate director saw it and he said, I loved the commercial. He said, It's like being back at the monitor with you when we're shooting. And I thought, You take yourself so seriously.

But you know the damned thing is, you've got to be serious about making a picture. Yet you've still got to have that sense of humor.

RS: What's going on in *After Hours* is really "Oh, my God, this is the worst evening." Yet it starts out really—

MS: Promising. But there's also a technical thing about the film. I always liked those two farces by Allan Dwan—*Up in Mabel's Room* and *Getting Gertie's Garter.* I liked the way their multiple stories enfolded upon each other, and how these people found themselves in these ridiculous situations, with everybody speaking so fast and moving around. To me, if you put any kind of reality into it—I mean, who cares about Gertie's garter?—you're not going with the game. You've got to go with the game.

RS: I think that's true. In this film there is a logical step-by-step descent, no? It starts with an innocent encounter in a lunchroom. And by the end—

MS: —he winds up encased inside some statue. I'm always interested in the ancient world, what it was like to be living in the Roman Empire or among the Greeks before Christianity—their relationship to their gods, and, in a sense, their relationship to life; their sense of the chaos in the world and their acceptance of it. I read a lot about the ancient world, for pleasure. I get into that mindset, and understand that the world is chaos, and understand that there may or may not be gods. And if there are gods, they're not really interested in us very much. I understand the cruelty and understand that death can happen any second.

That's the key thing to me—that idea of being a pawn, that the gods really don't care and we've got to make a life in spite of that. It comes down to accepting the reality. Rather than complain about it, we deal with it. We try to live a morally good life on this basis.

RS: So that's what *After Hours* is about.

MS: In a sense. It should just be a good black comedy, and you shouldn't have to think about this. But that's the impulse behind a lot of the things I do: I just find it fascinating to imagine what it would be like meeting an ancient now. I'd like to see what their similarities to us are as human beings, what they cared about, what they felt was right and wrong.

THE COLOR OF MONEY

RICHARD SCHICKEL: *The Color of Money* seems to me your most conventional picture to date: a sequel starring a major older star and a younger one very much on the rise. How did that happen?

MARTIN SCORSESE: My agent, Harry Ufland, helped put the movie together with Mike Ovitz, then, of course, the famous superagent. Paul Newman liked *Raging Bull* and wrote me a letter. So it was basically worked around Newman, that's how we got it made. By the time the film was being edited, Tom Cruise had come out in *Top Gun* and he was suddenly a big star. The film came in a day under schedule and a million dollars under budget and it did very well.

RS: How did Tom Cruise get involved?

MS: Michael Ovitz at that time was representing Cruise. He called me and said, "Why don't you use Tom Cruise?" Cruise had been in [cinematographer] Michael Chapman's film *All the Right Moves* [as a high school football player fighting with his coach]. And I thought he was very good. I said, "Sure, let's put him in as the young pool player."

Still, there were issues. You know, *The Hustler* [by Robert Rossen, which

In *The Color of Money* (1986), Paul Newman returned as an older version of Fast Eddie Felson, whom he played in Robert Rossen's memorable *The Hustler* of 1961. This time he was rewarded with a long-delayed, long-deserved Academy Award.

starred Newman as the young pool shark, Eddie Felson] is a masterpiece, so I couldn't emulate that. But I always loved Newman, and he was giving us a great chance.

At that point my main goal was to try to get *The Last Temptation of Christ* made. I knew I had to make it Italian style, in the style of Ermanno Olmi, Pasolini—

RS: Especially Pasolini. It put me in mind of his Christ movie—

MS: Especially Pasolini. Exactly. And the *Trilogy of Life* films. Anyway, I was out in L.A. and Ovitz had me come to his house. He told me he wanted to represent me. He explained to me that I could get paid for what I do [*laughs*]. He literally said that: "You know, you can get paid for this." Because at that point I never got a salary, I didn't care. Sometimes I just took scale. In *Raging Bull,* De Niro and I split our salaries, out of a bond of trust.

RS: Really?

MS: We just did it. We didn't care that much about our salaries; we wanted to make the movie. But in any event, Mike said, "What do you want done most?" And I said, *"The Last Temptation of Christ."* And he smiled. Mike was a genius at what he did, and a person who likes challenges. He said, "I'll get it made for you." I didn't think he would. I didn't think he could.

Within a few months, right before I signed with Ovitz's agency, he said, "You know, Tom Pollock has just become the head of Universal. And he signed a deal with Garth Drabinsky, of Cineplex Odeon Theaters from Canada. And they want to make the movie, for a price. What's the price?" The producer was with me, and she said about six or seven million dollars, whatever it was. Ovitz said, "They want to do it." I remember, we were on our way to Tahiti to visit with Marlon Brando. He'd invited me to his island; he wanted to make a movie. So we stopped over in L.A. and had lunch with Pollock and then we flew off to Tahiti. We came back, had another lunch with Pollock. And by that time, the picture was almost a reality. I couldn't quite believe it. I mean, I was a little nervous the night before I met Pollock. I remember Ovitz called me and said, "How are you feeling? Get in there tomorrow and do your lunch meeting, and give them your idea." Usually I was burning to tell the story, and I would talk for hours about it. But, sometimes, you know, you're just down. You just know how long the odds are. I said to Ovitz, "I don't know. I really don't know if I can . . ." He said, "What do you mean, you don't know? You're going to go in and you're going to tell them you're going to make the best picture ever made. That's how you do it." It wasn't a pep talk, really, but he helped realign my thinking.

RS: I often find that with something you really want, just before you pitch it, you feel like hell. You doubt yourself.

MS: Oh! [*Laughs.*] You'll never do it!

RS: I don't want to be here. I don't even know why I wanted to write this, or to make this.

MS: Maybe it's a mistake.

RS: I mean, it does happen.

MS: Michael, though, was very unique. He can grab your attention, convince you of practically anything.

RS: Yes.

MS: In any event, Pollock was an interesting man. He wanted to make special kinds of films. In two years he made *Temptation of Christ*, *Do the Right Thing*, and *Born on the Fourth of July*. Three pretty strong statements.

RS: Yes. Tom is a very interesting man.

MS: And Garth Drabinsky was a very unique character. Do you know him?

RS: I never met him, but I heard a lot about him. Didn't he go to jail?

MS: I think he might have. I don't know. But that was his moment. He had the biggest theater chain in Canada and America. And the only thing I had to do was go to Vancouver to have a press conference for the film, which is what I did. And go to Toronto for the opening. Garth was really great with us.

RS: He liked you and respected you.

MS: A very interesting man. But that's how *Temptation* got made.

RS: *The Color of Money* made some money, right?

MS: It made a lot of money.

RS: And finally it got Paul Newman his Oscar.

MS: It did. Richard Price was nominated, Paul, Mary Elizabeth Mastrantonio, and Boris Leven. I wrote the *Goodfellas* script with Nick Pileggi after that and was ready to shoot it, but then I got the money to do *Last Temptation*. We did that and then came back and finished *Goodfellas*.

Mary Elizabeth Mastrantonio gets up close and personal with the director.

RS: What was Newman like to work with?

MS: It was a great experience. We shaped the story around him, to emphasize those qualities that he had in him, at that point in his life.

RS: Which were?

MS: He was a man who was getting older, he understood the nature of it. Fast Eddie Felson was at a point in his life where he had to accept a challenge, go back to what he had done.

He had to stop gambling. He had become a different kind of hustler in a way, selling liquor. But he couldn't resist the joy of the game. I mean, not just pool, but livening up the game of life, which is the real gamble. But he had also to deal with his limitations as an older person. I wanted it to be a story of an older person who corrupts a young person, like a serpent in the garden of innocence.

RS: I see.

MS: The corruption of the younger person is really what I was interested in. Richard Price, the writer, and Paul formed a companionship working on scenes together, rewriting in rehearsals. The whole film was rehearsed. Paul wanted to rehearse like a play. I had never done a play, so he took me to a rehearsal hall. Basically I blocked the scenes there and the movie was shot very quickly because of that. All the pool games were designed in about two or three days in September and we were way ahead. The rehearsals with the actors were word-for-word from the script. It was a different way of working for me, very different.

RS: Did you find any constraint in that way of working?

MS: Not really. Don't forget, it's a sequel to a very strong picture. So you can only go so far.

RS: What was Tom Cruise like in those days?

MS: Wonderful. Enthusiastic and, I thought, a damned good actor.

RS: I think he's a wonderful actor.

MS: My mother and father were there—we were shooting in Chicago—and he became good friends with them. Very often, years later, he would go to their apartment on Third Avenue and 19th Street and have dinner in their apartment. He would just go and hang out with them. They loved him.

RS: I met him two or three times and found him very agreeable.

MS: I'm telling you, the kid was great. And in *The Color of Money* he was wonderful. And we had a great time. With Mary Elizabeth Mastrantonio, the three of us together working. I used to tell him about Stanley Kubrick all the time, about *Barry Lyndon* and other movies. Then, of course, he got to work with him in *Eyes Wide Shut.*

RS: I recently was reading a review of some star bio about him in *The New York Times.* It said that maybe Tom Cruise is looking for a father figure, because he had a very bad relationship with his dad.

MS: It's interesting he played that part in *Magnolia* then.

RS: Right. I forgot that.

MS: You know, about the father. He did a great job in that.

RS: Yes. Maybe the way he surrendered himself to Kubrick on *Eyes Wide Shut* had something to do with a father figure, too.

MS: Maybe. But I found him very warm, with a great sense of family.

THE LAST TEMPTATION OF CHRIST

RICHARD SCHICKEL: Frankly, I had a lot of trouble with *The Last Temptation of Christ* when I first saw it.

MARTIN SCORSESE: Well, it's a long picture.

RS: I'm a born atheist, I mean.

MS: Yeah, okay.

RS: I liked the movie better when I saw it again. I haven't seen it for some time, though.

MS: I haven't, either. I'm going to wait.

RS: You said that as a kid you loved all those sword-and-sandal epics, like *The Silver Chalice.*

MS: Yes. But they're bad.

RS: Perhaps, but I've always remembered *The Silver Chalice* because of the way it's designed.

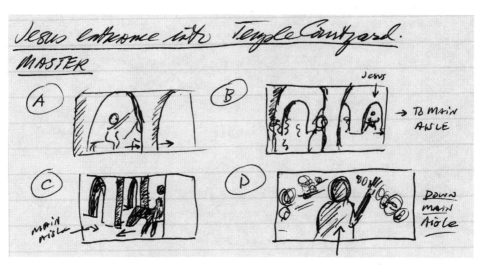

Marty's sketches for Jesus's entrance into the Temple in *The Last Temptation of Christ,* a film he had obsessed over making since the beginning of his career.

MS: Exactly. It's not a good film, but I love the look of it. We were working class, we didn't go to theater. We went to movies. That was the first time I saw real theatrical design in a movie. It was fantastic.

RS: What I was getting at was that somehow you were at least thinking about all those big, corny American biblical epics, very much a part of the 1950s moviegoing experience, when you made *Last Temptation,* even though it was a totally different kind of film.

MS: Always, yes.

RS: It's interesting to me how you got from *The Robe* and *The Silver Chalice* to *Last Temptation.*

MS: Well, by seeing them many times, and by accepting their conventions. And then realizing that the time was right, in the early eighties, for another approach— just to deal with the idea of what Jesus really represented and said and wanted, which was compassion and love. To deal with this head-on. To do it in such a way that I would provoke and engage the audience.

The only way you can do that is to not make your films look and sound like the old biblical films. In those films, the characters were speaking with British accents. The dialogue was beautiful, in some cases, and the films look beautiful. They were pageants. But they had nothing really to do with our lives, where you "make up for your sins at home and in the streets, and not in church." The transgressions you have to undo are with people. It's not about going to church on Sunday. Very often people think, I'll go to church on Sunday and I'll be okay. They know Jesus suffered, but they don't really ask what the suffering was for. I was upset when *Last Temptation* came out and people were claiming it was harming their faith. I never want to injure anybody's faith. If you have faith, that's a good thing. Whether I have my faith or not, personally, is a constant struggle. But there's a difference between faith and evolving in a spiritual way, a big difference.

Faith, a certain kind of faith, is a dangerous thing. If you take faith to heart and it affects in a positive way the way you treat people around you, that's great. The question of faith also brought me to make *Kundun*—about the Dalai Lama—the idea of a man or a woman leading a life of spirituality, what that is. The moment I went into preparatory seminary, I was only fifteen or so, I was determined. It was one way of escaping the hard world I was born into, to separate myself, to not have to deal with the moral issues of the streets and what I was involved in there.

But I shocked myself. I couldn't even take the first minor step toward the spiritual life that I had in mind. I was very disappointed in myself about not being able to take that step.

Jesus lived in the world. He wasn't in a temple. He wasn't in church. He was in the world. He was on the street. The picture I wanted to make was about Jesus on Eighth Avenue, something like Pasolini's *Accattone* [about a pimp attempting to reform, with tragic consequence]. The pimp represents all of us. He's our mortal condition. He dies. It's like Jesus when he dies, in a sense.

RS: I think there's something of Pasolini's Saint Matthew Passion movie in your film, too.

MS: Oh, there certainly is. I loved that film. Pasolini's *Saint Matthew* is absolute poetry—the idea of an engaging Christ who provokes and is tough. You know, I've come to bring a sword, I've come to set father against son and mother against daughter-in-law. It's a very strong piece and completely surprising, and has an immediacy you really feel.

But to go back to my idea of a modern-day Christ film: It would be black-and-white, and we were going to set his crucifixion on the New York docks. The images would have been good—in the tenements with people in black suits and white hallways. Palm Sunday and the crucifixion under the West Side Highway. In cinema verité style. Then, of course, I saw the Pasolini, and that was the top of the line. He understood it—faith versus a spiritual change that you have to undergo in yourself, whether there is or is not a God.

Marty of Arabia: The director on a Moroccan location for *Last Temptation*. It was, he says, the most physically arduous picture he ever made.

RS: To me there's something breathtaking about the film's basic conflict. I know it's not your idea.

MS: It's [Nikos] Kazantzakis's—the whole thing. Kazantzakis's idea, a beautiful one, is that the gift of life is a gift from God, so he is tempted—the ultimate temptation—to become us, just to live a normal life. The idea, of course, is that Jesus is all God and all man. That is the dogma, and that's the way I approached the film. I thought that if God is removed from us, is on a piece of wood somewhere, on a stained-glass window, a lot of people misunderstand those images. We don't, as Catholics, worship them. They're representations of the suffering.

And this is what Kazantzakis was dealing with, I think: If Christ is God, and man, too, then where's the sacrifice? When is the moment when he says, I've caused trouble everywhere, and now I'm going to have to be scourged and crucified, and I don't want that to happen. God could easily say, Well, there's not going to be a problem. I know what happens after death, and I know what happens with pain. But as a human being alone, Christ would have had to make the decision.

RS: I think that moment occurs in the scene with Harvey Keitel as Judas, where Christ asks what good his martyrdom is going to accomplish. I think it's a fabulous scene.

MS: That *is* the wonderful scene for me, when Jesus and Judas are in a granary and Jesus turns to him and says, "Isaiah came to me last night." "What did he say?" Judas asks. Which in itself is kind of funny, that they're living in a world where Isaiah could actually come to them at night. Or Jacob could struggle with the angel. And Jesus says, "I'm to be the Lamb, to be sacrificed. I'm to be crucified." And Judas, who has been following Jesus all along, thinking he was going to make a revolution, looks at him and says, "What good is that going to do?" He literally says that. What good is your being killed going to do for us?

RS: It strikes me as a very good question.

MS: Exactly. So Judas is speaking for all of us. What does that sacrifice ultimately mean? These were things that were just delicious to work with. It's the only word I can think of. If I had been allowed to edit it a little longer, maybe I'd have trimmed it down a bit ... But, being so close to it, I'm more negative than other people might be.

I loved the idea. I'm not saying I did justice to that idea in the film. But I understood that it had to work by way of a style so different from the biblical epics of the fifties and early sixties. Sometimes, I'd say, Oh, I wish I had three extra days, or I wish I had $2 million more. But we had to keep it small scale.

RS: Getting back to that crucial scene between Jesus and Judas—

MS: There's no doubt that was the key. That's why I thought it was so interesting in Kazantzakis's book that Judas is almost the hero. The whole concept was that the betrayer, Judas, was the key player, because if there is to be a sacrifice, and if there's to be this extraordinary redemption, then everybody around Jesus is part of a plan. Nobody's to be blamed, nobody's to be cursed, it's all got to happen. And by the way, Judas, you're the one who's going to have to be the fall guy. He's the only one Jesus can trust, so he's got to betray Jesus. And make him understand that he would be damned for the rest of eternity as the worst person in the world.

RS: Betrayal is one of your great overarching themes—maybe the most important of them.

MS: Remember that they called Bob Dylan Judas. [*Laughs.*] I mean, that word has power. That's one of the reasons I made the Dylan film [*No Direction Home,* his documentary about the singer-songwriter]—I heard him called Judas. I wondered what the nature of his betrayal was. My father, the stories of betrayal from the Old World, they helped shape me. These things obsessed me. And so, finally, in *The Departed,* it's all betrayal.

Then there's the whole question of the crucifixion, which implies a sort of acceptance of death. Well, yes, he was God. So there was no suffering, there was no problem. But if he's man as well, man suffers, is afraid of death. How does one deal with that issue? If you have the body of a man, how do you deal with the urges and feelings of a man?

RS: Certainly in the early passages of the film, he's very reluctantly embracing the notion that he's anything but a man, isn't he?

MS: Exactly. I thought that was interesting, too, and another Kazantzakis idea, that slowly the plan is revealed to him by God. Now, one could look at that and say, Well, that's a person slowly losing his mind.

RS: Indeed.

MS: I get fascinated by certain side issues, like imagery, in this case the fashioning of the crown of thorns, which wasn't in the book. The Passion Week, though, was something that had to lead to the real story, the temptation on the cross. I wanted to get past Passion Week as quickly as possible. But I couldn't, or I should say I wouldn't. I had to show him being presented to the crowd. We had to see the scourging. The viewer had to see the beating by the soldiers, all that suffering leading up to the crucifixion. I think that's all right. There are a lot of things I would have done differently now, but that was done with a real passion. I think that's why I embraced the story, why I was burning to make it. Keitel was burning for it, too. So was Barbara Hershey, who had given me the book when we were making *Boxcar Bertha.* In fact, the code name for the film was "Passion" when we were shooting and editing it.

RS: Surely, of all the pictures you've ever made, that's got to have been the hardest one to walk into a studio boss's office and say, Here's what I want to do.

MS: I had to learn to accept the fact that I could not get bigger, more expansive films made, the way I got them made in the seventies. I tried in 1983 with *The Last Temptation of Christ.* I pushed the studio to the limit, and the studio backed out on Thanksgiving Day. Right then I started thinking about what else I could do in life. Brian De Palma and I were talking about it one night. He had just shown *Scarface* and the Hollywood audience didn't like it. He said, "What are we doing here? What could we do, become teachers maybe?" I said, "I don't know. What the hell are we going to do? We can't go on like this. They don't want to make pictures that we want to make." We were in Hugo's restaurant on Santa Monica.

RS: I know it well.

MS: Then I realized I honestly didn't know exactly what else I could do. I wished I had learned to write music. I wished I could express myself in language and literature. Or that I painted. I took some time, went to China, did a symposium there in 1984. I found the script of *After Hours* and realized I had to teach myself how to do lower-budget pictures, and try to finally get *Last Temptation* made for a lower budget.

RS: What else could you do?

MS: Barry Diller asked why I wanted to make the film. We were in a hotel in New York. I said, "Because I want to get to know Jesus better." He smiled, then said, Okay. He went with it for a while. Then, at a certain point, he told me, Marty, the reality is that U.A. theaters wouldn't show the picture. I'm sorry, I'm going to have to pull the plug on it, because if we spend $18–19 million on a movie, it has to be showing someplace.

I became friends with Jeff Katzenberg and Michael Eisner. They had left Paramount at that point and had formed Touchstone. After I did *After Hours,* I got a deal at Touchstone. We did *Color of Money, New York Stories.* They felt *Last Temptation* was unfeasible. So I realized, Okay, you can't do it for $19 million, you've got to do it for five. I don't know how to put it in a nice way, but if they're fighting you, you have to fight back another way, you've got to be a guerrilla, come in under the radar.

If you look at the crucifixion scene in *Last Temptation,* you'll see that every shot is cut from one to the other as designed on paper. It was part of shooting so low-budget, so fast, that I had to actually visualize the whole picture in my head, like *Boxcar* and *Mean Streets.*

Another example: When Jesus is in the desert, I said that because of the outgoing scene, for the incoming scene he should be coming in screen left. I knew that would work, because I saw it in my head. If you're pressed for time you've got to get it immediately.

Crucifixion: Willem Dafoe was a powerful Jesus in this alternative to *The Greatest Story Ever Told.* But the film's sober virtues were buried by the controversy it engendered.

I tried to be very specific in lighting. I had some scenes that, unfortunately, I had planned for night. I had to shoot them in daytime. I didn't see any rushes—there were no projectors. Michael Ballhaus [the cinematographer] was so depressed sometimes—but he kept our spirits up.

But Thelma Schoonmaker was calling us up—it wasn't easy for us to make phone calls from Morocco, where we were filming. I'd ask, What does it look like? Does this or that happen in the scene? She'd offer her opinions. I did the film blind.

RS: I'm interested, of course, in the firestorm that blew up when the picture went into release. You probably thought it would be a controversial movie. But were you at all prepared for the outburst? I remember going to the movie and seeing grim Catholics marching around, carrying crucifixes and hateful placards.

MS: I had no idea. I thought there would be some people who would be set against it completely. But I also thought it would open up a healthy discussion.

RS: Really? Something as polite as that.

MS: Let's think about the nature of Jesus and what Jesus represents in our lives and the world and what the essence of Christianity is. I don't know what the answer is, but let's talk about it, and look inside ourselves to how we live.

I think that was something Rossellini hit upon in *Europa '51*. I've been told it was based on Simone Weil. He had made the film about Saint Francis of Assisi, from the medieval period. He asked, What if there was a modern saint? And was led to her.

She ultimately comes to the realization that it's a question of one step at a time, and that literally the person next to you may be the one in need. That's what she's there for. That's what we must do. I thought we could discuss that. I thought we could do that without making it the center of a media circus. Yet some people said that I was just aiming for box office because of the controversial nature of the picture.

RS: If I ever saw a movie that had no box office written on it . . .

MS: I thought it would get enough people interested to break even. That was it. I was in debt for years after that. I only came out of debt by doing *Cape Fear*. I put everything into it we had. The same thing happened with *Gangs of New York*. I overcame those debts after making *The Departed*. It took that long. But that's the gamble I take—everything goes!

RS: Did you really think you were going to get your money back on either of those?

MS: Of course not. Paul Schrader [who wrote the screenplay] knew we would have trouble. He was much more prescient that way. I'm always very much of the moment. He said people would be upset. I didn't think so.

RS: I suspect it had something to do with the fact that everybody knew you were raised Catholic. So for you to poke your head up and say, You know, let's consider this whole matter in a nontheological, or, rather, a nonideological way—I think they were lying in wait for you. The church has a keen eye for apostates. Surely you had some hint that you were going to get a reaction.

MS: I was hoping to get some thoughtful reaction, but I didn't make the film for money. I was just burning to make it.

RS: I know that.

MS: I expected *some* controversy. But I expected it to be intelligent. I expected discussion and dialogue.

RS: Not in America, pal.

MS: It was amazing.

RS: You were at the beginning of the period we're in now. The fundamentalists, both Catholic and Protestant, were already feeling their oats at that moment.

MS: It was, of course, condemned by the church from the pulpit, and they sent out their army, so to speak.

RS: But I certainly saw some very cretinous people picketing it outside the theaters.

MS: I know.

RS: So, all that came as a considerable shock to you?

MS: Very much so. By the time I appeared on *Nightline* on TV, where I was supposed to confront our critics, I realized what was happening and I stopped. Just let the film play. I was just satisfied that the picture had been made.

RS: It's quite a good picture; I was almost surprised that I felt that way.

MS: I hope so. I think it could have been cut more. We didn't have enough time, Thelma and I, because we had to release it pretty early. But I was satisfied. We had gone through an experimental process successfully. And it became a religious experience for all of us. I really mean that.

It was the worst shoot; you can't imagine. Joe Reidy, the assistant director, could tell you. Harvey Keitel could tell you, Willem Dafoe, Barbara Hershey,

Michael Ballhaus, all the actors. We had a very low budget, so we were stuck all the time. There were weather problems, too.

By the time I finished editing the film, I didn't know quite what they expected to make of the experience. Was it, as I told Barry Diller, that I want to get to know Jesus better? But after *The King of Comedy*, I wanted to go back to my own interests. I wanted to look into the development of the Gospels. The reality was that they chose which books were going to stay and which weren't. Why were those books written? How did some books go into the New Testament, and others not? The Gospel of Judas has only recently been found—but it was mentioned in other Gnostic gospels. A lot of these books were written eighty, ninety, a hundred years after the events they describe.

RS: That has always bothered me, too.

MS: With God, yes, you're talking about revelation and that's what we have to deal with. But we wanted to talk about those other things—about Jesus, Judas, Mary, too. At the end of *The South Bank Show*, when Melvyn Bragg asked, "What did you think they'd be most concerned about?" Paul Schrader said, "The dirty parts." Funny.

RS: What dirty parts?

MS: Well, the concept that Jesus would have sexual feelings.

RS: Oh, that.

MS: This was the big issue. That's what the critics claim it was.

RS: But this character is, for better or worse, half man and half God.

MS: Oh, no, he's full man and full God. You have to be careful, Christologically speaking.

RS: Whatever.

MS: That's the beauty of it. Let's accept him as completely God and completely man, and therefore he's going to feel everything a man feels.

RS: Of course.

MS: As I said earlier, some people would say, "Well, he's God, therefore he's on the cross and he'll get through death all right." But the point is he's going to be afraid of death because he's a man.

RS: And if he's a man, that particular death is going to hurt.

MS: Of course. That's why I directed as I did the scene when he raises Lazarus, and Lazarus takes his hand and pulls him into the tomb, and he's afraid to go in. Lazarus has said, This is where you're going. You're coming with me. Do you want to go through this? Jesus doesn't know what his role is until it's revealed to him slowly.

I think the key to it, as I also said earlier, was the relationship of Jesus and Judas. Why did he do what he did? For thirty pieces of silver? Thirty pieces of silver is nothing. It's not for the money. Something else had to have gone down, was going on. And then it goes back to this issue of loyalty and friendship.

One of the first films my father took me to see was [Sam Fuller's] *I Shot Jesse James,* in which Jesse's best friend kills him. My father was always talking about loyalty.

RS: I didn't see that film till fairly recently, but I liked it a lot—belatedly.

MS: Me, too. And this betrayal led me eventually to *The Departed.*

RS: Would your father have thought *Jesse James* was a western you might enjoy, or do you think he knew what was going to happen in that movie?

MS: He just thought it was a western. I wanted to see it. It had a great title. I was about six years old.

RS: So, were you satisfied when *Last Temptation* came out? I mean, forget the controversy—did it in some way do what you wanted it to do? Or did the controversy spoil it all?

MS: Something odd happened. The physical process of making the film, editing it—putting the man on the cross, the crowds coming in—was so intense I feel I just missed grasping it all. It got out of my hands. The process itself removed me from what I thought I would experience.

But it led to *Kundun,* which led to *Bringing Out the Dead,* which is leading to *Silence* [a film about Jesuit missionaries in feudal Japan—a film Scorsese has been struggling to get made for many years]. As I said, there are certain things I would have liked to have done better. The night I was on *Nightline* I realized there's something very special about faith, for everyone. Yet I wasn't intending to shake anybody's faith.

RS: I know that.

MS: Apparently people felt threatened. To them, there was an issue that was obviously much more important than whether it was a good movie or not. I finally realized that with all this clamor, it would be very difficult for anybody to engage in what I hoped the picture would create. Andrew Greeley tried in *The New York Times,* and a few other people wrote interesting things about it. But in most cases it was just dismissed. And that was that.

RS: Still, we shouldn't forget that in the movie Jesus is an interesting character, and he's nicely played by Willem Dafoe.

MS: Willem did a great job.

RS: Coming to it with my total lack of regard for religiosity—he engaged my sympathy, as does Harvey as Judas in his way.

MS: Yes.

RS: And I think there is, if you will, a kind of wonderful screenwriter's logic to that business. It's a neat twist and makes perfect narrative sense.

MS: Yes, and he said, "Oh, by the way, if I represent salvation, you'll have to represent the antithesis of that for eternity."

RS: For all eternity.

MS: All eternity. You'll be the one that they claimed hanged himself. And Dante will put you in hell in a certain place. It's fascinating. You know, I've seen parts of it on TV a couple of times. Maybe one day I'll screen it again. It's not a film I have bad memories of in any way. It's just when it opened, when all the controversy developed, that it was a nightmare. There was nothing I could say or do. I also couldn't be shaken, because I believed in what I did. In the end, I think *Last Temptation* was out of my grasp because I naïvely thought I was supposed to have taken some sort of a spiritual journey with it. But it may have been the wrong material to deal with in that way—dealing with Jesus as a man, the carnality, the physicality.

NEW YORK STORIES

RICHARD SCHICKEL: Let's talk about your contribution to *New York Stories* ["Life Lessons," an episode in an anthology film in which Nick Nolte plays a womanizing painter, both exploitative and needy of his protégée-lover-assistant (Rosanna Arquette)]. There's a sort of weird charm to that movie, but it also works out pretty brutally.

MARTIN SCORSESE: It does. It is funny, because he takes himself so seriously. Let's assume that he's a great artist—that's what the story tells us—which means he has to take himself seriously. Yet I think he's amused by having to do so.

RS: Oh, really?

MS: I think the one scene where he looks up to the floor above him, when she's up there with another young man, and the opera is playing, I mean he's just enjoying that, I think.

RS: What's he enjoying?

MS: He's enjoying the emotional turmoil, maybe the pain of the whole situation, which he has induced.

Marty's contribution to *New York Stories* (1988), an anthology film, was "Life Lessons," about an egomaniacal, sexually avaricious action painter (Nick Nolte) and his protégée-lover (Rosanna Arquette). The piece was funny and, at times, quite savage. The other directors involved in the project were Woody Allen and Francis Ford Coppola.

And ultimately it feeds into his work, you know. At the end, when he looks at that beautiful young woman behind the bar and we sense that he has to make a play for her, Nick Nolte turned to me before we shot it and he said, "Why don't we give this guy a break?" I said, "No, he's going to have to go with her."

RS: And what was the break he would have imagined giving him?

MS: To pass that one up and not get into a situation where he gets into a relationship with someone not on his level. It's simply not going to work. They're young. The women have a whole life to get through before there's a chance at an equal relationship.

RS: You're talking about his mentoring relationship with Arquette's character.

MS: Yes, exactly. I think he's done it repeatedly. And I think he's in a cycle in which he's doing that and which ultimately feeds his work. I think he feels he has to suffer to work.

RS: So he has to have these hopeless relationships?

MS: Hopeless, yes. I think so.

RS: That's an interesting way of looking at it.

MS: And also, you know, they're very beautiful young women.

RS: Yes, they are.

MS: And it's very enjoyable, up to a point. And then he has to go through that pain of the separation and find another one. But that's what Nick meant when he said, "Should we give him a break and not have him go with this new young lady at the end?" and I said, "No, that's not the story." He's not going to learn for a while longer. Maybe he never will. But maybe that's what he needs to work. Or at least that's what he tells himself. Maybe it's about feeling that emotion, feeling that you're alive, even if it's negative. And that goes on the canvas somehow.

RS: So his only real life is on the canvas.

MS: Yes.

RS: And his life is not a life at all.

MS: That's all used, in a sense, as material. It was enjoyable to do, and I have Richard Price to thank for a really good script.

RS: Who came up with that idea?

MS: I did. I had this idea for years. Back in the early seventies I had a copy of Dostoyevsky's "The Gambler," because I liked Dostoyevsky a lot, and I thought maybe we can do a version of "The Gambler," but that wasn't really for me.

But we took a scene right from "The Gambler" and put it in there, where he says, "You don't exist for me," when she's in the kitchen. "I can do anything 'cause I'm the invisible man to you," he says. That dialogue is from "The Gambler." The diary of the woman, Anna, was the inspiration for that character in "The Gambler." She was, I think, twenty-one years old and she was the mistress of Dostoyevsky, who was about fifty-three, thereabouts. And we literally followed the diary.

RS: Oh, how interesting, these—to me, at least—hidden analogies between these two stories.

MS: And from what I remember he was forced to write "The Gambler" because he had debts to pay, and he took a secretary in the room with him and I think it took about four weeks or five weeks. He dictated it. And at the end of those four to five weeks he married the secretary. And the only thing the wife says is "I never want to hear the name Anna again." Because in that room it all came out and went into "The Gambler." And his letter to Anna was interesting because he's so apologetic, and he waits until the third page to write that he's married the secretary. But she's twenty-one years old and she even wrote a short story; it's in there, too.

RS: How amazing.

MS: It's not very good, but it's fascinating because she calls him "F.," and she says "F. is here again. It's such a bore." And it's Dostoyevsky.

RS: Possibly he was a bore.

MS: Yeah.

RS: Obsessed guys like that can be very boring.

MS: Boring, you know. She would write: "Oh, he's going to cry again. I can't take it." The poor guy.

RS: But having said all this, it seems to be a very well-observed look at the New York art world, too.

MS: Richard did that, because he realized that we couldn't make the writing process visual. So he said, Well, make him a painter.

RS: The painting is great, yeah.

MS: Richard's wife is a fine painter, and basically that was the inspiration for it.

RS: One of the things I thought about the movie, too, was that very often in movies about painters, when you get to the painting it always looks faked.

MS: I know. I agree. Chuck Connolly did those paintings. They're quite interesting. He's still painting—in fact there was a documentary on HBO about him.

RS: Well, of course one of the things about abstraction is you can slather that paint around and it's very active—it's action painting literally—and at the same time you don't know whether it's good or bad. Whenever you show painting in a film it never feels real. I mean that's the downside, let's say, of *Lust for Life*. What I can accept, though, in your movie is his passion for it.

MS: Yeah, exactly. But we decided we had to show the paintings. And playing music—you talk to one artist, he says, I never played music; and you talk to another artist and he says, I play music all the time.

RS: And you opted for the music—which helps the painting scenes immeasurably.

MS: "A Whiter Shade of Pale," the elegiac tone of that song.

RS: And what of her? What will become of her? That interests me.

MS: I know.

RS: Will she one day . . . ?

MS: Maybe. Maybe.

RS: Because he has certainly insulted her gift or whatever talent she had. But yet she has the passion.

MS: She's got it, but does she have the ability, and does she have the toughness? That you can't teach anybody. You just can't.

RS: No.

MS: The more you do, the worse it gets. It's very hard.

RS: You're talking about protecting—?

MS: People who want to be artists. I mean whether you're an actor, whether you're a painter or writer, whatever. It involves a toughness that you have to have. You stand up and you take the blow, you know.

RS: It's true.

MS: You don't like it. And you've got to do it again and again. And you think, Well, why do I want to do that? But, you know . . .

RS: But it goes on and on, your whole life.

MS: It goes on and on, yes. Constantly. Some people even have the talent, but talent's not enough.

RS: No, never.

MS: You have to have a kind of defiant attitude, I think, in such a way that you cut out everything else. You just work and you do what you do. You don't listen to anybody, you don't read any criticism, you don't take any opinions, and . . .

RS: Well, then what comparison and contrast could we make between you, Marty, and Nick Nolte in that movie?

MS: Well, I guess . . .

RS: I mean, you're tough enough.

MS: I don't know. I try to be. I try to be—

RS: We all try to be.

MS: Yes, we all try to be. That's about as close as I can get, you know.

RS: Isn't it the truth, though, however much you say "I don't read the reviews," or "I don't pay attention to the reviews," the truth of the matter is you do notice them. You can't help but notice them.

MS: You can't help it, and there are some people who—in a friendly way—send you some good ones.

RS: There are also people who write and say, "You'll be interested in this notice in Memphis," and it's a devastation, you know.

MS: It's terrible! I learned that the hard way. I did that to a few people back in the late sixties—I said, "Oh, this was written about you," and I gave it to them and they said, "Thank you. I wish you hadn't." I didn't understand until I started really making my own work. It would happen sometimes, too, with very close friends of mine saying, "You know, what he said about you in the paper," and then they repeat it and say, "I'm against that, and I really think it was outrageous." And I would say, "Well, why did you tell me? Let it go. I know it's not good." Not everybody's going to like you. What can you do? You go back and you make another picture. If you can.

RS: Don't you feel that's the one thing they don't tell you when you're a kid starting out? You're aware that people give you good and bad reviews, but they don't really tell you how much you can be hurt.

MS: The pain is extraordinary. But I mean some people, some wonderful filmmakers, have asked me, "You don't read reviews. You don't pay attention to any of that, do you?"

RS: Really!

MS: I don't want to mention any names, but they're much more secure than I am, I guess. But the insecurity is part of what I do, and who I am. But I must say that when young people ask me what's the most important thing, I do use the word "tenacity," and that means, no matter what, you've got to be like Odysseus tied to the mast.

I can't say "Don't listen"—you're going to hear it, and it'll be with you for fifty years. You'll always hear it, even if they change their opinion. But if you get a lot of praise very often, there has to be an attack, or many attacks. There has to be. And then you just weather that, and you have to have confidence in yourself, and that's the tenacity.

RS: It is impossible, I think, to sustain a career of any length without that quality.

MS: Yes.

RS: You may be tenacious, but nobody's going to erase the terrible shitty things that have been said about you.

MS: By people close to you, too. And also then there's the praise, too—there's praise, but maybe praise for the wrong thing, for the wrong reason. But praise helps the financing of another picture. Also box office, to a certain extent, depending on the kind of movie you want to make next.

GOODFELLAS

RICHARD SCHICKEL: Your next full-length feature after *Last Temptation* was *Good-fellas* in 1990, which I suppose with *Raging Bull* is one of my two favorite movies of yours. Perhaps part of my feeling for that is based on the fact that most of us share a sort of love for gangsters as outsiders, or rebels. I mean, we always sort of sympathize with the gangster Jim Cagney, or people like him.

They seem to have such a nice, rich life: lovely meals they're always making for each other, a certain amount of friendship, brotherhood, and all that. They enjoy the good life, and at the same time they get to whack people.

MARTIN SCORSESE: When I was doing *The Color of Money* in Chicago, I was reading *The New York Review of Books* and saw a review of a book by Nick Pileggi called *Wiseguy*. It seemed like Nick was taking us through the different levels of purgatory and hell in the underworld, like Virgil or like Dante. Irwin Winkler said, "Are you interested in that?" I said yes and he bought it for me. I said yes because I thought Nick was telling the story in a different way. It's about that lifestyle, and the dangerous seduction of that lifestyle.

I remember I was talking to Marlon Brando from time to time, and he said,

Goodfellas was Marty's masterly portrait of low-level New York mobsters. Among those present in this "rollicking road picture" were Ray Liotta, Joe Pesci, Robert De Niro, and Joseph Bono. The film was released in 1990.

"Don't do another gangster picture. You've done *Mean Streets,* you did the gangsters in *Raging Bull.* You don't have to do that." I came to feel the same way. So I said to Michael Powell, "I think I don't want to do this *Goodfellas* thing," or *Wiseguys,* as it was then called.

Michael Powell went back to his apartment with Thelma Schoonmaker, whom he'd married right after *Raging Bull.* He couldn't see anymore, so she read the script to him. I was in the editing room, I remember, in the Brill Building, and suddenly he called and said, "This is wonderful. You must do it. It's funny and no one's ever seen this way of life before. You must do it." And that's why I did it.

RS: Well, there's a William Wellman story on *Public Enemy.* He found the script and he took it to [Darryl] Zanuck, who was running Warner Bros. It was then called "Beer and Blood." He loved it—these young writers had lived in Chicago and knew some of the mobsters. But Zanuck said, I can't do another one of these. I've just done this, I've just done that. Tell me one good reason to do it. And Wellman said, "Because I'll make it the toughest one you ever saw." And Zanuck said,

"You got it." You could argue that, of all the modern gangland things, *Goodfellas* is the toughest one of all. Was there some aspect of *Goodfellas* for you that was like Wellman's attitude, that you could do it tougher?

MS: I thought of it as being a kind of attack.

RS: Attack?

MS: Attacking the audience. I remember talking about it at one point and saying, "I want people to get infuriated by it." I wanted to seduce everybody into the movie and into the style. And then just take them apart with it. I guess I wanted to make a kind of angry gesture.

RS: Why were you angry?

MS: I guess I used to feel I was the outsider who has to punch his way back in, constantly. Some people don't have to do that, but I do. I'm not just talking about films, but everything.

I get angry about the way things are and the way people are. I get very involved in stories and the way a character behaves and the way the world behaves. More than anger, I think, maybe it's caring about how characters behave, how the world behaves. I'm curious about those things. I still get excited by the story. I still get upset by what a character does. And the anger is something to get me working. I have to get sometimes rather upset with myself or a situation before I can really start working, thinking clearly.

In the Rolling Stones documentary, I do a takeoff on myself for the first ten minutes. It's about everything that could go wrong for me as the director. And things do go wrong. And they affect you.

I remember a priest told my father to come to talk to him and bring me with him to the rectory one day. I wondered why, what I did that was so bad? I must've been about twelve. He said something about me going around with the seriousness and the weight of the world on my shoulders. At that age I shouldn't be that way, the priest said. I should have been enjoying my life.

But then later, when they threw me out of the preparatory seminary, the monsignor told my father, "Your son? You tell him, 'There's a brick wall. Don't hit your head against it, you're going to get hurt.' And your son will get up and hit his head against the wall." Then the monsignor got up and mimed hitting his head against the brick wall, and that was the end of it.

Everybody cares about what they do. But I get emotionally involved with everything, and over the years it became funny—over the top—like grand opera. Except when it's not. In my mind, whether it's the stroke of a pen or a bullet, a lot can happen to people. In our America, businesspeople are slaughtered every day. People are robbed every day.

RS: Well, there's that whole theory of Robert Warshow, about "the gangster as tragic hero."

MS: I was going to mention Warshow.

RS: I'm not sure I completely buy into that in a movie like *Goodfellas;* there's actually nothing very tragic about those guys.

MS: No.

RS: What happens to Henry Hill is not tragic; he's just not having fun anymore.

MS: Right. Too bad for him!

RS: And it's not a tragic ending.

MS: No, he's still breathing.

RS: I guess I need you to explain where you're coming from with that because it really is a unique movie, I think. You've said you can't see *The Sopranos* in it, but I see a sort of precursor in it.

MS: A lot of the wonderful actors in *The Sopranos* were in my pictures, so we always talk about it. A lot of the people in *Goodfellas* are not on the upper levels, so they're not tragic. It's just everyday tragedy. These guys are dealing on the everyday level. I knew them as people, not as criminals. If something fell off the truck, you know, we all bought it. It was part of surviving, part of living. Some of those guys were smarter than others. Some overstepped their bounds and were killed. That was based on reality.

There's a danger in idolizing that world, but many of the police who were down there in that neighborhood were on the take. I was surprised the first time I saw the American system at work, which was in *Twelve Angry Men*, Sidney Lumet's film. Today, I credit the priests in the neighborhood who screened a 16 millimeter print of it down in the basement of the church for some of the kids. It was like being on Mars.

RS: The surrogate in your film, practicing that idolization as a kid, is the Henry Hill character.

Marty directs Ray Liotta in *Goodfellas*.

MS: Yes. If you engage in that life, certain things are expected of you. First of all, to make a lot of money for everybody. Or to be the muscle. You have to perform, and you have to be careful: the scene that Joe Pesci asked to be put in, and improvised with Ray Liotta—the "You think I'm funny?" scene—shows that you could be killed any second. They don't care who's around. The trick in the picture was to sort of ignore that danger, make it a rollicking road movie in a way—like a kind of Bob Hope and Bing Crosby picture, with everybody on the road and having a great time.

When the Sicilian police finally broke up the Mafia in the early nineties, they arrested some guy—I forget his name, but he was the second in command—and an Italian reporter asked him if any movie about that world was accurate. And he said, Well, *Goodfellas*, in the scene where the guy says, "Do you think I'm funny?" Because that's the life we lead. You could be smiling and laughing one second, and [*snaps fingers*] in a split second you're in a situation where you could lose your life.

RS: Quite an amazing anecdote.

MS: That is exactly where you live all the time. That's the truth of it. Now that happened to Joe Pesci, originally, with a friend of his. He got out of it just by doing what Ray did. So when he told me the story, I said, "We've got to use that. That really encapsulates it completely. That's the lifestyle."

Remember when Jimmy Cagney got the AFI [American Film Institute] award, he thanked somebody I think was called Two-Times Ernie and the other street guys he knew as a kid. Because they taught him how to act. The kids in my neighborhood who told stories on the street corner, they'd have you enthralled, and often with a sense of humor about themselves. And these were some tough kids.

I'll never forget one of the toughest I'd ever met telling a story about losing a fight in such a funny way, and not being embarrassed about it. [*Laughs.*] Not losing any dignity. I thought, That is brilliant: to accept the fact that he was knocked down so badly, had to get up again, get knocked down again. We were all laughing, and he was laughing. I'll never forget it.

In the *Wiseguy* book, Henry Hill speaks that way, almost like a standup comic. He's got his own rhythm. There's a truth to it. Someone owes you money, and he doesn't pay you. So you go to him, and he says, "Oh, my wife got sick." "Fuck you, pay me." "My daughter is—" "Fuck you, pay me," a guy like Hill says. "My mother—" "Fuck you, pay me."

RS: De Niro in *Mean Streets* has no conscious sense of consequences, always living in the moment. That's symbolized in *Goodfellas* by the great tracking shot into the Copacabana, when they all go out on the town. That's the privileged moment they pay for in blood and death.

MS: Well, the Copacabana—that's the top of the line for Henry—it was Valhalla. When you were able to get a table there, it was like being in the court of the kings. The Mob guys were really the ones in charge. The Copa lounge was always more significant because the real guys were up there. That's why you have a lot happening in *Raging Bull* in the Copa lounge. My friend's father, the one who would read and listen to opera, his father was the head bartender there. We have him in *Raging Bull.* Nice guy.

Everyone paid for the privilege eventually. The danger of the picture is that young people could look at it and think, Hey, what a great life. But you've got to see the last hour of the picture when things start going wrong in a big way.

RS: I think in one of the voice-over lines Henry Hill says, You only have it for maybe ten years.

MS: That's right.

RS: That made me think about celebrity. Ballplayers, for example, only have maybe ten years.

MS: Right. Actors, filmmakers, you've got about ten years. Some of the greatest filmmakers had a run for ten years. It's part of American celebrity.

MARTIN SCORSESE: Sometimes I try to make a picture for purely entertainment reasons, like *Cape Fear.*

RICHARD SCHICKEL: *Cape Fear*? But it says so much about the American marriage going to hell.

MS: Well, that's what we added. The original script didn't have that. There's something that Nick Nolte's character had done, Mr. Bowden, that he would never be forgiven for by his wife and his daughter: There was nothing that he could ever say or do. You feel bad for him, and for them. That's the feeling we brought to the film, because it was so awful what they were going through. There was one particular scene when we were laughing because it was so pathetic. Nick says, "I can't do this scene." I said, "Well, we have to do it!" He said, "No, now he's going to ask her to forgive him. It's never going to happen."

RS: Right.

MS: Then they're put through this trial by this larger-than-life character, Max Cady. It really did start for me as pure entertainment, but then I changed it to be about the dissolution of the family unit. When you're coming out of the sixties, as I did, and thought about changing society, you had to think about changing the family unit. Does that work? Apparently it doesn't.

So here the family unit is being decimated. The husband is trying to hold on. His wife is barely holding on. Watch what she does with those cigarettes, Jessica Lange. The daughter has come of age. The scene in the old version where [Robert] Mitchum chases the young girl in the school? Wesley Strick wrote a very beautiful chase scene, very suspenseful. I said, "I can't do that, I just don't know how to do it." I could try to do it, but other people would do it much better than me. So I said, "What if the scene is about Max Cady just taking whatever last vestige of trust or feelings for her father that the daughter had?" That's what the scene should be about—spiritual pain as opposed to physical pain. And so Wesley worked on it and worked on it and worked on it. I think we got it [the scene where Max Cady and the daughter are alone onstage at her school]. Then we shot it with two cameras. The first take is the take we used. We only shot four takes. And De Niro was wonderful. Juliette [Lewis], too. But I didn't enjoy a lot of the making of it.

RS: I gather you really didn't want to do the big scene at the end, where De Niro is stalking the family, on the boat, in a hurricane? That's a tour de force.

MS: The scene that got me hooked actually was the one I just described. Then I said, You know what else? It was in early 1991. I wasn't even fifty yet. I was still thinking I wanted to make the films being made in Hollywood—big entertainment films with lots of action scenes. I thought there was room for me there, if I ever could enjoy just making a film that is only action. *Cape Fear* turned out not to be only action.

RS: I'll tell you, it's a lot better than Lee Thompson's version in 1962.

MS: Well, there were a lot of people who said that it wasn't as pure as the original B film. My view is that the B film comes from one time and place, and we come from another time and place.

RS: It really wasn't such a B film, not with Gregory Peck and Mitchum starring in it.

MS: Maybe so. But one thing I can tell you: Now that I'm older, I don't know if I would do a picture that's purely action, just for the sake of doing action.

RS: The family in *Cape Fear* is your most dysfunctional family.

MS: They really are.

RS: She's miserable. He's playing around, has played around. Their child is a basket case.

Cape Fear is a twisted—and far more interesting—remake of the 1962 original, which starred Gregory Peck. Now the family being terrorized by the psychopathic Max Cady (Robert De Niro, shown here with Scorsese) is anything but the loving unit portrayed in the earlier film.

MS: I just wanted Nick Nolte to play it as a guy who did something once or twice and no matter what he could say or do, it would never be the same. He wanted it to be an "I'm home, honey" kind of life. But the mother and the daughter will have nothing to do with him. He's trying, but he can't get it done.

That was the biggest change we made from the original script. In the original film the family was a very wholesome, together family. They were singing songs together, stuff like that.

RS: As far as I know, it's your only WASP family. So I think you're saying something there, pal.

MS: Maybe. I don't really know much about that. I know something about Mediterranean families. The only thing I knew of WASP families was what was coming out of Hollywood movies, which I could never identify with.

I'd see these movies—you know, Andy Hardy, and his father, a judge, little white picket fence. To me that was fantasy. I'd never met people like that, until maybe when I got out of NYU, and started to meet people who were not ethnic.

RS: Well, I think this film references those movies to a degree—the white picket fence and so forth. But I think the key scene is the one between the daughter [Juliette Lewis] and Robert De Niro [Max Cady, the psychopath who believes he was wrongly prosecuted by her father] at the high school, so let's go back to that. What the hell was going on there?

MS: It was about the betrayal of trust. As I said, it was the final blow against her father. In the original, with Peck and Mitchum and Polly Bergen, there's a scene where Mitchum shows up at the school and chases the kid through the halls, as I said. In the original draft of our picture, Steven Spielberg, who was the producer, and Wesley Strick, who was the writer, had a terrific chase sequence, a scare sequence. The kid was on kind of a ledge hanging on to a shade and the shade is starting to break off. And I said I could do it, but I'm not the best at that, I don't really do that as well as other people. Maybe you're looking at me for the wrong picture.

I said, I'd like to make that scene about the violation of the kid. It should be quiet. It should not be a chase. You know, a genre film—I always think I can make one and then I always work against its conventions. But Steven said to me, Marty, you can do anything you want. You can rewrite the script if you want with Wesley.

Did I want the family to live or die? "Well, the family's got to live," I said. Steven said, "Fine." I got hold of Wesley, and we started talking about this idea of a scene that was very quiet, but one where he could really destroy the family by taking the last vestige of trust that the kid had in her father, which wasn't very much, and destroy that. And do it as a sexual violation in a way.

Right before we shot, Bob De Niro had this idea of putting his thumb in her mouth. I said, Just do it, don't tell her.

RS: Everything Nolte does in that movie is a failure.

MS: He tries, though. He really tries, and it should work. But it doesn't. He's completely powerless.

RS: Because he is up against, what, absolute evil?

MS: I think so. I think that's what Bob really wanted to play. And the whole idea of him hanging on to the bottom of that car—I mean, you couldn't actually do that. But at that point in the movie, it really becomes a heightened kind of reality, particularly ending in the Götterdämmerung of the storm sequence, which I always wanted to try.

It was a technical thing for me. I wanted to see if I could do a real action sequence with boats, and that sort of thing. It took us quite a while, but we did it—Freddie Francis on camera—and it was quite something. It has a lot to do with *King of Comedy*.

RS: How so?

MS: Well, the intrusion. The violence of the intrusion. You know, in this case Cady was wronged.

RS: And so was Rupert Pupkin, I suppose, in a way.

MS: Exactly. Jerry wronged Rupert to a certain extent—in Rupert's mind, anyway. Jerry talked to him in the car, so therefore he's his friend. So when he says to the assistant, "Are you speaking for Jerry?" he's turning toward retribution. He's got to get even. In *Cape Fear* Bob was even more interested in the violation of the family—of the Juliette Lewis character in that "theater scene," where he destroys the last vestige of trust she has in her father. Then he also wanted to play Max— almost like *The Terminator*, like a machine. Ultimately, at the end of the picture, he's the incarnation of everything they ever did wrong or felt wrong or thought wrong. He's putting them through it.

I don't know if they ever will be the same after this story ends. Some viewers thought, Oh, the family's back together. Yes, they're back together, but think about what they're going to be like afterwards.

RS: You can't quite imagine them, two weeks later, sitting down and having a nice roast beef dinner together.

MS: Nope.

Twenty years ago, on television, I saw a British series called *Survival,* black-and-white documentaries. It was about people who had gone through a great deal of suffering, being stranded on mountaintops and the like. One was about a family being stranded in a lifeboat—a mother, father, daughter, and son. The family was talking about it years later. The parents were divorced. They had been the closest family until they got in that boat. They spent four weeks in that boat, and they described everything they did. Just the matter of moving a foot into one another's space, for instance, was huge. They are intelligent people, educated, filled with love. But they had to divorce after that. It was absolutely shocking.

MARTIN SCORSESE: I think *The Age of Innocence* is interesting because it has to do with responsibility.

RICHARD SCHICKEL: But no one in it is in the classic sense nurturing.

MS: No. If they are nurturing to anything, they seem to be nurturing to their class, their society. Do you see what I'm saying?

RS: Yes.

MS: Which is better for Newland Archer [Daniel Day-Lewis, whose passionate, yet unconsummated, love affair with Ellen Olenska (Michelle Pfeiffer) threatens the comfortable class structure of 1870s New York]. He doesn't realize that because passion has taken over. In the long run it's better for him. It goes back to the idea of responsibility.

RS: But then what about the Polish countess? Does she have any nurturing in her?

MS: Well, I think so. But would he be able to benefit from that, the kind of person he was bred to be? Would he be able to handle being in Europe with her, and dealing with the situations she would be dealing with?

The Age of Innocence was seemingly Scorsese's most anti-Scorsesean film: an elegant yet large-scaled adaptation of the Edith Wharton novel about a blighted romance in nineteenth-century New York high society. The director, seen here in costume for his small role, saw analogies between the social controls exerted by his muscular mobsters and these more subtle guardians of the status quo in another insular society.

RS: Interesting point.

MS: I don't think he was meant to be that way.

RS: The standard line on *The Age of Innocence* is that its people live by a rigid code of conduct, so intensely that analogies between them and the Mafia have been drawn. These people wouldn't kill you, but they could isolate you.

MS: Ostracize you. The more I learned about that world, working on the film, the more shocking to me it became. We tried to get the authenticity of Visconti, even though I couldn't hope to achieve the beauty of *The Leopard* or *Senso* or *The Innocent.* I loved those pictures, I watched them over and over.

But, anyway, the brutality of the flanking movement that is put upon Newland Archer by his wife, and by the heads of the family, the van der Luydens and his wife's mother, was extraordinary, I thought. There is that wonderful revelation when he finally understands that everybody knows what's going on between him and Ellen, when he sees his wife smile at him at that party. Everybody's known all along. Two people are in love with each other, and they think nobody else knows and everybody knows. It's the slow and agonizing and brutal way in which they undo him—and it's all done extremely politely. It's pretty brutal, I think.

RS: But he's so passive.

MS: That's what everyone said. You know, that was the last film of mine my father saw and I dedicated it to him. When I was making the film, I was thinking very much about my father's sense of obligation and responsibility—what he did for us, whether he was massaging me with alcohol to get a fever down or going through all this madness with doctors, not having an education, not knowing how to deal with all this. I thought that Newland Archer, when he decides to stay, is demonstrating that kind of responsibility. The boy says to him at the end of the film he knew they would be safe because his mother told him that when it came down to it Archer would give up the thing he loved most to stay with them. I admire that. Now whether he's passive earlier in the film or not, that's something else. But his decision—I admire it.

So I think he's much maligned. Jay Cocks said later—he gave me the book originally—that people never forgave the fact that Daniel Day-Lewis and Michelle Pfeiffer don't get to make love in the film. But that's the story.

Even at the end, when we were shooting in Paris, Michael Ballhaus, my DP [director of photography], looked at me, and goes, Oh, why can't he go upstairs? When, at last, he could safely embrace Ellen, I said, He can't. He can't go up. That's what she loved about him. What are you going to do, be inconsistent at the last minute? But the thing with the children was very touching, I thought.

RS: For me, it was something that only had impact when I saw the film a second time.

MS: Maybe it is too studied, the homage to Visconti. But Jacques Tourneur's in there. There's the influence of the beautiful narration of *Dorian Gray,* and the narration of *Barry Lyndon,* of course—how the narrator's voice helps get you to a certain contemplative state, almost like reading a novel from the nineteenth century. You hear the voice of Joanne Woodward, as Edith Wharton, right in your ear.

RS: It seems to me a beautifully judged and measured film. I seem to recall that its release was somewhat delayed.

MS: I'll never forget it. We finished shooting in May, June 1992, around then. The studio would like to have gotten it for Christmas. But it was a tricky film. The energy was held back, the emotion was underlying. And then my father died during that period.

RS: Right.

MS: It was too held back. The question was, Did expressive camera moves break the form of the traditional costume movie? We did some things which people considered inappropriate for that type of story, as if that type of story should be told only in one way. We did a two-hour-and-forty-minute cut of it. The studio said the picture was going to come out the following year. An article came out in the papers, *Variety* or somewhere, explaining that the film was being postponed; there wasn't anything wrong with the film, it said, it was just that the director has an "obsessive attention to detail." Excuse me.

RS: Every worthwhile director has that obsession.

MS: I usually take things to the reductio ad absurdum. If I'm not complaining, then I'm not thinking it through.

RICHARD SCHICKEL: When you got to *Casino,* you said, you'd gone as far as you thought you could go with just plain brutality—the way people kick people around, beat them up, blow them up. It's relatively speaking a late gangster movie. I have no idea about the origins of that project or why you feel it exceeded what you'd previously done in the realm of brutality—especially when they're burying poor old Joe alive out in the desert.

MARTIN SCORSESE: I know, it's awful. It's done by his friends. And this is something that is so disturbing.

RS: This theme of yours of betrayal, right?

MS: Yes, yes. And the closest people turn on him. Now, he did behave badly.

RS: Yes.

MS: And he abused his power. And he was a killer. But it's the world he's in. There is no other world. And you have to stop him from breathing. It's an extraordinary thing how people could do that. But the thing is the calculation. You have to trick him. Then you have to follow through, you have to do whatever you're doing, whatever violence you're committing—until he stops moving and breathing. And did he, as a human being, deserve that from his closest friends? From his closest collaborators and family members almost. When I shot the scene, I shot it very straightforward, very flat. And I figured that's the final curtain in that world. That's it. That is my final statement.

The cornfield beating of Joe Pesci in 1995's *Casino,* a film about the Mafia's rise to control of Las Vegas and the decline of Ace Rothstein, played by Robert De Niro, who masterminded it.

RS: Does that scene at all analogize to the scene in *Goodfellas* where they've got the guy in the trunk? I mean, you know, he's suffocating before they kill him.

MS: I think it's different—I mean, murder is murder. But the murder of Billy Batts in *Goodfellas* is out of hotheadedness.

RS: Right. They're like young heedless guys—

MS: Yeah, drinking. They're like barbarians at the gates. I don't think they planned on doing it. They knew they were gonna beat him up. They knew they were gonna commit an act of punishment on him. But the point is that it's like many murders, it happens moment by moment. Unpremeditated murder usually happens where it's almost inadvertent, where you take one step and the other person takes another, and then you have to keep going.

RS: I see what you mean.

MS: You have to keep going. The scene doesn't start that way. The scene doesn't say, I'm gonna kill you. No. They're talking and the next thing you know, the gun is around. And then they become angry and passion takes over. But in *Casino,* it's planned.

RS: Just tell me, how did *Casino* come to you? How did you get involved?

MS: That was kind of a commission. I had a deal at Universal. We did *Cape Fear* there and they wanted another film. Tom Pollock and Casey Silver were there. And Nick Pileggi brought this newspaper article to me about the car blowing up with Lefty Rosenthal in it. [Rosenthal was the brains behind converting Las Vegas from a pure gambling center to a kind of family playground.] And the revelation of the story of the triangle between Rosenthal, Ginger (his wife), and Nicky, Lefty's best friend. In any event, that story seemed so vivid—two friends, one was the brains, one was the muscle. And sometimes the brains would use other people's muscle. And sometimes the muscle also had brains. But primarily they controlled this empire for the Mob; so it's a story of empire. And the story of, again, the seeds of destruction in our own selves. And the poor woman who's stuck in the middle. In fact, quite honestly, everybody who was there in Vegas when we were doing the film liked the Nicky character a lot. They didn't like the Ace character at all.

RS: Why didn't they like Lefty?

MS: They just felt he was cold, tough, and the feeling was that if he had to use violence, he did it through other people. Whereas Nicky was, you might say, up front, hands-on. And the cops, the policemen, who were part of that task force that was supposedly set to get Tony and all his men in Vegas, the kindest words they had were for the woman.

Scorsese and Sharon Stone, as Ginger, the tragically touching showgirl of *Casino*.

RS: Really?

MS: They said that she was the one who got the worst of it all. They treated her badly.

RS: Of course, she becomes this drunk and—

MS: Oh, horrible. And she died exactly that way in the motel hallway.

RS: Is that so?

MS: Yeah. And that night, I remember Sharon Stone was trembling. She felt she had to channel the woman. And there were so many people who knew her and they were all around us. They were acting in the film. It was kind of strange. I mean, strange in a good way. It worked on her beautifully. And it was quite something— you can't imagine some of the stuff that went on. We just scratched the surface, and it's going on now, too.

RS: I thought the Mob was gone from Vegas.

MS: It's just in another place.

RS: That's America's family playground.

MS: It's America's family playground. Yes. What does that say about our values? So the end of the picture is really about us and about our values—that's what I thought. The last statement on that way of life and that world is the killing in the cornfield.

RS: I kept thinking—and I reran it just a few weeks ago—I kept wondering: Did you think at all about *The Godfather*? Because, you know, in this film, whenever they go back to the Mob, they're sitting around in some garage.

MS: That's where the real stuff went on, you see.

RS: Yeah, right. And I'm really laughing at it, because here are these powerful guys and they're sitting around—

MS: This dirty place with the oil, the smell of the oil and the grease.

RS: Yes, and eating really low-level Italian subs.

MS: I know.

RS: And I was thinking, this is Marty making a little comment on the Corleones, who have fancy homes and all that . . .

MS: I always said, I just knew the person on the street corner who had just robbed a carton of cigarettes and was selling them to somebody else. I can never imagine the Corleones, I couldn't even imagine the Sopranos living in a big house in New Jersey. I only saw a few of the shows, and it's not the world that I knew.

RS: Do you think these guys, like back when you were a kid on Elizabeth Street, do you think they went home from their social club to wonderful houses like the Corleones'?

MS: No, they lived in apartments in the tenements. There were a few who had nicely appointed apartments. It was decent, it was nice, especially if they had families. But basically, I got to tell you, it was very plain.

RS: Well, that's interesting. The American fantasy is that these guys lived these big lives . . .

MS: Even if they lived in those tiny apartments, they were the bosses of the neighborhood. If there was a problem, they'd take care of it. They had a florist shop. Somebody had a butcher shop. So they were part of the family in a way. So it wasn't that they were the men on the hill. It wasn't like they were separate from us. They were all mixed in together. There was one who had a house out in New Jersey, and I was friends with his son. And they would take us out there every now and then. It was like an excursion.

RS: A little outing in New Jersey.

MS: That was a big deal. And they'd put us in this Chrysler Imperial. It was amazing, with the biggest fins you could imagine. And that was the year that the song "Volare" was out. You heard it everywhere. It was so great to go to the country and to be in a swimming pool just for a day. And all these men were in this house talking, sitting at tables, making phone calls.

By the way, they're dead now. They were killed two years, maybe four years, five years, later, those people I'm talking about. They lived in the neighborhood, but they were killed. The son was killed first—he was twenty-two or twenty-three years old.

RS: Let me ask this, kind of drifting back to *Casino.* It seems to me that its uniqueness in your body of work is that it's the closest you come to very high-level criminality.

MS: But that's about it, I can't go any further. That's about as high as I could go, because first of all I'm not that interested in that highest level. It might be more interesting to do a film about the senators' families in ancient Rome right at the decline of the republic before Julius Caesar, and the machinations of which family worked against the other family causing the death of Caesar. They go into a civil war, and they wind up with an empire. They wind up with an emperor. Okay. But it's interesting why the republic fell apart. And it has to do with Renaissance politics then. But I'm more interested in the incremental moves. It's a wonderful thing when Lefty keeps his trousers in the closet, because he doesn't want to ruin the crease. Person comes in, he puts on his pants. That's no problem. But that little detail reflects something much bigger that could be very damaging to him. The small moves are what I'm interested in. And the personal relationships. *The Godfather* I never thought of.

RS: I think it's a great movie.

MS: I do, too.

RS: But it's a total fantasy.

MS: It is, yes.

RS: I mean, Mario Puzo just made all that stuff up. I don't think it's observed reality on his part.

MS: But does great art have to be reality? No.

RS: So when we're talking of a movie like *Casino,* I think you're saying that some part of you just doesn't want to go further up the hierarchical ladder. I mean, there's something in the relationships at a lower level of criminality than Don Corleone that is more interesting to you.

MS: It is more interesting because I think ultimately it's the same mind, only the decisions are smarter. The decisions are better informed at the top.

But I'm also interested when they make the wrong decision, the wrong alliance. They're like Cicero in the Roman republic when everything did fall apart, how he had to take as allies his enemies. And he wound up having to kill himself ultimately. He was a great man, yet he made the wrong move. And it's very interesting, because it's life and death.

RS: So did you hesitate at all on *Casino?* Did you think, This is kind of out of my familiar range?

MS: Vegas, no. That was okay—the brashness of it. People enjoy it, fine. I just don't enjoy it myself. I don't really gamble that way. I'm not very good at it.

RS: You gamble in other ways.

Tilling the field: Marty directs the cornfield scene. He says it is the most brutal sequence he's ever made and believes he will never make anything like it again.

MS: Right.

RS: I've often said to people, What does it mean to me to go to a slot machine? My whole life is a slot machine.

MS: Are you kidding? Every minute I open that door or pick up that phone. And on top of that, I've got a family now and I'm getting older. It's hard, every gamble you take.

RS: It's absolutely true.

MS: Okay, it's all right. We can do it. But the interesting thing was the blast of Vegas, the idea of Vegas, especially in the seventies. In the fifties and sixties, Vegas was for people who liked to gamble. But later you have Sinatra and the Rat Pack and all. And it gains a swagger: Listen, you don't like it, don't come here. You can't take the heat, get out. Fine.

But by the seventies, it went further, and a lot of it was due to Lefty Rosenthal. He brought in Siegfried and Roy. He made it into one big Crazy Horse Saloon, and also got the place to make a lot of money for back home, for Chicago. But what was interesting to me is that it just reflected a complete embrace of excess.

And that's why the first image in the film has to be this beautiful car. Man walks out in wide-screen and color, he's wearing salmon-colored pants. In fact, we had to tone it down from the actual clothes that Lefty had. Anyway, he turns the key, and the car blows up. That seemed to me what we're doing in our society—the values that we have. Anything that's good has to make money. How is cinema judged today, aside from a few critics or reviewers? Basically it's judged by how much money you make on a weekend. Is cinema serious anymore? I don't know. At the time when I was making certain films, I took cinema seriously.

RS: You still do.

MS: Yeah, I still do. But the next generation doesn't, because of the excess.

RS: That's a good point, because of all your movies, this is the one that's most satirical about excess. I mean, the décor in Lefty's house is just amazing.

MS: Toned down.

RS: There comes a moment where there's no humor or horror in it for you.

MS: Nothing.

RS: No frisson, as we might say.

MS: There's no enjoyment.

RS: I guess it's saying something that you hadn't quite said as openly in your previous excursions into this world.

MS: I think so. And at Universal, Tom Pollock really wanted me to make the film, and Nick had that story. He hadn't finished the book yet, and so we worked on the script together for about six months, in a hotel, and we ordered transcripts and whatever other interviews we could get. And we had papers everywhere. And I decided it had to be an epic—a three-hour epic, but very fast. Very fast, because in the world that they're in, things go faster. You get more—it's consuming, consuming, consuming. It represented to me—I've got to say—what we're doing in this society. It really did.

RS: But it's gotten much worse.

MS: Yes, much worse. In *Casino* there's no such thing as law, there's nothing. It just goes. And then they self-implode.

RS: One of the things that, again, seems significant, re-looking at the movie, is there appears to be within the city limits of Las Vegas not a single person of any moral stature.

MS: I agree.

RS: I mean, who do you tell, what cop do you call?

MS: Who knows, I can't even say. It feeds, I think, the worst part of our human nature. But continually. And it's very hard on the people working there.

RS: So, even though you made *Gangs of New York* later and it's historical, I mean this in a certain sense completes . . . You have the criminal element of, let's say, *Mean Streets* as it's perceived by quite a young guy. Then you move on to *Goodfellas* and then this. And one of the significant things about the *Casino* guys is they're all mature guys, unlike even the guys in *Goodfellas*.

MS: In *Goodfellas* they're younger and brash . . .

RS: They're younger and feistier and unable to recognize consequences.

MS: They never fully become members of the Mob, either, because they weren't considered sharp enough. They weren't considered trustworthy enough. So definitely *Casino* was the final one.

RS: You're not drawn to doing another one of those?

MS: No; if anything, it would be something that would be from a perspective of somebody who's in their seventies, looking back.

RS: That would be interesting.

MS: I'm talking about working on something like that.

RS: Because you don't naturally think of any of these guys living into their seventies.

MS: A lot of them did, though.

RS: But the thought is "Live fast, die young."

MS: But they do. The ones who think that way get killed right away. You know, they really do. That's it. It's like the old Wild West, with the young kids trying to make a name for themselves. Or in Hollywood. Different kinds of producers or studio execs come in and you know what it's like. They have to make a mark, really, and that's understandable. It's just some people go about it in an interesting way.

RS: In ways that are very self-destructive. There are not so many of them, but they preoccupy outsiders looking in.

RICHARD SCHICKEL: With regard to *Kundun,* you mentioned earlier your looking out your window, down on some guys hanging around the social club.

MARTIN SCORSESE: Yes, looking down at something going on. God knows what.

RS: Well, the story of the Dalai Lama, from childhood through his exile from Tibet, I saw a lot of you in the main character—the young boy observing life through a telescope like you on your fire escape observing life on the street. That young boy with the telescope is also observing, and I thought, Is that Marty?

MS: Well, yes, that interested me a lot. His always looking through that telescope, through a window. The action he's observing, when he's a child, is a little bit removed from him, as in a movie. But he wanted to be part of it. When he left Tibet, he asked who said Tibetan Buddhism was going to continue to exist the way it had the past sixteen hundred years or whatever. It's now gone from there. He was taking it out to the world—he is taking with him the moral authority of who he is. He is now out in the world, stirring conversation, making people listen. That's what I thought was so interesting.

Melissa Mathison's script was mainly told from a child's point of view, and we

The chosen one: The new Dalai Lama takes up his duties as Tibet's spiritual leader in *Kundun* (1997), one of Scorsese's most surprising films.

tried to make the picture as much as possible like that. For instance, he sees the adults whispering, and the next thing you know, his teacher is gone. It obviously implies a lot about what was going on in Tibetan politics.

RS: Another source of information for him is his little movie projector.

MS: Movies.

RS: Among other things, he was watching Laurence Olivier's *Henry V.*

MS: He was watching newsreels, too. It has to do with my own puffed-up ideas of becoming a spiritual person and a priest, and of course I hadn't even gotten to first base. But this boy was raised as a person whose life *is* a spiritual one. That's why I was interested in this character. The question for me was and is: Do you have to be religious to be a spiritual person?

RS: The movie has a stately pace.

MS: Yes, it does.

RS: You could say the same thing about *The Age of Innocence,* but in the form of easily grasped emotions, more familiar elements. I think that in *Kundun* you were taking a huge chance. First of all, it's got a Buddhist theme, not exactly in everyone's top ten. Second, the film is set in remote Tibet. You could say *Goodfellas* is quite obviously in-your-face daring. This film risks alienating the audience in quite another way, almost the opposite way.

MS: This was much, much tougher. For example, when he's told that the Chinese have invaded, the camera pans to him, and he just stands there. Its inaction is the action. It's antithetical to what we know as Western drama. But why can't there be a film where the drama happens internally? Does a story have to be made the way films are being made in this country? Is there room for a story to be made here a different way? I say yes. In the seventies, you got a fairly good budget for doing it. Now you don't.

In this case, there was the CIA's involvement and Chinese intrigue. I wasn't interested in that. I was interested in the boy's journey as a spiritual being, when he took Buddhism outside Tibet.

RS: In purely visual terms, a lot is said about that character when he separates the two fighting insects. And there's not a word of dialogue.

MS: It was a very interesting movie to cut, because I felt ritual was so important in it. I thought by showing the rituals in the film, and by dealing with the color and the texture, the tone of the ritual, the sound of the ritual, the body language, that the movie could build to a point where for some people it might be a kind of religious or spiritual experience.

RS: I love the moment where Chairman Mao leans into him and says, in effect, You do understand, religion is the opiate of the masses.

MS: Yes, he says, "Religion is poison."

RS: It's the turning point in the movie, because what he says is very powerful. And we've already seen the Chinese marching through. He's putting poison into his ear.

MS: He's telling the Dalai Lama it's over, that his system is no good, that theocracy is out of date. The Dalai Lama says he's going to institute reforms. Mao says it can't be done fast enough, it's not good enough. Everything's got to go. Because religion is poison. And the Dalai Lama said all he could look at was Mao's shoes—the shine on his shoes. He watches the shoes go by and he knows he's finished.

I mean, it was the end of the world for them. I'm always interested in people who lose their world. Like in *Mean Streets,* or *Goodfellas,* or *The Age of Innocence.* Here the Dalai Lama is losing the Tibetan Buddhism of the past sixteen hundred years, wiped away in a very cruel way.

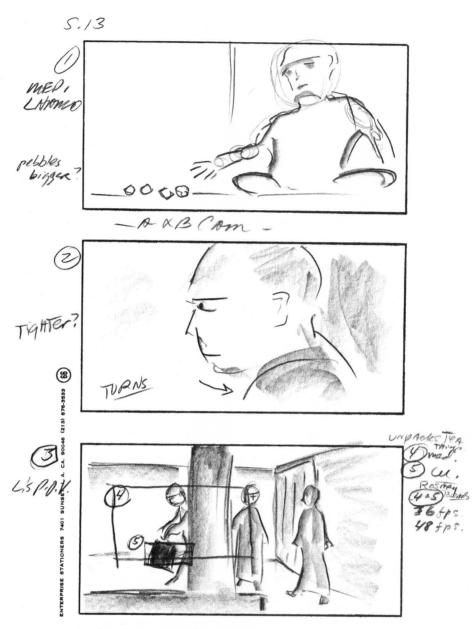

Marty's storyboards for a key *Kundun* sequence.

RS: That's actually a theme I hadn't thought of.

MS: In *New York, New York* they lose like mad. But they learn. I mean, we hope they learn.

RS: Henry Hill is a big loser.

MS: Yeah, but he came out the other side.

RS: He should perhaps use some of his extensive free time to see *Kundun.*

MS: Oh, good Lord. In one of the first two shows of *The Sopranos,* I was supposedly coming out of a car with an actress going to a preview, and one of the guys from *The Sopranos* says, "Hey, Scorsese, Marty, we love *Kundun*!" I loved that.

RS: When worlds collide . . .

MS: I went to a ceremony in Washington, where the Dalai Lama was getting a gold medal. There was a Tibetan gentleman, a very small man in golden Tibetan robes. I think he was a monk. He had little glasses and a very chubby face and he had written a book. I forget his name. As we were streaming out of the rotunda, he saw me, took my hand, and said, "I thank you so much for making that film. Thank you so

On the *Kundun* set Marty directs Tenzin Thuthob Tsarong, playing the grown-up Dalai Lama.

much." He was very sweet. Then he went on: "I saw your other movie, *New York, Gangs.* Violent, violent." I frowned, apologetically. "But it's all right. It's in your nature." [*Laughs.*]

RS: Very funny.

MS: I had tears in my eyes.

RS: Really?

MS: The acceptance of it. If it's in your nature, okay, it's in your nature.

I mean, that's the movie. That's the feeling. That's why it's dedicated to my mother. The Dalai Lama spoke the next night in Washington and said it doesn't matter if you're Christian, Jewish, Muslim. You're talking about the same thing. It's compassion. It's in the New Testament, when they ask Jesus what the most important commandment is. He says, "To love God, and love your neighbor as yourself."

That's it. For me, it comes from my interest in the priesthood. That's why *Kundun* is so important to me. It's about the changes in you as a person, as a filmmaker, whatever; the change in your body, the change in your heart and your soul as you grow and embrace new ideas. And the tendency to fight those instead of accepting them.

BRINGING OUT THE DEAD

RICHARD SCHICKEL: *Bringing Out the Dead,* though it's radically different from *Kundun* in setting, style, and subject matter [it's about emergency medical teams trying to save lives on the streets of Manhattan], has, I think, some thematic relationship to *Kundun.*

MARTIN SCORSESE: Scott Rudin [the producer] sent the galleys to me and I thought, It's *Kundun,* but in a modern urban setting. It was the first contemporary film I had made in years. It's the same thing that brought me to *Kundun:* the spiritual nature of the Dalai Lama's life is the same theme I saw in Joe Connelly's novel.

RS: The Dalai Lama doesn't think you can bring people back to life.

MS: No, but there are spiritual figures who can be a bridge between ourselves and the spiritual nature of existence. So you may be able to open a door in our consciousness.

RS: Maybe.

MS: There's a more searchable longing in Nick Cage's character, the ambulance driver who can't save all the victims he's supposed to attend. And there's the spiritual conflict in him, expecting too much of himself—his pride, the idea of being able to bring back the dead.

RS: Pound on their chests and they'll breathe.

MS: I thought that was an interesting state of mind to be in: (A) to have the compassion to be able to do that on the street, and (B) to lose sight of what you're really there for, which is, as he says, to witness and to share the experience with the victim, learn from it, as much as possible.

RS: But witnessing is different from bringing them back.

MS: Well, yes, you can't bring them all back. None of us is God.

I think what Joe Connelly is saying is that not bringing somebody back to life is a loss. When you lose them, you feel responsible. Another person may go through it and lose ten, twelve people and still be able to continue, but this particular man—

RS: It's an interesting risk, isn't it? On the one hand it offers you the chance to be the person who gives the gift of life. The risk, though, is that you are unable to save them. You're always poised on that terrible precipice.

MS: That's why the character's breakdown occurs. That's why I was drawn to the story. I wanted to explore what we expect of ourselves.

It's very difficult for me to fully understand the nature of people who devote themselves to a spiritual life—the kind who deal with their own spirituality and don't deal with others. But there's the other kind—like Nick's character—who, literally, lay healing hands on others.

RS: These are people whom we admire almost in a perfunctory way. We say, A schoolteacher does the most important thing, but is underpaid . . .

MS: We believe it. But we don't live it. Yes, you're right that these people should be paid more, but it's more than that.

RS: All I'm saying is that that is the conventional way to look at people who do nasty, ugly, underpaid jobs, that often involve them with death, and drugs, and terrible things: We admire them, but we don't really support them.

MS: Right, we don't support them. It's interesting that Joe Connelly, who wrote the novel and the screenplay, went back into EMS [emergency medical service]. He's still dealing with things we would never go near.

I relate this to my Skid Row experience—my self-criticism for, as a child, thinking of those people as subhuman, while around the corner in the church they were talking about compassion and love. I was frightened and wanted to move away from those Skid Row people as much as possible.

Are we all capable of that reaction? Think of World War II. Think of the genocide. I am amazed by those people who confront the problems, face them, deal with them. Anyway, when I read the book, I thought it was extraordinary—moving, and funny, and tough. And not cynical—they were dealing with life and death. The characters have a certain hard edge to them.

Nick Cage's character is cracking. At the beginning of the story he begins a three-day-and-night crack-up: it's been two or three weeks and he hadn't brought anybody back to life. He knows he's not God, but there's a pride because he has the power to bring someone back to life. He thinks he is divine to a certain extent, and it's very moving when it strikes him that he may not be.

As I mentioned before, at one point he says, "I'm there to be a witness." Maybe that's all it is. It's like the Tibetan who told me what was in my nature. You have to accept it. If you fight it all the time, you'll be extremely unhappy. I mean, if you have this violence in your nature, it doesn't mean you have to act it out.

I'll never forget when Nick says, "You know, I'm a grief mop." He's saying, I

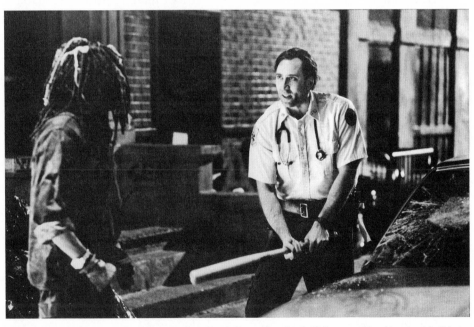

Taking back the night: Nicolas Cage, as an emergency ambulance driver, fends off demons, real and imagined, in *Bringing Out the Dead* (1997).

just stand there and I witness the grief. But there's too little of that. Coming from where I came from and remembering listening to certain priests who were important to me, I just think there's too little of it in our society. We're being inundated with so much information, and yet numb to suffering around the world.

That made it a highly difficult picture to shoot because it put us in dangerous areas, shooting at night—seventy-five nights of shooting.

But Nick Cage was great. All the actors were great—with great senses of humor. It was a good script by Paul Schrader, too, I thought.

RS: In some of its tonalities—don't laugh now—that movie reminded me of *After Hours.* Do you know what I mean? It's New York at night.

MS: Crazy things happen.

RS: Well, of course. And it is someone being pushed—

MS: —to the limits.

RS: Yet this movie is not unfunny.

MS: It's terribly funny, and kind of audacious. I mean, you have the drug dealer impaled on a fence, hanging off a twenty-two-story building. And as he's talking to Nick Cage—the actor's name is Cliff Curtis—suddenly there are fireworks over the city. And he just shouts, "I love this city!" [*Laughs.*]

RS: It's one of the great crazy scenes.

MS: Yeah, that's sort of my homage to Manhattan. With the fireworks at the end of *Manhattan.*

RS: You mean, your homage to Woody's *Manhattan?*

MS: No, my Manhattan, but referencing Woody's film.

RS: That may be the essence of Marty Scorsese right there. [*Laughs.*]

MS: [*Laughs.*] He's crucified! [*Laughs.*] Twenty-two stories up. Why save a drug dealer—he's such a creep? But he's got to be saved.

And Nick is just taking his blood pressure, holding on. "They're sending up relief, they're sending up people, relax." And, actually, this is true, a lot of this really happened.

They had to use acetylene torches to break the wrought-iron fence. They take the guy to the hospital with part of the fence in him. He's sitting there forever waiting for the nurse to come by. And she goes, Well, hopefully, you'll go to the ER.

He says, Hopefully I'll go? What do you mean? I'm sitting here with a fence up my ass. Let's go. I mean, there's street humor in that.

RS: Absolutely.

MS: But Joe Connelly told me stories that are not that funny. The hell nights in the emergency room when everybody is freaking out. The horror of what he described to me—a terrible subway crash about ten or fifteen years ago, for example.

RS: I remember it.

MS: Some of the things he described seeing you can't talk about. And the self-doubt: If you had taken your finger and held it in his heart long enough, you could have stopped the bleeding. I mean, this is real stuff. This is happening every night, every day.

They have patients they call frequent fliers, people who keep coming back, homeless people. Or people who drink too much. "Just put him over there. It's George again." We've seen those people. I've been in hospitals—I tell you, a lot of that film came out of taking my mother and father, my father particularly, to the emergency rooms for over ten years. In and out of hospitals, getting phone calls: Something has happened, come down.

Then when my father died, the same thing happened to my mother. Three years of that. You walk into an emergency room at two in the morning. I'll never forget one place, it was run by nuns. One of them must've been four feet tall, about seventy years old. She had wrinkles in her face. She was Italian, really tough. She said, "Come in-a-here. Come in-a-here. Here's your mother!" I just followed her. It was like the nun who took the guy down from the tree in *Amarcord.* She just climbed up and hit him in the head and brought him back down. This nun was tough.

It was almost surreal. I walked by a room and I saw a man bandaged, full of blood, who had cut his own throat. It was one of the most horrific images that I ever saw. And these people deal with that every day. And nobody wants to know about it. We, as a society, don't want to know about it. It's like *Europa '51*, the Rossellini film, the woman who tries to help people in different ways. Ultimately she realizes you just can do one thing at a time, the best way you can. I'm not saying everybody has to go out and do these kinds of things. I'm just saying we need to be aware of it.

RS: Yes, of course. But there's something else about the film. It's very New York— you see the humor of it within the horror. People from other places don't see the world in quite that way.

MS: I see what you're saying. No, I am an urban person, there's no doubt, a New Yorker, really, Manhattan.

RS: In a way, it's one of the things you had in common with Elia Kazan. He used to say to me, "Oh, for Christ's sake, how do you live out there [in California]?" I said, "Well, I don't like it, Elia. But you know . . ." "Ah!" he would say. "I walk ten minutes around my house and I see more life in that ten minutes than I see in a month in Los Angeles!"

MS: It's true. You're sitting in a car out there, isolated. But I tried to be Californian, I really did.

RS: You talked about how horrible it was shooting *Taxi Driver.* And here you are, right back in the same environment!

MS: You're right, you're right!

RS: I mean, it's maybe not quite as intense as *Taxi Driver.* They're at least a lot of the time up in their cab, kind of at a height looking down.

MS: Drifting through, and looking down.

RS: But they have to get out of the cab, and they have to deal with people who are grievously sick or injured.

MS: I rode with them one night. It was quite something. And the music's playing, you know.

RS: Is Nick Cage's character, or, for that matter, Joe Connelly, fated to be there?

MS: Let's say there's a pattern to life. There probably isn't, but there's supposed to be a pattern. And Joe Connelly is out there on EMS right now. It is like fate for him to be dealing with these people.

RS: Going back to *Bringing Out the Dead* now, I see much more in it than when it was released. But speaking of fate, it seems to me, looking back, that the movie was sort of fated to fail, both critically and commercially.

MS: The picture was tough for audiences, and that was a moment [1999] that those kinds of films weren't being supported by the studios.

RS: That one was not supported by the studio at all, I believe.

MS: Not at all. And it was gone.

RS: But here's the only thing I know for certain: History is the only judge of movies, books, paintings, anything.

MS: I know.

RS: Whatever they said at the moment may or may not be correct. The real truth is revealed when we look at a movie fifty years later and think, God, it really is terrific. And lots of times, of course, the film is really not as great as I remembered it.

MS: I agree. But you know, it was tough, the film disappearing, but it was also a great time because two weeks after the film came out, my daughter Francesca was born. *Bringing Out the Dead* was the end of something that was very special, though.

RS: Was it the end of a kind of New York obsession?

MS: No, I think it had more to do with a philosophical cycle of my own. It had to do with trying to evade the fact that you're going to die, we're all going to die. You know, when I was staying at a hotel while my house was being renovated, even forty-one stories up, I heard the sirens constantly, from eight at night until about two in the morning. It got to the point where I had to use earphones to shut the sounds out. It was like the city was screaming in this agony and this pain.

GANGS OF NEW YORK

RICHARD SCHICKEL: I suppose the most tormented project you ever did is *Gangs of New York.*

MARTIN SCORSESE: *Gangs,* and *Last Temptation. Last Temptation* was the worst shoot.

RS: *Gangs* at least didn't present the same kind of powerful religious conflicts that *Last Temptation* did.

MS: What I'm referring to is the physical making of the production. *Temptation* was a matter of shooting time and the weather. We all had a kind of passion for it and just kept pushing through. Whereas in *Gangs* we had the sets and the actors— everybody was there. It was a different kind of pressure.

I'm too close to the pictures. A lot of them are too damn personal. I'll always be negative at first, but then I'll talk to some colleagues and think, Well, this was pretty good, even on *Gangs of New York,* which, at times, was nightmarish. Still, some of it was the best time we had in our lives, for a lot of us who worked on it.

RS: Why was it the best time?

A dream realized: Marty developed *Gangs of New York* for over two decades and finally realized his ambitions in 2002, in a flawed, brilliant film bedeviled by cost overruns and compromises.

MS: Just the nature of what we were able to put together, the world we created, and the enjoyment on the set.

Everybody was exhausted. There were conflicts all around. We had language problems—there were stuntmen from Yugoslavia. We didn't know what was happening sometimes. Yet somehow it was a wonderful place to be at that moment, whatever you may think of the film.

RS: I think the film has brilliant stuff in it.

MS: But as you've said to me, If I could have finished the Draft Riots . . . But we never got the money to do the Draft Riots [in massive opposition to the Civil War draft laws, which permitted the well-to-do to buy their way out of military service].

RS: I think it festered so long with you—well over a decade—that something got lost in the festering.

MS: Yeah, if I had maybe done it earlier. But in any event, even knowing that, still they were some of the best times we ever had. And some of the worst, really.

RS: What was so hard about making the film?

MS: The fact that we were running out of money. The pressure to finish. People were leaving, props were being taken away. Extras were leaving. We still had to shoot certain things and I wasn't sure we could shoot them with only three people or whoever was left. We managed, but it was hard. Did I use those shots? Maybe not, but still . . . To be honest, I could've kept going. It was almost like some of the big films in the seventies where directors just kept shooting.

But I couldn't go any further. The studio and my backers tried to help me. But at a certain point they said to me, We don't have any more money. That's when I put my money in. And it was swept up within a few days. It was just an obsession for me. I think of the world that I was in when I was making it. And that affects saying whether I like the film or not.

RS: Why did the movie take so long in the conceptualizing and writing stages? I mean, it became kind of a legend.

MS: Well, obviously, I grew up in that area. And when I became aware of St. Patrick's Old Cathedral and the graveyard around it, with the names on the tombstones, I realized the Irish were there before the Italians. I became fascinated by the history of the New York City downtown. The cobblestones talked to me. I started doing research on it in libraries—on the church, on Archbishop [John] Hughes, the power of the Catholic Church, the Irish at that time. And in 1970, on New Year's Day, I was house-sitting with some friends on Long Island somewhere and I found this book called *Gangs of New York* by Herbert Asbury, and I started reading it. Clearly it related to where I grew up. The section we took from the book was from the 1840s to the 1860s. There also were sections on the Bowery, where I grew up. Raoul Walsh drew on that for *The Bowery* with Steve Brodie jumping off the Brooklyn Bridge. Everybody still talked about that when I was growing up.

RS: Seriously? That was a long time before you were a kid.

MS: Oh, I remember, my father used to talk about Steve Brodie, some guy jumped off the bridge on a bet, and he lived. The whole struggle between the Irish and Italians was part of my youth in that neighborhood.

RS: So when you were growing up there were still Irish-Italian tensions?

MS: No. There were no more Irish—but we heard about it. We heard stories of how rough it was. My father was growing up there—he was born in 1913—and there was a lot of fighting, a great deal of tension. When we were living there, the Puerto Ricans were moving in. So it was a similar thing, but not as strong. Elizabeth Street at the turn of the century, after *Gangs* is set, was the street that had the highest infant mortality rate in the city—cholera, all kinds of disease. I didn't know that. Growing up, my father would tell me about different politicians, about Tammany Hall. My father would talk about Al Smith. My father was a Roosevelt New Dealer, until the fifties when he became more conservative.

What I'm saying here is that I never really was able to focus on how much of the story I wanted to tell, how much the story of that area reflected the overall city, the growth of New York, the growth of America. When I got together with Jay Cocks in the seventies and started working on it, Jay came up with a very beautiful script. It was almost like a novel: 179 pages. At that point, though, I was going through *New York, New York,* I was going through *The Last Waltz,* I was going through my own difficulties. I came out the other side through *Raging Bull,* even though I had thought I was going to come out of it with *Gangs of New York.* Maybe that was good, because I still hadn't gotten my hands around what Jay's story was, I couldn't quite grasp it. We became very influenced by the way Fellini did *Satyricon.* He said to Danilo Donati, his great costume designer, "We're walking in the streets of Rome and we lift one of the stones on the street, and underneath you see crawling around the ancient Romans." Fellini said about *Satyricon,* "It's science fiction in reverse." And there's a similar thing with aspects of [Sergio] Leone's *Once Upon a Time in the West.* All these styles were converging in our minds, and there are aspects of them in *Gangs.*

It eventually straightened itself out about 1990, when Jay and I worked on the script again and shaped it down to the story of Bill the Butcher and the young boy, Amsterdam, whose father Bill murdered and who wants to gain revenge. Then we came up with the idea that, for some reason, he can't kill Bill. But we knew that at the end we had to have the Draft Riots, and we moved the killing of Bill back to that part of the story. We made all kinds of adjustments—streamlining the story, developing set pieces that gave us the opportunity to depict life at that time, the way people lived. There had to be, for instance, a scene in which there was a theater riot. Because there were theater riots all the time. The working class and the gangs had no recourse to newspapers, so they all showed up at the theater to make themselves heard. There was a famous Astor Place riot where something like a dozen bystanders were killed.

RS: You've said to me that however horrendously you portrayed those times in your movie, you can't touch the reality of it.

MS: No. Even Dickens, when he came here, in his *American Notes,* said it was worse than anything in the East End of London. And I don't think we can even begin to fathom what it must have been like, what was going on in those cellars, in those caves below the streets—the pure evil of that criminal life. There were tunnels under 253 Elizabeth Street.

RS: Really?

MS: They're probably closed off now. But if you go into what used to be old Chinatown, there are still sweatshops below the ground.

RS: I had no idea—

MS: You can go there. Jay will tell you, he went with a policeman one night, because he was doing research on something and they took him through these sweatshops—illegal immigrants working there. I mean, that's a very old part of the city. It's filled with all these things.

What if you were really poor and there was no money, there was no work? The girls were dying at fifteen, drunk and having been prostitutes at twelve years old. People were just being washed away like garbage in that world.

That world was also reflected in the politics of the time, with Boss Tweed and others. So we had to fit those characters in, ending with the Draft Riots, which destroyed a lot of the city. Soldiers came in, howitzers were used. The soldiers had just fought at Gettysburg, you know. Nobody knows how many were killed in the riots.

RS: It seems to me that *Gangs* is harmed in a curious way by its greatest scene, which is that huge fight—

MS: —at the beginning. That was in the script from the very beginning in 1979. You never know where you are, and then finally you realize it's New York City.

RS: That fight is one of the great sequences—

MS: —and maybe we never topped it.

RS: That's what I was going to say. The Draft Riots just can't compare to that fantastic scene.

MS: Yeah, I know. But as I said, when it came to the Draft Riots, there were tensions with the money. We had focused on violence at the Colored Orphans Asylum in the script and then we couldn't shoot it. That's not an excuse; we just didn't have the dough, and we had to drop it, and it's therefore flawed. Maybe we should have shot the Draft Riots differently. But somehow it fell together that way, and that's all we were able to get. We knew it all had to end in some sort of conflagration of the whole city, like the volcano erupting in *The Last Days of Pompeii*. We did not get enough of that done.

RS: Whereas I've never seen anything better than that opening.

MS: That was shot at the end of January 2001, and after that, the money ran out. The studio said to just finish up the movie. I'm not blaming them. If I had planned it differently, if I'd rewritten it right, we could have done more. But I took a chance. I wanted to get the opening the way I wanted it, and the pagoda scene, too—the center of the film. That had been shot around Christmas 2000. I knew we would have to fill in the rest and try to get as much of the Draft Riots as possible.

RS: Is it right to say that intensely action-oriented scenes are much better done in a limited area, and that the Draft Riots are—

MS: Massive.

RS: So that's almost an endemic problem in doing the Draft Riots?

MS: Right. We had specific incidents—it is all very well documented. But we were only able to shoot a few. That's not an excuse—we chose them. We had to have the elephant go by, for example.

RS: Right!

MS: Harvey Weinstein was very funny about that. At a certain point he said, "Marty, out of these ten scenes, we can only afford three. What do you want to do?" I said, "Three, okay." But I squeezed another two out of him. He turned to me and said, "Okay. You can have the elephant, although we don't really need the elephant." I said, "Yes, we do, because it's probably the most surreal shot." When Barnum's Circus blew up and the animals were running in the streets [an event that occurred two years later but was incorporated into the film]. Can you imagine? But it reminded me of the bombings of Berlin in '45, when the zoo was hit and the animals ran out. Civilization in Berlin was gone. That's what it must've felt like in the Draft Riots.

RS: Earlier, you said this was manifestly a movie you just had to do. You said it reflects the history of your people—

MS: Well, New York. And how it reflected the country overall. As I did more research over the years, people kept saying that if democracy didn't work in New York, it wasn't going to work anywhere else in the country. Urban areas such as Philadelphia and Boston had similar gangs and troubles.

RS: I know you sometimes develop scripts for many long years, everyone does. But this one seemed to go on forever. Maybe it's just because I knew Jay so well. I think the first time I ever met him I asked, "What are you doing?" And he said,

"Oh, I'm working with Marty on *Gangs of New York.*" And thirty years go by and he's still—

MS: It's a good point. I don't think I ever wanted to finish it.

RS: Really? Why?

MS: I was obsessed with the story of the city. There were so many wonderful elements to it, so many anecdotes, different characters, so much I wanted to show. It just never settled satisfactorily in my mind. I felt I had to sacrifice too much of all that, and I never felt comfortable about it.

RS: Is it fair to say, no matter how much money you had, how much time you had, that it just had to be some kind of giant epic?

MS: Yes. It would have been a good five-hour picture. It's not that odd today. People see things in two parts. There are television shows like that. I mean, *The Sopranos* goes on and on and you have an almost endless film, really. People like that.

RS: But *Gangs* was conceived before the possibility of doing a *Sopranos*-like development, which might have satisfied you better.

MS: It *would* have satisfied me more. When television films started to be made in the sixties, especially things like Don Siegel's *The Killers,* we thought they would explore character: there would be a chance to do a twelve-hour film when needed. But it became a different medium. And, in a sense, not a director's medium.

RS: I was thinking of something like *Rome* on HBO.

MS: Yes, exactly.

RS: That has the sweep, and it's telling the story of that particular place and time.

MS: Or *I, Claudius* on the BBC. That would have been ideal for *Gangs of New York.* You'd just have to conceive the picture differently, like a television film where you shoot ten pages a day. I mean, the amount of money that was going into the costumes, the shooting, the extras, bringing people in from Ireland and from England—this could only go on for a certain amount of time. You have to be incredibly schedule-conscious.

But I still have part of my mind back in the seventies—when you were able to do an epic film, maybe a three-hour film, and the marketplace accepted it. *Apocalypse Now,* for instance. That's what I had in mind. I think *The Departed* is longer, actually.

RS: It is.

MS: There's nothing that I cut out of *Gangs of New York* that I would want to put back in the picture. Whatever I cut out I did better in another movie anyway. It's just very simply, as I said, that I never finished the script.

RS: It's almost as if you get trapped in projects. You want desperately to make a given film. You keep thinking of compromises that could get it made. But there's some part of you that doesn't want to make those compromises, you hold on to some unrealizable dream.

MS: Yes. There's no doubt of that. I mean, you actually said it. The other thing is that at that point we were able to do it, we were able to actually build a lower Manhattan in Rome, where we shot. And it behooved me to try to find a way to pull it together.

RS: Absolutely.

MS: Or at least, Part One. In my mind it was sort of like Part One. In a way, whether it's good, bad, or indifferent. There are some interesting scenes.

RS: There's a lot of good acting in the movie.

MS: The acting is wonderful.

RS: Particularly by Daniel Day-Lewis.

MS: He's great. I loved him in *There Will Be Blood.* He was amazing. At first, I didn't even know it was him.

RS: Those last minutes in the bowling alley are beyond the beyond. [It's a scene in which Daniel Day-Lewis—playing perhaps the most misanthropic character in film history—bloodily beats to death the preacher-son of his longtime business rival.] I've never seen anything quite like it in a movie. You're following this interesting story and then suddenly this outburst of insanity happens.

MS: I went with it, you know. It's pretty wild.

RS: It's astonishing. I said to Day-Lewis when I met him, "I've just never seen anything like it. I couldn't imagine where that came from." And he said, "It's funny, my mother said the same thing to me."

MS: They asked me to do the Q and A for an event in New York with Paul Thomas Anderson. There was only one other movie from my generation about oil discovery—*Giant.* And I said, I guess for your generation it's more *Chinatown.*

He goes, "No, no, it was *Giant*." He had seen *Giant* a number of times and loved it. And I said what I love about the picture is that it eschews the epic conflagration at the end which seems like it always has to happen.

RS: Right.

MS: In *Giant* there is this great scene where Jett Rink [James Dean] is fighting with Rock Hudson in the basement of the hotel, where he gets drunk and all the shelves collapse. And then, of course, the fight in Sarge's restaurant.

RS: That's a great scene. It's corny as hell.

MS: It's corny as hell and he loses the fight. Anyway, what was interesting here is that instead of exploding, the scene implodes. In this ridiculous bowling alley!

RS: A mansion having a bowling alley—it's almost the ultimate in conspicuous consumption.

MS: Oh, boy.

RS: I imagine you're drawn to *There Will Be Blood* in part because it's another father-son drama.

MS: In part, I suppose. But I have to emphasize again that by the last thirty years of my father's life, we became friends. I'm dealing with it still in the Kazan documentary Kent Jones and I are finishing, which is really more of a memoir, almost a eulogy. And it has, again, to do with Kazan's film *East of Eden*, which is a great exploration of the love and hatred of a son and his father.

RS: But your father wasn't anything like Raymond Massey's father in *Eden*.

MS: Not at all. But in the child's mind, I may have conjured up images of God the Father in the Old Testament.

RS: Well, if you see him in the documentary you made [*Italianamerican*], your dad is very silent, though kind of amiable.

MS: At first very secretive. And then he opens up, you know. It seems to be a well that I keep drawing from. There seem to be some primal feelings that I kind of feel comfortable with, and enjoy. Maybe not enjoy, but that seduce me into certain projects.

RS: Talking about Daniel Day-Lewis: There is the character in *Age of Innocence*, and then there's his character in *Gangs of New York*. It seems as if he is some sort of go-to guy for you when it comes to father figures.

MS: There's an element of my father in *Gangs*. Because of a kind of strict way of thinking, and, as I told you, my neighborhood was like a little medieval village.

RS: Daniel Day-Lewis is a fastidious man who's an absolutely great father, in a certain sense, in *Age of Innocence*. I find it fascinating that you would even think of the same actor for Bill the Butcher.

MS: Look at *My Left Foot*—the way he controls his body; the energy it takes to play that character, the energy it took for him to do a painting with his feet. He actually did one then.

RS: Did he?

MS: It's hanging in Jim Sheridan's house, the director's house, in Dublin. There's a kind of determination in that work. More than that, there's an anger that you certainly could tap into—a good, healthy kind of anger, not a self-destructive, King Lear–like anger, as there is in *There Will Be Blood*. He's shouting at the elements by the end of the movie. There's definitely that in him. I saw it in *My Left Foot* and I saw it in *Last of the Mohicans*. And the great sense of humor in *Room with a View*. So I said to myself, Well, the guy can do anything.

RS: From some things you've said, I gather that even as late as your parents' young years, some of the *Gangs* architecture and atmosphere still lingered in your neighborhood.

MS: When my mother was a girl, the horrible tenements still existed. You looked out at nothing. The first man who did a film there was Raoul Walsh. He shot some of *Regeneration* there.

RS: I've never seen that movie.

MS: It's magnificent, incredible. It's unrelenting, a tough movie, because he knew the people at Five Points, what was left of the Five Points. He put some of them in that film.

RS: Raoul was born in New York.

MS: His *The Bowery* is like my *Goodfellas* in a way. You know what I'm saying?

RS: Not exactly.

MS: Because he knew those people, knew their folklore. He knew how they went in a bar and how they ordered a beer, how they moved, the kind of clothes they wore. He understood Chuck Connors, the famous racketeer, who coined the phrase "rackets." He threw big dances the police would come to. There's some-

234

Leonardo DiCaprio and Marty on the *Gangs* set.

thing about all that that was second nature to Raoul—similar to the way I grew up around that area of Italian Americans. He was Irish. He really had the line on post–Civil War to turn-of-the-century New York—of the New York Tenderloin (up in the Chelsea area), the New York underworld. I think he had it down cold.

There's something about the way my parents described their lives—I have that script that Nick Pileggi and I are working on, "Neighborhood" it's called now, and it's about them and that period of time. It's partly the way they described their lives and the way they lived and the way they dealt with just the basics of living—how everybody would take care of each other in the tenements, where the toilets were, where they had to wash, a sink, one faucet, if they had any at all. The way people lived, and the way they had grocery stores, the kind of food you would get, that really had ties to the way people lived in early New York. It's the same as Orchard Street, the same with the Jewish area. I felt—

RS: Some living connection there—

MS: Yes, absolutely. You could feel it in the walls of the tenements. There were ghosts. It had a history and it had character. We knew so much of what had happened in that area.

RS: It's as if that history didn't exist when the official history of those times was written.

MS: Well, I guess it's like picking up *The New York Times,* the Metro section, where you see small articles that are front-page news in the tabloids. I remember back at NYU, people used to say, Read the tabloids, because they talk about real life. Because poor people don't have educations, that doesn't mean they don't struggle and suffer.

One guy I knew made page one in the *Daily News.* He was a nice kid across the way, maybe sixteen or seventeen. He was the son of the lady who ran a soda fountain at 240 or 238 Elizabeth. She was really nice, let us hang out there. And he was always very quiet. In 1950, '51 maybe, he took part in a robbery, had guns, and got shot. It was on the front page of the *Daily News.* And, you know, his mother was in that luncheonette for another thirty, forty years—next to the butcher. It's just you get into situations.

RS: Why?

MS: No education. That kid probably needed money. Probably there was peer pressure. He was very quiet. He wasn't an aggressive kid. The next thing you know, they were going in with guns. They come out, the cops are there. They see a kid with a gun, they start shooting.

RS: It's obvious that that kid—or the modern mobsters in your other films—are in some way the inheritors of the world you portray in *Gangs.*

MS: I was always drawn to a world that seems so strange, almost like the ancient world, yet still filled with the same kind of people. We haven't changed.

The Bowery was the last dregs of the Five Points. You lived with people dying in the streets. It was what the Five Points must have been like.

RS: But how different was the *Gangs* underworld from the underworld you saw glimpses of?

MS: Very different. There was anarchy, more tribalism in the past. My grandparents were tribal, but not like what we showed in *Gangs,* where somebody would turn on you and betray you.

RS: You've said you feel *Gangs of New York* isn't as violent as some of your other movies.

MS: Nowhere near the violence of my other pictures. It does go on and on, a continual cycle of violence, though. It's as Daniel Day-Lewis's character says: A man robs me, I cut off his hand. He talks against me, I cut his tongue out. He tries to harm me, I cut his head off and put it on a pike so everybody can see it.

Maybe if I'd made the film earlier, it would have been horrendous in terms of graphic violence, but I don't really want to do it anymore—after doing the killing of Joe Pesci and his brother in *Casino,* in the cornfield. If you look at it, it isn't shot in any special way. It doesn't have any choreography to it. It doesn't have any style to it, it's just flat. It's not pretty. There was nothing more to do than to show what that way of life leads to. Not only what it leads to, but that it leads to this being done to you by your closest friends. It's brutal, it's nasty, it's humiliating, to say the least.

It speaks to some people. Joe Pesci was playing golf, and a couple of older men were on the same course. Afterwards, they were all in the locker room, and when they changed into their street clothes, it turns out that the two gentlemen are monsignors. They went over to Joe and said, We admire your work. Joe figures they are going to compliment him on *Home Alone.* But they said they really liked him in *Casino.* They said they really felt bad about how he died in the film. They really felt for him in that sequence.

And Joe said to me later, That's exactly what you wanted to do, right? I said, Yes—as mean and nasty as he gets throughout the whole picture, does he deserve his fate?

RS: It's pathetic.

MS: It really is pathetic and sick and terrible. I remember I showed a rough cut to John Kennedy Jr., and it upset him very much. When he got out of the screening room, he was walking in the hall. I said, What's the problem? He said, I just got a little nauseous.

But *Gangs of New York* is stylized, like choreography, I think, so the violence seems held back to a certain extent.

RS: It was more mass violence. The violence in *Casino* was pretty much one-on-one.

MS: It's happening right now as we speak, all around the world. In Iraq, in Afghanistan—the breakdown of society, the breakdown of civilization. We'll be reduced to chaos again.

We bombed Afghanistan into rubble, where, you know, warlords have taken over. Kids today don't know what happened in China in the 1920s. Just look at the beginning of *Lost Horizon.* The Chinese warlords. They cut off heads just for the equivalent of speeding. Read Edgar Snow's books.

RS: What you're saying is that we're witnessing a kind of fraudulent nationalism that's masking sheer chaos.

MS: You give a seventeen-year-old kid a gun and put him in a firefight, it's going to be rough. Kids often don't think they can die. Kids can easily become like animals, you know.

RS: By which I guess you mean a reversion to primitive tribalism?

MS: Yes. Definitely. The old genie is out of the bottle. We're in for hundreds of years of it.

I read ancient history to learn how the empires fell. The barbarians at the gates. Take *Gangs of New York*—their gods are Celtic war gods. It's not Jesus suffering on the cross. They're tough bastards. They're going to kill and maim. The reality is that the war gods are the ancient gods. The history of God, the development of monotheism, is warlike.

THE AVIATOR

RICHARD SCHICKEL: How did *The Aviator* get off the ground, so to speak?

MARTIN SCORSESE: At the time, I really wanted to do *Silence* [his script about Jesuit missionaries in Japan]. I tried writing the script with Jay Cocks in 1991 and it didn't turn out right. There were also problems with the rights. The other picture I really wanted to do was *Gangs of New York,* which eventually, obviously, got made. Meantime, I had to work, I had to find something.

When this script came to me, they didn't tell me what it was about. It just said "The Aviator." I don't really like flying very much. I'm fascinated by it, but I just don't like it. But there's also a kind of beauty to films about flying—like *Hell's Angels,* which is still the best work with planes in a picture [it was released in 1930, though begun some years earlier], Howard Hughes directing. Even William Cameron Menzies's design of the plane in *Foreign Correspondent* was terrific. So I've always had some fascination.

But I'd always stayed away from a work on Hughes because I knew there were many people, a number of excellent filmmakers, who had been trying to make pictures about him over the years: it was sort of their territory. Warren Beatty wanted to make a Hughes picture for years. He talked to me about it—he talked to *everybody* about it. Spielberg also wanted to make it. The legend of the strange-looking old man who lived in one room.

The only thing I knew of Howard Hughes was his involvement in *Hell's Angels,* and what a lot of people know of him today: that he was a very famous, very, very rich man who died holed up in a room somewhere, and looking kind of strange toward the end.

By the way, I didn't think the dramatic scenes in *Hell's Angels* were all that good.

RS: They were awful. But the flying was great.

MS: William K. Everson showed it in 16 millimeter at NYU, and I sneaked into his class to see it for the first time. Then I saw the restoration of it. It was amazing—especially the flying sequence. *The Outlaw* I didn't like. But I liked some of Hughes's other films, like *Scarface,* which he produced. I loved that film. Not as much as *Public Enemy,* though.

RS: You couldn't see *Scarface* for a long time. Hughes had it held back.

MS: You couldn't see it, right.

RS: It's a movie Howard Hawks directed, but never much liked. He said to me it was not in his style. He said, "You know, I'm hanging cameras from the ceiling and all around. My style is eye-level camera, real simple cutting."

MS: But he has the long tracking shot in the beginning which is very, very good.

RS: But, really, he wasn't a big tracker.

MS: No, but that really worked with the shadow. And then, of course, the bit of music from *Lucia di Lammermoor* that Paul Muni whistled whenever he killed someone in *Scarface.* We used that in *The Departed*—a reference to that. And we put the Xs all over the bar, one for everybody who gets killed.

RS: What do you mean, Xs?

MS: There are Xs in practically every frame in *The Departed* to reference *Scarface.* Every time someone is killed in *Scarface,* there's an X in the frame. But it's hidden—it's either a shadow or part of the set design. We literally put Xs on the walls with the shadows, and the light, even when they salute at the end, the two hands sort of cross.

RS: And why did you do that?

MS: So that if people ever go back, they would have fun noticing the Xs. I mean, it was too much, we put too much in. But you didn't notice. That's a good thing.

RS: Let's go back to your initial response to "The Aviator."

MS: It took me twenty pages to realize that at the beginning it's about Howard Hughes directing *Hell's Angels*. By the time I finished reading it, I saw that it goes from 1927 to 1947, which means it covers just twenty years of his life. It doesn't deal with his end, just elements of it. There are nervous breakdowns in the film that lead eventually to the big one at the end. And also four plane crashes—two of them in the film. And one car crash, which did a lot to his head. Then, too, it had a sense of the obsessive, which was important to me—the obsessive nature of his cleanliness, and how he got wrapped up in it.

But the main thing was this was a very vibrant, alive young man—aging over twenty years, going through hell, with more hell to go through when the film is over.

What I hadn't understood, but which John Logan's script made clear, was how important he was in aviation. I didn't understand what the XF-11 flight was like, or the H-1, or particularly, the nature of the Hercules, the giant plane he built and how he's affected a lot that we do in our lives.

The script had an upbeat feeling about him, before the illness set in. I think what John was trying for was something that had the spirit of adventure—a hope of what this country could be. It's about this spirit of the explorer—the spirit of

Meet the press: Howard Hughes, on the edge of madness, after getting the Spruce Goose into the air at the end of *The Aviator.*

someone who kept testing the limits and pushing and pushing, because this was the country to do it in. You know, when they got to California, there was no place else to go. That's it. Everybody who wants to make it big goes to California, because it's the last place, it's the furthest west you could be. You've got to make it there, or not make it at all. So you have everybody going out to be stars in California. That's part of America. And then the disease sets in.

RS: But these are also businesses that oddballs could go into. They were for outsiders, people who couldn't go to Wall Street and be in investment banking.

MS: They were going to do it on their own, they were going to make movies.

RS: Or build airplanes. Something visionary.

MS: "Visionary" is the word. And the thing about it, too, was the idea of the sky being the last frontier. When you couldn't go any further west, you go up in the sky. But then the sense of rapaciousness sets in. It's something we're dealing with in this century.

I thought the story was fascinating, and a good introduction to Hughes. There are other people who may want to do other aspects of his life, but this film deals with the young Hughes, who is not only flying, but making a picture about flying. It's crazy—you know there were four men killed making that film? He was shooting from the cockpits of those little planes, almost scooters. I was in one of them, though of course I didn't go up in it.

So it is Hollywood spectacle combined with internal conflict, and the destruction of this man—at least the seeds of it. Beyond that, of course, he was known as a great lover. From the year he was born, 1910, to about 1970, he had relationships with hundreds of important people. You mention a person's name, Hughes was with him, or her.

I found the script particularly interesting because of the relationships John Logan decided to highlight. He fictionalized at times to give the essence of what it must've been like to be around him, to be like him. He left out sections of the life so that the sections that remain resonate more.

I said to John, You've got to deal with all the things he did with the women. But which ones do you drop, which ones do you use? John already had in the script three women. Katharine Hepburn is one whole story. Ava Gardner is another. We added one scene where she attacked him, because that actually happened, and I wanted something more for her. Then there was the woman made up to represent all the other women, Faith Domergue. I felt those three women would be it. The prime interest, of course, is in the Katharine Hepburn relationship, because they felt comfortable with each other, yet ultimately had to break up.

A lot of the film has to do with the nature of wanting to be famous, the nature of wanting to be stars, the nature of what that's like for two creative people. He was creative and, of course, she was a genius at what she did. So you do feel something when they break up.

Also it's got Hollywood in the 1920s, Hollywood in the '30s. It's got the Coconut Grove in those days.

RS: It is interesting, the notion of Howard Hughes kind of having it all in his earlier years in an almost innocent way. I mean, I love it when he just swoops down on the beach and picks Hepburn up and takes her flying. What the hell, he can do anything he wants, he's so rich. And then he starts, almost imperceptibly, going crazy. That scene where he keeps repeating, "I want to see the plans. I must see the plans."

MS: Oh, that was scary. He just gets brain-locked. And don't forget, he had had two car accidents and two plane crashes; his concussions were bad, and that affected him.

RS: There's now all this research in professional football on concussions. And they're seeing these players who are addled from it and they don't even know it. They reach their forties and they're not completely with us any longer. I'm sure that happened to Hughes.

MS: I really believe that.

RS: Even though he was an oddball to begin with.

MS: Yes, absolutely. Some doctors told me, Oh, he had to be autistic, he was this, he was that. I don't know. Whatever it was, he was certainly odd. But also the empire contains the seeds of its own destruction. He represented that to me. That's why that repetition scene at the end—and the way Leo [DiCaprio] did it—was so good. And then, you know, "Moonlight Serenade" slips in.

That bland sound of Glenn Miller's that was so nostalgic in a way: America right at the beginning of empire. That's what I thought the movie was about. I thought it would be so nice to end it right before he flies the Hercules.

RS: But you let him have his triumph, getting the Spruce Goose [the Hercules] off the ground for a few minutes.

MS: I added the men with the white gloves, and especially John Reilly saying, "Everybody works for you, Howard." When John Logan came up with that line, I said, "Perfect." Whether it's a dream or not, that's what he's feeling: "Everybody works for you." And suddenly they're all closing in on him. It's the beginning of a long, long decline. He dies like an ancient Greek king, doesn't he? I mean, he had his own doctors. He's not going to go to a hospital. Why should he go to a hospital? His doctors give him the drugs he needs, the liquid codeine. And, you know, when regular doctors came in, if you read the reports, they said, "This isn't neglect; what can we tell you?"

RS: It's really a romance, often a dark one—the romance of flight, certainly, the romance of these beautiful women, and the romance as well of invention, where the individual inventor-genius could still make a difference.

MS: Right. It begins in the time of Edison. It's the time of America inventing everything new. Hughes was a pioneer.

RS: Movies and aviation were invented at around the same time.

MS: The same time.

RS: And they were run by the same kind of people. The WASPs did aviation, and the Jews did the movies. But in terms of ambition, of inventing businesses that had never existed before, they were the same kind of people.

The film has a wonderful conflict between Hughes's TWA and Juan Trippe's Pan Am, though, which I didn't know very much about. For some reason I remembered some old newsreel footage of a congressional hearing where they both appeared.

MS: Until I did some research, I didn't realize how interesting Juan Trippe was—curiously, my wife and her father were friends of his. As the head of Pan Am, he wanted to keep those international routes to himself, away from Hughes's TWA. The fight about the international routes was interesting to me. And then there's the climactic sequence when Hughes does, ultimately, fly, just for a couple of minutes, the Hercules. It was a plane that was five stories high, you know.

He was like an ancient Greek mythological king, like Croesus or Midas, in a way. In my mind, his obsessive-compulsive disorder is like the labyrinth that he gets stuck in—sort of like the Minotaur. He's got wings, like the ones Daedalus makes for his son, Icarus, the wings to get out of that labyrinth, but he flies too close to the sun and the wings melt, and he comes down. There's a Hughes metaphor there. His pride and his ego destroyed him, too. But it was still worth it, in his mind, whatever happened.

The film has a pretty dark character at its center, but it's a very light film in a way, too, in a good way, I think. It's an upbeat picture, except for the last half hour.

RS: But even then he at least gets the Spruce Goose off the water.

Crash and burn: Leonardo DiCaprio, as Howard Hughes in *The Aviator* (2004), faces one consequence of his passion for flight.

MS: Yes, he does. We felt, though, that we were doing a film about hubris, the kind of thing that made all our European forefathers want to get across to the other side, to California. But at a certain point it's going to stop. You know? [*Laughs.*]

RS: You run out of country, standing there on a beach in Malibu and wondering, What's next?

MS: What's next is that you've got to deal with yourself.

RS: Let's talk a little about the style of the film—the use of color in particular, which is spectacular.

MS: *The Aviator* is a good example of really embracing two-color and three-color schemes of shooting. And then the scene in the Senate hearing was a more neutral color in a way, which eased the film into the modern world.

RS: In the early passages it's very beautiful, and not just in the flying scenes. For instance, when he's courting Hepburn on the golf course, it has a kind of Hollywood-of-the-time look.

MS: It's two-color, Cinecolor. What we did was we dropped out the yellow. We had only red and green. And her lips are orange practically.

What she wears at Pantages Theater—the actual color of the dress is very different. In reality the dress is a greeny mustard color, but on film it reads as peach.

RS: Really?

MS: We made it into literally two-strip Technicolor. First of all, we did it in the costumes, in the color of the sets. Then, finally, it was enhanced digitally. Until we got to the 1940s, the scene where he takes her to an opening. She's with Louis B. Mayer, and he goes to the bathroom and can't touch the doorknob. That's when we slipped into three-strip Technicolor.

RS: Since two- and three-strip Technicolor don't exist anymore, how do you re-create that?

MS: Well, first I showed the crew many different films. Luckily, there was a color show in L.A. at the Academy, and they started with the beautiful nitrate black-and-white print of *Midsummer Night's Dream,* just to show how beautiful black-and-white was. Then they showed whatever extant examples of two-strip Technicolor and Cinecolor films were available—some very bad films, but some of the colors were just beyond belief. Then, of course, they went into three-strip Technicolor with *Robin Hood* and *Becky Sharp.* Ultimately, they showed a beautiful clip of *East of Eden* in an original Scope print. And they showed some clips from *Ryan's Daughter* in 70 millimeter, and it looked very beautiful. So we took the cast and crew to that Academy screening, and then I started screening films on big screens at the Sony studios—everything from *Divorce of Lady X* to *The Mystery of the Wax Museum* to *Dr. X* to *Blithe Spirit.* And then eventually *Leave Her to Heaven,* in color. Some of Ava Gardner's clothes in our movie were based on what Gene Tierney was wearing in that film. The use of blues and the reds.

RS: Oh, that film seems to me—

MS: Dazzling.

RS: I mean, that color is just—

MS: Lurid.

RS: Blinding.

MS: So *Leave Her to Heaven* became very important, and a film which I love called *Desert Fury*—Lewis Allen directed with Burt Lancaster, Lizabeth Scott, and Mary Astor.

RS: Oh, that's an odd, wonderful film.

MS: And having designed the costumes and the sets as much as possible in those colors, we then went the extra steps in digital. I would show the designers old westerns in Cinecolor, and say, "You see the way the light is reflecting off the gun? That's the blue we want."

RS: So what was probably pretty easy in the day of three-strip Technicolor becomes an enormous task now.

MS: It was crazy, but it was fun. [Robert] Richardson did it and Rob Legato did the visual effects. And the lab did a great job. So the color meant something special.

RS: Let me stop you right there. The average viewer is not going to know that's two-color or three-color. You could have done a completely respectable-looking movie that would have satisfied viewers and critics. So why go to all that trouble?

MS: I don't know. I never even thought of it that way. I mean, part of it is the enjoyment of doing something special and creating a look, a certain look. It's just the nature of the process. I just felt it was real important with *Aviator.*

I did it in *New York, New York,* too. I would get stills from *Band Wagon* and from all other films like it and literally say "duplicate this" to Boris Leven, and then he would add to it, including painting the sets. And we painted lipstick on the men. And the shoulder pads were exaggerated two or three inches. It was just the way I saw it. I mean, certainly, another person doing *The Aviator* or a Howard Hughes film could shoot it straight. It would be fine. It's just a different vision of it. But I thought Hughes had a great love for movies. He was there at that time when movies were making the transition to sound and color. I thought it would be nice to make a little history of the movies, to show the texture of the color changing as the film went on. It kind of fits with the subject matter, you know.

RS: I hadn't thought of it that way. But it's a nice touch—well, more than a touch, considering the effort that went into it.

MS: It's a history of color in a way.

RS: Certainly, though, looking back on the film, it did have a lot of the quality that I imputed to life in Hollywood in that age, maybe even the way you thought of it when you first went out there as a kid—just the way the personalities come into the premiere, for example. It had more excitement than I think those events actually had in life.

MS: But even when you saw the black-and-white newsreels of the *Hell's Angels* opening, it was pretty stirring. I mean, at a certain point we colorized some of that. He's sitting in the back of the car with Jean Harlow and, if you notice, the color seeps in. And it gets richer as he gets out of the car. Every shot was manipulated.

RS: In postproduction?

MS: Some of that was post. But her dress was exactly what she wore that night, though the color of it was different. It was photographed the way we wanted it. We filmed it one way knowing that the color would look another way. That was part of the texture of the movie. It was one of the incentives to make it. Hughes loved movies so much, and he made all those terrible ones later at RKO in beautiful Technicolor.

RS: I know.

MS: I mean, I think if he had been around twenty years ago, he'd have colorized all those old black-and-white pictures.

RS: He might have. Eccentric billionaires get to do that.

MS: Yeah, they get to do whatever they want.

RS: Was there something in the contrast between *The Aviator* and *Gangs of New York* that attracted you? You know, the feeling that you could be beautiful and elegant in the old Hollywood manner?

MS: That *was* part of the attraction. But I liked John Logan's script a lot. And also in my mind there was a somewhat religious aspect, flying like a god in the air.

RS: I never thought of that.

MS: Being closer to the final mystery, so to speak, of who we are and what we are.

Happy days: Hughes and Katharine Hepburn (Cate Blanchett) at the Cocoanut Grove nightclub.

RS: You're up there, you feel that much closer to it.

MS: You're much closer, and you become like a god.

RS: Now that I think about it, in your *Hell's Angels* flying sequences you show him up there in godlike command of the sequence.

MS: It was amazing what he did. I don't say that that's good, I'm just saying he did it. It took us about a year to do the whole sequence. We finally found that Leadbelly song that's on at the end of the film. Listen to the lyrics of Leadbelly singing about Howard Hughes: "I'm going to that world up there." It's beautiful because he has someone just drifting away into the stratosphere, flying away, never coming back. Which is what happened to Hughes in a way.

RS: Did you analogize at all between yourself and the obsessive Howard Hughes who's driving everybody crazy with making *Hell's Angels* or getting the Spruce Goose built or whatever?

MS: No, not really.

RS: What I'm asking is if there is something similar between the way you approach a task and the way Hughes did.

MS: We were getting the last shot, and there was something going wrong. They had begun to shoot before I had seen the setup. I said, "Stop! This has got to stop!" I said, "This is not worthy of Howard Hughes." I found myself jumping up and down on the tarmac, with the whole crew surrounding me in a semicircle. They were saying, "What is he talking about?" And I'm yelling, "We're not doing that shot! Get it out of there!" I had designed the shot according to the structure of what John Logan wrote in the script. It was the shot of Leo getting into the XF-11 cockpit before he takes off for the test flight that ends in the Beverly Hills crash. I wanted to boom down, but they just shot him getting into the plane. I said, "No. It has to be a boom down when he gets in to the cockpit."

Then someone said that we were going to have to do the shot again anyway, against a green screen. But I had a feeling—the kind of feeling that builds up in your mind, like paranoia. We were all working together, we were not enemies. But you never know what a studio is going to do. Let's say we go, God forbid, three weeks over schedule, four weeks over schedule. At a certain point, in order to satisfy the schedule, I might start to feel, You know what, I think I'll use that shot we did by accident on the set. And we'll forget the boom down.

But I didn't want to sacrifice that shot. I felt it would have been one of the worst things you could do—making aviation scenes not on the highest level. Basically, I was saying, Let's not sacrifice that shot. Let's not compromise here, because in desperation to finish, I may sacrifice that idea and use the less interesting shot.

I had a feeling that day. Maybe it had something to do with the hotel we were in. It was an old Spanish mission, and it was haunting. I couldn't sleep.

And I wasn't the only guy. Everybody felt it. I looked out the window and across the courtyard there was a monk, a Franciscan monk with a crucifix pointing at me. And I closed the curtain right away. We had just gotten there. It was early evening, and Joe Reidy came by. I said, "Joe, come in the room." Joe is an old Irish Catholic. I said, "I just want you to look out the window and tell me what you see out there." He opened it, and he looked. "Son of a —" I said, "Look at that. It's a clock tower, and they're life-size effigies of monks." I took another look and I said, "Wait a minute, it's a different monk." They had different ones. And it was turning. And they were all aiming their crucifixes at me.

I kept wondering why they gave me this suite directly across from the clock tower. Then, that night, Leo and the producer of the film went to Leo's room and they were talking, and the producer says, "What do you want to do? Do you want to go to sleep now?" "Oh, I don't think so," Leo said. So they watch a film. After the film was over, they looked at each other and one of them says, "Why don't we watch another film?" They didn't want to go to sleep! There was just something creepy about the place. And everything around us was burning.

RS: I find I'm very uncomfortable living in California. I find the place very spooky.

MS: I do, too.

RS: I feel much safer in New York.

MS: Me, too.

RS: There's very little chance that an earthquake will wipe your house out in New York.

MS: Or a major fire.

RS: You're always on the edge in L.A.

MS: All that potential for catastrophe.

RS: Not that a solipsist like Hughes would have noticed that. Not that he would have noticed that he was living a kind of perverse American epic. Finally, *The Aviator* is your American epic.

MS: Maybe.

RS: What you're saying is that a Howard Hughes would not arise in France or England. He had to come out of something that's—

MS: Intrinsically American.

RS: Profoundly and even inexplicably American.

MS: That's what attracts me and repels me about the whole story, that it could only happen here. You're right about it being an American epic—coming off another one, which was *Gangs of New York*. It was scary to do a picture on Howard Hughes because many people asked why I wanted to make a film on him. He represents certain things that aren't the best in the world, and about our country, and about what is it to be a human being. But I thought all of that was fascinating, because of the relationship that Hughes had in my mind to the country itself—about power and the corruption of power. It's also about the dream of the country, as I said.

RS: There were all those Mormon guys around him at the end, serving his obsessions. They obviously hoped they'd get at least some of his money. I know it's outside the scope of your film, but do you know where the money went?

MS: It's partly in one of the greatest research centers right now in Southern California, where it's doing great things for diseases like Parkinson's, and neurological research. It's amazing: somewhere down in the southern part of L.A. you pass by the Howard Hughes Research Center. There are big pictures of him, his name is all over the place.

RS: Go figure. But given the way his life ended, there's something profoundly, ironically right about that happening.

MS: Absolutely right.

NO DIRECTION HOME: BOB DYLAN

RICHARD SCHICKEL: Your Bob Dylan documentary [*No Direction Home: Bob Dylan,* released in 2005] came between *The Aviator* and *The Departed.*

MARTIN SCORSESE: It was a special one for me.

RS: I'm not a big Dylan fan, but I think it's very, very good.

MS: I love Dylan.

RS: Did you love Dylan way back when?

MS: I came late to Dylan. I didn't go to Gerde's Folk City, which was literally around the corner from the Greene building, where the NYU group was; he was there at that time. But I didn't know him. I first heard Dylan when he recorded "Like a Rolling Stone." Then I listened to the older stuff.

   I wasn't politically oriented. I became aware of different kinds of politics at NYU. As I said earlier, my father was a Democrat—until he voted for Eisenhower in 1956.

RS: What changed for him?

MS: Worried about money, maybe. How to pay for me to go to college. The Cold War, too. We really believed we were going to be bombed any second. The nuns in the school would have us go through that duck-and-cover routine. We had to wear dog tags every day. A nun would tell us whenever you hear a low-flying plane, that may be it.

RS: I think maybe urban Catholics with their hatred of Communism were more prey to those feelings.

MS: We were going to get it. We did get it eventually. September 11, we got it.

RS: Never thought of it that way.

MS: We're going to get it again. At some point it's got to happen. We're the center in New York.

RS: Possibly.

MS: Anyway, that period shaped me. I heard Dylan's record "A Hard Rain's a-Gonna Fall" and I found it so stirring, so beautiful and moving. I get chills even thinking about it now. The lyrics—and musically I liked it. My father said he didn't have a voice. But my mother would say that he didn't need a voice, that it was the way he sang. She said it was like Al Jolson, who didn't have a great voice. "It's a performance, the way he puts over a song," she said. She loved "Ain't Gonna Work on Maggie's Farm." She understood it. She was the one who had to go to work in the garment district, where your boss always won.

RS: Actually it's a very interesting point.

MS: Jolson's voice was kind of odd. It really was the performance.

RS: Absolutely.

MS: It was the shape-changer onstage—Jolson himself. Like Dylan, the shape-changer.

RS: That's right. One of the points Gary Giddins, the jazz critic, made about Jolson in *The Jazz Singer* was, to paraphrase, You look closely and he's shimmying like Elvis.

MS: That's right. A little later Cab Calloway did the same. When Jolson did "Toot, Toot, Tootsie" in *The Jazz Singer,* it was amazing. I used a bit of it in *Goodfellas.*

RS: I remember.

MS: I dislike *The Jazz Singer* in terms of the—

RS: Oh, it's an awful movie.

MS: It's terrible. But my mother and father loved it. They loved it because they identified with the family, the breaking of tradition.

RS: It's old country tradition versus new-style Americanism.

MS: Yes, and my father was feeling that we were losing the tradition of the family, the Sicilian family. And here were the Jewish people, who lived nearby, sticking to their family. Don't forget, the immigrant groups—the Jewish, the Italians, especially the southern Italians—had so much in terms of the family as tradition.

And we're losing it. My oldest daughter, Cathy, knows, because she was born in 1965. She remembers. She stayed with my parents. She knows the old family. Until Aunt Fanny, who lived in New Jersey, died in 2010, Cathy visited her quite often. She spent Christmas with her. Fanny was the last of the last. My daughter Domenica knows the tradition a little bit. She's thirty-one. But my little one will never know the world that *Mean Streets* came out of.

So I come from that. So when Dylan was singing protest songs, like "Gates of Eden," I didn't quite get it at first. But I loved his sound, the music itself.

RS: I agree with that. My problem with him is that I mix up the persona, which I don't care for, with the music, which I respond to.

MS: I didn't really get involved with the persona that much. Everybody has their own idea of who Bob Dylan is. That's why when Jeff Rosen brought it to me, again through Jay Cocks, who is a friend of Rosen's, it was hard to take it on.

RS: So what did Rosen bring to you? Just the idea of doing it?

MS: He brought to me the fact that he is the archivist and the producer of Bob Dylan. He said he would open up the archive to me, all this footage, years and years of footage. He said, "I finally did a ten-hour interview with Bob." He said Bob told him, "I will do this with you, but I'm not doing it again. I'm not sitting down and going over this stuff again."

Jeff said, "I'd like you to see just a little of the interview. I'd like you to see some interviews that we've gotten over the years that are in the archive of one of the old Broadway producers, some of the old record producers, Allen Ginsberg's interview. I'd like you to see a little of that, maybe an hour of it put together." I looked at that hour, and I loved the idea of Tin Pan Alley clashing with the folk-rock scene, the folk scene, the politics. But, still, I didn't realize some of the intensity of it, what happened at the Newport Folk Festival, when people reacted so badly against Dylan as a Judas for playing the electric guitar.

RS: It was quite something.

MS: It's betrayal again. Imagine having somebody yell "Judas!" as you're playing music onstage.

RS: I never understood what was so terrible about it.

MS: It's in the film; they actually have the footage, that moment when the guy yells "Judas!" Apparently it was only heard on bootleg records. But Jeff and Dylan had the footage. It's in the film.

RS: All because he was playing an electric guitar. Big deal.

MS: It was because he betrayed the cause.

RS: The cause being pure folkism?

MS: No. The political cause. Woody Guthrie played the acoustic guitar and said his "machine" kills fascists. Dylan had to play what people wanted him to play. He could make a difference, because people listened to him. He started to feel he didn't want to be pigeonholed. It's interesting how a man like that had such influence, which disturbed him.

RS: So it wasn't just the new technology.

MS: Not at all. Pete Seeger said, "This is music that's just for kids to dance to. We're not going to be able to change the world with this."

RS: He was right, pretty much. A movie, a song, or a poem cannot change anybody in any profound way.

MS: There is one thing, though, in that film. There's a scene with Dylan, when Pete Seeger took him down south, playing at the back of a truck. It's quite beautiful. They're taking it on the road.

I didn't realize that Pete Seeger, among others, had been blacklisted. "Good Night, Irene" was an important song in my house because my brother would play it on guitar, and you could hear it all through the neighborhood through the windows in the summertime, people singing "Good Night, Irene." My little one— I put it on her CDs, and the other day she said, "I can't get 'Good Night, Irene' out of my head." [*Laughs.*]

RS: Why is that such an important song?

MS: It just took over the country. Seeger made a big hit of it. It's in the film. At that point Seeger was blacklisted. He lost ten years of work. People felt Dylan was the new voice in that tradition. But apparently he didn't want to be that voice. He just wanted to explore what he wanted to explore—his own soul, his own heart, whatever.

The thing I discovered in watching Jeff Rosen's footage was that there was something about his face, the way he was answering the questions. He was telling as much of the truth as he could at that moment.

There's a story in the film about him stealing some records. It's quite funny. Well, let me explain about those records, he says. Those records were as rare as hen's teeth, so me, being a musical expeditionary, I felt it was okay to steal them.

He had the right. That was his obsession. He was going to do what he wanted. I found that interesting. But really the key was having this footage by D. A. Pennebaker of the 1966 tour. Robbie Robertson is on it. He told me they were playing, and people were yelling, "Trash, it's rubbish," that sort of thing.

So I got the idea that he would start playing "Like a Rolling Stone" and the young English fans would be saying, "Oh, it's awful, it's trash, he's sold out." I asked David Tedeschi, the editor, what would happen if we went right into conflict. Like a drama.

Then we would go back in time. And then he talked about his being in Minnesota, about the cold.

RS: Believe you me!

MS: And he said, "It was too cold to rebel." And then he heard that beautiful piece of music "We're Drifting Too Far from the Shore," too far from God, you know, on the Victrola in his house that his father bought. He felt that he wasn't born to the right family. He thought he came from somewhere else. So we just went on a journey with the movie. David Tedeschi and I—the film evolved as we worked on it.

RS: It has that feeling about it.

MS: We had to find the thread of it, which was that he had to be himself wherever it was going to take him. Ultimately he was going to disappoint a lot of people, make them angry by doing that, but he did it. That's important, I think, for an artist.

RS: I've been coming around on Dylan. It's a little like your father said; I don't like his voice. But now I'm coming a little more to your mother's point of view: "He doesn't need a voice." Still, Dylan doesn't strike me as a natural fit for you.

MS: Probably not.

RS: I mean, he's this middle-western Jewish person, far from your experience.

MS: I think of the lyrics, you know. I think of the lyrics.

RS: That's it?

MS: I think of the lyrics. I like the way he sings, too, and I've liked his presence in all the different incarnations he's had over the years. But in putting the film together, I could not bring any preconceived ideas. I didn't want to listen to anybody else's opinions.

That's very important, because he meant so much to so many different people at different times—they want him to be this, they want him to be that. The hard thing is to follow your own path.

RS: Especially in the world he lives in.

MS: And you have all these people pulling at you.

RS: That's right.

MS: You have good people pulling at you—Pete Seeger, Joan Baez, you know. And I wondered what made those other people so angry and bully him from the stage by calling him Judas. What did he do that was so bad? Some of those people were planted, from what I understand.

RS: Oh, really? So he picks up an electric guitar, big deal. I mean, I still don't fully understand it.

MS: The electric guitar actually made me listen to the old stuff.

RS: Why would his life turn on this one simple, stupid little question?

MS: Phenomenal. And where did it take him? The motorcycle crash. He just stopped playing then. He realized he had to take care of himself. He wasn't going to listen to anybody. He didn't want to be a voice for anybody's generation. He would do what he had to do.

RS: Anybody who wants to be anybody's generational voice is full of crap. There is no such thing.

MS: I know. But younger people put that on him.

RS: Obviously he wasn't part of your growing up musically?

MS: No. But I did use a quote from him on the title page of the script of *Mean Streets*—from "Subterranean Homesick Blues": "Twenty years of schooling and they put you on the day shift."

RS: In a funny way, then, the Dylan movie was a learning experience.

MS: Yes.

RS: More so than doing the Stones movie?

MS: Yes.

RS: Or *The Last Waltz*?

MS: Yes. The humor of it. And also then I began to realize, you could re-create for a younger audience what it was like in the late fifties, early sixties, in the Village, in Tin Pan Alley with its characters, on Broadway. They all contributed to the new music of the time.

RS: That's probably true.

MS: But also they're like Damon Runyon characters. These kids are not going to see people like that on the screen anymore. We only wanted to go up to the motor-cycle crash in 1966. We just intimated what was to come. I wanted to show that if you lived that life, this is what you would do. You take chances. Some people make it and some don't.

RS: That's absolutely true.

MS: You know, I didn't want to do things about his personal relationships. Dylan, a young boy in his teens, going on the road. Like with The Band: People got very annoyed because Ronnie Hawkins told Robbie, You come with me on the road, you'll get more pussy than Frank Sinatra. Some people were furious. [Film critic] Penelope Gilliatt was furious about that.

RS: Was she?

MS: And the film got an R rating because of that.

RS: I can't imagine Penelope Gilliatt—

MS: I was told a bottle rolled down the aisle at the screening.

RS: I wasn't at that one, you know. But Penelope, by the end of her career, was drunk at every screening I was ever in with her. And when she first came here, she was one of the most beautiful creatures I've ever seen. She had a beautiful little body and that red hair.

MS: And she was a great writer.

RS: Poor old Vince Canby, you know, kind of just holding her together for years.

MS: But those young guys, there was a bravado to their lives.

RS: Well, sure. Of course.

MS: And so the Dylan thing became for me—

RS: —what you said before: you trying to find this guy.

MS: The artist.

RS: And you do find him by the end of it.

MS: I think so, by the end. Especially that long line of people waiting for him, and finally his saying, "I want to go home. I want to go home." It's all there, I think. It's interesting to me that he was able to follow his own impulses creatively, he seemed to just find his way. Now, you may ask, What's so great about that? Well, he just evolved and kept working and working and working. In spite of all the criticism.

RS: There was always a lot of phony piety associated with the criticism.

MS: I only began to discover that as we were doing the film. But in any event, the Dylan film was a lifesaver for me, because I felt creatively satisfied with that picture.

RS: In a way that you had not lately felt satisfied?

MS: No.

RS: This is coming right after *Gangs*?

MS: Right after *Gangs* and all through *Aviator*, and after *Aviator*. Even right before *The Departed*.

RS: Were you frustrated after *Gangs of New York*—did you feel you needed to do something somehow purer or more authentic?

MS: Maybe. I don't know if I did it intentionally. But I felt good when I finished the Dylan film. I feel that the power, sometimes, of a documentary moves me so much more than a feature. Who knows if they're better than the features I make? I have no idea. What I know is that I felt emotionally and creatively satisfied having gone through two, three years of working on the Dylan film. It was very exciting to me.

CONVERSATIONS WITH SCORSESE

RS: Well, there is something, I've got to say, even in the kind of documentaries I do, where you do an interview, and somebody says something to you that you feel is unique.

MS: Yes, and *you* got it. The same thing happened with the Italian film documentary, which we were doing when we were finishing *Bringing Out the Dead.* It brought out quite terrific stuff, which I was not going to get again.

RS: That's correct.

MS: It's like when an actor does something in a film—an improvised move or line, or in many cases a written line—and it's sublime. I'm talking how I feel when I watch it. I'm not talking about critics or the audience.

RS: You have to have been there.

MS: Yes. And documentaries do that for me. They free me, in a way, to hope and pray for those moments in the features. It's what [Elia] Kazan did. In *On the Waterfront,* where the moments between the actors were so powerful—it's something I said when I started making films—it would be something just to be on the set, just to be in the presence of a moment like that. That was reinforced by my mother in the beginning of *Italianamerican,* when I started to run the camera to try to get them used to the film. My parents sort of took over the film. And I went with them. I asked my father a few questions as we went through. I realized once again—I always talk about this—that the close-up of the person speaking, that's cinema.

RS: You know, that's something Andrew Sarris wrote years ago; I think he was writing about one of the Eric Rohmer films, *My Night at Maud's* perhaps.

MS: I liked that.

RS: It's a wonderful film. He said, and I think I'm quoting him absolutely accurately, "The cinema has no greater spectacle than that of a man and a woman talking."

MS: He's right. It's something I hope for in each one of my pictures—somehow to get moments like that.

RICHARD SCHICKEL: *The Departed* was based on a pair of Japanese crime movies that were quite well received critically. And, of course, it eventually brought you your long-delayed Oscar. I gather you hesitated about making it at first.

MARTIN SCORSESE: For me to make a movie I have to become really enthused about a project. As excited as I was by the script by Bill Monahan, after a few weeks I decided I didn't want to do it. By that point the studio, Warner Bros., was very interested in doing it and Leo DiCaprio was involved. And they said, We really think you should do it. But it didn't seem right for me.

RS: Did you feel that you been here before, done it before?

MS: To a certain extent. Not on the level of the schematic of the story, the nature of the plot; I hadn't done that before. And the characters were interesting to me, even though they weren't fully there yet. But I just didn't know what I would do with this story.

RS: What conclusion did you come to?

MS: I had an anger about the story, about the world it's set in and how it reflected the world we're in now. That's the emotion and the energy that I worked from.

RS: Explain that a little more.

MS: It has to do with the nature of betrayal. The nature of a morality which, after 2001, has become suspect to me. I'm concerned about the nature of how we live, how we're living in this country and what our values are. This new kind of war is going to continue. Our children are going to inherit it. It's not going to be over with by the time we're dead. It's like a worldwide civil war. How does one behave in that context? What's right and what's wrong in that war? On the street level of *The Departed,* no one can trust one another. Everyone's lying to each other. It fueled me in a way. It got me angry, it got me going.

RS: So how nuts was Jack Nicholson by the end of that movie?

MS: Just as you saw on screen. Jack is very interesting because he will stay that way off camera, in the daytime and nighttime—always coming up with ideas, always pushing and shoving to the point where the other people in the picture come up to that level. That's where you experiment a lot, you try things.

He was always inventive. We knew we had to embrace this character in a different way from other characters like him in other movies I've made.

RS: I felt that Nicholson's work was very underappreciated. I thought he gave a superb performance.

MS: I thought so, too. Maybe it's the same kind of thing that happened when some people first saw *The Shining.* They thought Nicholson's performance was over the top.

RS: I thought it was great.

MS: Me, too.

RS: It was great in part because he can make you laugh without the laughter yanking you out of your involvement.

MS: I was stunned by the performance. I must say, though, that the first time I saw *The Shining,* I was taken aback. I didn't quite

Double agent: Leonardo DiCaprio pays a price for the dangerous game he played in *The Departed* (2006), the film for which Scorsese finally won his directorial Oscar.

know what to make of it. Then the second time, I was locked. I mean, yes, there are problems in the ending of the film, but the nature of his performance with Shelley Duvall is just . . . I don't have the words for it.

You know in *The Departed* he found things to use from his own past and his life. Jack's interesting in the way he'll go off in different ways. It's fascinating to try to jump in and hang on and go with it. He always struggles with the issue of whether he's gone too far. He's always asking, Should I go further?

RS: In a way, that's the art of acting.

MS: It is.

RS: I'll never forget one thing Elia Kazan said to me about Jimmy Dean. You know, I'm not a big James Dean fan—

MS: Yes, I know. But I was probably the right age to see *East of Eden.* Maybe you were a little older.

RS: There's just something in that performance that I never fully buy. Anyway, Kazan said, "Brando had technique. If he would do something good"— the kind of thing you're talking about Jack being able to do—"he could go on doing that as long as you needed him to do it." The over-the-shoulders, the close-up, the medium, whatever. "Dean had no technique. He would do a great thing, but that was it. If you came around for the side angle or whatever, he couldn't do it again."

MS: I was surprised when I worked with actors who were able to repeat. I'd always worked with actors where we would just sort of find things together, because I never had any training in acting school or any theories of any kind.

It's the actors who taught me. I was in love with performance from Kazan's films, and from John Cassavetes's *Shadows* and *Faces,* so I just like to be there when I see an actor do something that is so powerful, moving, and surprising— whether it's Bob De Niro, Harvey Keitel, Jack Nicholson, Leo DiCaprio, or Cate Blanchett, when she says "I'm leaving" to Howard Hughes in *The Aviator.* "And so there we are."

Look at her eyes when she says that. It was a medium shot. I didn't have to go in close for that. I was stunned when she did that. She's remarkable. At another point he says, "You're just a movie star," and the look in her eyes is just a killer. And there were no camera moves, nothing. It was just the actor, and I just loved it. I don't come with any preconceived notions. And I'm often dealing with characters in my movies who have a kind of looseness to them.

RS: Who are also, of course, capable of excess.

MS: Yes.

RS: Maybe that's one clue as to why you keep going back to these people, because ultimately they do act out their hostility, their aggression, their murderous impulses.

MS: There's no doubt there's a kind of catharsis in it for me, as I'm watching it happen, then as we put it together in the editing, and sometimes when I'm watching the film. When it's there on the set, it's an amazing thing. Even if it's Cate and Leo in the bathroom when she's fixing his foot and she says, "They'll think we're freaks." And he embraces her. It's very moving to me because it's very real. I buy it. The actors make me buy it.

RS: I think it all comes down to the director being an intelligent audience for the actor. You don't necessarily need to know how they got there. You just have to recognize that they got there.

MS: Yeah. Sometimes I'm almost honored by an actor, Bob De Niro in particular, because we've worked together so often, when he comes up and says, "Do you think I got there? Do you think I was there?" You discuss it, you try to guide, but it's a very fine line. And I learn by mistakes, by saying too much, by not saying enough.

RS: When I was writing a review of a biography of Otto Preminger, I was thinking: He was not a good director—in the sense that he made everybody so frightened that they couldn't do their work. On the other hand, I do very much like *Anatomy of a Murder.*

MS: It's brilliant, it's really something.

RS: That may be, in part, because of the star acting of Jimmy Stewart. You know, he's just going to damn well do what he does. He had been doing it for twenty-five years at that point.

MS: And what he did worked.

RS: It's perfect because the context is perfect for it. It doesn't feel false.

MS: It's a grounded story, so Preminger's style is simpler.

RS: The man who wrote the novel had lived in this country all his life, so it has some authentic texture, which got into the film.

MS: Robert Travers, right? The fishing, everything. Is Arthur O'Connell Stewart's partner?

RS: Right.

MS: What he wears, the vest, everything, it's all just right. And the great Eve Arden.

RS: Eve Arden is the secretary. It's all shtick in a way, everyone operating within their long-established acting conventions, which Otto couldn't terrorize them out of.

MS: I just learned not to terrorize the actors. I learned it from De Niro, Keitel, Ellen Burstyn. I learned it just behaviorally with them.

RS: Well, you know, I've talked to a ton of directors now, having made nineteen film profiles of them. And there's not a single one of them who's ever been able to tell me anything about how to direct an actor. Howard Hawks: Maybe he would say something to Cary Grant like "Well, Cary, that's kind of boring. Can you do something else?" And Cary would say, "Let me try," and he'd do some mad, wonderful Cary Grant kind of thing.

The director explains it all on the set of *The Departed*.

MS: But that's Cary Grant. It's his command of the frame.

RS: Or maybe Jack Nicholson?

MS: Well, in *The Departed,* we were in the fifth week of shooting, I'd say, and suddenly all of it came together. We found the stride, you know.

RS: You're talking particularly about Jack? I should think in a way he has to set the tone for anything he's in. He's something of a sacred monster.

MS: Yes, but that's the adventure of it. That's what you want. I've known him over the years, and I was always looking for a film I could work with him on. This one was tailor-made, in a way, because of the Irish-American underworld, particularly out of Boston. He's got an Irish-American background. And in one of our first meetings we talked about that. He understood it. He would tell me things like "The Irish have been given the words, the Italians the music." He'd be quoting Joyce, he'd be quoting Yeats. He'd go on talking about old friends of his. He'd be telling me different stories, tons of stories. Eventually he said, "What kind of a person should my character be? If I do this," he said, "I need to have something to play."

The script was excellent, but the part that Jack played, Frank, and the part that Vera Farmiga played were the ones that we worked on the most. We changed them all with the actors, and the writer, together, although Jack did a lot of his own changes on set, and with me.

But it was extremely collaborative. For instance, he had a little beard, and he said, "Should I shave this? Do you mind? Or should I keep it?" And I said, "Keep it on." I came to realize that there was something about this character, this idea of a man slightly coming apart, that was different from my other films. If you think of the way De Niro dresses in *Casino* or the way the actors dressed in *Goodfellas, Mean Streets, Raging Bull*—the underworld characters were all impeccable in a certain way. This had to go another way. Once I made the comment about the beard, it sort of set him free. Eventually it led to the scene with Leo and him at the table. We did five takes in one day, two cameras simultaneously, pretty much as written. That night I said to Jack, "You know, we have the setup for the next day. We have the camera. I just don't see shooting tracking shots of Leo coming in, and exterior shots. It's just about you two." I told Jack, "Anything you can think of, come in and we'll just do a couple of takes tomorrow, and that'll be it, and then you can go home."

So that morning I was walking to the set, and the street was alive—there were all these people rushing around, and it was a hot, hot day. All of a sudden some-one comes up next to me and says, "I've got ideas, I've got ideas!" It was Jack. [*Laughs.*] And that became the scene that you see in the movie where, basically, he does the sniffing of the brandy. And he sniffs at Leo, and he says, "I smell a rat." Then he uses the gun on Leo, without Leo knowing. And without me knowing! I didn't know whether he was going to fire or not. Even if you use blanks, it's very dangerous, and I didn't quite know what was going to happen.

That kind of thing leads to a different level of reality. When he pulls a gun like that, you see Leo's face and you know that's the candid reaction—nothing's edited, nothing's cut out. I didn't know where the scene was going to go next. Because Leo was the rat, and he had to get out of that room.

But how is he going to do it? I was holding my breath. Then he does it. He convinces Jack. Jack as an actor felt at a certain point Leo's desperation, seeing it in his eyes and the way he asks him, "You know, Frank, how many guys around you want to plug you?" It got Jack back on the rails again.

That was very interesting to me, being in a situation where I didn't know what was going to happen. I had a sense. After this take was over—there was one take that was even more extreme—I trimmed it down with the five takes from the night

DiCaprio and Jack Nicholson in a tense moment from *The Departed*.

before and recut with Thelma. In fact, that scene took months to cut. People liked it; some felt Jack was King Lear. To me, in reality, nothing satiated the man. Not drugs, not women. Some killing, maybe. And what's his relationship with Leo anyway? What's his relationship with Matt? Is Matt really his son, maybe? And, in a way, that was the moment where the picture came together for me.

RS: Really? That one scene?

MS: That was a long process, maybe five or six months with Jack. Sometimes you don't know exactly how that story is going to end up, or where it's going to go.

RS: Of the major actors you've worked with, does Jack present the most radical challenges to you as a director in keeping the film more or less on the track that you intended?

MS: I think so. But on the film it was mitigated by the fact that we really didn't work together that long on it. So ultimately, no matter what happened, the tracks were there for me to move along on in the editing. There was nothing wrong with taking chances, trying different things. As long as we had the time. But we only had twenty-five days.

RS: Yes, right.

MS: He had to be God the Father gone mad, you know, the whole world coming down around him. And it did.

RS: It sure did.

MS: And if it looks like he's going to go flying off—well, he should. I could pull it back. But you never know with those situations. It reminds me a little of the kind of energy that I saw with Pesci and Ray Liotta in that *Goodfellas* scene I keep referencing, the "What's funny about me?" scene.

I don't know what would've happened if I had made a picture with Jack ten or twenty years ago. I only know his working as he is now. I would have liked to have known what it was like to be with him in the period when he did *Five Easy Pieces* or *Carnal Knowledge*. People change in their behavior in their work, you know.

RS: That to me is one of the more interesting challenges that a director faces. There are certain things Jack can do that no one else can do.

MS: Right.

RS: But that's quite a challenge, because someone like Jack, people with those special skills, also have the potential to wreck your picture.

MS: Totally. But that's the battle, that's the war. In this picture Jack's character controls everything. He has a power of life and death over everybody around him, Leo, Matt, Queenan [the head of the police team trying to bring Nicholson down, played by Martin Sheen]. Some people feel there is sometimes too much here or there; others feel it all works. You feel your way through it.

I was around a very powerful man—a boss in the underworld in the old neighborhood in the fifties and sixties. At that point everything was changing. I saw the effect this had on him when he started to fall apart. The first people he killed were his closest friends. They buried the bodies in a restaurant.

People would come to my father to talk about it. They didn't know what to do. The fear was palpable. My father's younger brother, Joe—the one who "went wrong"—worked for this guy. I recall vividly him rushing into our apartment on Sunday morning out of breath, saying, "I just almost got killed. He pulled a gun on me." Then my father had to go and deal with certain people my uncle had been ostracized by.

My father always warned me, "These guys are bloodsuckers. Don't ever, ever, let them do a favor for you, because you'll never be able to pay it back. Stay away. Just smile, say hello, be respectful." He was stuck in that world. He was oppressed by it. But he was apparently a person they liked and listened to. My uncle, by the way, lived, but the boss was killed. Apparently the police took the body out of the funeral parlor to determine the cause of his death. It wasn't natural.

That boss had been very nice to me. I was close friends with his nephew. I would play around his house all the time. But when he turned bad, so to speak, the people around him went down fast. Ultimately he was taken out by his own people. All that went into Jack's character.

Another scene I really liked was when Jack started singing "Mother Machree" to Ray Winstone, egging Ray on, and Ray was trying to egg him on. But Ray at a certain point pulled back; he had decided that his character, Mr. French, was going to be a wall. The only one that Frank, Jack's character, trusted was Ray's character.

Frank is called Francis only by Ray in the picture, if you notice. He is the only one who is trustworthy. Watch what Ray is doing: he's just staring at other people. When Leo comes in the room, he stares at Leo. Jack starts singing "Mother Machree," and I thought it was too much, but then in the editing, I said, "Why don't we cut from 'Mother Machree,'" which gives this wonderful end to the line, filled with energy, and cut to the two bodies of the people he had gotten killed.

There are some people who say, "Oh, that's too much." Well, I've seen people sitting in bars who all of a sudden start singing.

It's all a matter of how you craft it. And the bottom line with Jack is that I saw him take his role places that were both interesting and liberating.

His obscenity, his equation of obscenity and violence, was liberating, for instance. He said, "Listen, after I hit the kid, break his hand, why don't I then go to my girlfriend?" When he does, she goes, "What's got you all hot and bothered?" He says, "I'll tell you in a minute. Come in the car, I'll show you." It's the direct relationship between the violence and the sex.

Jack was saying, That exists, let's show it. I felt it wasn't only a film about Frank Costello. It's the obscenity and the violence that he represents that permeates the picture, permeates that world. But as I say, if I had been able to work with Jack on a twenty-week shoot, I don't know what it would have been like. Or if I had worked with Jack in this picture ten years ago, maybe it would have been different.

Sly psychopath: Jack Nicholson as Frank Costello in a rare relatively calm moment in *The Departed*.

RS: My impression of Jack, and I don't know him at all well, is that at his age, he is going to do what he wants to do. You're hiring him for a certain kind of dangerousness that is completely unpredictable.

MS: That's right.

RS: And you have to give him that privilege.

MS: You discover that the first day you walk on the set. You think it's going to be fortuitous for the movie, though, you think the picture's going to be taken in a better direction—and that you're going to go with it.

RS: Well, is that one of the aspects of your nature that sets your work apart from other directors, that you will take those chances with actors who are, let's put it as politely as possible, unpredictable, and may do things that are very difficult for you to handle, because they are going to push the picture in directions so that you may not actually be able to put it together sensibly?

MS: Yes. I had to take that chance.

RS: You've done it more than once.

MS: Yes, I have. And when you do, it's always a battle. Sometimes a picture gets away from you and sometimes it doesn't. What I felt about the first four weeks of shooting *The Departed* was that it was not going smoothly, it was not going as planned. I knew Jack was bringing new stuff in, because we had been working on it before I started shooting. So I was very interested to see what was going to happen when we got to his scenes. But I do like to take the chances, although it can be nerve-racking.

RS: The language in *The Departed* is as brutal as some of the action, it seems to me, and even in today's world, dangerous to employ.

MS: I'm not going to say it doesn't exist, because it exists. It's not about giving a bad image to some ethnic group. That is the reality, that is what happens.

RS: You know, that fits my theory of what was really so loathesome about movie censorship.

MS: Oh, my God, it was so crazy.

RS: Not talking about the sexual revolution on film made it much harder to deal with than if they were just talking on the screen like normal Americans talk.

MS: I think you're absolutely right about that. I was part of that revolution, or, to put it another way, I was probably the only one who wasn't sexually liberated.

RS: If you say so. And then everybody went nuts about that, as if America was about to fall into moral shreds.

MS: It's like what Chairman Mao said, or was it his wife: If the revolution stops revolving, it's no longer a revolution. Therefore we must continue with the Cultural Revolution.

It became an obsession, and the next thing you know, town houses are blowing up on 11th Street.

RS: Two houses from where I lived.

MS: Geez. This is why I liked a lot of Julie Taymor's film, *Across the Universe*. It touches upon all these elements, and you get to see how it all fits together. And somehow the lyrics, the music, give you the period. What a decade! What a time!

RS: That's for sure.

MS: What a time to have gone through. That's why at the age of thirteen or fourteen, whether you liked the Kramer films or not, he did tackle certain subjects that made you think, subjects that weren't being talked about elsewhere.

RS: The censorship was far worse than just sexual censorship. It came up in the course of my history of Warner Bros. For example, in the late thirties they wanted to make movies that warned America about the threat of Nazism. The Breen Office [the censors for the movie industry] said no. Breen wrote a letter to Warners and said, "We feel you can't make this movie, because how can you say these terrible things about Hitler? Look at all the good he's been doing for the German people." To their credit, they told him to go screw himself. It was more than that you couldn't show a woman's breasts or you couldn't say "hell" and "damn." They were interfering in real issues, political issues. It's very disturbing.

MS: Yes.

RS: Because you keep this lid on.

MS: Certain philosophical and political points are made in the storytelling, and if they're softened or skipped—well, it just shouldn't be allowed to happen. Art is art. So the censorship concept is very important, because we were—many of us are—formed by mass entertainment.

RS: Of course.

MS: That's why when in *The Departed* Jack equates sex with violence as part of the thrill, that was liberating. I don't know if there was enough of it in the film, quite honestly, because there was a whole struggle going back and forth with the studio on that. The nature of his language, the obscenity of his language, was different from the kind of vulgar language that we used in *Goodfellas* or *Casino.*

RS: Can you characterize the difference?

MS: It had kind of a mean edge to it. I'm saying he got something in there that directly equated language with violence.

RS: There is a specificity in his language. It's not just a casual "Hey, motherfucker."

MS: No. There's a meaning there.

RS: What he says is probably literally going to happen.

MS: It's going to happen. In that scene when Jack says, "You like little Miss Freud sucking on your dick," it's very specific. Jack was saying, If you do your job, these are your benefits. You get them from me. You enjoy it? Good. But where the hell were you? You were supposed to be there, you weren't there.

The specificity cuts away all the nonsense. That's the nature of the world they're in. What I loved about Matt's character: he tries to pretend he's in a somewhat different world—an apartment that's a little more upgraded, and he buys croissants, you know, and dies.

That's why I love what Bill Monahan did in the script at the end, when Mark Wahlberg is there with the gun pointing at Matt Damon, and Matt looks at him and he says, "Okay." And then he gets shot. Okay, he's saying, I'm so tired. I made it as far as here. Now just take me out. I'm not up to this. I was never up to it. Just finish me off.

He even tries to pretend otherwise. In the scene in the theater, he tries to say, Frank, what are you doing? What are you, crazy? And he's trying to actually talk to him. He's trying to put on the appearance of a responsible citizen. Yes, I work for you. But I'm still a policeman, and I still have some power.

Jack pointed out to me, "He's sitting behind me." He mentioned the word "confession." And I realized he made the porno theater the confessional. If you look at it, he's like a priest. The priest doesn't see your face when you're in the confessional. It was wonderful, I told him.

RS: Did you just instinctively stage it that way?

MS: Well, he couldn't sit next to him, so he had to sit behind him. Then we looked at it and he looked like the kindly old priest that Barry Fitzgerald played in *Going My Way.* Only a slightly more demented version. And there's this guy, you know, leaning over, recounting his sins, so to speak, to him. And the priest is another kind of priest, really.

RS: Putting it mildly.

MS: The whole porno theater takes on a very different aspect—very Catholic—about sex and guilt and confession, and it all seemed to come together there. I think Jack understood that. I don't know his personal life that much. But some of the stories he told me made me think he understood the impact of Catholicism on the Irish and the Irish American. And also the differences between Irish Catholicism and Italian Catholicism.

RS: It sounds as if the picture, on the whole, was pretty satisfying for you.

MS: I was just hoping for some sort of financial success with *The Departed.* I figured pretty much that that would be it for me, that I wouldn't do any more studio pictures.

RS: What would you do?

MS: More independent films. I didn't see where I could fit into the system anymore, given what the system needs at this point in time. Having come off *Gangs of New York* and then *Aviator,* I just didn't know anymore that I could go on making films under corporate control. I don't say that the people who made the film with me at Warner Bros. were difficult to work with. It was a matter of whether I have what they need, what the corporation needs. And how much of an effort it will take.

    The Departed came out the way I wanted it to come out. Below the line it was an average budget of a Hollywood film, and there were stars in it, and therefore I had to work with the studio very closely. Screen it, argue, discuss it, you know. We stuck to our guns. We got pretty much what we wanted, though there were a couple of things here and there which we didn't get. That doesn't really matter. The thing is, I don't know if it's worth going through the process again. Because, ultimately, the marketplace for big-budget films means there will be less experimentation in them. It's the old story. Now, even more so.

    At my age, having gone through what I have, I don't know whether it's worth it anymore.

RS: I understand. It's a wearing process, even when everyone's being pleasant.

MS: When I was finishing *The Departed,* I said, "I'm out of here." I barely saw the answer print. I was off shooting the Rolling Stones film, *Shine a Light.*

SHINE A LIGHT

RICHARD SCHICKEL: *Shine a Light* is pretty much pure heedless performance—it's not like *The Last Waltz* or the Dylan doc.

MARTIN SCORSESE: Pure rock 'n' roll. They didn't touch up any of the music, except one note, I think.

RS: There's no social commentary in it. Aside from the incredible lines in Mick Jagger's face, he's still moving the way he used to. That's an inspiration rather than a commentary. I mean, my knees ache in the morning when I get up.

MS: After Jagger saw the first cut of it, he said, "You know, I'm still tired from the film." He said, "It's one thing if I did two songs in one day. But I did all that in two hours." I intended to keep him part of the group—to show how they play off each other onstage, the energy and the exchange of physical and psychic energy, the intimate nature of it all. Keith Richards moving out onstage, bending, kneeling down.

RS: In some weird way it was, as I said, kind of inspirational. Every once in a while you see the audience and they're very young as a whole. There are very few old gents like you and me in the audience. The Stones are now kind of old guys, too, so it was good that you put in the footage when they were busted for pot, or whatever the hell it was, in the old days. It reminds you of where they came from.

MS: David Tedeschi and I had to balance that. Every time I put too much of that footage in, it took away from the music. It was a very delicate balance.

RS: I could see that. But the picture needed something to ground it historically.

MS: Yes. At the end you see Keith Richards, when he finally stops, hanging on to his guitar, trying to catch his breath.

RS: He was flat out of breath.

MS: Gone, and then he resurrected himself! It's just stunning to watch.

RS: I have to tell you, I have gotten belatedly to like rock 'n' roll much better than I did back when I was supposed to love it.

MS: Maybe because it's not forced on you now, as it was when your peers expected you to love it.

RS: Maybe. But I like the beat of it. And with better recording, I can hear the lyrics better. So I know what the songs are about. They don't just sound like a lot of noise.

MS: There's something very interesting in what Jagger does, what they all do, onstage—Mick, Keith, Charlie Watts, Ronnie.

RS: I love watching a drummer like that.

MS: You know, his back straight, his hands moving, and calm, cool. He's the very core of the group.

RS: There's a moment in there where he just goes [*makes whoosh sound*].

MS: We did movie lighting, and the stage was very hot. Jagger at one point is sort of fanning with his shirt on a reverse shot, laughing at Charlie. Basically he was saying he was hot. When they left, they just took off. We didn't talk after the show. I left a message for Mick saying it was wonderful, that kind of thing. The next day he called me from San Francisco and said, "Have you recuperated yet?" I said, "No." He said, "We've been working arena shows, and stadiums. So imagine if you had been shooting a spectacle film for a year, and then you were told to do a play by Eugene O'Neill for two nights on Broadway."

What drove me in this film is just the nature of the energy itself, which can't be stopped. Primeval almost.

RS: That comes through very strongly.

MS: I sort of forgot about their age. I just saw this movement.

RS: Let's talk a little about coverage. How did you assign it among your fifteen cameras?

MS: Just by luck and determination. I drew up all kinds of shots but basically I didn't use any of them.

RS: But you had cameras assigned, right—one on the group, one on the drummer, one with a side angle?

MS: Yes, but because Keith moved a lot and, certainly, Mick did, there had to be several cameras assigned to each guy. And the cameramen asked, "Aren't you going to be shooting yourselves, shooting each other?" I said, "It doesn't matter."

RS: I think it was fine to see a few of those cameras. I've seen a lot more cameras in other docs.

MS: I said, "Just go with it. Don't worry about picking up other cameramen, don't worry about it." Sometimes we were able to carry out our design. There was a big camera in the center, on a crane. And at certain points in songs it would pull back, or it would come in. That was rehearsed, and we were able to get some shots I really wanted—especially the one where Mick got Keith to sing into the same mike with him.

RS: Right.

MS: There's always been something special between Mick and Keith. The people who really know the Rolling Stones love to see Keith and Mick singing at the same mike again. Mick said, "I think I could do 'Faraway Eyes' if I get him on the stage, but I don't know where he's going to be." He said this in a very sweet way: "You'd have better luck predicting the Grand National." If you ever look at the film again, you'll see he's looking for Keith.

RS: Yes, that's quite clear. It makes you think about all the years they've shared.

MS: The "making of the film" material we managed to get on there I thought was good.

RS: I loved that stuff. I wanted more of it.

MS: Me, too. I tried, I tried. But we had to stay onstage.

RS: There's a little contentiousness going on there.

MS: Yes, actually.

RS: Between you and Mick.

MS: Yeah.

RS: I mean, first of all, he obviously wanted the film to be made.

MS: Yes.

RS: But what did he think you were going to do, sit in the corner with a little hand-held camera and shoot?

MS: They're flying around the world. I'm busy. I've got cameramen coming in. I don't quite know what songs they're going to play. In other words, I can't control what they're doing onstage. But I have to control. So does Mick. He controls what he does onstage, I'm controlling what I'm doing. Somehow the cameras and the performers had to meet. And it was a wonderful kind of chaos. I just started shooting everything. You know? It's not designed. There was literally a rhythm we developed. And the rhythm of the world today, certainly in America, is that images can't stay on for more than a few seconds.

RS: Right, I know.

MS: Still, you've got to stay on somebody for a while, let it play, to feel the effectiveness of it.

RS: That is what I felt watching the film.

MS: Me, too.

RS: There is in the preliminary stuff where you're getting hassled—

MS: You know, the funny thing was when Mick finally saw it, the telephone sequence with his voice coming through like the voice of God, he said, "Well, Marty, you know that conversation was over an hour." I said, "Yes, I know. But I cut it down." It may have been over an hour, but there was still frustration because the two of us could not get face-to-face in a room for any period of time.

RS: It mystified me that you keep asking, "Could I see the playlist?"

MS: They wouldn't let me see it. You know why?

RS: Why?

MS: Because, ultimately, they have to gauge the audience, gauge how they were all feeling. We never, ever went backstage or dealt with them later than twenty minutes before they went on. I just let them do it. Most performers do it. They tend to make it up at the last minute. I'm feeling this tonight, I'm feeling that.

The second day was generally the same as the first night. I knew Mick was going to make changes. And if he was going to make changes, I needed to know what those changes were. On the other hand, because I'd already shot the earlier concert, I could wing it. You know, what the hell? Okay, oh, it's a different song, all right. I had a little bit of a problem getting a camera to cover somebody, but basically I was okay. It wasn't that bad.

RS: Okay. But here's my point, applying to both nights: You've got your fifteen cameras. Obviously, at least ten of them have a specific thing they're covering, right?

MS: I think so, yes.

RS: Someone is on Mick from the front of the stage. Someone is on Keith from wherever—

MS: Keith. Somehow, yes.

RS: But I was struck by the fact that at very, very crucial moments, you chose a close-up of the strings of a guitar—not necessarily Mick's or Keith's—but some other musician's in the back somewhere.

MS: Ronnie Wood.

RS: That was kind of amazing, because you had so little chance to prepare for that.

MS: There was not one song I feel that we lost. I never had that problem. It's like dance. Sometimes I'm on the movement in the frame, even if it's just a hand on a guitar or the string being touched, or the string being plucked. It reflects something at that point in the song that was more important to me than watching one of the people.

RS: How did you know to be there at a particular moment?

MS: Great cameramen do that. And great focus pullers. John Toll, Andrew Lesnie, who did *Lord of the Rings,* and Robert Richardson did all the lighting, designed it, and was on a camera. Ellen Kuras. And Bob Elswit, who did *There Will Be Blood.* We had some of the greatest cameramen. They just had a great time. And also I was in the back with fifteen or eighteen screens, whatever it was, in front of me. I was saying, So-and-so, see if you can get in tighter. Don't forget, cover Keith here.

RS: You were acting almost like a sports director.

MS: Yes. But sometimes I just sat there and was mesmerized by some of the action, and didn't say anything. Sometimes I was pointing and saying, "Get me a reverse, get me a reverse, and get it wide." But the stage was small. And they have a lot of equipment back there. I didn't realize that. That was our biggest issue. When the Stones go on tour, they have like a medieval village that they take with them from place to place. They set it up overnight, you know. And they have their way of doing things. And you have to fit in with their way. But they had to fit in with what we were doing, too. It's kind of absurd. Like Mick almost being set on fire because the lights were too hot.

RS: And you were going, "He's going to burn up."

MS: Yeah! [*Laughs.*] I said, "Obviously, we can't have that happen." Another example: Somebody said, "Well, you need to shoot Mick from behind when he opens the door," and I said, "But we can't, he's wearing a feather coat." I mean, what are we talking about? On Halloween Mick is going to leave the stage, go out in the alley, and change costumes. I said, "On Halloween night, in New York City? [*Laughs.*] He'll never get back to the door." Anything could have happened. But there were a lot of police, all kinds of security. They had it locked down. You see Mick in the film and he says, "Hmmm, all these cameras." That was the way it was. There was one point at which he was talking on the telephone, with all those cameras buzzing around. I thought, What happens if the camera moves the wrong way and he slams right into it? What if it hits one of the people?

RS: He also mentions that all you were doing was going to bother the audience.

MS: But what could I do? The only thing we could do was put the cameras on the stage and try to work it out in rehearsal. Unfortunately, we didn't have much rehearsal: a lot of their rehearsals were private.

Ultimately, I did find out what songs he was going to play that night. I won't say how.

But for me the energy was great, like a dance, and the editing was fun. I love watching music films. It could be classical music, it could be opera. I would love to have done an opera on film. But I think I probably would have done too many angles, too many cuts, too many special shots.

RS: Maybe you should become another Billy Friedkin, go around and stage operas in opera houses.

MS: I don't know. People have asked me to do operas, but I don't even know if I know opera that well. I don't have the imagination to take advantage of the proscenium. It all seems like a wide shot to me. I would have to be very careful.

Mick and I had been talking for years about another project. That's how I got to know him a little bit. He came to me about a project about the music business, which we're still involved in. The main thing, though, is that when he was on tour I would go and see the show. At a couple of the shows, when I got real close, I thought, I've got to get this on film. And I did.

RICHARD SCHICKEL: How did *Shutter Island* come up? Somebody says, "Hey, here's a Scorsese film"?

MARTIN SCORSESE: We were going to do *The Wolf of Wall Street.* It's an extraordinary true story. Leo DiCaprio as this young man who created this empire on Wall Street with junk bonds and wound up in jail. And it's a story of excess again. I was hesitant about it, but the script was written by Terry Winter, and I agreed to work on it and in a sense what happened was it wasted about five months of my life.

RS: On what?

MS: Waiting for them [Warner Bros.] to agree. I pointed out that although everybody was well-meaning in the situation, it's just that tastes are very different. And so I said, "You know, there could be a problem," because we had some problems on *Departed.* That worked out well, but it was a process. And I said, "I don't know if I can handle that process again. I'm getting maybe too old for it. I don't know if I can handle it, if it's worth it." But I did try. And they tried.

But ultimately five months went by. I turned around, nothing had happened. And at that point I had to work. And right around that time, there was talk of this story. [Ostensibly it is about a pair of federal marshals (Leonardo DiCaprio and Mark Ruffalo) who appear on the eponymous island, which houses an insane asylum, to search for a patient who has gone missing. Though shot realistically, this turns out to be pure fantasy, the mad imaginings of DiCaprio's psychopathic character.] This story of these two men who are going to an island. And I said, "Hmm, yes, I want to do two men going to an island, but in Japan." [He's referring again to the long-delayed project *Silence*.] So, in any event, they sent the script to me and said, "Well, just read it and see what you think." But, you know, a lot was invested in it.

RS: It's not a hugely expensive picture, is it?

MS: It's up there.

RS: Really?

MS: I was very aware each day of money. And when the weather went against us, halfway through the shoot, it was a very difficult process because every decision we made—based on the best meteorological advice, logistics, everything you could think of—we lost, every choice we made. It's a miracle it ever got finished. But I read the thing and it was late at night and I was very moved by the ending, the last scene.

RS: What was so moving in that for you?

MS: The impact of his decision to go to the lighthouse. He makes a choice to wipe out his false memory, in a way.

RS: I found myself very lost in this movie. And not in a good way.

Shutter Island (2010) is a vision conjured up in the mind of its mentally disturbed protagonist.

MS: I don't even want to talk about it because it's like I can't handle any more criticism of it. Sorry.

RS: I don't mean it as criticism.

MS: You either go with it or you don't.

RS: There was some reality I couldn't embrace in that movie. I don't know how to explain it in any other way.

MS: Maybe that's it. Maybe it's no good. I don't know.

RS: I'm not saying it's no good, Marty.

MS: No, maybe it isn't. I really don't know. All I know is that we're in his mind, we have to see the world through his mind. And the world in his mind is post–World War II/early fifties paranoia, which is real. Yet it all seems like some scenario from some old story. There is a storm, it is a dark night, there are suspicious doctors. Anyway, I could go on for hours about it or not at all, because it depends on how it hits you. Some people were really stunned by it. Others can't get into it at all—can't feel, as you say, the reality.

RS: Well, he's not crazy for a long, long time in the movie as far as we can perceive.

MS: Right. It's about how you perceive the reality around you.

RS: It's a funny movie, though, because it's not a typical Dennis Lehane novel—compared, let's say, to *Mystic River* ...

MS: But from what I understand he did it based on his anger at the time of the Iraq war.

RS: Really?

MS: Yes, basically he said, What was the worst period for paranoia? He looked back and everything seemed to converge in McCarthyism. The Communist Party in America, what that meant about our relationship with Russia, and, psychiatrically, the use of these drugs as opposed to lobotomies.

RS: And they're back, lobotomies.

MS: Yes, I know they are, because you can map the brain perfectly. It's amazing what they do—whether that's right or wrong. I'm just talking about the ability to do it now. And also the use of drugs and the use of talking therapy. Drugs, lithium—very important, very important. Thorazine—very important. And the talking therapy. And these converged, especially the paranoia, during the Cold War. I took it at the face value of a man who's going on an island to find this woman who is lost, who has left, escaped. And then it's not about that. And then it's about something else. Then it's not about that, either.

RS: In reality, if there is a reality in this movie, he's a federal marshal. And that portion of the movie where he comes to the island, is that real?

MS: No, that doesn't ever happen.

RS: But it seems so real . . .

MS: Well, if you were him, it would be real. If you were mad, it would be real. I grew up amidst homeless people on the Bowery, just a few blocks away. They hear voices, and the voices tell them to do something. They go and kill children because the voices tell them to. They really hear that. So the guy is looking. He's thinking about all these scenarios, and the scenarios are like films in a way. This is his reality.

RS: So is it fair to say that this entire movie is only that character's reality? There is no island reality at all.

MS: I think ultimately in the top room it's real. When they explain it all to him.

RS: Oh, really?

MS: A lot of people choose not to see it that way. They become so invested in the way DiCaprio played it that they don't believe he's crazy even at the very end, when he says, "My name is Andrew Laeddis and I killed my wife in the spring of '52." They just don't believe him. And that's what the beauty of it for me was, that he takes responsibility for his violence, for his violence in the war, too.

How do we expect men to live like this, when they come back from war? How many men have come back from Iraq and killed their wives?

RS: Probably quite a large number.

MS: We don't even know the damage that's been done. Now whether the war is right, wrong, whatever, that's a whole other issue. But what do we expect from people who are put into a war situation when they come back and try to fit into normal society? Quote, "normal society," unquote. But the other thing that really surprised me in the script was that the story kept changing. It started as a mystery, then it became a detective story. Then it became Cold War conspiracy theory. Then it became something else. And the next thing you know, they're in a graveyard. Why are they in a graveyard? We were trying to explain it at one point. We tried in the cut and said, You know, nobody is listening to the exposition. Drop it.

RS: I suppose, for me, when they're in the graveyard is when you start thinking, Wait a minute.

MS: Exactly. You see where this is going. You realize that there's a doctor with him. He's getting out of hand in the graveyard. They shouldn't be there in the storm. Then he disappears. But in any event, what really held me was when he meets Patricia Clarkson in the cave. I really believed it when I read it.

Leonardo DiCaprio and Mark Ruffalo experience the dark dream that is *Shutter Island*.

RS: As a reality?

MS: As a reality. And I said to myself, Well, it's okay, this is seriously a conspiracy issue. I was young, but the Cold War made a great impression on me—the sense of being taken over, like in *Invasion of the Body Snatchers*, it was worse than being killed in a way because they took your soul. They took your mind away. This is what we were told as children about Communists, because they were "godless."

RS: Well, an enormous amount—I hate to say it—of what we call McCarthyism certainly had a fair amount to do with Catholicism. I don't mean in any narrow religious sense—

MS: Well, yes, because—

RS: —but in the sense of their position in society.

MS: Yes, because if the Communists deny God, well, who's going to be annihilated? The church. Any religion basically, but primarily the church. I remember that feeling of the soul being taken away, the idea of soldiers coming back from Korea who had been "brainwashed." It's best presented in *The Manchurian Candidate*. And, there was Cardinal Mindszenty, the way they broke him down, the story told in *The Prisoner* with Alec Guinness and Jack Hawkins, all of these things contributed to living that experience. And I thought, Well, all right. I'll go with that. So I shot that scene totally real, three angles with a wide shot, that's it. I thought, So what is our reality in cinema, too? Who do we believe in a film?

RS: It seems from what you've said that the essential trick, if you will, of that movie is that there is no actual reality in it.

MS: Right.

RS: It's all in his mind in some way. But the movie doesn't have any wavy dissolves—oooh-oooh, we're into crazy now.

MS: No, because you can hallucinate, and it seems very real. I mean, I never took hallucinogenic drugs, but more than a couple of times in the seventies, I could swear I saw something that wasn't there. It reaches its peak really in *Raging Bull*—the paranoia.

RS: Well, paranoia is a big deal with you, isn't it?

MS: I guess it is.

RS: I mean, I don't think of you as at all paranoiac.

MS: No, not anymore. Again, I guess part of it is where I came from. As I've said, we lived in a world where you don't say anything. To this day, there are people I know—somebody walks up to them in a restaurant and says, "Are you So-and-So's brother?" He goes, "Excuse me?" "You have a brother who lives on Mulberry Street, name is Al?" And my friend will say, "I'm sorry, I don't know what you're talking about. You probably have somebody else in mind." You become a very good actor. And it's almost like a friend of mine, a guy I grew up with, who just wrote to me about this thing we're talking about, and he said, "They don't understand. You had to reinvent yourself every day. You had to act in the street every day," and he said, "Also, the church was there. It was basically like being under the Taliban."

And it implies a lot. If I were a writer, I guess I could write several volumes about it. But what my friend wrote me last week was true: People don't get it. They never will. You can't describe it. You could call it paranoia, but discretion is better. "Discretion" I'm using sarcastically; I couldn't say anything for the first fifteen years in L.A. about where I came from.

RS: Really?

MS: And by the way, this whole thing of me with noir images: Oh, you're always doing noirs. But when I grew up, when I looked out the window some mornings the light would be beautiful; other mornings it was dirty and filthy. Or I would see life through the fire escape. So in other words, what we consider as noir images is what I grew up with. It was my reality. That's why I wanted to see the westerns.

The thing that really is the epitome of it all is the one shot in a tunnel in *Raging Bull* with Bob and Joe and Egan, Mr. Egan, asking if he was going to throw the fight. And Bob and Joe were wearing these big hats, and they have this tunnel that we shot somewhere in Brooklyn. And I thought, Oh, look at this tunnel. Always shooting in a tunnel, shooting in a hallway, but the narrowest hallways. In my old neighborhood, the hallways were amazing. You could also sing in them. And my friends played cards in them—and a lot of money went down.

RS: And where were these hallways?

MS: Everywhere. They're still there. Now they're chic. They're charging a lot of money for them.

RS: Just to take it back to *Shutter Island*—

MS: I want to leave *Shutter Island,* but okay.

RS: It feels to me in this movie that Leo's character is literally among the least rooted characters in the history of the movies, because you don't know in all of this what actually happened to him.

MS: No. We don't even know if he really killed that many guards, and if there were that many guards killed in Dachau.

RS: I understand that, yes.

MS: But the idea of the madness of the killing at that moment, where the shot goes on just a little too long, was an expression of what it must be like to lose your senses in killing. You've had your finger on the trigger for like five minutes, and you've killed about forty people, fifty people, maybe more.

RS: And you believe that is a reality of his life?

MS: No, but he feels he did it.

RS: But he did kill the wife.

MS: Oh yeah. That we know. And also when he says, "I should have helped her and I didn't. I'm responsible for the killing of the kids too." He feels responsible for the killing of the children.

RS: So that portion of the movie may have a bit of reality in it.

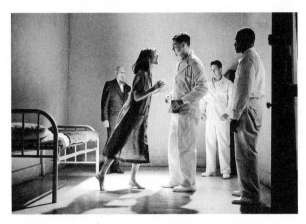

Mad scene: DiCaprio confronts one of *Shutter Island*'s inmates.

MS: I think it does, yes. At the end, when he decides, I'm checking out. Sorry, Doctor. I know this may ruin your plans, all your theories, all your experiments. But I can't take the pain anymore. And it's better to go out this way, you know, and the doctor knows.

RS: Knows?

MS: He knows that he's not crazy at that point. The look in his eyes was that he knows it's not Teddy, it's Andrew who's going out. It's not Teddy. Teddy is the person he made up. It's Andrew that's going out, Andrew Laeddis.

RS: So in other words the reality of his war is the reality that totally unhinged him.

MS: I think that set him off. And that's why I say it has a lot to do with returning veterans and what they call now post-traumatic stress syndrome. The reality is you can shape a young person into becoming a killing machine. Now, how do you turn it off? But people have come back and have been able to do it.

RS: Just a crass question while I think of it. Are you astonished by the grosses on this movie?

MS: Yes—although "astonish" may be too strong a word. But I can't say I didn't think about it. I had a very difficult experience making the picture, particularly in postproduction.

RS: Really?

MS: And I still haven't gotten past it.

RS: What is the nature of the problem?

MS: It's just that depression hit. I don't know what happened. Living in that world, with those people, was very upsetting. And also the pressure of getting it done. And then I said to myself, I don't want to do it again. I always say that when I make a picture, but it's just not right anymore for me to do.

RS: I hear what you're saying.

MS: It's just, at a certain point, well, life is complicated. I didn't even want to think about it, quite honestly, especially when the film was held back from its original release date—wisely so, I've come to think.

RS: I'd almost forgotten that.

MS: That's what finally did it. You're sort of running a marathon and suddenly, bang! You're about to hit the finish line and somebody just has a baseball bat and hits you in the chest. And like wham, you go down and—

RS: I'm going to assume you didn't believe that was malicious or that they were selling out the movie, that they really thought it would do better in February.

MS: Absolutely. But it's still someone pulling a rug out from under you. And so you're spinning.

RS: I remember the posters were up, the trailers were playing.

MS: Yes, it was ridiculous. But the time they chose to open it was very, very good. Hopefully they're happy, everybody's happy.

RS: Of all your movies it's the one that appeals most directly to the prime movie audience, the kids, who love ugga-bugga.

MS: But those places were genuinely weird. That's an abandoned hospital where you could feel, from the walls, the pain and the suffering that it contained. The whole thing had a very strange, eerie feeling to it.

RS: Which hospital, where was that?

MS: A place called Medfield about an hour outside of Boston. But he saw the world that way, and he heard things that way, including the music. In his mind that's how dramatic it is. The way the book was written or the script was written, but particularly where we shot it, lent itself to the thriller or the horror genre. But the place was really uncomfortable, to say the least. You can have all the people you want running around, you can have all the coffee and all the crafts services tables, it doesn't matter. If you have any feeling at all, you want to get out of there.

RS: While you were working on this, did you at all look at *Titicut Follies,* Fred Wiseman's movie about the criminally insane?

MS: Well, *Titicut Follies*—I didn't have to see it again. I knew it very well. I saw it when it was playing at the 34th Street East Theatre.

RS: I was very involved with that. I testified on its behalf in Boston, because they banned it, and there was a big court case when I was a very young film critic. But I knew Fred.

MS: Yeah, he's great, a great filmmaker. He's the great documentarian. He has chronicled everything. Five hours, six hours, it doesn't matter. And he doesn't intrude on it. He holds back. And I once saw *Titicut Follies* on a big screen, and I've seen it a couple of times over the years. Those were the days when documentaries were shown as a regular feature. In fact, there are moments that the actors [in *Shutter Island*] took directly from certain people in *Titicut Follies*.

RS: I felt a lot of that in the film. And it's been many years since I've seen *Titicut*.

MS: And the other thing was that Dr. James Gilligan, who was our technical adviser, was one of the men who went in after Bridgewater [the prison-hospital where Wiseman's film was shot] was exposed. He was part of the group that revamped Bridgewater and other places. And he pointed out that Ward C is actually a smaller version of the places he knew at Bridgewater. Pretty horrifying.

RS: So that reality has infected his imagination.

A light moment in a dark place: Ben Kingsley, Marty, and Max von Sydow on the *Shutter Island* sets.

MS: Very much so. However, Dr. Gilligan did say that he many times worked out scenarios with the patients and acted out different scenes for different lengths of time. I guess psychodrama is what you would call it. But even more intense.

The directorial problems in the picture were interesting. For example, there are guards in the frame all the time when you see Leo. There's always somebody there in the background. That's the way he sees certain places. We took some chances every now and then by cutting a certain way. If you see it one way, it's just reaction shots. But if you see it another way, it's complicity. Everybody knows what's going on. Everybody except Leo. He walks into a room and something's going on, but he's not part of it. Everybody's talking about you. Or at least you think so. But you're right, he's not rooted in reality. By the time you get to that cave, with Patricia Clarkson, his pretended reality has gone completely.

And that put me in touch with the thoughts I was having, when I talked about the idea of cinema being not real in a sense. It's something not tangible because it's projected electricity, images on a wall. And it's that we somehow make up the film in our own minds, in a sense. Yes, the images are created by some people, but you never see them. You don't know their context even. Maybe you see a film forty years later, you don't know where it's from.

RS: That's one of the things I think about a lot nowadays in the digital age. I mean, at least at one time there was a physical object called a film.

MS: Now, it's in cyberspace. Does it really exist now? And as you get older, too, you wonder, do we exist? I mean, in a sense, I guess, we do. But what is existence and what is consciousness?

RS: For that matter, what is moviegoing? How has that changed in the modern world? You know, we go to movie theaters where we have our popcorn. We're watching, but we're not as focused maybe as we should be. You probably are, but I'm sometimes not.

MS: I used to be. Now, I don't know. When I was younger, probably the prints we looked at then in these old theaters, if we ever saw them now, we'd think they were terrible. But as a young person if the story took you in—whatever the hypnotic or the dreamlike qualities of the picture—it didn't matter what the circumstances were.

RS: There was the shimmer of them too, the sheen of them.

MS: Particularly all those prints we were seeing in the early fifties were nitrate.

RS: Yes.

MS: They glowed, you know. It was like the dream life of the Aborigine, who believes his dreams are real and what we're living in now is a dream. But it's nice to think about it, because of the nature of our destiny, the passage we have to make, life into death. You know, existence and non-existence.

RS: It's interesting that these things you make, which may or may not be digital, are going to outlive you.

MS: Yes. I hope so. It seems in a way, at this point, I just want to keep working and making more films—even the documentaries are interesting to me. You can hear one being made now, the George Harrison music. Maybe by doing so many pictures at once, it's an attempt to prolong life. I don't know.

DRAWING DREAMS

RICHARD SCHICKEL: I want to talk about the processes by which you make movies—designing them, shooting them, editing them.

MARTIN SCORSESE: Maybe it began with those drawings that I made as a kid. They were attempts to visualize a story, using drawings in sort of a cinematic way. At this point in my life, I'm sort of happiest when I'm in a hotel room doing those designs. We don't use all of them, but it's the first attempt at telling a story through pictures. So it's exciting.

When you move from one frame to the next, you're making a cut in your mind. I didn't know I was doing that as a kid. But in a way, I was already in control. I didn't see any other way. I knew I couldn't be an actor. I didn't know about cinematography. I couldn't tell you anything about light: I always make a joke about it, but where I grew up, there was no light. There were brick walls. And if you look at my movies, there's a bulb.

RS: Let's begin where you began, with drawings, those sort of storyboards. Did you know that your idol, Mr. Kazan, had contempt for people who made storyboards?

MS: I'm sure. But I like to draw pictures. It just turned out the pictures started to move. What can I tell you?

RS: In his autobiography, Kazan says he was very insecure when it came to making *The Last Tycoon.* He says he found himself making "shot lists." He saw that as a symbol of the insecurity that had begun to afflict him.

MS: Part of it *is* insecurity. I know what he means—you can't lock an actor into a frame, you know.

RS: That's his second point. He says you've got to be alert to the fact that somebody's going to do something wonderful that you haven't storyboarded.

MS: You can't lock it in. You can't. This is the tension I play with. I have to have the ability to realize when something's not working, and to change it—to go for the truth, the emotional impact. There are a lot of great directors who have total contempt for storyboards.

RS: Yes, I know.

MS: There's one great director who actually said on one film, "I had a laundry list of shots but I threw it out." What I do or what I learned to do is not necessarily the only way you make a picture, as we know. I have no theater background, I didn't have a very broad literary background; the only thing I know to do is think in terms of pictures.

RS: Kazan was not a picture guy. He was a word guy. At least at first, or so he said to me one time.

MS: He became a picture guy, though.

RS: He did become one, yes.

MS: He really became one in *East of Eden,* and certainly in *Splendor in the Grass,* and in *Wild River.* It all culminated in *America, America.*

He came to NYU around that time. In Lincoln Center Theater he was doing *After the Fall.* Professor Robert Gessner got him to come and speak and students asked him questions. One I remember was "Would you do anything differently if you were starting now?" He said, "Yes. Now I'd start in the editing room."

RS: Coming out of the theater, where words are so important, shaped Kazan's initial approach to movies—so he said.

MS: Words and also the blocking of the actors. But then, if you look at stills from the theatrical production of *Death of a Salesman,* his use of flashbacks, his use of scrims, is just phenomenal. It's very cinematic.

But for me, I love the drawing. I love seeing these pictures. I love making the frame and seeing something in it. I stopped taking drawing lessons at a certain age. I wish I had continued, because I could have really done very pretty, interesting storyboards. You know, the look of the wide-angle lens, of an 18 millimeter in an Orson Welles film, is so important to me. Or how an actor in the foreground is distorted a little bit.

I could draw that. I could draw that with pencils, the Eberhard Faber Ebony, Jet Black, Extra Smooth, 6325. I've been using them since the fifties. They no longer make them. I bought the last box of them on eBay for a couple of hundred dollars. It turns out there were a number of people around the world who have been using these pencils for years. There are new versions of them, but they aren't as good.

I found that with these pencils the shading is wonderful. As I draw, I'm figuring out the lighting, I'm figuring out what lenses to use. I'm thinking, Maybe that should be wider? That character should definitely be in the middle of the frame. This arrow means that he comes in a certain way—he comes into the frame when you least expect it, and I've got to do separate drawings of him, and of the other characters in the scene. In something I'm working on now, he's a deputy warden of a prison. Two marshals are in the scene, and they start walking forward. The warden has got to step into the frame and say, "Hold it." That's the image I want. The idea is that these pencils are the ones I've used over the years. This one has the word "Design" on it—and that's the new kind. And that isn't as good, the shading isn't as good. But they stopped, because they found a way to make them cheaper. Now I only have a few more of my preferred pencils left.

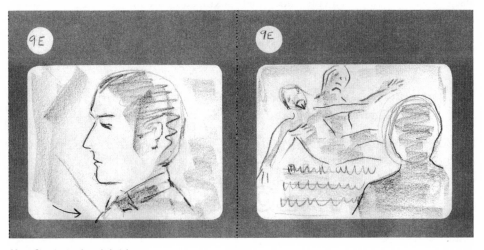

Mean Streets storyboard sketches.

RS: Then what are you going to do?

MS: A friend of mine asked, "Marty, how many pencils does it take to make a picture?" I answered, "One or two." "So, okay," he said, "you may have enough, then."

I had also Paradise color lead pencils. I loved the way the lines were made. I loved the impression that they made on the paper.

RS: Kazan found himself frightened by that kind of process.

MS: I always felt I could express myself better with drawing. I get pleasure from making the drawings, which even help me design editing sequences, too. I draw the shots, we get those shots, I put them together. Thelma knows now how to do it because she's worked with me so long. So it goes, "Remember, we did this in *Last Temptation*, the hammer came up and you cut it three times?" And she goes, "Yeah, but it was a bitch to cut." And I say, "I know. But let's try it again."

RS: You spent two weeks drawing your little pictures for *Shutter Island*. And you mentioned doing that as early as *Boxcar Bertha*. Storyboarding.

MS: I used to storyboard everything, literally. *Taxi Driver* was completely storyboarded. *Raging Bull*—storyboarded. Literal drawings, I mean.

RS: I assume all the boxing stuff had to be a little bit improvised.

MS: No, that was all drawn, every shot.

RS: Every shot? That's amazing.

MS: I saw the boxing on a videotape, the blocking, and then I broke it down. Bob's body language would give me an idea for a camera move. I would do the shots as if they were bars of music, as in the editing of *The Last Waltz*. You see? We did the song "The Weight" on *Last Waltz* in a studio, because we didn't get it on the stage. If you look at "The Weight," you'll see that there's one shot for maybe two, three bars, and it cuts. That's what I brought to the boxing scenes. I wanted them to be very special, taken from the point of view of the boxer in the ring.

RS: Another picture with pretty good boxing material in it is *Body and Soul*, don't you think?

MS: Excellent.

RS: And, you know, Bob Rossen had Jimmy Wong Howe [the cameraman] on roller skates.

MS: It's brilliant. If you look at the Robert Wise film *The Set-Up*—I screened it on a big screen when we were doing *The Aviator*—the boxing scenes, the whole picture, stands out.

RS: It's a great little movie.

MS: It was shown in the history of cinema class I took at NYU. Haig Manoogian showed that as an example of modern American cinema.

RS: Deservedly so. It makes me crazy that the high critical fraternity looks down on Bob Wise.

MS: I can't believe it.

RS: Bob made five or six movies that are terrific.

MS: Even a ghost story, *The Haunting*, is one of the greatest.

RS: I think his little one for Val Lewton, *Curse of the Cat People*, is excellent. It's the first movie I ever saw that scared me witless—with such simple devices.

MS: Excellent. Robert Wise was underrated.

RS: He was a consummate craftsman, you know.

MS: *Odds Against Tomorrow* is very good.

RS: Quite good.

MS: *Born to Kill.* And he did one of my very favorite westerns, which my parents took me to see at the Midway Theater in Jamaica, Queens, when we were living in Corona—*Blood on the Moon.*

RS: Excellent movie. Barbara Bel Geddes and Robert Mitchum were in it.

MS: I had never seen anything like it. I was five years old.

RS: It's a little like Raoul Walsh's *Pursued.*

MS: Exactly.

RS: It has the same kind of mood about it. It was also with Mitchum, of course. But back to you and drawing: You never brought in a storyboard artist?

MS: What I did was not good drawing, but I did it myself.

RS: And then put them up on a bulletin board?

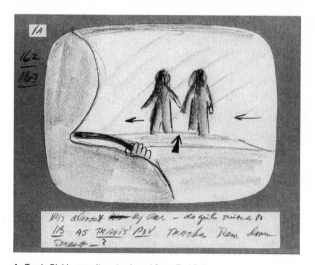

As Travis Bickle sees it: a storyboard from *Taxi Driver*.

MS: Yes. When I was doing *Taxi Driver,* I was at the St. Regis Hotel and I put all the drawings all around the room. Michael Chapman [the cinematographer] came in and we looked at them all from scene to scene to scene. I had to have it that way because I was always concerned about final cut. I had no final cut. I don't think I had final cut even on *Goodfellas.* Years later they gave it to me, but none of my pictures were giant box office successes. *Taxi Driver* was successful, but not like a *Star Wars* or a *Jaws.* So I had to be very precise. I had to know exactly what I wanted to do, and still have room for improvisations. I had to know that we would pan from left to right, that we moved here or there, that we started the scene with the actor coming in from the right. And sometimes you get on the set and someone says, "He can't come in from the right, he's got to come in from the left." So I've got to change my screen direction in my other cuts. And so the storyboarding now has come down to a process of making notes, which are in the margins of the script.

In some cases, a big action scene like the one in *Cape Fear,* the boat scene, I did all the drawings—little drawings, some bigger drawings—and made notes, and then an artist came in and did real storyboards based on my drawings. In the case of the action scenes in *Aviator,* I did the storyboards, which became these wonderful new visual storyboards on a computer. I forget what they're called . . .

RS: Previsualizations?

MS: Yes, that's it.

RS: How does that work? I've never actually seen one of those. I gather it's a crude little animation that helps you to imagine the shots you're eventually going to make.

MS: Well, I drew a little note, or I drew a little drawing. And Rob Legato, the second unit director, came in with Joe Reidy and we had a model of the plane. He had a little camera on a cable. We moved it on the plane for an angle. I could see

298

that in life size we would need to move the camera a little more to the left, perhaps, or lower. Maybe we could see that the plane didn't have the right kind of seat to film from behind the actor's head. That kind of thing. He took a black-and-white picture of what we agreed on. Then Rob previsualized based on that. I'd see maybe five or six or seven other cuts together on previz, and I'd say, "No, that first shot is not low enough, a low enough angle. Make that lower." Then he added a guy coming in from the right. I said, "Okay, keep that, but the next shot should be more to the left." It's very, very specific. We literally had a little movie of the storyboards of the action scenes.

That was broken up into four different sections, sections that I would do with Leo in real time and a real place—against the sky in a parking lot in a mock-up of the plane. Then shots with a double. Then shots that were going to be done by Rob Legato that were digital. So maybe a couple of hundred shots were shot over a period of four or five months as we were shooting the rest of the film, and then we ended with him on a green screen. It was all based on the previz, which were based on my notes and drawings.

RS: So on all your films you'll draw notes on your script?

MS: Yes. On *Goodfellas,* for example, I pretty much designed the film on the script as Nick Pileggi and I wrote it, even designed the freeze frames in those sequences in the beginning. It was all there. I always say that the film was like an afterthought. But the actors contributed so much. And the paragraph about the Copacabana was just the way Nick had written it. I said, "It's going to be one shot." I just wanted to leave it the way it was in the script. There was nothing to draw. We had to go to the place and actually lay out the shot. Which is what Joe Reidy and Michael Ballhaus and I did at the Copa. We got that shot in three-quarters of a day. We got another shot that day, too.

They worked it out. They designed with me. I said, Now we're here, now over here this happens, that happens. And they would suggest something happening, and I would say, Right, let's put that in moving this way. All culminating with the camera ending up on Henny Youngman. That wasn't drawn. That was worked out in my head, then on the set.

RS: But something as rough, as seemingly improvisational, as *Mean Streets* wasn't drawn, or was it?

MS: That was mainly drawn, because I couldn't take a chance. If I had six shots and we didn't have enough time to get two or three of them, I had to be able to say, Okay, do these two. We can redo this in another location if we just take the wall out here or whatever. We had to move so fast. I had to, literally, visually, see what I needed to get from the beginning.

RS: And you always carry the drawings, the notes, in the script?

MS: On the pages of the script. I often have drawings on a separate piece of paper for a scene. I have an assistant who gives me that in the morning, or the night before. And basically I work with that. Then there is improvising on the set. Like, for example, in *The Departed*, I said, "I want glass walls. But they have to have the blinds"—you know, rather than shooting against blank walls. The blinds had to be a little bit open. I knew that when they report to Marty Sheen behind the desk in the beginning of the film, it had to be a wide shot, I knew it had to be head to toe. I knew the cadets had to be on the left, the other actors on the right. We did the same kind of thing on the rest of the shots.

RS: Does this, among other things, free you to work a little more emotionally with the actors, because you know where you're at?

MS: It definitely gives you more time with the actors. There are other benefits. For instance, that long sequence that cuts back and forth in *The Departed,* when Mark Wahlberg keeps attacking Leo DiCaprio, is composed of specific camera moves, all of which were designed in my notes. So I knew that the lines of dialogue would be good for a certain kind of camera movement. And the actor would act knowing that. We didn't have to overlap, shooting twenty-five different angles or whatever.

RS: This can be a more efficient way of shooting, then?

MS: Yes, it is very precise in the camera moves and cuts. Leo had to be in the frame in a certain way. His eyes had to be seen a certain way. It gets that specific. You can see it in Kubrick films; I like watching how he cuts, and when he decides to cut, and what the size of the framing is. It specifically influenced the way I did the scene in *Goodfellas,* where De Niro tells Ray Liotta in the luncheonette near the end of the film, "I want you to go down south, and take care of this guy for me." Then it freeze-frames. And Liotta says, "That's when I knew I was going to be whacked." That was very specifically influenced by shots by Kubrick, where the actor is almost looking in the lens. That is very difficult for the actor because the other actor he is working with can't be where the camera is, so the actor has to put his face against the lens. I've worked with some people who have said, "Look, I can't do that. I'm not going to do it." We have to get them comfortable. But De Niro and Liotta went with it. It has an immediacy that I think draws the audience in, without the audience understanding why. You see it a lot in Kubrick.

RS: Yes, you do.

MS: And you see it in Hitchcock. I like watching the angles and the way he cut *The Birds*—just watching the sequences without any birds in them. It's interesting to watch how the camera moves and how Tippi Hedren approaches when she drops off the love birds as a gift. If you watch her coming up the deck, the camera is pulling back with her, and then it intercuts with tracking shots of her point of view of the barn. Nobody's there, but it has a little bit of creepiness to it, even though it's before that part of the movie that takes off.

RS: He was good with those creepy little moves—the almost subliminal hint of menace in them.

MS: *The Wrong Man* was another film where he did that so well.

RS: I love that movie.

MS: Watch the camera moves in there. I screened that when we were making *Taxi Driver*. I designed a lot of *Taxi Driver* based on that.

RS: Based on what aspect of it?

MS: The paranoia of the people. The way the camera reflected the paranoia. It was making Travis feel guilty about something he didn't do.

RS: Right, it did.

MS: Which was perfect for my themes. I like to deal with characters who have that sense of guilt about them.

RS: *The Wrong Man*, which is about a man wrongly accused of a crime, is a canonical film for me, and to most people it's not. I think it's a great movie.

MS: I think it is, too.

RS: Because Hitchcock rarely went to that realistic working-class place in other films.

MS: I screened it for *Aviator*, too, for Leo and all his friends. I pointed out to watch when Henry Fonda sits in that jail cell after he's finally booked, when he sits on that cot and looks up at the corner of the ceiling. Then when he looks at the sink. Then when he looks over at the bars. Look at the inserts. It's not just a shot of the ceiling. You have to figure out exactly how he looks at it, which corner of the ceiling.

The inserts tell you things. For instance, the inserts in *The Aviator*, when the man who has polio is in the bathroom and asks Hughes to pass him a towel, and Hughes refuses. It's the way the towels are looking at him.

RS: The towels are looking at him?

MS: If you look at the insert, the towels are saying, Touch me. Come on, touch me. You can't do it. The angle of that shot was important. Bob Richardson and I fooled around with the angles; we shot the full day. I think we shot more than forty angles—of everything. Forty-two setups. Even the toilet paper, the soiled towels, the towel in the basket. Hughes realizes that all the towels are gone, and he looks in the basket, and the basket is almost beckoning him: Touch me, touch me. And he couldn't do that.

As I said, the angles on the inserts are very important. They are all designed and worked on.

RS: It's possible, isn't it, that Hitchcock was the most meticulous storyboarder?

MS: Oh, yeah. I loved his stuff. I remember doing my comic strips when we were living in Queens. I did them in 1.33 aspect ratio. It was square. That was like a movie for me. I must've been five or six years old. Then, when I was in Manhattan, in 1950, about eight or nine years old, I would watch *Suspense Theater,* or something like that, on TV and try to do my version of it in drawings. I'd paint them with watercolors. I had a whole bunch of them. Then one day my father saw me playing with them and I hid them, threw them away, as I told you before.

RS: There are really none of those left?

MS: No. I guess I felt ashamed of them. A year or two later, I said to myself, You know what? The hell with them, I'm going to do them again. Those I have.

By that time I was a teenager, seeing things on the wide screen. As I said earlier, I drew Roman epics, one of which was called *The Eternal City.* I drew gladiatorial combats. They were in wide-screen. I was already thinking in terms of how to do a scene. I still have the same problems framing close-ups, in anamorphic, today.

Watching *Million Dollar Movie* on TV, I could revisit a film every night for a week. I was determined to figure out the camera angles, though I didn't know that terminology. I thought about how the camera was closer or further away from an actor, whether the camera seemed to move in or out.

But I was dealing with that when I was doing these little drawings. There would be one panel with three images on it—the beginning, the middle, and the end of the shot. For example, in the opening credits of one of these Roman stories, I drew the soldiers outside on the Appian Way beginning a triumphal march, soldiers coming in and the camera up in the sky. Then I had the camera coming down, the army getting closer. Then I showed the wall on the right, the army on the left. As I came to my name as director, I had the camera boom over the backs of the soldiers, going through the gates with them. I would say to myself, We start here, but we've got to wind up there.

RS: In animation, those shots are left to the in-betweeners, and you're not an in-betweener.

MS: No, I'm not.

RICHARD SCHICKEL: We haven't yet discussed color. Is there a typical Martin Scorsese palette? I mean, some of the films strike me as pretty saturated. But you can't say that of *Age of Innocence.* I don't think you can say it about *King of Comedy,* which has a nice glow.

MARTIN SCORSESE: *King of Comedy* was a big departure. As I've said, it was a very difficult film for me to make for many different reasons, and that was one of them. I had to try not to do too much camera work that drew attention to itself.

RS: Is there a relationship between that reluctance and the film's palette?

MS: *Mean Streets* is very saturated. *Alice,* too. *Taxi Driver* not so much. *New York, New York,* definitely. *Kundun,* definitely. I tried somewhat in *Age of Innocence.*

RS: *Kundun* seems to me very Asian—soft and even misty at times.

MS: The colors are strong, I think, but it might not be as saturated as some of the others. There's no doubt that three-strip Technicolor had a big influence on me. As a young person, seeing a film that employed it was the most magical experience—seeing *Duel in the Sun* in color or seeing the rerelease of *Robin Hood* in color, and

"Happy Ending": Liza Minnelli enjoys her stardom in *New York, New York*.

those old westerns in Cinecolor. It was hyper-real. It's the antithesis of *On the Waterfront*, which kind of wiped the board clean for me.

RS: Hyper-real?

MS: It was good for stories that weren't on a naturalistic level. And so I associated color with that type of picture. But by the late sixties, Andrew Sarris was writing that the norm for every film would be color. It was hard to believe at the time, but he was right. That's why, when we started working in color and designing in color, the color fading issue came up. When you design a film in color, the color has to remain stable, the way you originally imagined it.

RS: Hence your passion for film preservation.

MS: We had so much trouble getting the money for *Taxi Driver* that Michael and Julia Phillips and I were talking about doing it in black-and-white video. We were that keen to tell the story. Of course, eventually we shot in color, but the palette in it was really muted compared to *Mean Streets*, which is almost operatic, almost like a musical at times.

I tried to adapt the color palette from *The Red Shoes*. I was trying for a three-strip Technicolor look. I couldn't do that, of course; *Godfather II* was the last film printed in Technicolor. After that the processing machines were gone. For *Taxi Driver* and *Alice Doesn't Live Here Anymore* I preferred a warmer look. *Taxi Driver*, though, was the key. That was a film that ordinarily would have been made in black-and-white, there's no doubt about it, but you had to use color, and the colors had to be muted. And so that became a big issue.

RS: I'm trying to imagine *Taxi Driver* in black-and-white. I like it in color.

MS: Don't forget the last sequence, when we took the color down for the ratings board [in order to de-emphasize the bloodiness of the violence]. That was my suggestion, to desaturate the color. I guess I was obsessed with what Oswald Morris and John Huston did on *Moby Dick,* and with *Reflections in a Golden Eye.*

RS: That's quite a beautiful film.

MS: I wanted to do something like that with the whole picture. But I couldn't. Oswald Morris and John Huston had access to a three-strip negative. So it was a little different. I couldn't desaturate ours like that. So each shot I had had a basic color—green, brown, or blue. I chose brown. And then the color was fused in, 20 percent color, 80 percent brown. The next shot might be 60 percent full color, 40 percent brown. I wanted to do the whole movie that way. That would have been great.

RS: It would have taken a long time to do that.

MS: We did it fast—in a week or two. The opticals were going real fast. We did some trims that satisfied the ratings board, and I liked the way it looked. I remember when we screened it in full color, the blood looked fake to me. Paul Schrader had imagined more of a Japanese film, where the walls would have been drenched in blood. Sort of a samurai look. Paul was very much into those films. He had just written *The Yakuza.*

That's when I began to have a real problem with the color palette. In *New York, New York,* I embraced the full saturation

Battered Bull: Jake LaMotta after a long day at the office.

again. And in *Raging Bull,* I decided no color, because I just couldn't continue with color anymore. That also helped the period look of the film.

RS: Absolutely.

MS: When I did *King of Comedy,* the art director, Boris Leven, and I decided to keep it really muted, really down. An uptown New York, Seagram's Building sort of quality.

RS: That's what it looked like.

MS: You know, it has a nice, early sixties kind of feel. Boris put a dash of red in, here and there. I love looking at those buildings. That's New York.

We shot right in the building where the iconic restaurant La Brasserie is; it's supposed to be where Jerry's character lived. That was enjoyable to do. After that, *After Hours* was full, straight color. We didn't have much of a problem with the color in *The Last Temptation.* There was a whole ancient world of dust in the desert. In *Goodfellas* we went garish; you just had to go full blast.

RS: Those guys weren't going to wear a lot of Brooks Brothers suits.

MS: No way. They made me a suit from the picture, the one that Bob wears when he walks in the first time. Kind of a French blue silk suit. It's hysterical; I can't wear it, of course. But it was really wonderful, and I thought the colors were just eye-popping. That was the nature of the beast, the nature of that world.

RS: Yes, it was.

MS: Then I got up to speed, so to speak. Except in *The Departed.* I wanted all the color out of that.

I got very upset. Everybody was wearing black anyway, for God's sake. In the modern world, the use of black is ubiquitous. There's no more style the way I like it. I sound like an old man, but the way I like style on screen is with suits and ties and that sort of thing. Conservative, conventional.

RS: If you look at older pictures, the actors going in and out of a nightclub are always incredibly elegant.

MS: Elegance is a very different idea now. I decided to drain the color out of the damn thing. I thought, It's so ugly. That matched the way everybody was behaving in the film.

RS: Yes, I can see that.

MS: Anyway, I scouted locations in the winter. I had never been in Boston, but the snow there was beautiful, trees with no leaves on them, black. I thought that would be great for *The Departed.* I don't really know the modern world in color. I just don't get it.

But then Matt Damon had agreed to do De Niro's film, *The Good Shepherd.* There was a question as to when he would be available, and I thought, You know what? *The Departed* really doesn't depend on seasons. Bob's film did. So I moved my picture from the fall to April. When I got to Boston, I was shocked by the green leaves in the trees. Then I realized, these guys get cut up, they get shot, they betray each other under green trees just as well as under bare trees. So with *Departed* I became at peace with the color process. I accept now that a color film is made the way they used to routinely make black-and-white films—that is to say, I try not to think about color at all.

SHOOTING

RICHARD SCHICKEL: When you're on the set—particularly when you're isolated on a location, with everyone away from their normal lives—don't you feel that the company often becomes a little surrogate family?

MARTIN SCORSESE: Coming from a very tribal place, the real bond for me was one of blood, of family. Very Mediterranean. When I made the crossover to New York University I brought that expectation with me. I expected that the people around me, the new people I met from all different parts of the world, would become family. I don't think they saw it that way. I expected from them things they could not provide.

RS: But still, don't you feel that any movie company, or most movie companies, while they are up and running, are little families?

MS: Absolutely. Like Ealing Studios in the old days, or the way Raoul Walsh worked at Warner Bros., or William Wellman, and Frank Capra and Harry Cohn at Columbia.

RS: They had the same crew, the same cameramen. Very often the same actors. There *was* a familial feeling.

MS: You know, some of the best times are on the location scouting; everybody has lunch together, you all talk, everyone gets to know each other. There's Fellini wanting to make a series of films on the actor, the producer, and so on. One of the lines in his treatment was that the location scout is very important. It was always important, he said, to scout a location near the best restaurant. It was just an excuse to get to those restaurants. Very Italian.

But a familial feeling is a very important thing. Henry Fonda and John Ford, or Anthony Mann and James Stewart—these were extraordinarily complex, important relationships. When there's a rift, the fallout could be very upsetting. For example, Irwin Winkler told me in 1994 that Michael Chapman didn't like *Raging Bull* [which came out in 1980].

RS: Didn't like the story?

MS: Didn't like the way it turned out. Just that. I don't think he ever told me that. Now everything is fine. Paul Schrader doesn't like it, either. I was surprised, because we worked so closely on it. But Michael—the film didn't hit him. He didn't get it. He didn't like it. [In later years, Chapman came to regard the film much more highly.]

RS: He did a beautiful job on it.

Lining up a shot in *Raging Bull*.

MS: Absolutely. It's one of the best-photographed films. But not everybody has to like what you're doing. Very often it's hard to know what goes on around you. In many cases people are being polite and just not telling you what they don't like.

RS: I know that happens very often.

MS: A funny thing happened on *Raging Bull.* I was on the set waiting for a shot to be ready. There were some crew members there, real Hollywood pros. Nice guys. They were sitting there talking behind me; they didn't know I was there. One of the guys asked of the others, "What are we doing next?" Somebody answers, "Who knows, who cares? It's all a bunch of crap anyway, Jesus."

That guy was so nice to me on the set. He was a real pro, but he hated everything we were doing. He couldn't care less. [*Laughs.*] They were called to go back to work, and they went at it like men on the chain gang.

RS: Let's talk more about cinematography. You've said you're not as confident about lighting as you are about some other aspects of your work. Yet your pictures seem very well lit to me.

MS: I don't have it.

RS: What do you mean, you don't have it?

MS: I don't think in those terms that much. Yet, it's true, when I look at something, I'll think, My God, it's far too bright, or too dark, or whatever. But then I'll look at, let's say, *The Informer*—the streams of light, the dust particles in the light—and I'm in awe. I'm not talking about sentimental value. You look at any Ford picture and there's a depth to the imagery, a power to the lighting, even in the one that's considered a failure, *The Fugitive.* It's more than being pictorial—no matter who the cameraman was.

RS: I actually like that film, no matter what its reputation is.

MS: Me, too. Gabriel Figueroa's lighting was great. I'm talking also of Kazan's lighting of the whorehouse hallway in *East of Eden,* or the lighting of Boris Kaufman in *On the Waterfront*—that scene at night where you see Brando running in the back alley, the truck is about to get them, and he breaks in the window—the way the cobblestones are lit. It became an iconic image for me; I always wished I could take that image and put it up on a wall.

RS: Are you saying that you feel you have never, or rarely, in your pictures gotten that kind of depth?

MS: No, I think I may have. I certainly tried on *Mean Streets*, I can tell you that. I knew that the red gels had to be a certain way. There are a couple of scenes in *Alice Doesn't Live Here Anymore* where Alice walks into bars to do auditions. Look at the light. I said to Kent Wakefield, the cameraman, Let's do it like John Ford. And he said, Absolutely. But I don't tend to think of it, unless I go to a location and I have a fairly good rapport with the director of photography. Then it becomes something I focus on. I had to be very specific on *Mean Streets* and *Alice*. And with Michael Chapman on *Taxi Driver*. I guess it's something I focus on when I'm doing it, rather than thinking about it beforehand. Whereas editing, I tend to think of it way beforehand—the framing, the blocking.

RS: In other words, you sort of look ahead to the edited film; a vision of that is tentatively in your mind.

MS: More than tentatively. Shot number one will cut to number two, and number three, and number four, and that should give you a movement based on the images. I was startled sometimes by the editing in Eisenstein's films—*October*, and of course *Potemkin*. There was some editing in Carol Reed films that I liked, and Orson Welles. And I really liked the way certain things were edited in *Force of Evil*.

Moments come to mind, and I think, How was that done? Then I use that insight. Remember that scene of Howard Hughes seeing an old man sweeping up in the factory, and he says, "Who is that man? Get rid of him"?

RS: Yes, of course.

MS: Well, what I tried to do was to intercut moves in on Leo's face. I do that all the time; I move in on somebody, then you cut back to what he or she is seeing. I tried to do something simple in this scene, but it didn't quite work. I wanted to intercut it with a tilt up on the old man with the broom. A camera is focused on the broom, then you're moving in on Leo, then back to the broom. You're seeing a little more of the broom, you see a hand with these funny fingernails. You're moving in on Leo tighter. You cut back, and you reveal the face of the old man. By that point you should have moved in on Leo fully. The problem was that the motion was too jagged.

I think I shot the man with the broom for about four hours one night. The crew was laughing at a certain point. And I said, I'm not sure about that tilt. I don't know. And Thelma and I tried it different ways. Finally Thelma had the idea of intercutting Leo's hand from the scene in the future, in the screening room, putting on the tape recorder, and then it worked. That's an example of something that didn't work exactly the way I wanted.

RS: Right.

MS: All the fight scenes in *Raging Bull* were basically filmed that way—except for the big moment when Sugar Ray Robinson finally beats up Jake, who is hanging on the ropes.

I designed all those scenes. I was given a black-and-white video. I broke it up into parts, like music, like for *The Last Waltz*. Two or three of the fight scenes were cut in a couple of days. We put one shot next to another; they were very easily put together.

That Sugar Ray Robinson scene I just referred to, by the way, was based on the shower sequence from *Psycho*. I had every frame of that. And I designed corresponding shots of what it would be like in the ring, based on those elements. I shot it in about ten days. And then when we edited, we moved shots around, because each one had its own energy. A glove coming into frame is different from a knife. So in the process of trying to make the glove have a similar effect to the knife, the use of undercranking and overcranking and other techniques came into play. Unpredictable things happen when you're doing that. In this case, the glove has a certain amount of light on it, and there are sprays of water and sweat flying. It created things in the frame I just didn't expect. One frame of light cuts better to another frame of light. That sort of thing. So basically, I feel much more comfortable designing the editing than the lighting.

There were lighting ideas in the storyboards for *Raging Bull,* but then I listened to the cameraman and sometimes that's when I had to ask, Can we do this? What about that?

I always tell the story of Spielberg making *Empire of the Sun*—that incredible shot of the sunrise, the last kamikaze silhouetted against it. I asked him, "How did you get that? It was so beautiful." Well, he told me he got there an hour or forty-five minutes earlier, before the crew, and he looked around the set. He saw that there was mist on the ground and knew how the sun would come up, and that was the effect he wanted. He got the assistant cameraman and shot before anybody else got there. He grew up in Phoenix, Arizona.

Michael Powell was able to tell the time of day by where the sun was. But he grew up in the English countryside. For me the elements were inhospitable. I don't understand natural light. So I never really thought of lighting in those ways.

It changed with Michael Ballhaus, by the way, whose lighting for the Fassbinder films interested me.

RS: How so?

MS: They had a kind of almost neorealistic look, though the films were framed very carefully. But the lighting was higher key. And yet it was a very dramatic film. I don't know if I understand a lot of the Fassbinder pictures. I'm not quite that kind of person. But *Merchant of Four Seasons* influenced me a lot—the toughness of the whole, the toughness of the frame, particularly in the scenes where his wife is making love to another man, and he comes in. Or he has a fight with her. It was done with such unflinching honesty. The lighting was so honest. Yet there are other moments where the lighting was almost like Douglas Sirk. I wanted to work with Ballhaus. He could be amazing.

King of Comedy is another good example of lighting that gave me a different look. Coming off the extraordinary work Michael Chapman did in *Raging Bull,* I was rethinking how to make movies—going back to no camera movement for the most part. There are about two or three shots that have movement in them. Basically, everything is medium shot, close-up, medium close-up, wide shot. Functional tracking.

RS: Who shot that one?

MS: Frederick Schuler, who was the operator for Michael Chapman for years. Freddie was able to give me the look that I wanted, which was almost like a television film.

It took me a long time to come around to the film for many different reasons. Each day I had problems working on it and shooting it. The actors were all great. There were no problems with the actors. But it was very difficult for me to be there. And part of the Rupert character, I realize, I had in me. Part of Jerry [Lewis] I had in me. And I didn't want to face it at that moment. As I mentioned earlier, I was struggling personally when I was making that film, so I designed it so the shots would be hermetically sealed frames. Rupert was in Jerry's frame a lot of the time. He's after Jerry, he wants Jerry. That was my thinking. And I wanted it to have kind of a flat, high-key lighting.

RS: It's appropriate to that film.

MS: That was a good example of being very, very specific about lighting in a picture.

RS: When you're working away on your script, I would think, it's primarily on where the camera will be placed, where the camera is going to move in the shot, that sort of thing.

MS: In a lot of cases. Although sometimes you're just planning on what you need to do to really cover properly.

RS: So as you're doing that, vaguely, even specifically, is the overall look of a film coming into your mind?

MS: Yes, it is. I definitely have images in my mind's eye. But you get on the set and you have to adjust—suddenly it's brighter than you imagined, for example. That's always a problem for me. In the old days, before there was video, someone would give me the filter to look through. I would be told, "That's the way it will look." I didn't want that many things overlit.

RS: I always find looking through the viewfinder that it looks brighter than I thought it was going to be.

MS: I agree with you! And I'm almost embarrassed to say at times, Is this a little too bright in the corner here? No one will see it. It's barely going to register. But I have to ask. I go through a constant process of question and answer: Should we try this, how about that?

Kundun was a whole other experience with Roger Deakins, who is a master. His lighting was fantastic.

RS: It's a beautiful film.

MS: I'd watch him work—meticulous. We talked about style. We talked mainly about the lighting—we always do a lot of screening of films for lighting. For example, for *Taxi Driver* I screened *The Wrong Man* and also *Salvatore Giuliano* [Francesco Rosi's 1962 drama about political conflict in postwar 1940s Sicily], Gianni di Venanzo's photography in that film. I told Chapman, I want that in color, the philosophy of it. Michael understood that. We got it for *Taxi Driver,* I think.

Anyway, for *Kundun* I remember we talked a lot about the lighting in Zhang Yimou's films, and Chen Kaige's films. We also talked about the lighting in *Fat City,* which he liked a lot.

RS: Really? I would never have thought of that film in this context.

MS: Those were our touchstones. I didn't see a lot of the rushes for *Kundun.* I saw most of them when I came back. I just had total confidence in what he was doing.

RS: At what point in your career did you start using monitors?

MS: There was a one-inch monitor on *King of Comedy.* For *After Hours* there was a black-and-white monitor. There was definitely a monitor, black-and-white, for *The Color of Money.* I tried to use a color monitor on *The Age of Innocence* for a few shots, but I didn't like it, so I stopped using it. For *Goodfellas,* I think the monitor was black-and-white, too. Then we started using color monitors and that's what we're using now.

Prior to that, you would design the shot, work it out. And then I'd physically ride the shot, frame it, say what I wanted, and then they would do it. You really had to have a lot of confidence in the camera operator, because he would eventually be the one who could tell you what you got, what the best take was.

The director overcome by Michelle Pfeiffer's beauty in *The Age of Innocence.*

RS: A lot of directors still don't always use monitors.

MS: I think that's good.

RS: So then what's the advantage of using a monitor from your point of view?

MS: The exact framing. I can tell the energy of the camera movement that I want. I can tell if I have the right cut points.

As far as acting is concerned, it helps a little, too. But, believe me, when you screen the rushes, that's when the acting pops out. And it's a dangerous thing. Some actors like to look at the tapes, and that can be a problem. There are a couple I trust. Nicholson, though, never looked at a take. He had total trust that way. There are a couple of actors who see the rushes and know how to handle it, how to assess them and move on.

I don't think I've ever been involved with an actor who wanted to study them over and over and redo things. I point out to them, That's a tape. It's a small monitor. Even if the film is on television later on, it's not going to look like that.

There are pictures of Kubrick working on *Eyes Wide Shut* and other films with actors around him, looking at videotape playback, and he's improvising with them. He improvised with Peter Sellers in *Lolita*. Imagine if they had video playback at that time. I think he would have done that with Sellers, or in *Dr. Strangelove*. It really depends on the person making the film.

RS: Can you contrast that with your way of working with actors?

MS: By the time I did *New York, New York*, I expected more from actors like Bob De Niro, because they brought so much to their work to begin with. But I expected a lot from everyone. I kept pushing and pushing everyone, sometimes into very bad states. In a funny way, I didn't understand the nature of what they bring to their work. They go through a great deal before they get on that stage that you don't even know about.

Yet I'm aware of and ultrasensitive to everything a performer goes through as he is doing it. In fact, my set is, very often, attuned only to the actor. It's always very quiet. If the actor wants to do ten takes, usually, if I have the time, we do it. If he doesn't want to do any more takes, that's it. Early on, everything was about what I wanted, and I thought everybody would just snap to and do it.

DIRECTING ACTORS: AN EXAMPLE

RICHARD SCHICKEL: Through the years you've been closely associated with four leading actors in several films apiece—Harvey Keitel, Robert De Niro, Daniel Day-Lewis, and, lately, Leo DiCaprio. These are very disparate actors. But do all of them give you a comfort zone, an ease of communication? What?

MARTIN SCORSESE: The explanation is in part that making films with your friends, spending time with them, gives you the opportunity to share feelings with them about many different things.

RS: What about Leo, for example? Did you see him and say to yourself, I love this kid?

MS: Bob De Niro told me about working with him on *This Boy's Life.* A couple of other people told me about him, too. Then I saw the movie, in which I thought he was excellent. But then I saw him in Lasse Hallström's film *What's Eating Gilbert Grape.* I thought he and Johnny Depp together were fantastic.

RS: They're both very good.

MS: But really, it was just that Bob said, This is a young boy who has that something special. You've got to work with him.

RS: There's something different about him, though, in one respect: Unlike your other leads, when he first came on the scene, he was a big teenage rage.

MS: Not for me. I was going on what I saw in *Gilbert Grape,* and *This Boy's Life. Titanic* sealed his popularity. But I still saw him as the young actor who was so extraordinary in those other movies. Mike Ovitz put us together. It turned out that Leo liked the pictures I made over the years, he wanted to work with me. Hopefully, we can do a few more.

RS: How would you characterize him, compared to Keitel, De Niro, and Daniel Day-Lewis, as an actor?

MS: I see a great similarity.

RS: In what way?

MS: In the way he works. He's very specific, and if you need some powerful emotion from him, it's going to be there. I don't think he necessarily needs to spend three hours on preparation for certain kinds of things. He's a real pro. He gets in there and he gets it done. When I least expect it, he finds an emotional level I didn't think was there. He surprises me, moves me. Which is very hard to do when I'm on a set.

You know, I've got lights around me, I've got the producers yelling at me because they want me to finish. All these problems. As you get a little older, you have to be in great shape and you have to be focused. And I found that Leo's very similar. His instinctive feeling about the world around him is a lot like mine. The major difference is I'm thirty-five years older, a totally different generation, and he grew up in California. But we think similarly.

I always tell a story about what happened on *The Departed,* that scene where Marty Sheen gets thrown off the roof, and he's lying in a pool of blood. We had to go back to that location a thousand times—it was just one of those pain-in-the-neck shoots. It was very difficult for other reasons, too, including the actors' schedules and finishing on time.

So I needed to go very quickly that day. And I needed a medium close-up of DiCaprio's reaction. He comes running and the body falls right in front of him. In the original Chinese film, apparently, the guy falls on a car. In *Collateral,* Michael Mann, whose work I admire greatly, has a character fall right on a cab.

RS: I remember that vividly.

MS: So I said we couldn't have that in this script. So how was I going to do it? I decided we would stay on Leo and never see Captain Queenan being pushed out a window; we just see him falling through the air. And suddenly, he would fall in front of the kid. So we got that shot, which was a problem because we had a dummy, and blood being sprayed—too much blood, not enough blood. Then I needed a medium-close shot with Leo as he went around the body. In the meantime, these other guys, these animals, are coming down the building. If he's late, he could be exposed as the rat. And, of course, he was just talking to Queenan on the roof, who was going to get him out of the whole thing.

On take one I should have been in front of the camera and watching the actor. But I was a little tired, so I was watching it on the monitor. And Leo did something in his reaction that suddenly moved me to tears. Son of a bitch, I said to myself. That's why I make these movies. That's why! [*Laughs.*] And I told him, "That was beautiful." And he said, "I think I can do it better." "Okay, let's do another," I said. We did three more takes, I think. But I decided [*laughs*] that first take was beautiful, and I used it.

RS: We're talking pure actor's instinct here, aren't we?

One of the several mad scenes in *The Aviator.*

MS: The instinct was extraordinary. And it was instinct under a lot of pressure. But the kid locked in, he had a certain kind of truth—he gave a whimper, like the whimper of a poor little animal that was stuck in this world, knowing it would get killed.

And that wasn't the end of it. Marty Sheen wanted to be off camera for him, in the blood, lying on the ground, you know. And Leo didn't want Marty to do that. But Marty was a pro, he was going to do it. And, bless him, he did it. Then, in editing, we struggled, Thelma and I, to work it out so that we stayed on Leo the right amount of time and didn't cut away too soon. We tried different cuts. I said, "Keep it the way I felt it that day." I said, "Let's keep it long." And then I had to struggle to keep all the sound out. They'd keep putting sound in, background noises. I said, "What's that? It's interfering with the sound in his throat."

RS: But there's even more to that sequence, isn't there? I recall that Marty Sheen's death is followed with shots of Matt Damon, back at headquarters, trying to figure out what's happening.

MS: Yes, Matt is in his office after Marty falls off the roof, and you cut back to Matt at the desk. He has the walkie-talkie on the desk, and he's listening, and he's saying, Who fell off the roof? What are you talking about? Every time you cut, it's a different angle and slightly different lighting, and the camera's moving a different way. Until finally you're in very close. All that was designed. And it was shot very quickly.

RS: And what is the editing saying?

MS: There's an implied tension in the frame if the sequence is working.

RS: So it's related, in some measure, to the dialogue he's speaking?

MS: And the intensity of how things are going out of control on the other end of the walkie-talkie. The more things go out of control, the more the camera is moving in closer to him, but off on an angle. The more he's worming out of it, the more he's taking the coward's way out, the more I felt that, instead of tracking in faster, zooming in, I wanted it to be slower—to convey the feeling that he's set in motion a series of events that are going to go out of control and everybody's going to die.

But the editing is very controlled, because the frame has to have that tension. It's almost as if you want to hit him with the camera. But you can't. The camera's holding back. The tension arises out of the contrast of its pace, enhanced by the editing, with the hugeness of the events going on in the sequence.

Normally, a picture like that develops into a big, climactic shootout—you know, a bravura set piece in terms of camera movement, lighting, explosions, this sort of thing. But we had that to a certain extent earlier when Jack gets killed in the car. So it's almost perfunctory, that scene. The only thing we could do was be as objective as possible about it. It didn't need any embellishment. There are a few cuts, and then basically it's a wide shot. It's the opposite of what Hitchcock does with suspense. Maybe the Hitchcockian way would have been to show Barrigan [one of Nicholson's hit men] coming up the stairs with the gun, Leo in the elevator with Matt, Barrigan getting closer with the gun, Leo in the elevator, the door opening, and Leo getting shot.

RS: Well, as you know, Hitchcock liked to give the audience information the characters don't have, to enhance the suspense.

MS: It *was* about suspense. But when I was growing up, I was in situations where everything was fine—and then, suddenly, violence broke out. You didn't get a sense of where it was coming from, what was going to happen. You just knew that the atmosphere was charged, and, bang, it happened.

In this particular story, I wondered what would happen if you just killed the main character. Then the audience has to think about who they have to care about.

RS: I was with both those boys. I didn't choose.

MS: No. But I saw an audience reaction in Chicago, a preview, where they were stunned. They didn't know who to care about. All bets were off. All plot points were thrown out the window. It was [*snaps fingers*] like a moment in time: You exist, then you don't exist. That is the nature of who we are and what we are as human beings. It happens that fast in life, whether it's a violent death or a natural death.

RS: Oh, God, yes.

MS: I think of that all the time.

RS: Me, too. But, you know, we've drifted kind of far from Leo. Any more thoughts on his work habits?

MS: Well, I really respect what he did in *Aviator* as Howard Hughes, how he worked with the Hughes accent, how he went through all the meetings with John Logan. The thoroughness of Leo's approach—I just know I can count on him.

RS: Is he an actor who does more research on his parts than other actors?

MS: He does very thorough research. We shoot a lot more than we use with him. Very often with him I'll shoot the psychological subtext. I did it with Bob, too. And with Daniel. You never know, the subtext may need to be seen. If we can squeeze it in, it's there. I found with him, in acting out the subtext, he goes through a process until he knows it's been fully absorbed. For instance, on *Aviator,* we all had discussions about whether we should or should not show the old Howard Hughes—Howard Hughes in Vegas at the end of his life. I had felt when I read the script originally that it was good that we never saw the old Hughes.

RS: That's one of the things I liked about the finished film. That crazy old coot in Las Vegas is about the only thing most people know about Hughes. What we didn't know was much more interesting, as the movie proves.

MS: Right, but the discussions went on about it. I wanted to at least entertain the idea of using a scene of the old Hughes. What scene might we do of him? What would be consistent with the rest of the picture? John Logan, who wrote the film, worked on so many different things—Leo, me, him, together. We came up with a couple of scenes. I wasn't totally convinced, but I would have shot them.

But about halfway through the picture we had to do the scene where Hughes loses his mind in the screening room, sitting nude in the white leather chair. The attendant comes in the door with his gloves on. Hughes says, "Bring in the milk. Bring in the milk."

RS: A great scene.

MS: But we spent, I think, nine days and nights in the screening room on that. It was hell, absolute hell. His body makeup took seven hours. With that much makeup, you cut into your shooting time. You can only shoot maybe five hours, as opposed to twelve hours a day, or ten hours. Leo felt it was the hardest thing he had to do.

RS: Well, that happens a fair amount of time with you, doesn't it?

MS: What?

RS: That the scenes take a lot of time. I'm just thinking of what some of your actors have gone through to make your pictures.

MS: Yeah, they do a lot. They're very committed.

RS: It's grueling.

MS: Absolutely grueling. But Leo's got the youth and the energy. And the curiosity for it.

Anyway, I saw the rushes of him in the screening room scene and I felt strongly that we didn't need to include the last Las Vegas scene. I looked at the scene we had and I said, Forget it. The next day I saw him on the set. I took him to my trailer and I said, "We did the old Howard." [*Laughs.*] "You have to see this stuff," I said,

The cinematically complex murder sequence in *Shutter Island*.

"it's beautiful—especially the blue behind his head." And when Leo saw it, he said, "Great. Okay."

So we didn't shoot the older Howard scene. But he had to go through a process, get the real knowledge of shooting that scene. Some people tell an actor they will do something, and don't do it. I was going to shoot it. Even if I shot it and didn't use it, I was still going to shoot it. But when he looked at the rushes, he agreed that there was no need to.

RS: Do you feel a little more mentorly toward Leo, as opposed to actors who are your contemporaries, like De Niro and Harvey?

MS: Maybe. But that would be presumptuous of me, I think. Besides he comes from another time and culture. I can guide a little bit, that's about all. There might be some specific things I'd tell him from time to time, to watch out for, or think about clearly. But that doesn't mean he'll do it. It's like any kid.

But no matter what you do, the difference in generations is there.

RS: Sure.

MS: It's just there. I mean, there are certain things that happened on the Howard Hughes picture which were interesting, and stemmed from the difference between a young man and an older man. For example, it's how the whole relationship ended with Katharine Hepburn by the screening room door. We went through a whole process there. It became more attuned to her. That took maybe eighteen or twenty takes. That's something we discovered together—for Leo to put the focus on her and not think about himself. Not to bring her into his goddamned world. Get her out of there. Say, Yeah, yeah, I'll go flying with you Tuesday. Don't worry about it. Rather than being, in that particular moment, a character who would be asking for her sympathy. That's a key thing. That's something he discovered while we were shooting that scene. I didn't know how to say it. But we kept working until I finally realized what it was.

RS: So that he wasn't asking for sympathy?

MS: Right, exactly. And then finally he did something, and I said, That's it. We've got to go that way. But it took me all those takes to get to it with him. It's the process. But he found it rewarding and so did I.

RS: Would you say, from what you hear, that you do more takes than other directors?

MS: No. That was a special scene. He's talking to her through a door and he's out of his mind. You just can't do it in two takes.

RS: I'm sure.

MS: You would be missing something. We had to touch upon every possibility, you know: all those spasms, which were related to his obsessive-compulsive disorder. We did different takes with different kinds of moves. Maybe he touched his legs too much in one take, so we did another one with less touching of the leg. That kind of thing.

RS: That's a lot to hold in your head. I'm talking about you, Marty, not him. Let's leave Leo out of the equation for the moment. How do you know when you've got it? What's the moment?

MS: In this case, I could hear it in his voice. Like that scene in *The Departed*, I knew immediately when we had it. I just felt we were going to cut to him and he was going to give the required emotion. I didn't know how he was going to give it, though, or that it was going to be that moving.

I heard something similar in the door scene between Hughes and Hepburn in *The Aviator*. It was in his voice when he turned to me and said, "Don't make it about me, make it about her," and I said, "Exactly."

I didn't know that from the beginning, though. Because, you see, there was so much that was going on in his body movements in every one of those shots. And maybe a third of that scene was cut out of the picture. It was almost mathematical. We had to measure how many times we used that tic in the earlier part of the shot; we didn't want it to be too much. And the tone of voice—a little too much of the twang: we had to take that down. We could loop that later, just in case we got in trouble, but I'd rather do it on the set.

Liza Minnelli commands Marty's attention in *New York, New York*.

All those choices meant really hard work, especially if you have a special relationship with the actor. But you just go through it.

We had a good time with it afterwards, particularly when he talked to Alec Baldwin [playing Juan Trippe] through the same door. Where he had the meeting, and he's screaming at one point, I wish you were there, so you could have seen how that plane flew. [He's talking about the moment when the Spruce Goose takes flight.] It was beautiful, you would've loved it. Because he knew that Juan Trippe also loved flying.

And Juan Trippe tells him, "Fly safe, fly safe," at the end of the scene. It's very moving.

RS: It's amazing to me, how you can stay on top of so many things.

MS: I stretched that screening room set like I did the ring in *Raging Bull.* We made the room much, much longer. We added wall space, added more walls, so that it always seemed bigger or smaller, or whatever. It's never quite one size. That took time. But it was something we had to try.

Making *Gangs of New York,* I felt there was a real bond created between Leo and me. So I thought that if there was a project that came to him, or one that I came across that he would be perfect for, or that was written with him in mind the way Ellen Burstyn was perfect for *Alice Doesn't Live Here Anymore,* or *Raging Bull* was for Bob, or Paul Newman was in *The Color of Money*—I felt it would be great to go further with him. When I saw the title on the script of *The Aviator,* I thought, That word hasn't been used in years. I was very dubious about it. Then I read the first scene with the mother bathing him and I thought that was interesting, about quarantine, and the strangeness in the mother. The next thing I know,

I realized it's Howard Hughes shooting this movie, and I thought immediately, I can't do this. But when I continued reading the script, I came to see it as an epic about an American pioneer.

RS: Right.

MS: And it was bold enough. John Logan had that fine perception of Hughes's creative energy and how that creative energy fueled the great American pioneers of the nineteenth century.

RS: I really feel *Gangs* and *Aviator* are related in some way. The American dream, if you dream it intensely enough, will make you nuts.

MS: That's the beauty of *Aviator.* The land wasn't enough for Hughes. He had to have the sky, too. But the real point is the end of the picture where he gets locked in his mind again and can't get out and he keeps repeating, "The way of the future, the way of the future." For me, ending it on Leo's face in the mirror saying that line was the reason to make the movie. We worked on that for the whole nine months we were shooting. To accept the future, knowing full well that for him it will only mean those men with the white gloves. For me, I must say, the way of the future is all about unrestrained greed.

RS: It's a very beautiful and ironic ending because, you know, you're also hearing a radio reporter saying, "Well, Howard Hughes has flown."

MS: He flew the Hercules for two minutes.

RS: It's a very interesting climax, isn't it? I mean, in some curious way. It's a triumph—an ironic one, of course.

MS: I thought it was great. That's really what made me do the film. The shaking of the plane and everything, that sound is on that audiotape. We used the actual audiotape. Hughes said, I think we're aloft, or something like that.

The reporters on board all started applauding and whooping. All that's from the actual tape. And they were terrified, those reporters, because he was supposed to be taxiing it, not taking off. They didn't realize what Hughes, the maniac, was going to do. After that, I thought that line about "the future" was a perfect way to end, because no matter what you could say about Hughes's descent, that scene intimates all the rest of the story for me.

But I also loved the idea in the script that the real battles in America, the real conflicts, are in the boardroom. Juan Trippe and Hughes at a table in the Coconut Grove talking about buttons or zippers—when I read that, I said to myself, That's the scene for me.

RS: It's a great scene.

MS: I felt that was also something for Leo. Remembering the way he placed himself into *Gangs of New York* for me, and the way he worked on that character. We had formed our friendship. And I wanted to do a film with him next that would showcase him as a character. As I said, I felt okay about the project because all the other ones about Hughes had to do with the older Hughes.

RS: The easy, moralistic part of his story. No one had dealt with the visionary part. They just wanted to deal with the crazy bastard in Las Vegas.

MS: I thought the visionary part was fascinating. It doesn't mean there aren't negative things about him, obviously. But still, to have flown in those planes . . .

OBSESSIONS

RICHARD SCHICKEL: I admire the different ways you match your obsessions with those of your actors. Otherwise, what they do is not going to be serious, it's not going to be worthwhile. It's going to disappoint you, ultimately. There are certainly directors, Eastwood would be a good example, who appear to be very casual—

MARTIN SCORSESE: Yes, but you can see he has a lot going on in him. You can see it in his films, his body of work. He is an extraordinary man, in part because he's very cool about it. Maybe Hawks was that way.

RS: Well, we're talking about a couple of real WASPy directors, you know.

MS: Maybe that's what it is.

RS: WASPs have got to stay cool. We cannot let people see us sweat.

MS: I'm really the opposite [*laughs*]. It's part of the enjoyment. I had a meeting here with Joe Reidy, my AD and the writer of this short film we're doing now, *The Key to Reserva*. We're going over every shot. I'm telling him, "No, it's a medium shot. This is his face. You're on him. The camera tracks around a door that opens, he doesn't know, and a figure comes into frame." Joe gets up and he says, "So he's here." And I say, "No, no, no," and he asks, "Are they moving?" I said, "No way." There was total confusion. It set me off. I lost patience. And after I fell silent there was a pause, and Ted Griffin, the writer, said—completely deadpan—"You see, he just takes all the joy out of the process." And we all started laughing. You know, niggling about every little detail, because ultimately, that's what it's about. I mean, if the protagonist is aware of the light, would he turn around? But then, again, if it's in the style of the films of the period— early fifties Technicolor—he may not turn around. Will I have a cameraman who knows how to do that light effect? Will the color be lush enough? All this sort of thing.

RS: Don't you feel, though, that there's a danger that self-consciousness is possibly going to creep in there?

MS: That's a point. Yet I don't ever like people hanging out behind me. I have a mirror, usually, over the monitor to see who's behind me.

RS: In case some actor—?

MS: No. I can't speak freely. I can't speak freely if somebody's behind me. Visitors to the set for me are not a good thing.

RS: I agree.

MS: If people have to come and say hello, or there's some political issue involving the studio, we usually do it at a time when it doesn't disrupt shooting.

But I haven't gotten the right mirror yet where I can see all that I want. I have one in the editing room. I sit with my back to the door, and the door opens, and I can see who's coming in the door. Otherwise I'd turn around all the time, and I'd be distracted. My eye can just glance now, and I can get back to work.

In the mixing room there's a door that squeaks. It's been that way for ten years now. Every time somebody goes in or out of the booth, I hear the squeak and it invariably makes me turn to my left. We make jokes about it now. The guys in the mixing room say they can't do anything about it. I say, You're mixing some of the biggest movies in the world in this room, and you can't fix the door?

RS: What about the exhaustion factor, especially when you're shooting? I haven't done anything like what you've done but I find if I'm shooting a documentary, and it's going pretty well and I'm really focusing, I come home just drained.

MS: My problem is not only am I drained, I'm up.

RS: Yes. Me, too.

MS: I wind up in such a high level of energy that it's very difficult for me to get to sleep and get enough sleep to shoot the next day. Of course, there are days when it's a wonderful tired, a wonderful fatigue, because you feel you did such interesting work. Or maybe the work was not so interesting, but at least you did it, you worked it out, you went

Marty directs Ben Kingsley in *Shutter Island*.

through the process. As you get older, naturally, it's a physically taxing job. I have to make sure I get eight hours' sleep. It wasn't true in the past, but now it is. So I've got to pace myself. But yes, the fatigue factor is enormous.

And your mind keeps buzzing. I may just be playing around with shots. I may have listed and drawn ideas for twelve to sixteen angles, when in reality we're maybe going to wind up with four, or in some cases, just one. You think about the scenes where the camera should creep in—creep in, not move in. Or I can focus on a line of dialogue, when there is something unsettling about it. And that gives tension to the rest of the scene. That's the way I think.

RS: Are we just talking there about the accumulated wisdom of the ages, a trained instinct?

MS: I think it's accumulated. If it's trained, it's trained from my own films. You can imagine the tension in a scene, or the warmth, or the humor. I think I know the size of the frame, and I think I know when to cut—and when not to. Somehow that comes out of the story, and the actors who are playing the parts. They determine, sometimes, whether you should move the camera or not, whether you should be in close-up, whether it should be a medium close-up. I try to translate all of that into visual terms—the feeling I'd like to get from a scene.

RS: But there's something that, to me, is mind-bending. A film is, after all, thousands of feet of celluloid long. A famous scene, something like the one in *The Letter,* where Bette Davis is screaming—

MS: "I still love the man I killed."

RS: That seems like kind of an obvious shot. But a lot of scenes in those thousands of feet of celluloid are not obvious at all. They might be as effective as a wide shot, a medium one, whatever.

MS: Absolutely. In fact, coming in on a close-up of her there may be wrong.

RS: These are big choices you are making. And a movie is composed of hundreds of those choices.

MS: That's the problem of visualizing it beforehand. Sometimes I'll be in a room for hours before coming up with an idea for one scene. Sometimes it flows for two to three hours. And all of this, in most cases, changes when you get on the set.

RS: So, theoretically, might it be as effective to start work on a film with maybe the first ten or fifteen pages outlined with your drawings, and then as the film develops its momentum, at night you would make the shot list and your drawings for the next day?

MS: A shot list you can make up anytime. That just tells you you need certain angles to cover the action, to communicate with the audience. But I never found that easy to do the night before a scene. Still, quite honestly, half *The Departed* was done that way.

RS: Which way?

MS: When I got there, I was saying things like "Change the locations. Forget it. We're not using this location." Or "It's okay, we're going to move over here. Put the camera here, come in this way, all you need is a close-up of him." Basically, the big choice there was to go with buildings that were being restored in the old seaport of Boston.

The choice to cut to Martin Sheen falling through the frame without seeing him being pushed out the window was not in the script. I decided on that in a hotel room. That was the editing point. When the audience sees his body falling through the frame—I had drawn a little picture of it—it gasps, because he's in free fall. They want to know what happened. I liked that, but I had the scene shot other ways, too—a little tighter, a little wider—to make sure. I had an idea to shoot it from above, to follow him down. So we shot a stuntman, in a kind of really dynamic angle. But there was no way to use it.

So the way it worked out, we used the shot I had designed. I'm not saying I'm on the money all the time in what I think of originally. And, yes, you have to be prepared to throw it out the window. I've been talking about this for years and other directors say, Oh, kids do that, you know. Well, maybe I'm still a kid making the drawings in a room. But the whole production works around getting that series of shots.

RS: That reminds me of something Howard Hawks used to say, that there are only six scenes in a movie that are worth a damn.

MS: Really?

RS: It was a conversation he used to have with John Wayne. The other scenes are just to get you from one of those scenes to the next of those scenes.

MS: True. But, still—

RS: So Wayne would say to him, "Howard, is this one of those scenes?" And Howard would say, "No, Duke, it's okay. Just walk in and pull your gun, it's okay."

MS: And yet John Wayne walking in and pulling his gun in a Howard Hawks–directed picture seems to have better energy, better framing, and be somehow better constructed. It seems to hold together better than other John Wayne films.

RS: I agree with you. Go figure.

MS: I don't know. I can't figure it out. But for me, there's no such thing as an unimportant shot. Hawks had a different way of telling stories. I think one of the few films that I've had with a plot was *The Departed.* And I did my best to destroy that plot.

RS: Wait a minute. What do you mean by that? There's a plot in *Goodfellas.*

MS: No, it was a story.

RS: Maybe we're just talking semantics.

MS: There was a kind of a plot point at the end in that Joe Pesci gets killed because he killed a guy. Basically, though, it's *Public Enemy,* the rise and fall of a whole system.

RS: Well, I see your point, without fully conceding it. But wouldn't you say that *Age of Innocence* has an enormous, quite intricate plot?

MS: I guess it does. I mean, that's Edith Wharton. I shouldn't say I don't do plot. But I do tend to be attracted to stories that are more character-driven. That's really it.

EDITING

RICHARD SCHICKEL: You did a lot of your own editing when you were starting out, but I wasn't aware of how much of it you did until we started talking. Did you just pick it up, learning to do by doing?

MARTIN SCORSESE: No, I watched it in the movies. I watched Eisenstein—

RS: No, I was thinking more about picking up technique—in those days it was Moviolas, right?

MS: Oh, yeah, Moviolas, and hot splices. And the thing was, the falling in love with the actual image in the frame itself, and the sprocket holes, and the flare between the sprockets, and the edge fog. I just fell in love with it.

RS: What do you mean you fell in love with it?

MS: Just that. I loved the way film looked. I still do. I look at Thelma sometimes— we'll stop on a freeze frame or on a section of the shot where the camera stops running—and you get half an image. You see white, red, yellow, and you see an eye. I say, "Look, that's a beautiful frame." I used a shot like that at the end of *The Last Temptation of Christ*. There was a take I wanted to use at "it is consummated"— but it was exposed by mistake and had edge fog on it. I was upset until I realized that it was the perfect ending. That was the take I needed. It's just the nature of celluloid itself and what light does to the image. I just love it.

RS: Thelma has been with you many, many years. What makes her your ideal editor? What qualities does she have?

MS: She comes from the late sixties. She was not a film student—she just did that six-week course at NYU, and then she went back to Columbia. I think she studied political science. There was something about the nature of what we all did in *Woodstock*—it was serious, particularly on all the filmmakers' part. I was still probably too conservative to fully embrace that freedom. I think Thelma still retains that view of the world, from the sixties, an open-mindedness. And she wants to protect—good, bad, or indifferent—the art.

Something we do may be a good film, or a bad film: it may not last, or maybe a hundred years from now somebody will still be looking at it. But whatever we're doing she will defend to the death. She's a very good ally. Sometimes you get tired, you start to waver, during the battering process, when you're first screening a film. It behooves you to listen to others, but often as you get near completion of a picture, you get bad advice, or pressure. Thelma's very good at steadying the course. A couple of times she's actually told me, Stay strong, we're going to get through this one. She respects the purity of the picture.

Thelma knows the way I choose takes, in rushes. The hardest work is done usually while I'm watching rushes. I will not watch them with anybody else but her, though when I was working with De Niro in the seventies, he would watch rushes, too, particularly on *New York, New York* and *Raging Bull*. He'd be in the room and sometimes he'd say, "I like that take," or whatever. I didn't mind that, because I had a very good relationship with Bob and that's what part of that collaboration was. We seemed to hit it off so well with choosing the same material. Not that we could articulate it. We kind of started to trust each other very strongly.

He just needed to know that I went through the process, tried things, worked things out. But the bottom line is, I never would have gone so far with Bob if it had been a situation where he said, "I want that scene cut," or "I think you should use another take," and demand another shot. There's no way I could do that. Watching the rushes only with Thelma, I can be open.

Thelma hardly comes on the set, you know. She reads the script only once. She just gets footage. Every day she gets to see what happens next.

Beginnings: Editor Thelma Schoonmaker works with Marty in the *Woodstock* editing room.

She doesn't get involved in set politics that way. She doesn't know that during a particular take somebody got sick, or somebody was angry. She simply writes down all the takes, in great detail, then types it all up. It's a long process. She knows my preferred takes, second preferred, third preferred, the possibility of a whole other way to go. Come back to the fifth take and she'll remember it. Then she edits it all together so that you just punch up the takes, they're all there. That takes a little longer, but when we're looking for something, she can always find it easily. And her comments are so helpful. She might say, Look at his eyes here. Look at her eyes there. We need some more emotional impact, we need some more warmth. There was another take where he seemed a little more that way. Things like that. And I'll look at what she is referring to and maybe say, I don't know if that's any different. She might look doubtful. And then I'll say, "Well, put it in. Let's see." She's very good with keeping the heart of the picture foremost, in terms of emotion.

Thelma usually doesn't cut anything until I see all the rushes. I go through the process with Thelma, and we don't like anybody with us if I can help it. I have to be able to say, for instance, "I don't like what he's doing there." Maybe later I'll say, "Oh, that's better. I see where he was going, okay." She writes all of it down, and we record it.

She types up all my notes and organizes them in her computer. So that if I say, "Scene 42, in the third shot," she'll punch it up and she'll say something like, Okay, your preferred is here, take 11. Your second preferred was take 8.

RS: It becomes like that American Express commercial you made, where you say, "Too dark, too light." And you're just looking at snapshots of your imaginary nephew's birthday party.

MS: Very funny, I think. I just took it to an absurd level. Which isn't that far.

RS: That's what I was about to say.

MS: Sometimes Thelma and I are laughing, sometimes we get depressed. I might say, We lost the entire dramatic thread of this. They should shoot the director.

That's why I don't want people to be there. It's for me. I want to be able to say what I feel about the actors, what they're doing in the frames, uninhibited by anybody. Thelma is the woman I trust.

RS: So Thelma knows all the secrets.

MS: Yes. Everything. Volumes. Anyway, almost inevitably we use the preferred takes; in many cases, even the third preferred.

RS: Is there any particular reason for that?

Endings: Schoonmaker and Marty went their separate ways after working together on *Woodstock* (1970), reunited on *Raging Bull,* and have been editorially inseparable ever since.

MS: Because the tone of the picture changes somewhat in the cutting. The look on this person's face makes it feel angrier here, or happier there, for instance. One take that I didn't particularly like at first may flow from the preceding scene better; we can only see that as the film is shaping up.

Thelma memorizes it all, and I memorize it, too, in the rushes with her.

RS: You've mentioned that you did a lot of your own editing when you were starting out, but I wasn't aware of how much of it you did.

MS: I edited *Mean Streets* myself. I don't have credit on it because I'm not in the union. Sid Levin put his name on the film for me, the editor of Marty Ritt's films.

Then I started working with Marcia Lucas, George Lucas's first wife. That was *Alice Doesn't Live Here Anymore, Taxi Driver,* and *New York, New York.* Tom Rolf did some of *Taxi Driver,* a couple of scenes, including the famous "Are you talking to me?" scene. He's a master editor. It's the one sequence where I didn't say to the editor I needed something changed. Yeu-Bun Yee worked on *Woodstock* with me, and he and Jan Roblee worked on *The Last Waltz.* That took place over a period of two years. After that I asked Thelma to do *Raging Bull,* because at that point Marcia had left the business pretty much. I hadn't really stayed in touch with Thelma—she was working in Pittsburgh. There was almost a ten-year gap. I think she came to look at *The Last Waltz* once or twice and gave some opinions on that. I wanted her to work with me on *Raging Bull.* I told Irwin Winkler that, but she was not then in the union. We were almost finished with the film—mixing it—by the time we got her into the union. She's been with me ever since.

The editors working in the system didn't want me in the editing room. Well, I am sorry, that's how I work. Thelma knows who I am, knows the best and the worst of it. Her loyalty to the film we're trying to make is the key.

RS: I don't remember your ever saying it quite that way.

MS: A loyalty to the film, to what my initial instinct was, what some people would call an idea, a vision, whatever. We are constantly being buffeted by all kinds of turbulence while making a movie. And you have to hold that plane straight as best you can. Thelma is very good at refocusing me. We'll think about someone else's idea, try it out sometimes, maybe even show it to the person whose idea it was. But, in the final analysis, it's my call. She's very loyal to that concept.

I've had editors try to make changes without my noticing. And I'll say, "No, something happened there." And the editor says, "I didn't think you were going to notice that." I don't need to play games. It's hard enough as it is. I have to work together with an editor I trust.

Thelma and I usually have a good time when we get into the editing room. The hardest time and the best time.

RS: Thelma asked me the other day, "How do you and Marty work?" I said, "Oh, we kind of go on until midnight or so." And she says, "Oh, we sometimes used to edit all night."

MS: We enjoyed that so much. We used to edit only at night. *Raging Bull* was edited only at night, so nobody would call us. *King of Comedy* was edited at night, and we got into a rhythm. That's when making a film is really the most fun.

RICHARD SCHICKEL: Music is almost as important to you as film has been over the course of your career. Did your father ever take you to the Metropolitan Opera or to a concert, anything like that?

MARTIN SCORSESE: No. But eventually my friends and I would see operas. We'd have seats way up at the top of the old Met.

A lot of classical music I learned from Hollywood films. The first LP I bought was Tchaikovsky—the *1812 Overture*. Some of my uncles had twelve-inch records of Tchaikovsky's *Capriccio Italien*, Debussy's "Claire de Lune," and I would listen to those, along with "M'Appari," the aria from *Martha* that Enrico Caruso sang. I listened to a twelve-inch record of "Sing, Sing, Sing" by Benny Goodman. There was a great deal of music around me. In the sixties, I brought into the apartment Stravinsky, *Le Sacre du printemps* and *L'Histoire du soldat*, things like that. They began to get on my parents' nerves a bit.

I took several music courses at NYU. I had a choice between the history of painting and the history of music, and I took music. I don't regret it. Music was more useful in filmmaking.

In *New York, New York,* Liza Minnelli played the naturally gifted band singer who marries Robert De Niro's driven bandleader, to their ultimate sorrow.

RS: So where does pop music come in?

MS: Well, my interest in pop music, I guess, was born of the swing music I grew up listening to—records of Django Reinhardt and the Hot Club of France, and Al Jolson: Jolson's records were rereleased for *The Jolson Story* at the time. His theatrical persona was amazing, extraordinary. Have you seen the restored version of *Hallelujah, I'm a Bum*?

RS: No, I haven't.

MS: I saw it on television as a young kid. It was a bad black-and-white, scratched, edited-down version. But they restored it about two years ago. It's a masterpiece.

RS: Really?

MS: Lewis Milestone was the director. The editing was almost like Russian editing. Sometimes, too, the effect is almost Brechtian. It was a major revelation. It's edgy and tough; it deals with the New Deal, and Marxism. It's just extraordinary.

RS: Even in Milestone's later films, which were sometimes banal thematically, there's some beautiful filmmaking.

MS: His films were part of a United Artists television package—all the Alexander Korda films, plus things like *The Shanghai Gesture,* which was repeated all the time. I became obsessed with it.

Of Mice and Men was repeatedly shown, and that too affected me a lot. Lenny and George were like brothers.

RS: It resonated with you because you have a brother?

MS: Yes. But Aaron Copland's music was also important to me. That was when my ear began to be attuned to scoring. We actually wound up using a section of that on the television in the background of the scene in *Raging Bull* when De Niro is fixing the TV, and he's questioning his brother, which builds to the moment when he asks, Did you fuck my wife? That's literally synced up to the end, when Bob's walking up the stairs to confront his wife—the ending music of *Of Mice and Men.* All the dialogue is there, too. My ear became attuned to that kind of music. I saw *The Red Pony* on its release in 1949, and that was Copland's music. My father liked guitars, and he bought some records. One record I still have is considered the first rock 'n' roll record, one of the first "boogie-woogie" records. It was made in the forties by a guy named Arthur "Guitar" Smith and was called *Guitar Boogie.* The flip side was something by the Tennessee Ramblers, which you can't get a copy of anymore. It was basically bluegrass. We had maybe twenty-five records and I played them over and over again. My father used to play ukulele, apparently; I never saw him do it live, but in my Italian documentary we have film of him that his brother-in-law shot. My father always talked about appreciating how people played guitar, banjo, bluegrass fiddling. My brother then started playing guitar, and sometimes my mother was washing dishes or something, and he'd be playing something, and she'd be singing along—songs like "When Day Is Done," standards that we all knew.

When I was growing up, my mother used to like listening to country western. I heard it in the morning in the late forties, early fifties—Hank Williams and others.

RS: How does an Italian lady get to like country western?

MS: She just liked country western because of the guitars. I remember that we liked "Clear, Cool Water," by the Sons of the Pioneers. Do you remember that?

RS: Do I remember it? Are you kidding?

MS: The thing about that was, for me as a kid, it was a very interesting story.

RS: [*Sings.*] "... don't you listen to him, Dan, he's a devil not a man ..."

MS: A devil, not a man, yeah. Then the guy dies in the song. It's a dramatic song. I guess the epitome of that kind of song is the "ride away" chorus in *The Searchers*. [*Sings.*] "Ride away." It clicks in there with the opening shot and the last shot.

RS: Given all that, did the rock revolution really hit you hard? I mean, did it just blast into your consciousness?

MS: It did—because it was 1953. The songs up to that point were, you know—

RS: "How Much Is That Doggie in the Window."

MS: Right. And Frankie Laine—"Jezebel"—or Perry Como singing "Round Round Round" and "Papaya Mama." These are the bad ones; Como did good ones, too. And Frankie Laine sang "That's My Desire," which was not bad. But you had that extraordinary singer named Johnny ...

RS: Johnny Ray?

MS: Yeah. "The Little White Cloud That Cried." You'd hear this echoing in the streets, the 78s. I was thirteen years old, the right age, when I first heard Fats Domino, singing "I'm in Love Again," and "When My Dreamboat Comes Home." And then Presley's "Hound Dog," "Heartbreak Hotel," "All Shook Up"—that was a key one. The other important singer for me was Little Richard—"Tutti Frutti," that was major, right at that same time. My uncles loved music so much, and when I would play that, one of them would say, "He's not singing. Listen. He's out of breath." They didn't like it.

The other key voice for me was Ray Charles—"Hallelujah, I Love Her So." That I have on 78, and on the flip side is a song called "What Would I Do Without You?," which was a seminal song for many listeners of that period. It was seminal for The Band, I know; they would refer to it. It's extraordinary. Only two, two and a half minutes, a blues number, but Ray does something with his voice at the end where it cracks, where it's just overwhelming. Everything in the early fifties was changing. And at the same time you had pictures that were dealing with subject matter that was previously taboo. By 1954 there was *On the Waterfront*. The year after *Blackboard Jungle* appeared. To me it's not a great picture, but once you hear—

RS: "Rock Around the Clock."

MS: Exactly.

RS: Richard Brooks had a wild story about that. He could have bought the rights to that song.

MS: He would have never had to work.

RS: You know for how much? A thousand dollars.

MS: Then there were the other films that came out of Hollywood about rock 'n' roll that were absolutely terrible.

RS: That one wasn't so great, either.

MS: No, no, it wasn't.

RS: But the opening is great.

MS: The only truly great rock 'n' roll film is *The Girl Can't Help It* [a 1956 comedy by comedy master Frank Tashlin, in which a gangster tries to make his talent-free girlfriend (Jayne Mansfield) into a singing star]. They actually took the care and the time. Not every performance in it is on the level of a Little Richard or Fats Domino or Gene Vincent and the Blue Caps. But that's an extraordinary movie in terms of musical treatment.

RS: There is the big scene in *Blackboard Jungle* when the delinquents break all of Richard Kiley's records.

MS: That was terrifying, very disturbing.

RS: It was, wasn't it?

MS: Because I had those records at home.

RS: Of course you did. So did I.

MS: We had those records from the older generation. Those are the records we grew up on.

RS: It was symbolic — "Rock Around the Clock" is our music, the records we're trashing are your music. And your music is moldy fig music.

MS: But you know, it wasn't. I had it all. I mean, I appreciated the old and the new.

RS: Of course. But they were trying to say something about that generation of kids.

MS: It was a very tough transition. Some of the rock music wasn't very good, but some was classic. The sound of a Fats Domino, for example, the New Orleans sound; it's very special. It comes from many different sources: Cajun, the Acadians from Canada, Creoles. It's a very special sound. Remember Professor Longhair playing jazz piano in Clint Eastwood's documentary, doing "Tipitina"? It's a great moment.

Leader of The Band: Robbie Robertson, who starred in *The Last Waltz*, became Scorsese's good friend and, often, a musical collaborator on the director's later films.

RS: Yes, it is.

MS: Some of it sustains itself better than others. For example, for me, the early Presley songs were fine. After that, once "Love Me Tender" came out, we rejected him. Some of my friends didn't like any of the films he made except maybe *King Creole*, and *Flaming Star*, Don Siegel's picture.

RS: I liked *Flaming Star*. It was a pretty good western.

MS: *Flaming Star is* pretty good.

RS: But he doesn't sing in it, except the title song. The one with Barbara Stanwyck wasn't so bad.

MS: What was that?

RS: *Roustabout*, I think.

MS: I hated those titles, *Roustabout* and *Viva Las Vegas*. By that time we wanted to see him transform as a performer. Those were the years of James Dean, and Montgomery Clift, and Brando, people coming out of the Hollywood cinema who spoke for the young.

RS: He should have adapted, he could have. If he hadn't been managed by that terrible man—

MS: Colonel Parker, yes.

RS: I think he might have instinctively found his way to it. But, you know, Colonel Parker wasn't having that.

MS: Oh, I know. They had to make their money with him. I helped edit the *Elvis on Tour* film. It was enjoyable. He certainly performed, there's no doubt about it. But he didn't develop or evolve. They just created something, and they kept him where he was.

RS: He just got fatter and crazier.

MS: I stopped listening to Presley, I think, after, oh, maybe 1958. I didn't take him seriously anymore.

RS: What were you taking seriously at that point?

MS: There was still Chuck Berry, as a sort of a chronicler of the time if you listen to his lyrics. He was an originator. And being a New Yorker, doo-wop was very important to me. I hate that term, but those were the songs that were sung in the hallways. We would imitate those songs. Buddy Holly was very important to us—really key. There was something about the country and western influence. Did you know that Buddy Holly's song "That'll Be the Day" comes from *The Searchers*?

RS: Sure, of course. That line of Wayne's.

MS: Because they saw that movie, and John Wayne does get those laughs when he says, "That'll be the day." The timing is perfect. I saw Buddy Holly at the Brooklyn Paramount in one big rock 'n' roll show that ended with Jerry Lee Lewis, whom I also took seriously at the time. Buddy Holly up there on that stage—the thin suits, the narrow, narrow lapels, thin ties, big glasses. He had amplifiers that went to the ceiling.

We were stunned. Buddy Holly only played three songs, but they were extraordinary. Then Jerry Lee Lewis came out and just destroyed the place, I mean, took it down. That whole thing of attacking the piano. If you go back, Jimmy Durante did the same thing. And Franz Liszt—Lisztomania.

RS: Yes, right.

MS: Liszt would do what James Brown did.

RS: Jimi Hendrix burning his guitar. I mean, there's a whole tradition of it.

MS: My father's favorite performer was Cab Calloway. He loved Louis Armstrong, and Ella Fitzgerald. You can't touch them.

RS: Oh, absolutely.

MS: I appreciated all that. But my father kind of stopped listening after swing music. He didn't really get into jazz. I bought some jazz in the fifties that was pretty interesting.

RS: But cool jazz is not emotional.

MS: You're right. That's the problem I had. But a lot of emotion did come in through the scores of movies—*Sweet Smell of Success, Man with the Golden Arm,* Elmer Bernstein. *Odds Against Tomorrow,* and Duke Ellington's *Anatomy of a Murder.*

RS: That's a very good score.

MS: In the early sixties, Quincy Jones did a good one for *The Pawnbroker.* I was trying to learn more about cool jazz. But I went another way. I'm too hotheaded for cool jazz.

RS: That's a contrast between you and Clint. The big, WASPy West Coast guy went for the cool.

MS: And I went for the grand opera or rock 'n' roll.

RS: Highly emotive music.

MS: Still, in the late fifties and early sixties, jazz was part of your everyday life. We had Dave Brubeck's "Take Five." We had Ahmad Jamal's "At the Penthouse." We had John Coltrane's "My Favorite Things." We were playing those albums. Rock 'n' roll was more powerful, but still, that music coexisted.

I may not have been delving into it as deeply as rock 'n' roll, but country and western, country rock, the Dylan stuff, George Shearing, the Modern Jazz Quartet, and Gerry Mulligan, Chet Baker, Jimmy Giuffre—I knew all of it.

RS: It was a sort of obligatory eclecticism.

MS: Very much so. The best concert film for me is *Jazz on a Summer's Day*—Bert Stern made it in the late fifties. I screened it again two or three times before doing the Stones picture. I said to myself, What are we going to do with the Rolling Stones since everybody's done them? Jean-Luc Godard had even done the Stones. So I decided the only thing to do was just to do the performance, just stay with the music and stay with the performance.

He had great tension in the frame. He was a still photographer, you know—he may have needed only two cameras, really. I never knew him. But I went to see the film and I loved it! And it really holds up. For me, it's the key music film.

Watch the opening credits, the way it intercuts the reflections in the water, the boats, the mist, the sails. Jimmy Giuffre is playing his saxophone. There is a medium close-up of him. As Giuffre plays, he keeps moving his head toward the bottom of the frame, because he keeps squeezing out those notes. You think he's going to go out of frame, but he doesn't. The tension is wonderful. And the camera doesn't move. It's all interior, in a way.

It really holds up. In fact, Jagger and I were talking about making a *Jazz on a Summer's Day,* about the Stones visiting New York. We came up with all these different scenarios. We went through a long writing process on that before we abandoned it.

RS: Did it ever occur to you that your burgeoning interest in film and your burgeoning interest in music would ever come together in any way?

MS: I think so. Music moved me. It literally makes us move a certain way. It makes certain things happen. It's equivalent to dancing, I guess. You know, you behaved a certain way. Some of the boys were able to swagger. Others pulled back. But the music scored our lives. I was taking it all in, pulling it together.

Robert Pupkin in full cry.

I mean, the music was scoring what was happening—in the summer the windows were open and you heard music coming from other people's apartments. The people were eating, or looking out the windows, and the music would be playing. There'd be a family fighting, and the music would be the background to that, too. Music was playing as you saw the derelicts on the Bowery.

It was a cacophony of all kinds of sounds, but I started to put it together. The piano music of Fats Domino, it felt like it was rolling, and the camera would move and move and move. That started something working in my mind. The Beach Boys were the furthest thing from my experience—California and surfing—but I appreciated them musically, it suggested certain movement and action to me.

RS: I went to see Tom Stoppard's play *Rock 'n' Roll* the other night. It has got a lot of great rock music in it, including a couple of Beach Boys numbers—Stoppard heard their music in Prague. Think about it.

MS: One of their key songs for me was "I Get Around." I designed a whole sequence to it in *Who's That Knocking,* though I didn't use it in the end. I used "El Watusi" by Ray Barreto in a scene where the fellows are playing with guns.

The camera panned from left to right. And every time we dissolved, the camera got up to a higher and higher speed. So the shots became more and more slow motion. But it was imagined from listening to "I Get Around" over and over again when nobody was home—and "Wouldn't It Be Nice" and "Sloop John B," which is still a song I want to use. "Sail On, Sailor" I used in *The Departed.* Just a little bit of it. Their harmonies are fantastic.

RS: So we have not only films like *The Last Waltz,* but also the passionate and knowledgeable use of contemporary music as scoring in so many of your films. Was that just a natural development for you, given your history?

MS: That's a good question. I think about it a lot right now, because I'm deciding what kind of music score to have in a new picture I'm making.

In the forties, those 78s were almost talismans. I'd see the label turning and I'd hear this sound come out of it. Music was a mainstay in our household. There was a lot of communication through music, listening to it, listening to the lyrics. Music was a constant part of my life from the earliest time I can remember up until the time I moved out of the three rooms on Elizabeth Street. After that, I took music with me everywhere.

RS: Rock 'n' roll wouldn't have interested your parents at all, would it?

MS: Well, my mother was very tolerant of Presley and some other rock singers, but my father didn't like it at all, especially the doo-wop and the blues.

RS: In making *Mean Streets,* for example, was it a natural tropism to say, Oh, we'd better score this with some rock songs and some pop stuff?

MS: I think that came even before we started shooting—a lot of the scenes came out of listening to the music. Certain songs were attached to certain scenes from my past. I remember listening to certain songs in my brother's car as we drove around the Bowery, seeing the alcoholics in the street. That music is playing over the appropriate images in the film. Music produced a kind of visceral energy which, being younger, I fed on—the kind of aggressive music that's used in *Mean Streets*—for example, the Ronettes' song "Be My Baby."

The movies of that time had scores by Miklós Rózsa, Dmitri Tiomkin, Bernard Herrmann. I collected all those. My scores had to come from somewhere else, because I was usually reflecting another world, another time. The first time I really needed something more traditional was *Taxi Driver*—it was so internal I needed something special, and I chose Bernard Herrmann. Later, I worked with Elmer Bernstein.

But the reality was that there was no other way to do it. The only thing that stopped us from doing it was not being able to pay for the music licenses. And so in *Who's That Knocking* some of the music isn't very good. But all the music that was supposed to go into *Who's That Knocking* went into *Mean Streets* ultimately.

At the same time, Kubrick was using *Zarathustra* and Bartók, that sort of thing, in *2001*. Kenneth Anger's *Scorpio Rising* was a shock because of the use of music, the images, the whole idea of youth culture, the death wish—all of these forbidden images all thrown together with that sound track. It was important.

RS: In many instances in your films the music is almost running counter to the action on screen. It's very calculated, but it doesn't appear to be calculated when you're in the theater listening to it.

MS: That's right. Sometimes I take that sync point [the place in the film where the music kicks in] and I go backwards. I create the sync point with another piece of music, not the usual sting, as they call it, though I have used stings. The first time I heard that word was when Bernard Herrmann used it.

The night before he died, working on *Taxi Driver,* I asked him for a punctuation, and he goes, "You mean a sting." And he gave me one. It was for when Travis looks in the mirror at the end, and he thinks he sees something. I said, "It sounds too straight." He goes, "Play it backwards." That was the last thing Bennie did.

In *Cape Fear* we have it. In *Shutter Island* we have a couple of stings. I'm trying to find classical music that has stings in it already.

RS: That's hard, isn't it?

MS: It requires hours of listening to music.

RS: When I made my film about you that went on the DVD of *The Departed,* our whole fee went to music licenses—over $100,000 just for the DVD rights.

MS: I know the problem. And when we did *Mean Streets,* the whole film only cost $650,000. Jon Taplin got that money, and out of that money he was still able to pay the Rolling Stones and still able to pay for Cream and Eric Clapton and the Ronettes.

RS: When you hear music do you think, Well, that would be perfect for a film?

MS: Some music just stays in my head. I still have my original records. And a CD library. I find that I'm listening to music that I heard back in 1949. I play it through and I listen. By 1985 I stopped really listening to popular music. But the earlier songs created images in my head. Somehow some of those images and feelings—not all of them—were able to be used in certain pictures. Certain scenes suddenly reminded me of a piece of music that I thought would be perfect for a film.

RS: Can you give me one example of that offhand?

MS: "Jumpin' Jack Flash" in *Mean Streets.* The moment of the downbeat, I knew that Keitel would be taking his drink and it would be slow motion. Exactly what speed I wasn't quite sure of at the time—I think we went with ninety-six frames per second. I knew that at that downbeat there was going to be a cut. A better example is when Keitel in the very beginning of the film wakes up and looks in the mirror, and then puts his head back down on the pillow. There are three cuts there, and if you listen, three drumbeats: that's the beginning of "Be My Baby," produced by Phil Spector.

The editing came to me by listening to the beginning of that song.

RS: So this is kind of a reciprocating engine: the music and the image, the image and the music.

MS: Exactly. It's very different from the way others use music, I think. Very often a song is played for nostalgia. It's played all the way through, without alteration. But you can see in *Raging Bull, Goodfellas,* and *Casino* particularly that I went in and cut within the song so that certain points of the music or the vocals will be hitting between certain lines of dialogue. Those lyrics are also commenting on the dialogue.

It's all through *Raging Bull.* You can hear the Ink Spots commenting on the scene where Bob throws the steak against the wall: the Ink Spots are singing "Whispering Trees." I used the Brazilian music in the kitchen scene with Joe Pesci and his wife, when he wants more coffee and is trying to convince Bob to take the fight. I did the same kind of thing all through *Goodfellas,* particularly Ray's last day as a wiseguy, when he is cocaine-fueled, and you hear Harry Nilsson singing "Jump into the Fire" — "We can make each other happy, we can make each other happy" — and he keeps stretching out "ha-appy." I just kept mixing that, overlapping Nilsson's voice, which became like a cry at night — a panicked cry about being happy, very aggressive and very dangerous.

I think that's the theme of that whole sequence. It starts with the beginning of "Jump into the Fire," with the guitar and the drumbeats. Then we used that as a refrain. We started to fold the song in, overlapping itself — when Nilsson's voice is wailing, we put more wailing over that, for a double, triple effect. After a while, it was like a frantic voice in your head, you just can't take any more, you're going to explode. The next thing you know, there's a gun at your head and a voice says, "Turn off the car." And Ray's happy. He says, Thank God, because if it wasn't the police, he'd be dead. The music was great in building up to that point.

There's so much effective music in that film. There is the scene when Ray slams the trunk down and you hear the guitar on "Memo from Turner" from *Performance* [the cult classic of 1970, in which a gangster and a rock star engage in a messy, drug-addled relationship]. Then you hear Mick Jagger's voice coming in. This comes after De Niro in his terry-cloth blue robe says to Ray, "I don't want the guns. The drugs are making your mind into mush." Bob slams the door on him and Ray says, "I knew he wouldn't want the guns. I knew it." And he slams the trunk. It's funny, too, because these guys are killers talking about selling guns, and they're getting so petty, getting on each other's nerves. After Ray slams the trunk, Ry Cooder's guitar segues into The Who until Ray almost crashes the car. It was an improvisatory guitar solo that's quite beautiful and it just stayed in my head. I thought that would be great because Ray almost crashes into the car in front of him. And I thought, Let's go right from "Turner" into that, and back into Harry Nilsson.

RS: Is that kind of thing worked out largely in the editing room?

MS: No, usually before. Very often I play the music on the set.

RS: I didn't realize that.

MS: Not all the time. But I started doing that on *Who's That Knocking.* I played music I couldn't use on the film—a song called "The Lantern" by the Rolling Stones—to get the feeling of a camera move I liked. That was 1968. On *Goodfellas,* on the first day of shooting, we did the scene with the pink Cadillac with the two dead bodies in it. I knew I was going to use the last section of "Layla," by Derek and the Dominos, Eric Clapton. So we played that on set. It was great, the music had a grandiosity and a stateliness about it.

RS: When you're playing the music on the set, do you communicate to the crew what's on your mind?

MS: Oh, absolutely.

RS: That the music was meant to enhance a certain kind of a move?

MS: Yes. Michael Ballhaus would understand it. Michael Chapman did, too. Making *The Departed,* too, I'd play him certain music.

RS: I've actually never heard of any other directors who do it this way—the intricate working out of the music during the shoot.

MS: We also do more with it in the editing.

RS: That seems to me a unique aspect of the way you work.

MS: Well, the music is inseparable for me. It can be nerve-racking to get it right. It was new territory for me to work with Bernard Herrmann, Elmer Bernstein, Howard Shore. But we developed a wonderful trust. Some of the films that had those scores were in a genre style. I had a burst of energy in the seventies and I felt I could do any genre I wanted. That's gone now. If I do a genre film now, I really have to think about what new perspective I could bring to the genre.

The found scores—composed of pre-existing music—seem to fit more closely with genre pictures. I feel more comfortable that way. Even in *Kundun,* which is a special kind of film, we played Philip Glass on the set.

RS: Really?

MS: Yes, a couple of times, to get a certain mood. It's funny: Your camera's moving to the music, and you think you've got it right. But when you put the music next to it later in the editing room, you say, "I went too fast. I should have done it slower."

On *Who's That Knocking,* the people are in a party or at a bar and there's music playing, and you have to stop the music so you can hear the dialogue. But everybody still has to act as if the music is blaring. I hated that.

RS: Why?

MS: I want the energy there. That's a battle I'm having all the time. I try to get the music played back on set as much as possible in scenes like that before cutting it off. I want the actors at a peak. I want the energy going.

RS: Another director would have dozens of takes because he wouldn't actually know how the music which he's already heard in his head would work. Or, worse, a composer is going to come in and write a score six weeks later.

MS: Exactly. I don't feel comfortable with relying on a score. I admire great scores, and they've saved my pictures in many cases. But I tend to want to try to create my own score. In some cases Robbie Robertson helps. But not every film I make lends itself to that.

RS: An obvious exception would be *Age of Innocence.*

MS: That had to have a wonderful score. That's part of the tradition that film belongs to. I thought Elmer's music was just glorious.

RS: It's a beautifully scored film.

MS: You know, I sent that film to Kurosawa. He sent back a note saying, "I do not like films about romance." He also said it was not his kind of film, that he just didn't like it. And here's the point: He also said, "I must caution you, I must admonish you on the use of music. Like all Hollywood films, you're using music too much."

But to me it was like *The Heiress.* I wanted Aaron Copland. That was a key film for me. I wanted a reference back to that. And also in the look of the film.

RESTORING AND COLLECTING

RICHARD SCHICKEL: In the course of these conversations you have often said, "I ran such-and-such before I did that picture," or "It's like the scene in . . . ," and then you name a picture as a reference.

MARTIN SCORSESE: Yes, I'm just giving reference points.

RS: I understand that. I understand you're not copying the masters—although there's no reason not to sometimes.

MS: It's not going to come out the way they did it anyway.

RS: That's the whole point.

MS: The inspirational aspect of it is interesting to me—the notion of staying in touch with film history, film heritage. I've been told I do that more than other directors do. I don't know, but the view of the movies I carry around in my mind has changed over the years. I now prefer seeing other Welles films rather than *Citizen Kane*. I've reached a certain limit with *Kane*. Other films now give me more to think about.

MS: Renoir's *The River.* And *The Life and Death of Colonel Blimp.* I keep finding more and more in that. But I'm kind of done with *Kane* and *The Searchers.*

RS: I can't look at those movies again. I've seen them too many times.

MS: I should say that with *Kane,* there are still moments I can watch. It's still a reference point even though I don't watch it in its entirety.

RS: Are there specific sequences or images that haunt you, maybe while you're actually making a film?

MS: A lot of films changed the way I perceived the world around me at certain key points in my life.

Forty years ago, when I saw Antonioni's *L'Avventura,* I didn't know quite what to make of it. I went to see it a second time, and a third time. And I thought that the filmmaker was forcing me to view life in a different rhythm or with a different frame.

Part of the initial problem I had with the movie was that I didn't know who those people were. It depicted a world I had no firsthand knowledge of. But once I got past that, I began to see that the images had a melancholy and a power to them. There was drama in every frame. And the panning was different, the tracking was different.

I've always tried to capture what Antonioni did, but I can never get it. I just have a totally different sensibility. There's no way I can get near it. He does it a lot in *Blow-Up,* though I prefer *L'Avventura* and *The Eclipse.* But still there's this parallel move that he makes which is so detached yet has such spiritual power. It's a very cool sensibility, very cool. It made me stop and look. He was showing the world in a different way.

RS: Is that what drives you, making people stop and look?

MS: Probably. For example, the biggest problem I had with *Shutter Island* was trying to figure out the scene when he's walking down that long, dark hallway, and there are no lights and he's got to light matches. He's holding them up, trying to see if there are people in the cells.

There are those glimpses of people whom he thinks he sees, but maybe don't exist. How was I to shoot something that doesn't exist? I mean, Buñuel did it the best. He just cut straight to a dream, even though the audience doesn't know it's a dream. The camera move, the lights, the cutting—what to do to rivet the viewer?

RS: The way you reference films leads me to your interest in film collecting, and now the Film Foundation, and restoration. It's admirable, and it's useful. And a little compulsive. But you don't do it just to solve your own moviemaking problems.

MS: No, I don't. It's another aspect of myself. That's the guy who thought he was going to be a studio director, and realized the studios were all over. And what could he do about it? Well, he could try to preserve that history. If I had never become a filmmaker, the difference those films made in my life might make a similar difference in somebody else's life in the future. I'm excited by that. I like teaching. It's so great when some younger people around you have the curiosity and you can talk, and they get excited. You show

First among many: Marty acquired this Belgian poster in Greenwich Village for perhaps $25, when he was a young man. It was his first such acquisition, and to this day it hangs in his editing room.

355

them certain things, you give them something to read, and two years later they come back with a film.

RS: When did film preservation become a priority for you?

MS: It began in the mid-seventies when I was just trying to get films for research—American films, Italian, British, whatever. We found the situation was dire. The films were falling apart.

There was alarm, really. I felt it, some film critics did. Spielberg would get a print and it had turned magenta and would be cut in five different places and panned and scanned [a process by which a wide-screen image is altered so that it fills the entire frame of a television screen; at the time, federal regulation forbade black space at the top and bottom of the screen]. Sometimes we couldn't even see the image. We knew we had to try to make sure that these films survived for the next generation.

When I started working on *Raging Bull,* we started to form a preservation group. A lot of emotion was attached to that effort. The studios and the distributors, who had made so much money on these films, needed to be educated as to their condition.

Films were no longer printed in Technicolor. Every film was being made in color, and the color of old films was no longer stable. Color is intrinsic to the design of a movie, its inherent texture. And within a few years the color was gone, it was disappearing. That was something we really felt intensely at that time.

I attacked it on an emotional level. Even those who disagreed with me, especially in Hollywood, saw that there was a genuine reason for what I was saying. It was not to advance myself, or the film I was making at the moment. I was fighting for the films of the past. Don't forget, I said, you're also making money. You want people to see these films.

RS: The artifacts of history in film are terribly important. I mean, the worst movie in the world will contain clues to how we lived, how we dressed, how we talked.

MS: That is what I was pointing out in 1979. There was a film called *The Creeping Terror,* a silly sci-fi film shot in the Midwest. They got everybody in some town to act in it. So you actually saw the way people dressed. And you saw how they behaved in everyday life. They were "acting," but they really weren't. The plot was not the point. What was important to me was what it said about America, and about our culture. It was very moving.

RS: It became a valuable record.

MS: It really is.

RS: Yet sometimes I feel that's not enough for you. However much you contribute through your work with the Film Foundation, you keep saying you don't feel you give as much as you should, or in the right way.

MS: It's the conflict of the selflessness with the selfishness. You can write a check to a charity and you feel better. But writing a check is doing nothing. You should be out there, if you really care about it.

RS: You're very stern.

MS: It's true. And it is coming from a person who feels he's been a failure in giving over the years.

RS: Wait a minute: For you to put what you put into the Film Foundation, the amount of work you do for it . . . You shouldn't feel bad if you support film preservation. It's a valid thing to do.

MS: I do think it's valid. I think it feeds the soul in a way.

RS: Well, it certainly feeds your soul.

MS: A good friend of mine recently said, to make a point about the necessity of art, "Let's sell the Sistine Chapel to a developer so the poor can eat for one day with the profits." But then what? They would eat for one day, but we would have lost the Sistine Chapel. And the Sistine Chapel may be of more value for people for the next ten centuries. It's food for the soul. It's spiritual nourishment.

RS: Saving a glorious film that's in danger of being lost or destroyed might also possibly sustain souls.

MS: I know it will.

RS: So you should feel fine.

MS: I *do* feel okay about that. Maybe it's just that we take ourselves too seriously in this business. How do you develop as a person? Am I in touch with what moves me at this age? Am I able to convey it through the films I make?

Lenses, nature, actors. This has to be enough to drive you at a certain age, to keep you believing in what you're doing. If you don't believe in it, then you can't do it.

RS: I'm entirely with you on that. I don't really have to work anymore, but I like to work. I know you like to work. What the hell else would you do?

MS: I tried thinking of it, and I don't think I belong anywhere else, really. Maybe I should make more documentaries, especially the music ones. I need to find new forms of expression, narrative expression. And music is enriching. Whether it's Dylan, George Harrison, or the blues musicians we featured on the PBS series.

RS: The other aspect of your collecting is the posters. They're fabulous. When did all that begin for you?

Marty particularly admired the gaudy color palette director John Stahl employed on this 1945 melodrama. Gene Tierney's lipstick alone was enough to blow you out of the theater.

MS: While I was doing the storyboards as a kid, I also did posters and movie ads.

RS: I didn't realize that. It makes me think of Walter Benjamin, the brilliant, tragic Jewish intellectual who died early in World War II.

MS: I know the name, but I've never read him.

RS: He wrote a very famous article called "The Work of Art in the Age of Mechanical Reproduction." His notion was that a great painting has an aura about it, and that the further you get from the original, through mechanical reproduction—newspaper lithographs and so forth—the more the aura diminishes, my point being that a movie is not a static object. It's not in any particular place. It's in thousands of places simultaneously. Almost intrinsically it can't have an aura the way a Rembrandt painting can. Whereas a poster of that movie can have an aura of some sort.

MS: That's right, exactly.

RS: It's possible that a poster in some ways can have a poignancy and a power that the actual movie may not have. It's showing you maybe the three or four images that are the best parts of the movie. Maybe that's why posters have a kind of a particular pull for you.

MS: By the early seventies I started to become obsessive about collecting them. It was part of this urge or impulse to possess the cinema experience. The posters promise something. They really do. A special dream.

RS: If a poster is a good poster, it encompasses the movie instantly for you. Especially if you've seen the movie.

MS: True.

RS: But you've also spoken to me about the promise of the poster outside of the theater.

MS: Yes, exactly.

RS: But now that you're collecting them, it's not the promise anymore, it's the memory.

MS: Yes. The poster of *Leave Her to Heaven* evokes the entire movie for me. It's not the greatest film, but it's one of my favorites; I like watching it.

RS: Gene Tierney's lipstick blows your mind.

MS: It just knocks you down. We studied it for *Aviator.*

RS: All the lipsticks in that film are terribly vivid.

MS: For years I lived with a part of a six-sheet of *East of Eden.* A six-sheet is a giant poster, basically. But the greater part of it was missing. I just had the one image from the middle of it. I framed it. It was over the couch in L.A. for a while. It's in the vault now, I guess. It was just James Dean and Lois Smith in a dark hall; he's getting ready to go down the hall to his mother's room. Kazan came to dinner one night and was so taken by that. It conveyed all the fear of finding out what was at the end of the hall, what was in the room. There was no calligraphy, nothing, just that image. The *East of Eden* one-sheet doesn't evoke the film for me in the same way.

RS: What got you started collecting posters?

MS: Well, it's absurd, in a way—you can't possess the film because you didn't make the film, and you can't possess the moment that the film was projected. It's like chasing a phantom. The only way you can try to possess films is to make your own films. But they don't come anywhere near the films that influenced you or impressed you when you were in your formative years. So you try to capture something of them.

RS: I guess you could say a poster makes an object of a film.

MS: It does. I think it was Claude Chabrol who did a documentary showing clips of films made by the Nazis during the French occupation in World War II. There is this sequence when the narrator says, in a very chipper way, "Your favorite films are being used and recycled. And, in fact, very often you may find that certain films are being recycled as shoe polish." For example, they show someone shining his shoes, and the voiceover reports, "There's his favorite actress smiling back at him from his shoe tip," and the man smiles back.

RS: The true essence of a movie doesn't exist in the real, physical world, as opposed, maybe, to a poster, which is a stand-alone physical object. Can you remember the first movie poster you ever bought?

MS: *Phantom of the Opera.* It's a Belgian poster. My brother and I happened to see that movie on a rerelease on Halloween night at the Jefferson Theater in the 1950s.

RS: I liked that movie.

MS: Me, too. And I never saw color like that before. And the way it's cut to the operetta *Martha*—it's as well cut to the music and as well designed to the music as some of the scenes in *Colonel Blimp,* or *Tales of Hoffmann.* It's a little silly at times, but it made such an impression on me.

RS: It's the only version of *The Phantom* that gives the Phantom a motive.

MS: I'll never forget the scene when acid is thrown into Claude Rains's face—turning his mild-mannered musician into the film's eponymous monster.

RS: It's one of the great scenes.

MS: And the poor guy goes into the sewer—

RS: I saw it when I was twelve years old and I've never forgotten it.

MS: By the way, the original one, tinted and slow, eighteen frames a second, is excellent. It's with Lon Chaney.

RS: Oh, it's a very good silent film.

MS: His movements are excellent.

RS: So how many posters do you have now?

MS: Three thousand maybe. They're mainly at the Museum of Modern Art, which uses them for different shows. If there's a film that's restored, or there's a special show for a filmmaker, I'm asked for certain posters. We just make sure they're presented in a certain way, and that we can get them back. Recently, for the Roberto Rossellini show, we loaned them a few.

RS: But your original motive was just that you wanted that first poster?

MS: Well, yes. I looked at the use of color on it, and I was so obsessed with that three-strip Technicolor.

RS: Where did you see it?

MS: The poster was somewhere in Greenwich Village. It cost me maybe $25. Some years ago I found another copy, and that's in the editing room. I always look at it.

RS: Those Belgian posters, originally, all that same odd size.

MS: And they are in both French and Flemish.

RS: And what's the first movie you collected?

MS: I think it was *Citizen Kane.* And then I got *8½. 8½* is still very watchable for me.

RS: It's a wonderful film. Somebody said to me the other day that I had given it a bad review. I said, "I couldn't have. I love that film." But maybe I did, being young and stupid. I don't even remember actually reviewing it.

MS: I remember reviews people wrote in the sixties, even the fifties. I remember the *Daily News* review for *The Night of the Hunter,* two and a half stars. I went to see it anyway. I remember the review for *Forbidden Planet* in the *Daily News*—two stars, "a waste of electricity."

RS: Well, to be honest with you, I wouldn't have given more than two and a half stars to *The Night of the Hunter,* either—at the time.

MS: There are people who don't like it, there's no doubt about it.

RS: At the end of the day, if you liked it, and I didn't like it, it doesn't make any difference. That's just opinion.

MS: It has to do with different generations as well.

RS: Absolutely.

MS: As I mentioned, some people say *Fight Club* is *The Clockwork Orange* of its generation. Whatever you may think of the film is neither here nor there. It's the way it has affected many young people under the age of thirty right now.

RS: How many films have you collected, do you think?

MS: About four thousand.

RS: No wonder you're broke all the time!

MS: I've stopped. I was living comfortably, I'd say, until we did *Gangs of New York.* And then *Gangs* put me way in debt.

RS: You put your own money in it?

MS: I threw most of it in. I only got very little of my salary. I put the rest back into the movie. I was obsessed. I kept pouring it in.

MOIRA SHEARER

The Red Shoes

One of the ornaments of Marty's poster collection. *The Red Shoes* (1948) was co-directed by Michael Powell and Emeric Pressburger; the former became Scorsese's friend and mentor later in life, as well as Thelma Schoonmaker's husband.

I mean, they weren't even delivering *The New York Times* to the house. It took me until *The Aviator* to balance out the financial damage that I did to myself. That's why I did a lot of publicity. I had to; I had to follow it through. I didn't necessarily think it was going to win awards, but I had to follow it through in terms of box office.

I felt I might not be able to make another film again, in the sense of getting Hollywood backing. If you agree to do a film for a certain amount of money, and if you as director go way over budget, you have to pay overages. I don't know if I can afford it anymore. But somehow I have to do the films. I'll find something, I'll find a script, or a commercial, just to tide me over sometimes.

RS: I cannot tell you how much garbage I have written in my life for exactly that reason. I have done it all my life. It's only in the last five years that I don't have to do it. It's so hard to do something you're not really passionate about.

Yet sometimes when people give you an assignment, it turns out great.

MS: Look at De Niro forcing me to do *Raging Bull.* Very often some people know what's better for me than I know myself.

ASPERGER'S SYNDROME

RICHARD SCHICKEL: I read an article in *The New Yorker* once that made me think of you, and not you alone—other movie directors I've known as well. It was by Tim Page, a music critic, who suffers from Asperger's syndrome. He quotes David Mamet from a new book he wrote about cinema in which he says if there weren't Asperger's syndrome, there would be no serious movies in America.

MARTIN SCORSESE: [*Laughs.*] Why is that?

RS: Because the syndrome is a form of autism. Page says the symptoms that he suffers from include an insane amount of knowledge about a subject—in his case, music. He has an infinite capacity for detailed work. People who know him say he is out of his mind to do it. It would be like you mixing a scene for the twentieth time.

MS: That's the best part [*laughs*].

RS: As I read the piece, I was thinking, It's kind of like Marty [*laughs*]. You should read it—it explains what I think those priests recognized when you were a little kid. You're helpless, you understand.

MS: Yes, I think I know what you're saying.

THE ONRUSH OF TIME

RICHARD SCHICKEL: You're in your sixties now. You've had great success lately. But I wonder—are you beginning to feel age creeping up on you?

MARTIN SCORSESE: Of course, there's less time. And there are certain responsibilities. It's not a matter of luxury, but of keeping your nose above water and making sure my little girl's taken care of. The amount of work you want to do, the kind of work you want to do—your choices are different at this age.

RS: Looking at those choices, do you feel sometimes, I've done that, I want to move on, or is it, I've done it, but I can still do it better?

MS: That's the constant struggle, to decide.

RS: How do you look at it?

MS: When I talk about exercises in style, I don't know if there's any more time for that, because of the nature of the way I make a picture. Given the amount of time and effort I put into a picture, there's no sense in revisiting a similar one unless I can find another facet to the gem, if it is a gem at all—and maybe unless I can learn something from making the film. Sometimes you think you're learning from a film, and then sometimes you're just happy to get through a film.

Marty, at his Video Village, consults with Dante Ferretti. This is his vantage point on some of his sets when the cameras are turning.

RS: Every director has always said that.

MS: So the choice is, (A) Should I do again types of pictures I've done before? I have to ask myself what about it will be different, stylistically different. What is different about the themes? And (B) Should I enter wholly new territory—to try to do a spectacle of the ancient world, for instance? Should I try to do maybe a children's film?

But because of the way I make films, as I said, those would take longer. I don't know if I have that time to experiment. In the past ten years, I've kind of put them aside. I'm dealing with stories that are similar to what I've dealt with before. I think I'm finding new ways of telling them, finding new things in them to say, but maybe I'm kidding myself. I feel comfortable with what I'm doing—to a certain extent—and I feel impatient with it at the same time, because I want to move on in another direction.

RS: Some critics say, Marty is always doing criminals, he's always doing murderers. Then you go and do *Kundun* and they're not exactly happy with that, either. Does that get in your head? Do you ever say, Maybe they're right?

MS: Oh, yes, sure, when I'm in a weakened state. But I'm constantly testing myself. If the material is similar to what you've done before but you still get excited about it, that's the key: if you still want to deal with all the problems that you have to deal with to make any picture.

There are a number of scripts I've read, a number of books I've read, where I've said it'd be wonderful to do a film with this. But in the end I don't know if I could do them, something like John O'Hara's *Appointment in Samarra,* for example.

RS: That's the one nobody's ever licked. That would be a hard one for you, because it's dealing with a very small-town society.

MS: Exactly. I don't know if I have the time to put into exploring that.

RS: In effect, what you're saying is, If you weren't in your sixties—

MS: Maybe I would try.

RS: You could, perhaps, spend the extra time to absorb a different environment. Now you can't.

MS: I feel the onrush of time, but still, I have certain projects ahead of me, like *Silence,* which takes place in seventeenth-century Japan. I feel I can take the time on that, try to find the center of the picture. The shots are different because it's not set in a modern world. It's dealing with nature, and the evanescence of life, as opposed to it merely being about these two priests who are trying to sustain Christianity in Japan after the religion has been outlawed. They claim that God is demanding their—the priests'—martyrdom. And the Japanese are asking, What kind of a god is that? It's pretty interesting.

But the framing is the issue—whether it should be even a 2.35 aspect ratio. I honestly don't know. I mean, I saw a lot of Japanese films framed that way, but then I saw Mikio Naruse's films and he framed them in 1.33, which was fascinating. I can't use 1.33 today, but what I'm saying is, you think of Japanese films in the sixties, and immediately you think wide screen, 2.35.

RS: Since you brought this up, is framing the first question that occurs to you?

MS: You've got to be true to that world they're in.

RS: In other words, looking at that movie, we as viewers have to look at it with the eye of a character who's in the movie?

MS: No. The eye that I present that world to you with has to do justice to that world. I have to understand the layers of that world. You just don't photograph a house. I have to ask, Should there be a tree behind it? Should there be a river behind the house? What does the river really mean to these people? Should I include it in this or that frame? Should I wait for later? Should I track out from the river? Should I pan over to it? This sort of thing.

But it isn't second nature to me. Jean Renoir in *The Southerner* understood people, through the landscape, through their relationship to nature. It's very hard for me to understand that. You've got to be true to that world they're in.

RS: *Silence*—what is the film as you see it?

MS: Well, I don't want to give too much of it away, but it's about the very essence of Christianity. It's a true story about two Jesuit priests who steal into Japan to find a missing teacher who's become an apostate. The film is full of paradoxes. For example, one of the priests has to choose between his love of Catholicism and his love of a more broadly defined Christianity. Then there's a character he can't stand who keeps running around asking for confession, and keeps ratting on all the Christians. It turns out that's Jesus. Jesus is the man you can't stand. He's the one you've got to forgive. He's the one you've got to love.

The book was given to me by Archbishop Paul Moore of the Episcopal Church.

RS: How curious.

MS: He gave it to me in New York, the night after he saw *Last Temptation*. He said, The choices he makes are the very essence of his faith.

RS: It sounds like a really good story to me. Are you having trouble getting a studio to commit?

MS: I just think that in this day and age they'd rather do something more like *In the Valley of Elah* [Paul Haggis's 2007 film about a father's search for his missing soldier-son], which is more contained, and can't be misinterpreted as solely a religious story. It's about who we are as people. But, you know, it also behooves them to make pictures that make a lot of money.

RS: I'm not sure they make a lot of money all the time.

MS: No, they don't. But the risks, the gambles, are so big. It's amazing when you have meetings with the studio people and you hear their concerns and you try to make something for them and for yourself. You've still got two responsibilities. In this case it isn't that the studios totally don't want to make the picture, it's that it's not that attractive to them—put it that way.

RS: It's a tougher sell for them, when it comes to promotion and marketing.

MS: Yes, a tougher sell. Yet I could make it for a good price. It's very contained. It's

Marty directs Leonardo DiCaprio and Matt Damon on a Boston rooftop on *The Departed*.

not set in the shogun's palace. It's set in Kyushu, in southern Japan. It wouldn't be that bad.

RS: When you mentioned that you have a responsibility to the studio—it is, after all, their money and they're not necessarily your enemy—I thought of your father's lectures on responsibility.

MS: I know! It doesn't mean that I'm always responsible, and I certainly haven't always been responsible in the past. I try to be, I really do, but at a certain point if I'm getting something on film that's better than a studio ever thought it would get, then it behooves me to try to convince them to let me finish the job properly. A constant dialogue with the people who are financing the film is really important.

We worked very closely with the studio on *Gangs of New York*. The studio wanted to be kept abreast of what was going on, and I did every step of the way. They'd raise an issue, I'd discuss it with them, try to deal with it. Sometimes I couldn't. Sometimes I tried to and still couldn't. *The Aviator* was a very big movie, but it was on schedule, so I got a little bit of credit that way. The only difficulties we had were in the last month, over distribution. But that's a matter of one person's will over another. That's not about the film. That's something else. You just flail your way out of it, or into it. The only exception is if you're involved with the financiers. Sometimes you get into that kind of thing—like Selznick and Hitchcock maybe.

RS: Hitch and I talked about that one time. He really didn't like him.

MS: In *Rear Window* Raymond Burr [who played the murderer] is made up to look like him.

RS: I wasn't aware of that.

MS: Somehow Hitchcock came out of it stronger. Some people don't come out.

RS: It wasn't just that he became stronger. It was that Selznick became weaker, addicted to uppers and downers, that sort of thing.

MS: Yes. And then he made *A Farewell to Arms,* unfortunately. Oh, my God.

RS: Let's go back to you, Marty. Do you have a favorite or two among your films?

MS: No.

RS: Really?

MS: *Mean Streets* was very hard to make, but everybody was working well together and it was a good time in my life. I liked that. *Italianamerican,* the one on my parents, I learned a lot from that. I liked *The Last Waltz. Goodfellas* was like a rebirth. I was having a hard time. I sort of found myself again with it. *Kundun* is also a picture I like.

RS: I know that. But why, particularly?

MS: The mood, the tone of it.

RS: The spiritual quest?

MS: The quest of a person who is raised from a child to lead the spiritual life. That makes it a very interesting movie to me. I can't quite grasp it yet, though.

RS: Is it something in the selection of the child that's moving to you?

MS: No, it's the nature of loss, and the acceptance of it. The loss of a whole culture, a way of life. The loss of life, loss of friends, loss of relatives, the very transitory nature of our existence—accepting that, and moving on. That is where the texture and the color of the film come from.

RS: *Silence*—perhaps it has spiritual dimensions not unlike those of *Kundun*.

MS: Correct.

RS: When you were coming off an enormous success with *The Departed,* at some cynical, practical level, you could get on a crime story more easily than you could get on a Japanese movie. What I'm saying is that then you went to a studio and you said, I'd like to do the Japanese movie, they said, Yes, Marty, but we really love the one about the criminally insane set near Boston.

MS: Right.

RS: So, you know, that's the practical side of things.

MS: And you can't go on a set and say, I don't want to be here, even if you want to be on another set.

RS: But you have on your mind all those personal matters we've discussed.

MS: Yes, I'm getting older. As I said, there are certain responsibilities with the family at this point.

RS: That's the point I'm trying to make here.

MS: *Shutter Island* is about truth and illusion, too, you know. And guilt, a lot of guilt [*laughs*].

Marty, Elias Koteas, and Leonardo DiCaprio lost in the shadows of *Shutter Island.*

RS: A lot of guilt, as usual. I know.

MS: But my aim, finally, is to make *Silence,* the way my aim was to make *Gangs of New York,* and my aim was to make *The Last Temptation of Christ.* Or *Bringing Out the Dead.*

RS: Is the last temptation of Marty Scorsese to make something like *Charlie Wilson's War,* a political film?

MS: I'd like to make something that has some body—something that one would not only be able to enjoy as entertainment, but also to think about. That means being moved by it or repulsed by it at times. To leave the theater saying, You know what, that's a very interesting point of view. I guess that desire goes back to the impulse of a young boy looking at those American films in the theater, and then seeing the Italian films. And later being affected by seeing *Children of Paradise* for the first time. And then seeing Ingmar Bergman's *Seventh Seal* and *The Virgin Spring* and practically every Bergman film that came out every six months or ten months, whatever it was.

RS: They sure did come out in those days.

MS: If you ever look at what was playing back in 1960 in New York—I mean, it was amazing.

RS: I was at the movies three, four nights a week. You know, you'd go to 8th Street in the Village. You'd go to the Waverly, which played old American movies. I probably saw Sidney Lumet's *Twelve Angry Men* eight times.

MS: I saw *Treasure of the Sierra Madre* there for the first time. There's a part of me that loves European art. And there's a part of me that loves Hollywood film. Those are two very different traditions.

But always I want to communicate to an audience. I want them to enjoy the story, to go with it, to enjoy it.

I guess it goes back to that idea of good men doing bad things, and our not always judging them harshly. Creating a story around that. I believe I grew up in a world like that. A lot of my friends experienced it differently. But that's what I perceived. That's what I saw.

There's a Jacques Tourneur film, *Canyon Passage.* Did you ever see it?

RS: Yes.

MS: It's a beautiful film.

RS: It is.

MS: There's a wonderful moment where Brian Donlevy is in the back room—I think Hoagy Carmichael sees him—and he's weighing some gold out of a pouch. It's not his. He's just measuring it and marking the weight down. Then he looks at it again. He takes some for himself. That's where the problem begins. He's a decent guy, but he's got some business problems.

That kind of dilemma fascinates me. But I like entertainment in movies, too. I enjoy making an audience care about people, or laugh. I watch films from Africa, from South Korea. I see them as expressions from different cultures. I wonder about the value of a lot of the stuff that is being made here. I'm trying to look at other places for their personal expression—even the very, very long takes of Béla Tarr; at times it's a major investment, to sit down and watch *Satantango* for seven hours.

RS: No kidding.

MS: As I get older, I find I go back to early Carl Dreyer. I'll screen *Passion of Joan of Arc* and *Day of Wrath* [about witchcraft]. *Ordet* [a meditation on religious and profane love] is a masterpiece. What I guess I'm getting at is that I am still part of the American culture.

RS: You can't escape that.

MS: I've been looking at *It's a Wonderful Life* again.

RS: Frank Capra *had* a wonderful life. And he was a wonderful director.

MS: He saw America from the point of view of the immigrant coming over from a decaying European society. He flourished in the worst time, the 1930s.

RS: As long as you honestly put your experience into the work, it doesn't make any difference what your experience is, even if it's an unfashionably happy one.

MS: That's the key. Honestly putting your experience in. Crafting it in such a way that it has that honesty and the love from your heart.

RS: I agree.

MS: And you have to like the people you work with. That's why Capra was so great with actors—you could see he loved them.

RS: He was a very empathetic man, Frank.

MS: I never met him.

RS: I did, and I liked him a lot.

MS: *Meet John Doe* was on the other day. Thelma and I were looking at just a couple of cuts. The sound was down; I said, "Look at this," the scene where they choose Gary Cooper to be the American Everyman, when all those different men come in, looking to be cast as John Doe. I said, "Watch the cutting here." Barbara Stanwyck's face—it was great.

RS: Frank Capra was, technically speaking, one of the greatest directors who ever lived. The cutting—

MS: The frames.

RS: The way the shots are set up.

MS: That sequence in *Meet John Doe,* the rally at the ballpark in the rain, and the police. Do you know how hard it would be to set that up?

RS: It's one of the most complicated, brilliant pieces of filmmaking I've ever seen.

MS: What he was doing there was amazing. They shot eighteen months, they shot different endings.

RS: Yes, I know. And it's still not a movie that ends quite right. But up to that point there's so much fabulous shooting. And that rally in the rain sequence, if I were teaching film, that's one of the ones I would take and say, Look, guys. This is a gigantic sequence with thousands of people in it. Just look at it and die a little bit.

MS: I hadn't seen *Meet John Doe* in years when, one night, when I was shooting *The Departed,* I was in the trailer waiting. TCM is on with the sound off, and I watched *Meet John Doe.* I hadn't looked at that sequence in such good quality in years. That's when I realized what an amazing piece of filmmaking it is.

RS: Another great scene is the wedding at the end of *It Happened One Night.* It's breathtaking how he does that. You know, he has matching swish pans, cameras going, the girl going—

MS: People tend to overlook it because they only remember the characters.

RS: Well, you remember the funny, the sweet—

MS: But when you look at the film closely, the characters have a glow to them that's quite extraordinary. The lighting is brilliant. The editing is great.

RS: I had done the Frank Capra film for the series on TV, *The Men Who Made the Movies,* and they hired me to write another Capra show. Somebody else was going to direct it. I said, Sure, I can do that. The producer was a good guy, a former film editor, Carl Pingatore. We put the film together, and we took it to somebody at NBC, and he said, "But it's not funny." And I said, "Yeah, well, that's right, because, you know, Frank Capra isn't funny."

MS: I know.

RS: He's warm, but he's not funny. It's Depression America. I mean, what's funny in *American Madness*?

MS: Nothing.

RS: And look at the run on the bank sequence. It's beautiful, though.

MS: Fantastic, yeah. My wife heard his voice the other night on TV. She said, "Who's that?" I told her and she said, "He sounds like a nice man."

RS: He probably wasn't, entirely, you know, like all of us. But he wasn't the monster Joe McBride portrayed in that biography he wrote.

MS: You could feel the love of the actors, for characters they played; it's like a Jean Renoir picture.

RS: Frank was, at his height, when his was "the name above the title," a driven man, and an egotist, but he was also, I thought, a fundamentally good person.

MS: A work of art comes out of something, and it's got to be criticized, it's got to go in front of an audience. It has to be dealt with. This is its nature, its fate. You make your own meaning in life. Maybe works of art are attempts at this.

RS: The crisis, it seems to me, that has been more and more vividly played out in our time is existentialism versus the orderliness of organized religion. We are, most of us, now used to the notion that we live in a chance universe.

MS: Yes, exactly.

RS: I'm here with you. I ask you one final question that just happens to pop into my mind. I step out in the street and a car comes around the corner and kills me. If I hadn't asked that question, I'd have been across the street.

MS: That fascinates me. I actually think about it all the time. That's one of the ideas behind Nick's character in *Bringing Out the Dead,* thinking he can make a difference.

RS: Well, he does—to some degree.

MS: Yes, but he can't control the world. He can't control the cosmos. He can't control people's lives. He can't really bring people back to life, except almost by luck.

RS: It comes back to something that was so important in Elia Kazan's way of looking at the world. He said, Look, life is full of choices. If you married this woman, it means you didn't marry that woman. Marrying this woman your life goes in a certain path. But what would have been your path had you chosen the other woman? That's what we never know. That was the fascination for him. You know, he chose to testify at the HUAC hearings. Had he chosen not to testify, how would his life have been different? That was the most vivid example in his life. But the fundamental idea occurred to him in all kinds of situations, even very minor ones — I chose to shoot this scene this morning instead of that scene this morning.

MS: There are some who believe there may not be any design at all, that the design just works itself out. Where does God fit in this? Does He in any way? Is there some sort of a force?

My daughter comes into a room in Los Angeles. She flew out because we were going to one of these awards ceremonies. She was very happy to be there. She sits down and asks, "So why are we here?" Her mother says, "We're here for the event tonight." My daughter says, "No, I mean, why are we here on this planet?" I looked at the three of us and I said, "Well, if you weren't here, who's going to take care of the dog?" I said, "I'm here to take care of you, to take care of us, to take care of Mommy, we all take care of each other." That's it. It ends here.

RS: There appears to me to be some truth in that.

MS: That's all we know. And the next step is that the person next to you is somebody who cares about you. Maybe that is the nature of who we are.

RS: This has come up in different forms in a number of our conversations. It's obviously something you've wrestled with all your life. Now it seems to me, coming from a very different tradition from yours —

MS: Yes!

RS: I'm just done with it. I'm not having that wrestling match anymore. I believe it's a chance universe. I believe when I'm dead, I'm dead, I'm not going to some better place — which I bitterly regret, of course.

MS: We're going to miss it, you know. We're going to miss a lot. Except, following the logic of nothingness, we won't know.

RS: I have a friend who says, "What I hate most about it is you're asked to leave the party, and the party's still going on."

Marty lines up a shot in the danker reaches of the *Shutter Island* insane asylum. Cinematographer Robert Richardson is at his left.

MS: It will still be going on.

RS: They're going to be making movies—

MS: Pictures are going to be made, plays are going to be written, and books are going to be written. And I'll miss it all. It's not fair.

RS: You are finished, Mr. Scorsese.

MS: Oh, wait a minute, wait a minute, I have one more thing to say.

RS: It's funny, but it is not.

MS: Well, you have to laugh about it because that's what it is. Epictetus, I think, said not to be concerned with death, because life is the presence of feeling and emotion and awareness, and death is the absence of all of that, which means you won't have any awareness. So why worry about it?

RS: I've thought about the suddenness and the apparent motivelessness of violence in your films. There's a lack of—forgive the pomposity of this phrase—

precognitive awareness on the part of your characters in those situations. It makes your movies uniquely intense.

MS: I don't know. I don't mean them to be.

RS: Of course you mean them to be! What I'm saying is that I see a lot of movies and I admire a lot of movies. Your movies all characteristically have an enormous intensity to them. I'm not just talking about movement in the frame, the way you cut them, all of that technical business. There is a relentless, in-your-face quality to your movies. It's not present in the work of most of your contemporaries. I admire Spielberg, but he doesn't have that intensity. It comes out when we talk about, for example, your maniacal layering of music. It's in everything you do.

MS: Okay, it is in everything. It has to be worth saying to go through all this, to put it on film. And there's gotta be somebody out there it's going to say something to, to grab. It has to be that intense to accomplish that. It's got to be like DiCaprio's face when Jack Nicholson tells him, "I smell a rat." Leo has to convince him he's not the rat. Leo thinks, What am I doing here, what choice have I made in my life to get me in this position? It's all there in his eyes. It has to be.

RS: Well, where does the feeling that motivates that sequence spring from in you?

MS: You have to be selfless to be a good servant. Yet I have a giant ego. That's the way it is.

RS: It's the same with me. If I ask myself, What is the purpose of what I do? I have no idea. I think that's true of most people.

MS: People think in different ways. But you open up doors. That's the key, I think. Like the Walter Benjamin material we discussed. The business about the aura of the work.

RS: It's a fabulous piece of thinking.

MS: It's quite something. It's the kind of influence that a priest had on me when I was a kid, and he said, "Look at this book. Go see this movie. Listen to this piece of music." And suddenly people go off in directions they never would have thought of.

RS: Well, I guess that's the ideal. If you make a movie, or if I write something, that gets to a couple of people and—

MS: It makes some kind of difference.

RS: If it makes them think a little differently and behave a little differently, then I

THE ONRUSH OF TIME

377

guess we've fulfilled our purpose. I don't know what else we're here for. As you say, all the rest is ego.

MS: Yes, the rest is ego.

Kazan's *On the Waterfront* meant so much to me. People do affect other people. So many people go up to Bob Dylan and say, "Your work changed my life." What is he going to say to them? You can't say "I didn't mean to," because in some way you *did* mean to.

A lot of what I do comes from, again, what I perceived in aspects of religion. The nature of the male-dominated world that my father represented, and also the morality specific to that patriarchal religion—that whole way of thinking—as opposed to what I perceived in the "church," which represented to me a more nurturing, female side of the religion.

In my work, I've been trying to develop, over the past ten years, a nurturing compassion. Maybe it comes from guilt. I'm talking about guilt that comes from just being alive. That's what brings me to these characters.

RS: Guilt from just being alive? That's cosmic guilt!

MS: I just need to live with it and deal with it. Look again at Leo's face in *The Departed.* What is he guilty of?

RS: Really nothing.

MS: Yes, but in his mind, everything. He puts himself in a suicide situation. He's going to die. He's twenty-five years old. I've seen this happen, you know. I've seen people just condemn themselves. I've seen people destroy themselves over the years. Why? It's not that easy. There's something in our nature, something I gravitate toward.

RS: Okay.

MS: People say, You take yourself too damn seriously. But it's the reality. I'm stuck with myself. I've been taking myself seriously. I'd better listen to myself and deal with it.

RS: Well, you do take yourself seriously.

MS: I can't help that.

RS: All of us do. We can pretend otherwise. But the truth of the matter is almost everything we do is something that comes from some part of our souls.

MS: A basic core.

RS: A core, yes.

MS: Who we are, our heart.

RS: Do you have any aspiration—

MS: To make a love story?

RS: To put it simply.

MS: I keep thinking, Do I have to? But then I think, Well, if I'm able to do a love story, then I should be able to do an historical epic, I should be able to do anything else. In the time that's left, I would love to find a story like *Happy-Go-Lucky* [Mike Leigh's film about an amazingly cheerful schoolteacher's life in North London], for example, to deal with those two people—Eddie Marsan's character and Sally Hawkins's character, Poppy, in the car.

RS: Oh, that's a really interesting entanglement, isn't it?

MS: Yeah, it's wonderful. It's not a test or an exam, but it's like a canon of work that every filmmaker or novelist should be able to do.

RS: Alfred Hitchcock, to name another Catholic-raised artist, made the same movie a hundred times.

MS: Yes, but there were love stories, like *Notorious.* And *Vertigo,* the most extraordinary one, because Jimmy Stewart loses Kim Novak twice. If I finally do *Silence,* it will have no women in it, but it's about love. It's about love itself. And pushing the ego away, pushing the pride away. It's about the essential nature of Christianity itself.

RS: Is Christianity the ultimate expression of love? I don't know.

MS: It is the road I was given, the road that I was put on. If I had been born in the Middle East, I might have felt differently. I don't know. My first experiences with love, basically, were with my parents. Then the concept of love itself came through indoctrination by the church in the early 1950s.

I've gone through a lot of changes since then. But looking at who we are as a species, love does seem to be the only answer. So how is that nurtured? How is that developed in us as human beings? In our actions, particularly.

I often think of *The Bridge of San Luis Rey.* [There are five people on the bridge, all of whom are killed by an earthquake. The Thornton Wilder novel and subsequent film ask whether their deaths were part of some cosmic plan or merely accidents.] There doesn't appear to be a particular reason why they're there. The nurse at the end—a nun, I think—is taking care of all the other victims and she suddenly thinks, What if there is no God? Then she looks around and says to herself, in effect, They need your help one way or another, and she goes right back to work. That's the beauty of it.

The image of the dutiful nun attending to those wounded in the collapse of the bridge of San Luis Rey is one that often recurs to Marty. It's not particularly a spiritual thing. It's more a matter of the practical—and inordinate—demands that conscience and the accidents of fate place on the individual.

Alone among the world's major directors, Marty maintains an incredibly active life as a filmmaker in other fields. His documentary *Letter to Elia*, virtually completed before he began shooting the feature film *Hugo*, had its first film festival screenings, at Telluride and, later, at the New York Film Festival. It is a very personal tribute to one of his most revered directorial masters, Elia Kazan, and was meant for limited theatrical and wider DVD release. It followed by just a few weeks the HBO presentation of *Boardwalk Empire,* an historical epic about the criminal history of Atlantic City, for which he served as executive producer as well as the director of the first episode of the series. Beyond that he was directing the epic-length documentary *Living in the Material World: George Harrison,* about the life, music, and spiritual questings of the onetime Beatle, as well as the more modest *Public Speaking,* a very funny documentary about Fran Lebowitz, the comic writer, who is a personal friend of Marty and his wife, Helen.

Just recounting the range of his activities in the fall of 2010 leaves everyone except Marty a little breathless. He says that at his age (sixty-eight during this flurry of activity), he more and more feels the pressure of time and his own mortality. So much to do, possibly so little time. Moreover, he has never banked as much money as other directors of his stature have done; he's always plowing it back into film preservation, his collections of posters and film, his film foundation. He therefore worries about leaving enough money to assure his children's future, especially that of his youngest daughter, Francesca.

But more than practical considerations account for his pace. All of the work of 2010 and beyond has serious meaning for him; he wasn't and will not be bowling for dollars with any of it. Take *Boardwalk Empire,* for example. It may be full of menacing and bloody activity. But it is also a serious representation of the rise of organized crime in the early twentieth century. The New Jersey playground was, Marty says, "the template for Las Vegas," which means that it holds high intrinsic interest for him. I've never believed that he concerns himself so often with crime, both organized and disorganized, out of an impulse for sensationalism. It's the extremes of behavior found in the underworld that fascinate him.

And also the ironies it presents. For example, in *Boardwalk Empire* there is, of all things, the question of roads to consider. The rum runners needed paved highways to move their contraband from place to place. The result was the beginnings, at least in New Jersey, of an excellent road network that ultimately benefited the general public at least as much as it did the gangsters. It is this alertness to the curious by-products of criminal activity that distinguishes Marty's work in this field from that of his competitors. Comedy, like violence, is a form of extreme behavior, and there is a lot more of the blacker varieties of comedy in his films than most people perceive. It is an important factor in making *Goodfellas,* for instance, such an extraordinary experience. And *Boardwalk Empire* is a more than usually interesting television series.

But it is the documentaries that provide him with satisfactions not available in feature films. For one thing, the financial stakes in these pictures are much lower, which means the pressures on Marty are also lessened—especially deadline pressures. "You can approach the material carefully," he says. "You can let the film grow naturally. You are much more free to play with the form than you can with a feature film." The Kazan film provides a particularly good example. He and Kent Jones (co-writer and co-director) worked on it for several years, testing different approaches to his subject, making a multitude of rough cuts as he refined various versions of the piece.

Something similar, though with a different cumulative effect, occurred with the George Harrison film. He quite quickly determined that he did not want to think chronologically about the man's life. What fascinated him was Harrison's post-Beatles life, his disillusionment with celebrity follies, and, above all, the man's earnest search for some deeper, existential meaning in our passage through life. The film is very long (about three hours) and contains some interesting digressions on less-than-obvious matters. For instance, Marty suggests that Harrison's late music functions somewhat the way chanting does in Eastern religions, as an aid to meditation, which took Marty back to some of the ideas that underlay *Kundun.* Not that he wishes to proselytize for that notion. It is, he insists, just something that emerged as he worked with his material in comparative leisure.

As for the Lebowitz film, it is a much lighter exercise. "I couldn't resist it," he says. Interviewing her, bringing his cameras to her public appearances, he quickly realized that "you could make a different film every night," so mercurial is the persona she has created and plays with a sort of noisy subtlety. Making the film, Marty was often reminded of *Italianamerican.* However complex his filmmaking, both factual and fictional, becomes, he remains wedded to the idea that the world offers no more intriguing spectacle than that of a man and/or a woman simply talking to each other or to a camera. To invoke the cliché, such figures are capable of containing multitudes.

They are also capable of containing Marty—by which I mean that his work on nonfiction films is not just something that keeps a workaholic busy. It is, I think, central to who he is as an artist. It would be easy for someone like Marty to lose touch with reality, to succumb to the high flattery that is always dangerously available to "auteurs." This work on limited budgets, for (relatively speaking) limited audiences, on topics that are more interesting to him than they are to anyone else, keeps him grounded. It surely keeps him in touch with his modest beginnings, when getting any film, fictional or nonfictional, into release was a major triumph for him. They must, as well, remind him that maintaining your credentials as an artist in any medium requires that you from time to time devote yourself to topics that do not have broad popular appeal, that offer you more private satisfaction than public acclaim. This is, I think, especially true of moviemakers, who require so much more in the way of equipment and manpower to pursue their goals than do poets and painters.

So his documentaries are not sidelines or indulgences for him. They are, I believe, a crucial element in maintaining his sense of himself. Marty has lately found himself taken with the notion that there "is more democracy in our culture than there is in our society at large"—a willingness to take more risks, to experiment more radically with both form and content. His documentaries put him at the center of that sort of activity. They freshen and recharge his energies, grant him the opportunity for serious play, which is essential to any artist. It's an accident that so much of his work came to fruition in the fall of 2010. But it is no accident that the films were undertaken. They are of the essence as far as Marty is concerned. And they are a large part of what distinguishes his career from any other that comes easily to mind.

Scorsese was engaged from the latter months of 2010, through his usual lengthy postproduction period, which consumed much of 2011, on what turned out to be a bittersweet enterprise, the adaptation of a children's book called *The Invention of Hugo Cabret,* by Brian Selznick. The book, published in 2007, is something of a (deserved) instant classic, sparing on words but extremely rich in haunting black-and-white illustrations. It tells the story of the title character (Asa Butterfield), an orphan lad in 1930s Paris who haunts a train station, where he keeps its clocks running on time and seeks to reanimate an automaton his father was working on before his death. In the course of his adventures, Hugo runs afoul of a mostly hilarious Sacha Baron Cohen, playing a station police officer obsessed with sending parentless children to the orphanage, and, much more important, Georges Méliès (Ben Kingsley), the pioneering filmmaker, now forgotten, who is running a shop in the station. (This much of the story is true; Méliès did keep such a shop after he had fallen on bad times.) Asa makes common cause with Méliès's ward (Chloë Grace Moretz), and eventually they restore the filmmaker to history and achieve a happy ending, as well as a graceful tribute to the early history of the cinema.

Marty's film reversed the presentation of Selznick's book. It was made in 3-D and is mainly (and impressively) staged on a hugely elaborate train station set.

Producer Graham King initially budgeted the movie at $100 million, a figure that would soon be a distant memory. Marty says part of the overages were due to child labor laws in Great Britain, which prevented him from working with his leads more than four hours a day. But the real budgetary culprit was 3-D. The picture ran through three associate producers as everyone tried to solve the problems the process presented. The outside world will probably never know what the picture cost, but I have seen estimates as high as $170 million, and they don't seem unreasonable. As of the spring of 2012, the movie had grossed something like $116 million—nothing to sneeze at in today's movie world—meaning it had lost $54 million to that point, despite mostly good reviews and eleven Academy Award nominations (five wins in technical categories). By any standard, it would seem to be a notable financial disaster, though *Hugo* has been spared much of the gossip and recriminations that usually attend flops of such magnitude.

Perhaps it deserves to be spared such talk. To begin with, as Marty has observed, he does not *always* make crime pictures, as *King of Comedy, After Hours,* and *The Age of Innocence,* among others, prove. More to the point, the film itself is far from ponderous. It is, in fact, light on its feet, touched with humor and, above all, good spirits. You like these people, wish them well. And they return the favor. They have their frets, even their embittered moments, but they are always ready for redemption. And Méliès, at last recognized and publicly celebrated, has a truly privileged moment as he reclaims his place in the history of his art.

This says nothing about the sheer liveliness of the filmmaking. The script by John Logan is very faithful to the book; it is full of suspenseful chases and even includes some spectacularly staged train crashes. Yet the film never quite escaped the notion that it was a kid picture, that for all the care and sophistication of its making it was somehow an overgilded lily, or, as Joe Morgenstern called it in *The Wall Street Journal,* "a clockwork lemon." Pictures for this market tend to be about chipmunks, and animated ones at that. There is no perceived notion that anybody wants or needs more sophisticated filmmaking. Or that the accompanying "parents or guardians" need to emerge from the experience having felt other than that they did their duty. Manohla Dargis might write in *The New York Times* that *Hugo* was "serious, beautiful, wise to the absurdity of life and in the embrace of a piercing longing," and other critics would echo her, but it was, particularly at its price, a lost cause. If it was a cause at all. Maybe it was just a miscalculation.

What if Marty and King and Logan had stuck to the scale of the book? I don't mean making a black-and-white film, of course. But suppose they had made something on a more modest scale? Something more shadowed, less spectacular, maybe not in 3-D? Something, say, in the $75 million range?

There are dangers in that strategy, too. Such pictures are easily ignored, particularly if you are opening your film during the Christmas season, when the implicit demand for spectacle is at its height—in for a penny, in for a pound, and all that. Now at least its makers can console themselves with hopes for the long run: a classic that's rediscovered some time in the distant future (which, frankly, seems unlikely).

Marty was everywhere during awards season, nominated for prizes, even winning one or two. He was chipper when encountered on these occasions, and he seemed in good spirits on Oscar night. He had, I think, processed whatever disappointment the film brought him. He had had, God knows, other movies that had been enthusiastically received but had not done well at the box office. He would doubtless have more of them. That's the game as it's played. It may be that the only people disappointed by *Hugo* are those of us who thought it deserved not just respect but more enthusiasm than it got. There was something dutiful about many of those good reviews, something that didn't quite capture *Hugo*'s best spirit.

But, naturally, life goes on. Directors of Marty's stature tend to gain more sympathy than condemnation when they suffer a box office setback, especially when the film in question is as felicitous as *Hugo* was. As of the spring of 2012, his Sinatra biopic was languishing, apparently in the process of being rewritten numberless times. But Daniel Day-Lewis had been announced for *Silence,* that intriguing story of Jesuit priests in Japan, though it appeared that his next offering would be *The Wolf of Wall Street*, a fact-based story about a penny stock trader who becomes involved in Wall Street corruption. The film, starring Leonardo DiCaprio, was set to start shooting in August 2012.

Marty is, amazingly to me, seventy years old. But there is no diminishment of his restlessness or energy. I expect him to go on and on—with his features, with his documentaries, with his passion for film history, with his restorations. A few other directors are his peers, but he is, I think, peerless in the range of his interests, and the manic energy with which he pursues them. He is akin to—no other phrase will quite do—a force of nature.

R.S., April 2012

ACKNOWLEDGMENTS

Rather obviously, my gratitude goes first and foremost to Martin Scorsese, who embraced this book from the outset and devoted more hours to it than either of us imagined it would require. It's not just the time that went into our conversations that I thank him for, but for the time I know he spent thinking about and preparing for our talk when I was not present. I have interviewed many directors—Marty included—for a series of television programs I have made about them and their work. But I have never gone into quite the depth I did with Marty, whose patience, concentration, and openness were wonderful to behold—and inspiring as well.

My thanks for their assistance on this book go to a relatively small number of people, but they are all the more heartfelt because they are so few. In Marty's office, his co-producer, Emma Tillinger, became over the years not just an informal collaborator in my efforts, but a true (and unfailingly good-natured) friend. Lisa Frichette, Marty's personal assistant, has been a cheerful, blindlingly efficient presence as an arranger of meetings and source of information. She has been dauntless in support of a sometimes daunting task. Marianne Bower, Marty's archivist, has been wonderfully patient in answering my many questions and in providing most of the pictures that add so much to this book's appearance.

At Knopf, Jonathan Segal has been—as always—an ideal editor: incisive, demanding, and insistent that this book be as good as I could possible make it. I've known Jon for something like thirty years, and his friendship is one of the ornaments of my life. His tireless assistant, Joey McGarvey, has handled the multitude of details that go into making any book with unfailing good cheer and marvelous efficiency.

All these people have conspired to make this book a pleasure to work on and to make it better than I dared hope it might be. I hope that they will enjoy the results of our joint efforts.

Richard Schickel
Los Angeles
November 15, 2010

FILMOGRAPHY

Feature Films and Feature-Length Documentaries

WHO'S THAT KNOCKING AT MY DOOR (1967)

DIRECTED BY
Martin Scorsese

WRITTEN BY
Martin Scorsese

PRINCIPAL CAST
Zina Bethune..............Girl
Harvey Keitel ............J.R.

PRODUCED BY
Haig Manoogian
Betzi Manoogian
Joseph Weill

DIRECTORS OF PHOTOGRAPHY
Richard H. Coll
Michael Wadleigh

FILM EDITOR
Thelma Schoonmaker

BOXCAR BERTHA (1972)

DIRECTED BY
Martin Scorsese

WRITTEN BY
Joyce H. Corrington
John William Corrington
(Based on the book *Sister of the Road,* by Bertha
Thompson as told to Ben L. Reitman)

PRINCIPAL CAST
Barbara Hershey........"Boxcar" Bertha
Thompson
David Carradine........"Big" Bill Shelly
Barry Primus..............Rake Brown
Bernie Casey ....Von Morton
John Carradine ....H. Buckram Sartoris

PRODUCED BY
Roger Corman
Julie Corman

DIRECTOR OF PHOTOGRAPHY
John Stephens

FILM EDITOR
Buzz Feitshans

ORIGINAL MUSIC BY
Gib Guilbeau
Thad Maxwell

ASSISTANT DIRECTOR
Paul Rapp

MEAN STREETS (1973)

DIRECTED BY
Martin Scorsese

WRITTEN BY
Martin Scorsese
Mardik Martin

STORY BY
Martin Scorsese

PRINCIPAL CAST
Robert De Niro ....Johnny Boy
Harvey Keitel ....Charlie
David Proval..............Tony
Amy Robinson ....Teresa
Richard Romanus......Michael
Cesare Danova...........Giovanni

EXECUTIVE PRODUCER
E. Lee Perry

PRODUCED BY
Jonathan T. Taplin

CINEMATOGRAPHY BY
Kent Wakeford

FILM EDITOR
Sid Levin
Martin Scorsese (uncredited)

ASSISTANT DIRECTOR
Russell Vreeland

ITALIANAMERICAN (1974)

DIRECTED BY
Martin Scorsese

WRITTEN BY
Larry Cohen
Mardik Martin

CAST
Catherine Scorsese ....Herself
Charles Scorsese ....Himself
Martin Scorsese..........Himself (uncredited)

PRODUCED BY
Elaine Attias
Saul Rubin

ASSOCIATE PRODUCER
Bert Lovitt

DIRECTOR OF PHOTOGRAPHY
Alec Hirschfeld

EDITED BY
Bert Lovitt

ALICE DOESN'T LIVE HERE ANYMORE (1974)

DIRECTED BY
Martin Scorsese

WRITTEN BY
Robert Getchell

PRINCIPAL CAST
Ellen Burstyn.............Alice Hyatt
Alfred Lutter ....Tommy
Harvey Keitel ....Ben
Diane Ladd ....Flo
Vic Tayback................Mel
Kris Kristofferson .....David

PRODUCED BY
Audrey Maas
David Susskind

ASSOCIATE PRODUCER
Sandra Weintraub

DIRECTOR OF PHOTOGRAPHY
Kent L. Wakeford

FILM EDITOR
Marcia Lucas

PRODUCTION DESIGNER
Toby Carr Rafelson

ASSISTANT DIRECTOR
Mike Moder

TAXI DRIVER (1976)

DIRECTED BY
Martin Scorsese

WRITTEN BY
Paul Schrader

PRINCIPAL CAST
Robert De Niro ....Travis Bickle
Jodie Foster................Iris
Cybill Shepherd.........Betsy
Harvey Keitel ....Matthew "Sport" Higgins
Peter Boyle.................Wizard
Albert Brooks............Tom

PRODUCED BY
Julia Phillips
Michael Phillips

ASSOCIATE PRODUCER
Philip M. Goldfarb

ORIGINAL MUSIC BY
Bernard Herrmann

DIRECTOR OF PHOTOGRAPHY
Michael Chapman

SUPERVISING FILM EDITOR
Marcia Lucas

EDITED BY
Tom Rolf
Melvin Shapiro

CASTING BY
Juliet Taylor

ART DIRECTION BY
Charles Rosen

COSTUME DESIGN BY
Ruth Morley

ASSISTANT DIRECTOR
Peter R. Scoppa

NEW YORK, NEW YORK (1977)

DIRECTED BY
Martin Scorsese

WRITTEN BY
Earl Mac Rauch
Mardik Martin

STORY BY
Earl Mac Rauch

PRINCIPAL CAST
Liza Minnelli..............Francine Evans
Robert De Niro.........Jimmy Doyle
Lionel Stander...........Tony Harwell
Barry Primus..............Paul Wilson
Mary Kay Place.........Bernice Bennett
Georgie Auld.............Frankie Harte
George Memmoli......Nicky

PRODUCED BY
Robert Chartoff
Irwin Winkler

ASSOCIATE PRODUCER
Gene Kirkwood

DIRECTOR OF PHOTOGRAPHY
Laszlo Kovacs

FILM EDITORS
Bert Lovitt
David Ramirez
Tom Rolf

CASTING BY
Lynn Stalmaster

PRODUCTION DESIGN BY
Boris Leven

COSTUME DESIGN BY
Theadora Van Runkle

ASSISTANT DIRECTOR
Melvin D. Dellar

THE LAST WALTZ (1978)

DIRECTED BY
Martin Scorsese

PRINCIPAL CAST
The Band:
Robbie Robertson
Rick Danko
Richard Manuel
Levon Helm
Garth Hudson

APPEARANCES BY
Eric Clapton
Neil Diamond
Bob Dylan
Joni Mitchell
Neil Young
Emmylou Harris
Ringo Starr
Paul Butterfield
Dr. John
Van Morrison
Ronnie Hawkins
Mavis Staples
Roebuck "Pops" Staples
Muddy Waters
Ron Wood
Michael McClure
Lawrence Ferlinghetti
Jim Gordon

Tom Malone
Howard Johnson
Jerry Hay
Richard Cooper
Charlie Keagle
Larry Packer

INTERVIEWER
Martin Scorsese

EXECUTIVE PRODUCER
Jonathan Taplin

PRODUCED BY
Robbie Robertson
L. A. Johnson
Frank Marshall

DIRECTOR OF PHOTOGRAPHY
Michael Chapman

ADDITIONAL CINEMATOGRAPHERS
Michael W. Watkins
Vilmos Zsigmond
Bobby Byrne
Laszlo Kovacs
David Myers
Hiro Narita

FILM EDITORS
Jan Roblee
Yeu-Bun Yee

PRODUCTION DESIGN BY
Boris Leven

ASSISTANT DIRECTORS
Jerry Grandey
James Quinn

RAGING BULL (1980)

DIRECTED BY
Martin Scorsese

WRITTEN BY
Paul Schrader
(Based on the book by Jake LaMotta with
Joseph Carter and Peter Savage)

PRINCIPAL CAST
Robert De Niro.........Jake LaMotta
Cathy Moriarty.........Vickie LaMotta
Joe Pesci.....................Joey
Frank Vincent...........Salvy

PRODUCED BY
Robert Chartoff
Irwin Winkler

DIRECTOR OF PHOTOGRAPHY
Michael Chapman

FILM EDITOR
Thelma Schoonmaker

CASTING BY
Cis Corman

COSTUME DESIGN BY
John Boxer
Richard Bruno

ASSISTANT DIRECTORS
Jerry Grandey
Allan Wertheim

THE KING OF COMEDY (1982)

DIRECTED BY
Martin Scorsese

WRITTEN BY
Paul D. Zimmerman

PRINCIPAL CAST
Robert De Niro.........Rupert Pupkin
Jerry Lewis.................Jerry Langford
Diahnne Abbott........Rita Keane
Sandra Bernhard........Masha
Shelley Hack..............Cathy Long

EXECUTIVE PRODUCER
Robert Greenhut

PRODUCED BY
Arnon Milchan

DIRECTOR OF PHOTOGRAPHY
Fred Schuler

FILM EDITOR
Thelma Schoonmaker

CASTING BY
Cis Corman

PRODUCTION DESIGN BY
Boris Leven

COSTUME DESIGN BY
Richard Bruno

AFTER HOURS (1985)

DIRECTED BY
Martin Scorsese

WRITTEN BY
Joseph Minion

PRINCIPAL CAST
Griffin Dunne............Paul Hackett
Rosanna Arquette .....Marcy Franklin
Verna Bloom..............June
Tommy Chong ....Pepe
Linda Fiorentino ....Kiki Bridges
Teri Garr.....................Julie
John Heard.................Thomas "Tom" Schorr
Cheech Marin ....Neil
Catherine O'Hara .....Gail

PRODUCED BY
Robert F. Colesberry
Griffin Dunne
Amy Robinson
Deborah Schindler

ORIGINAL MUSIC BY
Howard Shore

DIRECTOR OF PHOTOGRAPHY
Michael Ballhaus

FILM EDITOR
Thelma Schoonmaker

CASTING BY
Mary Colquhoun

PRODUCTION DESIGN BY
Jeffrey Townsend

COSTUME DESIGN BY
Rita Ryack

ASSISTANT DIRECTOR
Stephen J. Lim

THE COLOR OF MONEY (1986)

DIRECTED BY
Martin Scorsese

WRITTEN BY
Richard Price
(Based on the book by Walter Tevis)

PRINCIPAL CAST
Paul Newman ....Fast Eddie Felson
Tom Cruise ....Vincent Lauria
Mary Elizabeth
    Mastrantonio ....Carmen
Helen Shaver..............Janelle
John Turturro ....Julian

PRODUCED BY
Irving Axelrod
Barbara De Fina

ASSOCIATE PRODUCER
Dodie Foster

DIRECTOR OF PHOTOGRAPHY
Michael Ballhaus

FILM EDITOR
Thelma Schoonmaker

CASTING BY
Gretchen Rennell

PRODUCTION DESIGN BY
Boris Leven

COSTUME DESIGN BY
Richard Bruno

ASSISTANT DIRECTOR
Joseph Reidy

THE LAST TEMPTATION OF CHRIST (1988)

DIRECTED BY
Martin Scorsese

WRITTEN BY
Paul Schrader
(Based on the novel by Nikos Kazantzakis)

PRINCIPAL CAST
Willem Dafoe.............Jesus
Harvey Keitel ....Judas
Paul Greco ....Zealot
Steven Shill................Centurian
Verna Bloom ....Mary, Mother of Jesus
Barbara Hershey........Mary Magdalene

EXECUTIVE PRODUCER
Harry Ufland

PRODUCED BY
Barbara De Fina

ORIGINAL MUSIC BY
Peter Gabriel

DIRECTOR OF PHOTOGRAPHY
Michael Ballhaus

FILM EDITOR
Thelma Schoonmaker

CASTING BY
Cis Corman

PRODUCTION DESIGN BY
John Beard

COSTUME DESIGN BY
Jean-Pierre Delifer

ASSISTANT DIRECTOR
Joseph Reidy

NEW YORK STORIES (1989)
"LIFE LESSONS" SEGMENT

DIRECTED BY
Martin Scorsese

WRITTEN BY
Richard Price

PRINCIPAL CAST
Nick Nolte .... Lionel Dobie
Rosanna Arquette ...... Paulette

PRODUCED BY
Barbara De Fina

DIRECTOR OF PHOTOGRAPHY
Néstor Almendros

FILM EDITOR
Thelma Schoonmaker

CASTING BY
Ellen Lewis

PRODUCTION DESIGN BY
Kristi Zea

ASSISTANT DIRECTOR
Joseph Reidy

GOODFELLAS (1990)

DIRECTED BY
Martin Scorsese

WRITTEN BY
Nicholas Pileggi
Martin Scorsese
(Based on the book *Wiseguy: Life in a Mafia Family,* by Nicholas Pileggi)

PRINCIPAL CAST
Robert De Niro .... James "Jimmy" Conway
Ray Liotta .... Henry Hill
Joe Pesci .... Tommy DeVito
Lorraine Bracco .... Karen Hill
Paul Sorvino .... Paul Cicero
Frank Sivero .... Frankie Carbone
Tony Darrow .... Sonny Bunz
Mike Starr .... Frenchy
Frank Vincent .... Billy Batts

EXECUTIVE PRODUCER
Barbara De Fina

PRODUCER
Irwin Winkler

ASSOCIATE PRODUCER
Bruce Pustin

DIRECTOR OF PHOTOGRAPHY
Michael Ballhaus

FILM EDITOR
Thelma Schoonmaker

CO-EDITOR
James Kwei

CASTING BY
Ellen Lewis

PRODUCTION DESIGN BY
Kristi Zea

COSTUME DESIGN BY
Richard Bruno

ASSISTANT DIRECTOR
Joseph Reidy

CAPE FEAR (1991)

DIRECTED BY
Martin Scorsese

WRITTEN BY
Wesley Strick
(Based on the novel *The Executioners*,
by John D. MacDonald)

PRINCIPAL CAST
Robert De Niro ....Max Cady
Nick Nolte................Sam Bowden
Jessica Lange ....Leigh Bowden
Juliette Lewis ....Danielle Bowden
Joe Don Baker ....Claude Kersek
Robert Mitchum ....Lieutenant Elgart
Gregory Peck.............Lee Heller
Martin Balsam...........Judge

EXECUTIVE PRODUCERS
Kathleen Kennedy
Frank Marshall

PRODUCED BY
Barbara De Fina

MUSIC BY
Bernard Herrmann

MUSIC ADAPTATION BY
Elmer Bernstein

DIRECTOR OF PHOTOGRAPHY
Freddie Francis

FILM EDITOR
Thelma Schoonmaker

PRODUCTION DESIGN BY
Henry Bumstead

COSTUME DESIGN BY
Rita Ryack

ASSISTANT DIRECTOR
Joseph Reidy

THE AGE OF INNOCENCE (1993)

DIRECTED BY
Martin Scorsese

WRITTEN BY
Jay Cocks
Martin Scorsese
(Based on the novel by Edith Wharton)

PRINCIPAL CAST
Daniel Day-Lewis .... Newland Archer
Michelle Pfeiffer .... Ellen Olenska
Winona Ryder.............. May Welland
Alexis Smith.................. Louisa van der Luyden
Geraldine Chaplin........ Mrs. Welland
Mary Beth Hurt........... Regina Beaufort
Alec McCowen............. Sillerton Jackson
Richard E. Grant .... Larry Lefferts
Miriam Margolyes........ Mrs. Mingott
Robert Sean Leonard ... Ted Archer
Siân Phillips.................. Mrs. Archer
Jonathan Pryce.............. Rivière
Michael Gough .... Henry van der Luyden
Joanne Woodward........ Narrator
Stuart Wilson .... Julius Beaufort
Carolyn Farina .... Janey Archer
Tracey Ellis................... Gertrude Lefferts
Norman Lloyd .... Mr. Letterblair

PRODUCED BY
Barbara De Fina

CO-PRODUCER
Bruce S. Pustin

ASSOCIATE PRODUCER
Joseph Reidy

MUSIC BY
Elmer Bernstein

DIRECTOR OF PHOTOGRAPHY
Michael Ballhaus

FILM EDITOR
Thelma Schoonmaker

CASTING BY
Ellen Lewis

PRODUCTION DESIGN BY
Dante Ferretti

COSTUME DESIGN BY
Gabriella Pescucci

ASSISTANT DIRECTOR
Joseph Reidy

A PERSONAL JOURNEY WITH MARTIN SCORSESE THROUGH AMERICAN MOVIES (1995)

DIRECTED BY
Martin Scorsese
Michael Henry Wilson

WRITTEN BY
Martin Scorsese
Henry Wilson

NARRATOR/HOST
Martin Scorsese

APPEARANCES BY
Kathryn Bigelow
Frank Capra (archive footage)
John Cassavetes (archive footage)
Francis Ford Coppola
Brian De Palma
André De Toth
Clint Eastwood
John Ford (archive footage)
Samuel Fuller
Howard Hawks (archive footage)
Elia Kazan (archive footage)
Fritz Lang (archive footage)
George Lucas
Gregory Peck
Arthur Penn
Nicholas Ray (archive footage)
Douglas Sirk (archive footage)
King Vidor (archive footage)
Orson Welles (archive footage)
Billy Wilder

EXECUTIVE PRODUCERS
Bob Last
Colin MacCabe

PRODUCED BY
Florence Dauman

ASSOCIATE PRODUCER
Raffaele Donato

LINE PRODUCER
Dale Ann Stieber

ORIGINAL MUSIC BY
Elmer Bernstein

CINEMATOGRAPHY BY
Jean-Yves Escoffier
Frances Reid
Nancy Schreiber

FILM EDITORS
Kenneth Levis
David Lindblom

CASINO (1995)

DIRECTED BY
Martin Scorsese

WRITTEN BY
Nicholas Pileggi
Martin Scorsese
(Based on the book by Nicholas Pileggi)

PRINCIPAL CAST
Robert De Niro ....Sam "Ace" Rothstein
Sharon Stone ....Ginger McKenna
Joe Pesci ....Nicky Santoro
James Woods..............Lester Diamond
Frank Vincent ....Frank Marino
Pasquale Cajano ....Remo Gaggi
Kevin Pollak ....Phillip Green
Don Rickles ....Billy Sherbert
Vinny Vella................Artie Piscano
Alan King...................Andy Stone
L. Q. Jones ....Pat Webb
Dick Smothers ....Senator

PRODUCED BY
Barbara De Fina

ASSOCIATE PRODUCER
Joseph Reidy

DIRECTOR OF PHOTOGRAPHY
Robert Richardson

FILM EDITOR
Thelma Schoonmaker

CASTING BY
Ellen Lewis

PRODUCTION DESIGN BY
Dante Ferretti

COSTUME DESIGN BY
John Dunn
Rita Ryack

ASSISTANT DIRECTOR
Joseph Reidy

KUNDUN (1997)

DIRECTED BY
Martin Scorsese

WRITTEN BY
Melissa Mathison

PRINCIPAL CAST
Tenzin Thuthob
   Tsarong...................Dalai Lama (Adult)
Gyurme Tethong.......Dalai Lama (Age 12)
Tulku Jamyang
   Kunga Tenzin........Dalai Lama (Age 5)
Tenzin Yesh
   Paichangi ....Dalai Lama (Age 2)
Tencho Gyalpo..........Mother
Tenzin Topjar.............Lobsang (Age 5–10)
Tsewang Migyur
   Khangsar ....Father
Tenzin Lodoe ....Takster
Geshi Yeshi Gyatso...Lama of Sera

EXECUTIVE PRODUCER
Laura Fattori

PRODUCED BY
Barbara De Fina

ASSOCIATE PRODUCERS
Scott Harris
Perry Santos

CO-PRODUCER
Melissa Mathison

PRODUCER, CANADA
Jeanne Stack

ORIGINAL MUSIC BY
Philip Glass

DIRECTOR OF PHOTOGRAPHY
Roger Deakins

FILM EDITOR
Thelma Schoonmaker

CASTING BY
Ahmed Abounouom
Ellen Lewis

PRODUCTION DESIGN BY
Dante Ferretti

COSTUME DESIGN BY
Dante Ferretti

ASSISTANT DIRECTORS
Rachid Gaidi
Scott Harris

MY VOYAGE TO ITALY (1999)

DIRECTED BY
Martin Scorsese

WRITTEN BY
Suso Cecchi d'Amico
Raffaele Donato
Kent Jones
Martin Scorsese

CAST
Martin Scorsese..........Host

EXECUTIVE PRODUCERS
Giorgio Armani
Riccardo Tozzi
Marco Chimenz

CO-EXECUTIVE PRODUCER
Raffaele Donato

PRODUCERS
Giorgio Armani
Giuliana Del Punta
Barbara De Fina
Bruno Restuccia

CINEMATOGRAPHY BY
Phil Abraham
William Rexer

FILM EDITOR
Thelma Schoonmaker

PRODUCTION DESIGN BY
Wing Lee

BRINGING OUT THE DEAD (1999)

DIRECTED BY
Martin Scorsese

WRITTEN BY
Paul Schrader
(Based on the book by Joe Connelly)

PRINCIPAL CAST
Nicolas Cage .... Frank Pierce
Patricia Arquette .... Mary Burke
John Goodman .... Larry
Ving Rhames .... Marcus
Tom Sizemore .... Tom Wolls
Marc Anthony .... Noel
Mary Beth Hurt .... Nurse Constance

EXECUTIVE PRODUCERS
Bruce S. Pustin
Adam Schroeder

PRODUCED BY
Barbara De Fina
Scott Rudin

CO-PRODUCERS
Eric Steel
Joseph Reidy

ASSOCIATE PRODUCERS
Mark Roybal
Jeff Levine

ORIGINAL MUSIC BY
Elmer Bernstein

DIRECTOR OF PHOTOGRAPHY
Robert Richardson

FILM EDITOR
Thelma Schoonmaker

CASTING BY
Ellen Lewis

PRODUCTION DESIGN BY
Dante Ferretti

ASSISTANT DIRECTOR
Joseph Reidy

GANGS OF NEW YORK (2002)

DIRECTED BY
Martin Scorsese

WRITTEN BY
Jay Cocks
Steven Zaillian
Kenneth Lonergan
Story by Jay Cocks
(Based on the book by Herbert Asbury)

EXECUTIVE PRODUCERS
Maurizio Grimaldi
Michael Hausman
Harvey Weinstein

PRODUCERS
Alberto Grimaldi
Martin Scorsese

ASSOCIATE PRODUCER
Gerry Robert Byrne

LINE PRODUCER
Laura Fattori

PRINCIPAL CAST
Leonardo DiCaprio ..... Amsterdam Vallon
Daniel Day-Lewis .... Bill "The Butcher"
                          Cutting
Cameron Diaz .... Jenny Everdeane
Jim Broadbent.............. William "Boss" Tweed
John C. Reilly .... Happy Jack Mulraney
Henry Thomas .... Johnny Sirocco
Liam Neeson................. "Priest" Vallon

ORIGINAL MUSIC BY
Howard Shore

DIRECTOR OF PHOTOGRAPHY
Michael Ballhaus

FILM EDITOR
Thelma Schoonmaker

CASTING BY
P. Larry Kaplan
Ellen Lewis

PRODUCTION DESIGN BY
Dante Ferretti

COSTUME DESIGN BY
Sandy Powell

ASSISTANT DIRECTOR
Joseph Reidy

THE AVIATOR (2004)

DIRECTED BY
Martin Scorsese

WRITTEN BY
John Logan

PRINCIPAL CAST
Leonardo DiCaprio ..... Howard Hughes
Cate Blanchett .... Katharine Hepburn
Kate Beckinsale............. Ava Gardner
John C. Reilly .... Noah Dietrich
Alec Baldwin................. Juan Trippe
Alan Alda .... Senator Ralph Owen
                                       Brewster
Ian Holm....................... Professor Fitz
Danny Huston.............. Jack Frye
Gwen Stefani................. Jean Harlow
Jude Law .... Errol Flynn

EXECUTIVE PRODUCERS
Chris Brigham
Colin Cotter
Sandy Climan
Leonardo DiCaprio
Volker Schauz (IMF)
Rick Schwartz
Bob Weinstein
Harvey Weinstein
Rick Yorn

PRODUCERS
Matthias Deyle (IMF)
Charles Evans Jr.
Graham King
Michael Mann

CO-PRODUCER
Joseph Reidy

LINE PRODUCERS
Dan Maag (IMF)
Philip Schulz-Deyle (IMF)

ORIGINAL MUSIC BY
Howard Shore

DIRECTOR OF PHOTOGRAPHY
Robert Richardson

FILM EDITOR
Thelma Schoonmaker

CASTING BY
Ellen Lewis

PRODUCTION DESIGN BY
Dante Ferretti

ASSISTANT DIRECTOR
Joseph Reidy

NO DIRECTION HOME: BOB DYLAN (2005)

DIRECTED BY
Martin Scorsese

CAST
Bob Dylan..................Himself

EXECUTIVE PRODUCERS
Jody Allen
Paul G. Allen
Barbara De Fina
Jeff Rosen
Martin Scorsese
Nigel Sinclair
Anthony Wall

CO-EXECUTIVE PRODUCERS
Gub Neal
Justin Thomson-Glover

CO-PRODUCER
Margaret Bodde

LINE PRODUCERS
Jessica Cohen
Tia Lessin

DIRECTOR OF PHOTOGRAPHY
Mustapha Barat

FILM EDITOR
David Tedeschi

THE DEPARTED (2006)

DIRECTED BY
Martin Scorsese

WRITTEN BY
William Monahan
(Based on the film *Infernal Affairs,* written by
Alan Mak and Felix Chong)

PRINCIPAL CAST
Leonardo DiCaprio ..... Billy Costigan
Matt Damon .... Colin Sullivan
Jack Nicholson .... Frank Costello
Mark Wahlberg............. Staff Sgt. Dignam
Martin Sheen................. Capt. Queenan
Ray Winstone .... Mr. French
Vera Farmiga................. Madolyn
Anthony Anderson ...... Brown
Alec Baldwin................. Capt. Ellerby

EXECUTIVE PRODUCERS
G. Mac Brown
Doug Davison
Kristin Hahn
Roy Lee
Michael Aguilar

PRODUCERS
Brad Grey
Graham King
Gianni Nunnari
Brad Pitt

CO-PRODUCERS
Joseph Reidy
Rick Schwartz

ASSOCIATE PRODUCER
Emma Tillinger

ORIGINAL MUSIC BY
Howard Shore

DIRECTOR OF PHOTOGRAPHY
Michael Ballhaus

FILM EDITOR
Thelma Schoonmaker

CASTING BY
Ellen Lewis

PRODUCTION DESIGN BY
Kristi Zea

ASSISTANT DIRECTOR
Joseph Reidy

PRINCIPAL CAST
The Rolling Stones:
Mick Jagger
Keith Richards
Charlie Watts
Ron Wood

WITH
Darryl Jones
Chuck Leavell
Bobby Keys
Bernard Fowler
Lisa Fisher
Blondie Chaplin
Tim Ries
Kent Smith
Michael Davis

EXECUTIVE PRODUCERS
Mick Jagger
Keith Richards
Charlie Watts
Ron Wood

CO-EXECUTIVE PRODUCER
Jane Rose

PRODUCED BY
Steve Bing
Michael Cohl
Lorne Orleans (IMAX version)
Victoria Pearman
Zane Weiner

CO-PRODUCERS
Joseph Reidy
Emma Tillinger

DIRECTOR OF PHOTOGRAPHY
Robert Richardson

FILM EDITOR
David Tedeschi

ASSISTANT DIRECTOR
Joseph Reidy

SHINE A LIGHT (2008)

DIRECTED BY
Martin Scorsese

SHUTTER ISLAND (2010)

DIRECTED BY
Martin Scorsese

WRITTEN BY

Laeta Kalogridis
(Based on the novel by Dennis Lehane)

PRINCIPAL CAST

Leonardo DiCaprio	Teddy Daniels
Mark Ruffalo	Chuck Aule
Ben Kingsley	Dr. Cawley
Max von Sydow	Dr. Naehring
Michelle Williams	Dolores Chanal
Emily Mortimer	Rachel 1
Patricia Clarkson	Rachel 2
Jackie Earle Haley	George Noyce

EXECUTIVE PRODUCERS

Chris Brigham
Laeta Kalogridis
Dennis Lehaneer
Gianni Nunnari
Louis Phillips
Chris Brigham

PRODUCERS

Brad Fischer
Mike Medavoy
Arnold Messer
Martin Scorsese

CO-PRODUCERS

Joseph Reidy
Emma Tillinger

DIRECTOR OF PHOTOGRAPY

Robert Richardson

FILM EDITOR

Thelma Schoonmaker

CASTING BY

Ellen Lewis
Meghan Rafferty

PRODUCTION DESIGN BY

Dante Ferretti

ASSISTANT DIRECTORS

Ron Ames
Joseph Reidy

HUGO (2011)

DIRECTED BY

Martin Scorsese

WRITTEN BY

John Logan
(Based on the novel by Brian Selznick)

PRINCIPAL CAST

Ben Kingsley	Georges Méliès
Sacha Baron Cohen	Station Inspector
Asa Butterfield	Hugo Cabret
Chloë Grace Moretz	Isabelle
Ray Winstone	Uncle Claude
Emily Mortimer	Lisette
Jude Law	Hugo's Father

EXECUTIVE PRODUCERS

David Crockett
Barbara De Fina
Christi Dembrowski
Georgia Kacandes
Emma Tillinger Koskoff
Charles Neuwirth

PRODUCERS

Johnny Depp
Tim Headington
Graham King
Martin Scorsese

LINE PRODUCER (PARIS)

John Bernard

DIRECTOR OF PHOTOGRAPHY

Robert Richardson

FILM EDITOR

Thelma Schoonmaker

CASTING BY

Ellen Lewis

PRODUCTION DESIGN BY

Dante Ferretti

SHORTER FILMS AND TELEVISION EPISODES

WHAT'S A NICE GIRL LIKE YOU DOING IN A PLACE LIKE THIS? (1963)
(NYU Student Film; Faculty Advisers: Haig P. Manoogian, John Mahon)

DIRECTED BY
Martin Scorsese

WRITTEN BY
Martin Scorsese

DIRECTOR OF PHOTOGRAPHY
James Newman

EDITED BY
Robert Hunsicker

CAST
Zeph Michaelis .... Harry
Mimi Stark .... Wife
Sarah Braveman .... Analyst
Fred Sica .... Friend
Robert Uricola........... Singer

IT'S NOT JUST YOU, MURRAY! (1964)
(NYU Student Film; Faculty Advisers: Haig P. Manoogian, John Mahon)

DIRECTED BY
Martin Scorsese

WRITTEN BY
Martin Scorsese
Mardik Martin

DIRECTOR OF PHOTOGRAPHY
Richard H. Coll

EDITOR
Eli F. Bleich

MUSIC BY
Richard H. Coll

CAST
Ira Rubin .... Murray
De Fazio .... Joe
Andrea Martin .... Wife
Catherine Scorsese ... Mother
Robert Uricola .... Singer

THE BIG SHAVE (1967)

DIRECTED, WRITTEN, EDITED, AND PRODUCED BY
Martin Scorsese

CAST
Martin Scorsese .... No Character Name

STREET SCENES (1970)

PRODUCTION SUPERVISOR AND
POSTPRODUCTION DIRECTOR
Martin Scorsese

CAST
Verna Bloom .... Herself
Jay Cocks .... Himself
Harvey Keitel .... Himself
William Kunstler .... Himself
Martin Scorsese.......... Interviewer

CINEMATOGRAPHY BY
Nancy Bennett
John Butman
Dick Catron
Frederick Elmes
Bill Etra
Tom Famighetti
Peter Flynn
Robert Foresta
David Freeberg
Tiger Graham
Fred Hadley
Tony Janetti
Arnold Klein
Don Lenzer
Ron Levitas
Didier Loiseau
David Ludwig
Harry Peck Bolles
Bob Pitts
Laura Primakoff
Peter Rea
Danny Schneider
Gordon Stein
Oliver Stone
Ed Summer
Bruce Tabor

Nat Tripp
Stan Weiser
Bob Zahn

FILM EDITORS
Angela Kirby
Maggie Koven
Gerry Pallor
Peter Rea
Thelma Schoonmaker
Larry Tisdall

AMERICAN BOY: A PROFILE OF STEVEN PRINCE (1978)

DIRECTED BY
Martin Scorsese

CAST
Steven Prince..............Himself
Martin Scorsese..........Himself
George Memmoli......Himself

EXECUTIVE PRODUCERS
Jim Wheat
Ken Wheat

PRODUCER
Bert Lovitt

DIRECTOR OF PHOTOGRAPHY
Michael Chapman

EDITED BY
Amy Holden Jones
Bert Lovitt

AMAZING STORIES (1986)
EPISODE: "MIRROR MIRROR"

DIRECTED BY
Martin Scorsese

WRITTEN BY
Joseph Minion

STORY BY
Steven Spielberg

PRINCIPAL CAST
Sam Waterston...........Jordan Manmouth
Helen Shaver..............Karen
Dick Cavett................Himself
Tim Robbins ....Jordan's Phantom

EXECUTIVE PRODUCER
Steven Spielberg

PRODUCED BY
Joshua Brand
John Falsey
Skip Lusk

ORIGINAL MUSIC BY
Michael Kamen

DIRECTOR OF PHOTOGRAPHY
Robert Stevens

FILM EDITOR
Joe Ann Fogle

CASTING BY
Jane Feinberg
Mike Fenton
Valorie Massalas

PRODUCTION DESIGN BY
Rick Carter

ASSISTANT DIRECTOR
John Liberti

BAD (1987)
(Music Video)

DIRECTED BY
Martin Scorsese

WRITTEN BY
Richard Price

PRINCIPAL CAST
Michael Jackson.........Darryl
Adam Nathan ....Tip
Pedro Sanchez............Nelson
Wesley Snipes.............Mini Max
Roberta Flack ....Darryl's Mother

PRODUCED BY
Quincy Jones
Barbara De Fina

DIRECTOR OF PHOTOGRAPHY
Michael Chapman

EDITOR
Thelma Schoonmaker

CHOREOGRAPHY BY
Michael Jackson
Greg Burge
Jeffrey Daniel

MADE IN MILAN (1990)
(An interview with the fashion designer
Giorgio Armani, for whom Scorsese also
made commercials in 1986 and 1988)

DIRECTED BY
Martin Scorsese

CAST
Giorgio Armani
His mother and father

DIRECTOR OF PHOTOGRAPHY
Nestor Almendros

EDITOR
Thelma Schoonmaker

MUSIC BY
Howard Shore

THE BLUES (2003)
(Television Series)

EXECUTIVE PRODUCER
Martin Scorsese

EPISODE:
"Feel Like Going Home"

DIRECTED BY
Martin Scorsese

WRITTEN BY
Peter Guralnick

EPISODE CAST
Corey Harris..............Himself
John Lee Hooker.......Himself (archive footage)
Salif Keita ....Himself
Willie King ....Himself
Taj Mahal...................Himself
Ali Farka Touré ....Himself
Otha Turner ....Himself

EXECUTIVE PRODUCERS
Jody Allen
Paul G. Allen

PRODUCER
Samuel D. Pollard

CO-PRODUCER
Richard Hutton

LINE PRODUCER
Daphne McWilliams

FILM EDITOR
David Tedeschi

LADY BY THE SEA: THE STATUE OF LIBERTY (2004)
(Television Documentary)

DIRECTED BY
Kent Jones
Martin Scorsese

WRITTEN BY
Kent Jones
Martin Scorsese

CAST
Philip Lopate ....Himself
James Sanders.............Himself
Martin Scorsese..........Host/Narrator

CO-PRODUCER
Rachel Reichman

ASSOCIATE PRODUCER
Edwin Schlossberg

"BOARDWALK EMPIRE" (2010)
(HBO Televison Series)

SERIES EXECUTIVE PRODUCERS
Stephen Levinson
Martin Scorsese
Timothy Van Patten
Mark Wahlberg
Terence Winter

SUPERVISING PRODUCERS
Margaret Nagle

"BOARDWALK EMPIRE" (SERIES PILOT)

DIRECTED BY
Martin Scorsese

WRITTEN BY
Terence Winter
(Based on the novel by Nelson Johnson)

CO-EXECUTIVE PRODUCER
Lawrence Konner

SUPERVISING PRODUCER
Howard Korder

LINE PRODUCER
Dana J. Kuznetzkoff

PRINCIPAL EPISODE CAST
Greg Antonacci ....Johnny Torrio
Pearce Bunting...........Bill McCoy

Danny Burstein ....Lolly Steinman
Steve Buscemi ....Nucky Thompson

DIRECTOR OF PHOTOGRAPHY
Stuart Dryburgh

CASTING BY
Ellen Lewis

PRODUCTION DESIGN BY
Bob Shaw

COSTUME DESIGN BY
John A. Dunn

Other Producer or Executive Producer Credits

Medicine Ball Caravan (1971) (associate producer)
The Grifters (1990) (producer)
Mad Dog and Glory (1993) (producer)
Naked in York (1993) (executive producer)
Clockers (1995) (producer)
Eric Clapton: Nothing But the Blues—an "In the Spotlight" Special (1995) (executive producer)
Search and Destroy (1995) (executive producer)
Grace of My Heart (1996) (executive producer)
Kicked in the Head (1997) (executive producer)
The Hi-Lo Country (1998) (producer)
You Can Count on Me (2000) (executive producer)
Rain (2001/IV) (executive producer)
The Blues (2003) TV series (executive producer)

The Soul of a Man (2003) (executive producer)
Frankenstein (2004) (TV) (executive producer)
Lightning in a Bottle (2004) (executive producer)
Nyfes (2004) (executive producer) aka *Brides* (English title)
Something to Believe In (2004) (executive producer)
Val Lewton: The Man in the Shadows (2007) (producer)
Lymelife (2008) (executive producer)
Picasso and Braque Go to the Movies (2008) (producer)
The Young Victoria (2009) (producer)
Untitled George Harrison documentary (2010) (producer)

Actor

Who's That Knocking at My Door (1967) Gangster
Boxcar Bertha (1972) Brothel Client
Mean Streets (1973) Jimmy Shorts
Cannonball! (1976) Mafioso
Taxi Driver (1976) Taxi Passenger
Il pap'occhio (1980) TV Director
Raging Bull (1980) Barbizon Stagehand
The King of Comedy (1982) TV Director

Anna Pavlova (1983) Gatti-Cassaza
After Hours (1985) Club Berlin Searchlight Operator
The Color of Money (1986) (voice) Opening Voiceover
'Round Midnight (1986) Goodley
New York Stories (1989) Man Having Picture Taken with Lionel Dobie
Dreams (1990) Vincent van Gogh

The Grifters (1990) (voice)
Guilty by Suspicion (1991) Joe Lesser
The Age of Innocence (1993) Photographer
Quiz Show (1994) Martin Rittenhome
Search and Destroy (1995) The Accountant
Bringing Out the Dead (1999) (voice)
   Dispatcher

"Curb Your Enthusiasm" (2002) As Himself
   (2 episodes)
Gangs of New York (2002) (uncredited) Wealthy
   Homeowner
The Aviator (2004) Hell's Angels Projectionist/
   Man on Red Carpet
Shark Tale (2004) (voice) Sykes

NOTE: Martin Scorsese received screen credits as an assistant director and film editor on *Woodstock* (1970), but was fired from the production before it was finished—an experience that to this day visibly upsets him. Subsequently, he was credited as an "associate producer" on another music documentary, *Medicine Ball Caravan* (1971), though most of his duties were as an editor. In 1972 he was credited as "montage supervisor" on *Elvis on Tour.* In this period he was the uncredited editor on several of his own films, including *Boxcar Bertha* and *Mean Streets*—because he was not a member of the editors' union—and he also worked anonymously as an editor on several Roger Corman films. In 2001 he directed "The Neighborhood," a segment of the television program *A Concert for New York.* His appearances as an interviewee on documentaries about movie history are too numerous to mention, and he also frequently appears as a presenter of DVD releases, as well on awards programs, on which he is often enough the honoree.

INDEX

Page numbers in *italics* refer to illustrations.

Japanese films, 60, 63, 117, 260, 306, 366
Jaws, 298
jazz, 343–4, 345–6, 348
Jazz on a Summer's Day, 346
Jazz Singer, The, 252–3
Jefferson Theater, 359
Jesuits, 177, 238, 387
Jesus Christ, 168–74, 216, 366, 367
   human vs. divine nature of, 170, 171, 174,
     176–8
   passion and crucifixion of, 169–73, *173*, 176,
     237
Jewish Americans, 234, 243, 253, 256
Johnny Guitar, 19
Johnson, Ben, 38
Jolson, Al, 252, 340
Jolson Story, The, 340
Jones, Kent, 135, 232, 382
Jones, Quincy, 346
Journey to the End of the Night (Céline),
   149
Joyce, James, 25–6, 55, 115, 265
Judgment at Nuremberg, 7
Jules and Jim, 65
Julius Caesar, 18, 54
"Jumpin' Jack Flash," 349–50
"Jump into the Fire," 350

K

Kael, Pauline, 110, 120
Kafka, Franz, 157
Kagan, Jeremy Paul, 88
Katzenberg, Jeffrey, 173
Kaufman, Boris, 311
Kazan, Elia, 8, 35, 51, 58, 123, 151, 222, 232, 259,
   262, 293–4, 296, 311, 359, 375, 378, 381, 382
Kazantzakis, Nikos, 170, 171
Keitel, Harvey, 123, 262
   in films of MS, 14, 26, 50–1, 68–74, *69*, *71*,
     98–104, *101*, 108, 109, 110, 111, 170, 172,
     175, 178, 349–50
   Marine Corps service of, 68–9
   relationship of MS and, 68–70, 83, 100–1, 264,
     318, 319, 324
Kelly, Gene, 29
Kennedy, John, Jr., 236
Kent, Rockwell, 18
Key to Reserva, The, 329

Killers, The, 230
King, Graham, 386
King Creole, 344
King of Comedy, The, x, xii, 86, 87, 139, 150–6,
   338, 386
   cast of, 139, 151–6, *154*, 307, 314
   MS's direction of, 151–5, 304, 314, 315
   script of, 150, 151
Kingsley, Ben, 290, *331*, 385
Knight, Arthur, 41
Knock on Any Door, 141
Kobayashi, Masaki, 117
Korda, Alexander, 341
Koteas, Elias, *370*
Kovacs, Ernie, 65
Kramer, Stanley, 7, 51, 271
Kristofferson, Kris, 109–11
Kubrick, Stanley, 42, 99, 166, 300–1, 317, 348
Kundun, x, xii, 54, 169, 177, 211–16, *214*, *215*,
   217, 304, 315, 352, 365, 369–70, 383
   script of, 59, 211–12
Kuras, Ellen, 278
Kurosawa, Akira, 60, 63, 352

L

Ladd, Alan, 38
Ladd, Diane, 108–9
Lafayette Escadrille, 45–6
Laine, Frankie, 342
LaMotta, Jake, ix, xiii, xiv, 104, *140*, 141, 143–6,
   155, *306*, 313
Lancaster, Burt, 245
Land of the Pharaohs, 53
"Lantern, The," 351
Last Days of Pompeii, The, 228
Last of the Mohicans, The, 233
Last Temptation of Christ, The, xi, 86, 92, 149,
   151, 162–4, 167–78, *168*, *170*, 186, 307, 367
   cast of, 170, 172, *173*, 175–6, 178
   controversy engendered by, *173*, 174–8, 224
   editing of, 171, 175–6, 296, 335
   financing of, 164, 171, 172–3, 174
   MS's direction of, *168*, *170*, 173–4, *173*, 175–7,
    224
   MS's obsession with, *163*, *168*, 172–3, 224
Last Temptation of Christ, The (Kazantzakis)
   92, 170, 171, 172
Last Tycoon, The, 294

427

Richard Schickel is the author, co-author, or editor of thirty-six books and the writer-director-producer of a similar number of television documentaries. Most of his work concerns filmmakers and film history.

Among his best-known books are *Elia Kazan: A Biography, D. W. Griffith: An American Life, Clint Eastwood: A Biography, The Disney Version, Brando: A Life in Our Times, Intimate Strangers: The Culture of Celebrity, His Picture in the Papers,* and his memoir, *Good Morning, Mr. Zip Zip Zip.*

His films include the epic five-hour history of Warner Bros., *You Must Remember This,* as well as *Charlie: The Art and Life of Charles Chaplin* and, most recently, *The Eastwood Factor.* He has also made twenty profiles of the major American directors, including Alfred Hitchcock, Howard Hawks, Elia Kazan, Woody Allen, Martin Scorsese, and Steven Spielberg. His reconstruction of Sam Fuller's *The Big Red One,* which restored forty-five lost minutes to the film, won many awards when it was released in 2004.

A film critic for *Life* and *Time* magazines for forty-three years, Mr. Schickel has held a Guggenheim Fellowship and was awarded an honorary degree by the American Film Institute. He has won the British Film Institute Book Prize, the Maurice Bessy Award in film criticism, the William K. Everson Award from the National Board of Review, and the Telluride Silver Medal, the latter two for his contributions to film history. He lives in Los Angeles.

A NOTE ON THE TYPE

This book was set in Garamond, a typeface originally designed by the famous Parisian type cutter Claude Garamond (ca. 1480–1561). This version of Garamond was modeled on a 1592 specimen sheet from the Egenolff-Berner foundry, which was produced from types thought to have been brought to Frankfurt by Jacques Sabon (d. 1580).

Claude Garamond is one of the most famous type designers in printing history. His distinguished romans and italics first appeared in *Opera Ciceronis* in 1543–44. While delightfully unconventional in design, the Garamond types are clear and open, yet maintain an elegance and precision of line that mark them as French.

Composed by North Market Street Graphics, Lancaster, Pennsylvania
Printed and bound by Quad/Graphics, Fairfield, Pennsylvania
Designed by Maggie Hinders